Food and seasoning go-togethers

Food	Spices	Herbs
Beef	Chili powder Ginger Paprika	Bay leaf Dill weed Marjoram Oregano Rosemary
Veal	Allspice Paprika	Dill weed Marjoram Rosemary Savory Tarragon Thyme
Pork	Allspice Cardamom Clove (ham) Curry powder Ginger Mustard Paprika	Basil Marjoram Sage Savory
Lamb	Cardamom Curry powder Mace Paprika Turmeric	Basil Dill weed Oregano Mint Rosemary
Chicken	Curry powder Ginger Nutmeg Paprika	Bay leaf Marjoram Dill weed Sage, savory, thyme, in stuffing Tarragon
Fish	Curry powder	Basil (salmon) Bay leaf Dill weed Marjoram Oregano Thyme
Green beans		Dill weed
Tomatoes		Basil
Coleslaw		Dill weed Celery seed

Foods for One or Two— or More

Foods for One or Two— or More

Amy G. Ireson
College of San Mateo

Shirley F. Lipscomb
Ohlone College

Houghton Mifflin Company
Boston
Dallas   Geneva, Illinois
Hopewell, New Jersey   Palo Alto   London

Photographs by Isago Tanaka

Copyright © 1978 by Houghton Mifflin Company. All rights reserved. No part of this work may be reproduced or transmitted in any form or by any means, electronic or mechanical, including photocopying and recording, or by any information storage or retrieval system, without permission in writing from the publisher.

Printed in the U.S.A.

Library of Congress Catalog Card Number: 77-75158

ISBN: 0-395-25820-0

Contents

Preface   xix

1. Food safety and sanitation   1

Micro-organisms found in food   1
  Molds
  Yeasts
  Bacteria
Food and infections   3
  Bacteria
  Viruses
  Parasites
Food and poisoning   5
  Bacteria
  Plants
  Animals
Control of food-related illness   7
  Cleanliness of food handlers
  Care of foods
  Sanitation for kitchen and equipment
  Sanitation in dish washing

Part 1 Food selection, storage, and preparation 15

2. Fruits 17

Nutritional value 17
  Effects of preparation on nutrients
  Effects of cooking and freezing on nutrients
Selection 18
  Considerations in selecting fruits
  Fruits and the consumer dollar
  Fresh versus canned or frozen fruits
Storage 20
  Fresh fruits
  Canned and frozen fruits
  Cooked fruits
Preparation 26
  Fresh fruits
  Frozen fruits
  Fruits to be frozen
  Dehydrated (dried) fruits
  Fruits in gelatin mixtures
Cooking methods 28
  Baking
  Broiling
  Poaching
  Stewing or Boiling
Serving suggestions 32

3. Vegetables 33

Nutritional value 33
  Effects of preparation on nutrients
  Effects of cooking and freezing on nutrients
Selection 35
  Considerations in selecting vegetables
  Vegetables and the consumer dollar
  Fresh versus canned or frozen vegetables

Contents

Storage 37
   Fresh vegetables
   Canned and frozen vegetables
   Cooked vegetables
Preparation 42
   Fresh vegetables
   Frozen vegetables
   Vegetables to be frozen
The effect of cooking on vegetables 47
   Green vegetables
   White vegetables
   Red vegetables
   Yellow vegetables
   Strong-flavored vegetables
Cooking Methods 48
   Boiling
   Steaming or waterless cooking
   Pressure-cooking
   Baking
   Stir-frying
   Deep-fat frying
   Microwave cooking
   Using canned vegetables
Serving suggestions 53

4. Salads   57

Nutritional value 57
Selection of Greens 58
   Considerations in selecting greens
   Salad and the consumer dollar
   Fresh versus canned or frozen ingredients
Storage of greens 61
   Washing
   Drying
Preparation 63
   Mixing salads
   Making molded and frozen salads

Salad presentation   68
   Size of pieces
   Garnishes
Salad dressings   70
   Vinaigrette (French) dressing
   Mayonnaise
   Cooked dressing
   Calorie content of dressings
   Selection of the dressing

5. Eggs   74

Nutritional value   74
Selection   74
   Considerations in selecting eggs
   Eggs and the consumer dollar
Storage   77
   Fresh
   Frozen
   Cooked
Preparation   79
   Coagulation of eggs
   Egg-white foams
   Emulsions
Cooking methods   81
   Baking
   Poaching, hard/soft cooking, and coddling
   Frying, scrambling, and making omelets
   Preparing stirred custards and puddings
Serving suggestions   87

6. Milk and milk products   88

Nutritional value   88
Kinds of dairy products   88
   Milk
   Cream

Contents ix

    Butter and margarine
    Cheese
Selection 91
Storage 93
    Milk
    Cream
    Butter and margarine
    Cheese
Preparation 96
    Milk
    Whipping cream
    Milk products
    Butter
    Cheese
Frozen Milk Desserts 99

7. Breads   102

Nutritional value 102
Ingredients 102
    Wheat flour
    Other wheat products
    Other flours
    Cornmeal
    Fat
    Liquid
    Eggs
    Leaveners
Preparation 106
    Flour
    Other ingredients
Mixing Methods 106
    Thick batters and soft doughs
    Thin batters
    Yeast doughs
Baking 109
Storage 112

8. **Pies, tarts, and turnovers**   **113**

   Pie pans   113
   Standard pastry   115
     Mixing
     Forming
     Trimming
     Baking
   Cookie-dough pastry   121
     Mixing
     Forming
     Trimming and baking
   Crumb crust   121
   Hard-meringue shells   123
     Mixing
     Forming and baking
   Prepared mixes and shells   124
   Fillings   124
     Fruit Fillings
     Custard filling
     Cooked-pudding fillings
     Meat and poultry fillings
   Toppings   129
   Turnovers   130

9. **Cakes and frostings**   **131**

   Nutritional value   131
   Ingredients   131
     Flour
     Liquid
     Fat
     Sugar
     Eggs
     Leaveners
   Altitude and cake making   133
   Mixing Methods   134
     Shortened cakes
     Chiffon cakes

Contents   xi

    Unshortened cakes
    Cake mixes
Cake Pans   137
    Selection
    Preparation
Baking   141
    Oven temperature
    Pan location
    Testing
Desirable characteristics   143
Fillings and frostings   143
    Fillings
    Frostings
    Spreading fillings and frostings

10. Grains, pastas, and legumes   148

Nutritional value   148
Cereals and cereal products   149
    Wheat
    Rice
    Corn
    Oats
    Barley
Dried Legumes   155
    Lentils
    Peas
    Beans
Selection and storage   156

11. Finfish and shellfish   158

Nutritional value   158
    Retail forms   159
    Finfish
    Shellfish
Selection   160
    Finfish

Shellfish
  Amount to buy
Storage 162
Preparation 162
Cooking methods 163
  Broiling
  Baking
  Frying
  Steaming and boiling
  Poaching
  Preparing chowders and soups
Serving suggestions 166

12. Poultry   169

Nutritional value 169
Inspection and grading 170
Retail poultry forms 170
Selection 171
  Grade
  Amount to buy
Storage 172
  Raw
  Cooked
Preparation 173
  Frozen birds
  Raw poultry
  Kitchen sanitation
Dry-heat cooking methods 178
  Roasting
  Broiling
  Barbecuing
  Frying
  Oven-frying
Moist-heat cooking methods 183
  Fricasseeing
  Stewing or steaming

Contents

      Poaching
      Serving suggestions 185

13. Meat   186

Nutritional value 186
Kinds of Meat 187
  Beef
  Veal
  Pork
  Lamb and mutton
  Cured meats
  Variety meats
  Sausage
  Luncheon meats
Inspection and grading 189
Cuts 190
  Cut and degree of tenderness
  Ground beef
Selection 192
  Quality
  Amount to buy
  Nutritional value and cost
  Soybean products
  Other considerations in selection
  Convenience meats and meat dishes
Refrigerator storage 196
  Fresh meat
  Cooked meat
Freezer storage 197
  Fresh meat
  Cooked meat
Preparation 197
  Tenderizing
  Frozen meats
Cooking Methods 199
  Dry-heat methods
  Moist-heat methods
Serving suggestions 209

Part 2 Nutrition and menu management — 213

14. Nutrition — 215

    Recommended dietary allowances   215
    Carbohydrates   218
      Food sources
      RDA
      Uses in the body
      Related problems
    Fats   220
      Food sources
      RDA
      Uses in the body
      Related problems
    Protein   221
      Food sources
      RDA
      Uses in the body
      Related problems
    Minerals   223
      Calcium and phosphorus
      Magnesium
      Potassium
      Sodium
      Chlorine
      Sulfur
      Iron
      Iodine
      Fluorine
      Zinc
      Other mineral elements
    Vitamins   231
      Vitamin A
      Vitamin D
      Vitamin E
      Vitamin K
      Thiamin (vitamin B_1)

Riboflavin (vitamin B_2)
Niacin (nicotinic acid)
Pyridoxine (vitamin B_6)
Pantothenic acid
Biotin
Folic acid (folacin)
Vitamin B_{12} (cobalamin)
Ascorbic acid (vitamin C)
Water 241
  Sources and requirements
  Uses and related problems
Digestion and absorption 242
  Digestion
  Absorption and transportation
Metabolism 243
Nutritional Summary 243
Food Labeling 244
  Ingredient listing
  Nutritional labeling
  Additive labeling

15. Meal patterns and menu planning 250

Factors affecting food selection 250
  Availability
  Family traditions and customs
  Habit
  Likes, dislikes, and preferences
  Diets
  Season
  Economics
  The meal-manager cook
  Other factors
Meal patterns 253
  Nutritional guides
  Nutritional requirements
  Caloric requirements
  Tailoring the pattern

Menu planning   258
    Individual situations
    Preparation methods
    Staying quality
    Flavor
    Texture
    Color and shape
    Temperature
    Problem areas
Serving suggestions   265

16. Organization and management of meals   266

Kitchen equipment   266
    Materials used
    Pans
    Knives
    Measurers
    Turning and stirring tools
    Beating and blending tools
    Miscellaneous tools
    Microwave ovens
Kitchen arrangement   273
    Preparation area
    Cooking area
    Cleaning area
    Planning area
    Reorganization of work areas
Food buying   275
    Basic knowledge needed
    Knowledge of alternatives
    The market list
    Store to storage
Meal management   282
    Organizational planning
    Evaluation

Contents xvii

17. Table appointments and meal service 293

Table appointments 293
 Tablecloths, place mats, and napkins
 Dinnerware
 Flatware
 Glassware
 Fondue pots, chafing dishes, and warming trays
 Decorative pieces
Setting the table 298
 The cover
 Serving dishes
 Buffet table
Service 303
 Plate service
 Family service
 Compromise service
 English service
 Russian service
 Buffet service
 Service for outdoor meals

18. Meals for special situations 308

Time-control meals 308
 Cooking methods
 Prepreparation
 Preparation of food ahead of time
 Equipment
Convenience foods 311
Dollar-control meals 314
 Planning
 Preparing
 Increasing knowledge
Food to go 318
 Planning
 Preparing

Meals for young children   320
   Undesirable foods
   Eating habits
   Atmosphere
   Meal planning
   Snacks
Weight control   323
   Underweight
   Overweight
Cooking as a hobby   327

Appendix A	Nutritive values of the edible part of foods	332
Appendix B	Temperature conversion for Fahrenheit and Celsius	386
Appendix C	Essential and desirable kitchen equipment	387
Appendix D	Equivalents and substitutions	389
Glossary		395
Bibliography		408
Index		411

Preface

This book was written for the motivated individual who seeks practical information on the basic principles and skills necessary in preparing nutritious, attractive, and enjoyable meals. Our motivation for writing this text came from the realization that many people face the responsibility of preparing their own food with little or no experience to help them. In addition our experience in teaching laboratory foods courses pointed up the need for a textbook in an introductory lecture-laboratory foods course that presents food selection, storage, and preparation in a concise, nontechnical manner.

We believe that laboratory experience illustrates cookery principles, helps the individual learn the desirable characteristics of well-prepared food, builds confidence in the ability to present meals within the constraints of time and budget, and encourages practice at home of the principles studied in the course. This book is dedicated to the accomplishment of these goals. Recipes are included in the accompanying manual, *Cooking for One or Two—or More,* to illustrate the principles and techniques. Many photographs are included in the manual to assist students in developing their skills.

In addition to the basic cookery principles, this book includes a brief survey of the fundamentals of nutrition, as well as meal-planning techniques that ensure inclusion of adequate amounts of the essential nutrients. Meal management—planning, preparation, and service—also is presented, to help the inexperienced individual develop skill in handling these significant aspects with a minimum of frustration and time. Appraisal and evaluation charts are included for use in planning menus, preparing products, and serving food. The attractive, appetizing, and artistic presentation of meals is emphasized.

The authors are deeply indebted to many people for their assistance in the preparation of the manuscript. Much of the material in the book has been used in classrooms, and students have been most helpful in pointing out ways to improve the presentations, explanations, and techniques. Staff members of the College of San Mateo have provided both support and encouragement for the work. Special thanks are due Grace Sonner for her direct assistance in many aspects of development. All users of this book and the manual will appreciate the outstanding photographic skill of Isago Tanaka, who always placed excellence of results over inconvenience and time. Sheri Becker must be singled out for special acknowledgment and thanks, because she rearranged her schedule to make typing of the manuscript her first priority.

We must also thank our families, especially our husbands, for their patience and understanding, as well as their encouragement and assistance in many ways. I, Amy, owe special thanks to my sons Randy and Rob, whose different approaches to meal preparation ("What's wrong with peanut butter sandwiches?") helped me recognize the need for this book, and to Rob for his assistance in writing.

The authors and publisher are grateful for the assistance of those who made professional reviews of the manuscript. These reviewers, to whom we give thanks, were Diana Halter, Dairy Council of California, Los Angeles; Dorothy Laubacher, University of Akron; Launa Morrow, Baylor University; Hilda Jo Jennings, Northern Arizona University; Rosa Poling, Glendale (Arizona) Community College; and Winifred Brunning, College of the Desert.

A.I.
S.L.

Chapter 1 Food safety and sanitation

Food provides enjoyment and, at the same time, satisfies two primary biological needs: it furnishes those elements necessary to the growth and regeneration of tissues, and it supplies the energy necessary to the sustainment of life. Although all forms of life need food, all do not need the same type of food. Green plants, for example, subsist on chemicals from the soil, carbon dioxide from the air, and sunlight. For plants, these three elements are food. Our bodies, through various chemical processes, convert the food we eat into the specific compounds needed for growth, regeneration, and energy, and we should not be surprised that our food also is capable of supporting nonhuman forms of life, as well.

Various microbes, often called *micro-organisms*, eat the same foods we do. Micro-organisms—molds, yeasts, bacteria—are found everywhere in great numbers. Some require oxygen to live; others require absence of oxygen. Many go into dormant stages when their environment becomes hostile and become active again when conditions return to normal. With few exceptions, we can assume that micro-organisms are acting on the food we plan to eat. This is not necessarily a bad situation, but since many micro-organisms are capable of causing sickness, serious disease, and even death, we should be aware of the potential hazards present in different foods and aware of the methods for eliminating the possibilities of food poisoning and disease. Experienced cooks will base many of their procedures on a clear understanding of this subject.

Micro-organisms found in food

Micro-organisms are so small, they can be seen only under a microscope. There are many different micro-organisms. Those that affect foods are classified as *molds, yeasts,* or *bacteria.* Some of these micro-organisms have two forms: a *growing* form and a *spore* (reproductive cell) form. The spore form moves from place to place in the air, and, if it comes in contact with a substance that provides the right conditions, it can develop into the growing form.

Many of these micro-organisms bring about desirable changes in food; others cause food to spoil, or make it unfit or dangerous for human consumption. Foods that are contaminated with undesirable or dangerous micro-organisms may or may not change in flavor, texture, color, or odor. In many cases, it is not possible to detect contamination just by looking at the food or tasting it.

Molds

Molds require moisture and food to grow. While they usually prefer a warm temperature, some are able to grow at the lower temperatures used in modern refrigerators. Most molds are not harmful, but they may change a food's flavor or texture, making the food undesirable for human consumption.

Molds grow in a wide variety of foods: fruits, breads, cheeses, meats, jams, and jellies. Boiling a food for a few minutes, although it will destroy mold, is not always necessary. Some foods, such as jams and jellies, are edible after the mold has been thoroughly scraped away. Other foods, such as cheeses, may be eaten after the mold has been trimmed away (with a thin layer of the cheese). Mold on country-cured hams should be scrubbed away with a brush and water or trimmed away before the ham is eaten.

Molds can be beneficial, and they often are used to produce different foods. Many cheeses, such as Brie, Camembert, and Roquefort, owe their distinctive characteristics in flavor and texture to the action of molds that are deliberately added to their ingredients. The action of molds on beet molasses produces the citric acid used in soft drinks and candies.

Yeasts

Yeasts also require moisture, food, and warm temperatures to grow; boiling temperatures destroy them. Yeast spores commonly are found in the air, on the ground, on plants, and on animals. Although they are not harmful to people, yeasts can cause undesirable changes in food. They are partly responsible for the white scum sometimes found on the brine in jars of homemade pickles.

Because yeasts convert sugar to carbon dioxide and ethyl alcohol, they are used as leavening agents (substances that make ingredients expand in cooking) for bread and other baked foods. Yeasts also are used to ferment wheat and barley malt in making ale and beer, and to ferment grapes in making wine.

Bacteria

All bacteria do not have the same requirements for growth. Although they all need moisture and food, some require oxygen and others do not; some grow best on one food, while others proliferate on another food. Also, bacteria grow at different temperatures. Freezing will retard their growth but will not destroy them; boiling, 100°C (212°F), will destroy most bacteria. (But see *Clostridium botulinum*, page 6.)

Bacteria grow very rapidly, particularly in unrefrigerated food. Meat, fish, eggs, and milk are the foods most likely to be affected by bacteria, because they have high protein and high moisture content. Bacterial action in food may or may not produce changes in flavor, texture, and odor. Therefore, do *not* taste any food that has an unusual appearance or odor; the food may contain bacteria that can cause illness or death. Dispose of such food immediately.

Lactic-acid bacteria have a desirable effect on food. They are used in the production of pickles, corned beef, cultured milk, buttermilk, butter, and cottage and cream cheeses. They are responsible for making cabbage into sauerkraut and for leavening salt-rising bread. In making vinegar, first yeast is used to ferment the sugar of apples or grapes into alcohol, then acetic-acid bacteria are added to produce the vinegar.

Food and infections

Bacterial, viral, and parasitic infections can pass from person to person through contaminated food—food infected by a human being or animal. Typhoid fever and tuberculosis are typical of the illnesses that are transmitted in this way, which are often called *foodborne infections*.

Bacteria

Salmonella Typhoid and paratyphoid are bacteria that belong to the *salmonella* genus. Because of sanitary regulations governing water and food supplies, typhoid is not widespread in this country; paratyphoid, however, still is a problem in some areas. *Salmonella* bacteria, which are found in the fecal matter of animals, fowl, and people, can be transmitted to food by carelessly washed hands or utensils, by contaminated work surfaces, and by insects and rodents.

Beef, which frequently is cooked rare, also can be a medium for transmission of *Salmonella*, particularly if the beef is cut on a contaminated surface. To avoid contamination, most butchers cut poultry and beef on separate counters or cutting blocks, or they use plastic blocks and counters and clean them thoroughly between use for each type of meat.

Salmonella bacteria can be destroyed by thoroughly heating the infected food to 65°C (149°F) for 20 to 30 minutes. However, usual cooking procedures often do not involve this length of time, so prevention is still the best control. Symptoms of *Salmonella* poisoning are headache, fever, nausea, vomiting, and diarrhea within 12 to 14 hours after eating the contaminated food.

Brucella A *Brucella*-infected cow will transfer the bacteria to her milk. Human beings who drink that milk may become ill with *brucellosis* (undulant fever). *Brucella* bacteria are destroyed by heat, which is one reason that milk is pasteurized before it is sold. Under federal and state testing programs, dairy herds are tested constantly to prevent the transmission of the bacteria.

Viruses

Infections of the respiratory tract, such as colds and influenza, may be transmitted by contaminated food. Usually, the food has been contaminated by an infected person who sneezed or coughed over the food or who omitted careful hand washing.

Food, water, and shellfish from contaminated waters transmit virus A, which causes viral infectious hepatitis. The virus is present in human fecal matter, so public-health measures—community control of water, food, and sanitation facilities—are imperative. The purity of water supplies must be maintained to prevent local outbreaks of infectious hepatitis.

Food safety and sanitation

Parasites

Trichinella spiralis This is a very small worm that commonly is found in pork or pork products, especially from hogs that have been fed on unsterilized garbage. The worm can be destroyed by heating pork to an internal temperature of 76°C (170°F). For this reason, all pork should be thoroughly cooked before it is eaten.

Endamoeba histolytica This is a very small parasitic organism that causes amoebic dysentery. The parasite is found in human fecal matter and may be transmitted to food or utensils by human hands, flies, or contaminated water. A temperature of 71°C (160°F) or over, however, destroys the parasite, and cooking heats usually do reach this temperature. Thoroughly wash foods that are served raw under running water, to ensure removal of any parasites.

Food and poisoning

Some bacteria found in food produce a *toxin* (poison) that can cause illness or death in people. In addition, certain plants and animals are toxic.

Bacteria

Staphylococcus aureus This bacterium, which produces toxin in foods, is responsible for the largest percentage of food poisoning in the United States. Staphylococci are naturally present in the atmosphere. They commonly occur in infected cuts, sores, and pimples, and in people's noses and throats. Usually, a food handler transfers the bacteria to the food, where they grow rapidly at room temperature. Their toxin causes nausea, vomiting, and diarrhea, generally within one to six hours after the food is eaten; recovery usually is rapid. Staphylococci are destroyed by boiling the contaminated food, but their toxin can withstand boiling temperatures.

Foods that are allowed to cool slowly or that are held without refrigeration are excellent substances for staphylococcic growth. Custards, cream puffs and éclairs, mayonnaise, potato salads, cooked chicken and fish, poultry stuffings, and ground meats are most susceptible to staphylococcic contamination.

Clostridium perfringens This bacterium is found in the soil and in the intestinal tracts of animals and human beings. Ordinary cooking temperatures often do not destroy the organism, which will multiply rapidly in food that is allowed to stand at room temperature. *Perfringens*-contaminated food can cause diarrhea, abdominal cramps, nausea, and headache.

A large mass of food, such as a stuffed turkey, cools slowly, even in a refrigerator. Therefore, it provides an ideal growth substance for *perfringens* bacteria. For this reason, never stuff a turkey or other large fowl without cooking it immediately. Do not refrigerate it or hold it at room temperature before it is cooked. After a meal, the stuffing from a roasted turkey should be removed and refrigerated separately, to hasten cooling. The stuffing also may be baked separately in a casserole or pan.

Clostridium botulinum In itself, this bacterium is not harmful; the toxin it produces when sealed in an airtight container, however, is lethal. The poisoning is called *botulism*, and its symptoms include nausea, vomiting, and diarrhea. Eventual muscular paralysis, respiratory paralysis, and cardiac failure generally lead to death.

It is particularly important to control this bacterium in canning nonacid or low-acid foods like meats, beans, corn, peas, peppers, or tomatoes. Because the toxin is not destroyed by boiling [100°C (212°F)], or usual preparation temperatures, all nonacid foods canned at home *must* be processed under at least 10 pounds of pressure for a specific time (for each type of food), to allow the food to reach 115°C (240°F)—a temperature that ensures safety.

It is extremely difficult to detect this toxin in canned foods because the foods may not appear altered in any way. Any food that produces gas, or caused a can to bulge, has changed color or texture, or appears in any way questionable should *not* be tasted. Such foods and their cans or jars should be discarded.

Although there have been cases of botulism from commercially canned foods, they are not common. Commercial food packers follow rigid sanitation practices to avoid this potential hazard. Still, any bulging or questionable commercially canned food is best discarded.

Plants

Some plants contain chemical substances that are toxic or lethal to human beings. Rhubarb leaves, the green sprouting parts of potatoes, and certain plants, like wild parsnip and deadly nightshade, are poisonous. The *Amanita* mushrooms' toxin can be fatal, and other mushroom genera are toxic in

Food safety and sanitation 7

varying degrees. Even experienced mushroom hunters have been known to make mistakes, so it is wisest to eat only those mushrooms that have been purchased in a store.

Animals

At certain times of the year, mussels, clams, and oysters may feed on plant life that produces a toxin in the shellfish. This toxin paralyzes the human respiratory center. Also, there are some fish in the Pacific Ocean that are poisonous only at certain times and other fish that have poison only in certain parts of their bodies. Some scientists believe that the poisonous condition is related to the coral reefs near which these fish usually live, while others think these fish eat certain foods that cause them to be poisonous temporarily.

Control of food-related illness

The best control of food-related illness is prevention, and the keys to prevention are cleanliness and sanitation—of food handlers, foods, kitchens, and kitchen equipment.

Cleanliness of food handlers

Anyone who handles food must develop good personal hygiene and working habits, to avoid accidental contamination. Before any food or utensils are touched, hands must be washed thoroughly with soap and hot water, and dried on a clean cloth or paper towel. While food is being prepared, hands should be washed:

1. after touching the body—nose, mouth, hair—or a visit to the toilet
2. after coughing or sneezing (the handler should move away from the food and cover both mouth and nose)
3. after wiping up any spills on the floor
4. after touching a telephone, doorknob, or any object that might harbor micro-organisms

If a food handler has a cut or infection on a hand, gloves should be worn until the injury is healed completely. This practice prevents any micro-organisms in the wound or bandage from being transmitted to the food.

Care of foods

Special care is necessary for each food type; and each is discussed in later chapters. Some general sanitary procedures do apply, however. Wash all fruits, vegetables, poultry, some fish, and dirty eggs before they are prepared and served. Handle high-protein foods with particular care, since many of them are excellent media for the growth of micro-organisms.

Refrigerate all perishable foods until they are prepared and served. Adequate refrigeration temperatures range from 0°C (32°F) in the coldest part of the refrigerator to 6.5°C (45°F) in the warmest part. Store foods that do not require refrigeration in clean containers, and keep storage areas clean and free of insects and rodents. Use a clean spoon or other implement to mix foods—a more sanitary method than using hands. Also, when testing for doneness or seasoning, use a *clean* spoon *each time* the food is sampled.

Sanitation for kitchen and equipment

Cleanliness of the kitchen and its equipment requires keeping everything in the kitchen scrupulously clean. The best practice is to establish a regular pattern for maintaining cleanliness and then to follow the pattern until it becomes habit.

The cooking surface, burners, and oven of the range require regular cleaning. Spills are easier to remove if they are wiped up as soon as they happen. Then, a general cleaning after each use is all that the range will need. Use a detergent, some water, a brush, a cloth, a steel scouring pad (if it will not mar the surface), and an ammonia solution or other liquid alkali to remove grease. An oven cleaner may be used, at intervals, but do not spray it on the thermostat-sensing rod, because it will affect the rod's operating accuracy.

Clean up all spills in the refrigerator at once. Periodically, defrost the refrigerator—even a frost-free model requires occasional defrosting—and wash the inside with a solution of baking soda and water (one tablespoon baking soda to one quart water). Always rinse with clear water.

Chopping boards and blocks may harbor micro-organisms, particularly after being used to cut meat, fish, or poultry. A chlorine-bleach solution or hypochlorite (calcium or sodium) is an effective chopping-board sanitizer.

Pour the solution over the board or block, then scrub thoroughly, rinse well, and dry. After chopping vegetables or other foods, simply wash the board or block with a detergent, and rinse it under hot water.

Thoroughly wash countertops after meal preparation and clean up with a detergent or soap and water. You may have to use a brush regularly to clean out crevices. Also wash the sink with a detergent and water and, if needed, a scouring powder.

A regular schedule for keeping the kitchen floor clean should be set up. Wipe up any spills immediately, and sweep or vacuum daily, if necessary. Wet-mop hard floors or shampoo the rug regularly.

Sanitation in dish washing

The main object of dish washing, of course, is to have sanitarily clean dishes. Soap or detergent and very hot water are required to clean off grease, food particles, and micro-organisms. In hand dish washing, a sanitizer is needed if hot water (49°C [120°F] for washing and 60°C [170°F] for rinsing) cannot be used. In machine dish washing, sanitizing is not a problem because of the higher temperature of water used.

Hand dish washing Time and energy can be saved and frustration avoided by adapting the following procedures to the individual situation.[1] The arrangement of sink and counter space will determine the exact sequence of steps, but each person should set up a hand–dish washing system.

The first step is to clean up as you prepare a meal. This not only helps to avoid a crowded counter at meal's end, but makes washing easier. Keep a sink or dishpan full of hot water and soap, and, as you finish each recipe, wash up any bowls, pans, or utensils you have used. Fill with water any pans or bowls that need soaking and set them aside. Place any spoons or small equipment that need soaking to loosen sticky foods in these pans or bowls. If food sticks tightly to pans or utensils, add a little detergent to the soaking water.

When you clear the table, a little organization will speed the process. Scrape, rinse, and stack the dishes to the right of the sink (Figure 1-1), with all like-kind dishes together. Stack glasses first, next to the sink, then flatware, then cups and bowls, then other dishes and plates, and, finally, pans. Place any greasy pans, such as frying pans and broiling pans, last.

If the sink has a garbage disposal, rinse the dishes quickly under cold

---

1. The instructions are for a right-handed person; a left-handed person should reverse the arrangements.

Figure 1-1 *Dishes scraped, rinsed, and stacked with like kinds together.*

running water. If the sink does not have a garbage disposal, scrape the dishes with a rubber spatula, pushing the garbage into a plastic bag or onto a newspaper for later wrapping. Then, rinse the dishes if necessary. Empty glasses and cups, and scrape and rinse any pans that were left to soak during meal preparation.

Prepare the dishwater in a sink or dishpan with soap or detergent and hot

Food safety and sanitation 11

water (49°C [120°F]). Place as many like dishes in the dishwater as is convenient. Then, pick up one dish with your left hand, and, while turning the dish, use a cloth, sponge, or brush in your right hand to wash it. Then, with your left hand, place the washed dish in a drainer (to be rinsed later with near-boiling water) or in a pan or second sink of rinse water, which is at least 60°C (170°F) or which contains a sanitizer. After you have placed several dishes in the rinse water, remove them to a rack to drain.

The water must be hot: for washing, 49°C (120°F); for rinsing, 60°C (170°F). Use a sanitizer if the water does not run this hot. Also, change the dishwater as often as necessary to keep it hot and clean.

If you have only one sink and do not have a dishpan (for rinsing), use the following procedure. Scrape, rinse, and stack dishes as described above, but wash and stack a number of like dishes on the left side of the sink. Then, rinse these washed dishes under hot running water and place them in the drainer. Because the rinse water dilutes the dishwater, additional soap or detergent is needed occasionally. And, since the water becomes very hot, fabric-lined rubber gloves may be necessary.

While the dishes are drying in the drainer, wash, rinse, and dry the pans. Clean burners, oven, chopping boards, and countertops. By this time, the dishes will be nearly dry, and the dishes, pans, and dish-washing equipment can be put in their proper storage areas. Wash, rinse, and hang the dishcloth and dishtowel to dry. And, finally, clean the sink.

Automatic dish washing Follow the directions given in the dishwasher's manual to load the machine correctly. The basic instructions will probably need to be personalized to fit the size, shape, and number of dishes used by the individual cook. Also, the order of loading will be determined by the arrangement of the dishwasher's racks.

Different dishwashers have different dish-cleaning requirements. All machines require removal of bones and large particles of food before loading. Most machines, except those with a soak cycle, require that you rinse egg, milk, butter, and dough from dishes before loading. Others may require that you remove all food before loading, especially if the dishwasher is not going to be run immediately.

Dish-washing precautions Certain items are best washed by hand. These include:

wooden equipment, such as chopping boards, salad bowls, wooden spoons
   and knives, and pans with wooden handles

knives with blades that rust
flour sifters, which may need cleaning with a brush
iron pans that will rust
lightweight plastic containers and measuring cups, which may become brittle, cracked, or warped from the heat

Most plastic dinnerware is dishwasher-safe, as is some novelty flatware, but many of these items cannot withstand either the high temperature or the long exposure to water. Aluminum pans and the handles of some pans will discolor slightly from repeated washing in the dishwasher. Fine china may be safely washed in a dishwasher with a detergent that does not contain a scouring ingredient. However, do not move china with a gold trim until it has cooled; the gold is soft while it is hot. Flatware will have fewer spots if removed before the drying cycle begins and dried by hand.

To save electricity, stop and open the dishwasher at the beginning of the drying cycle. Use a towel or sponge to absorb excess water from the tops of inverted glasses, cups, and other items, and leave the door of the machine open so the dishes can air-dry.

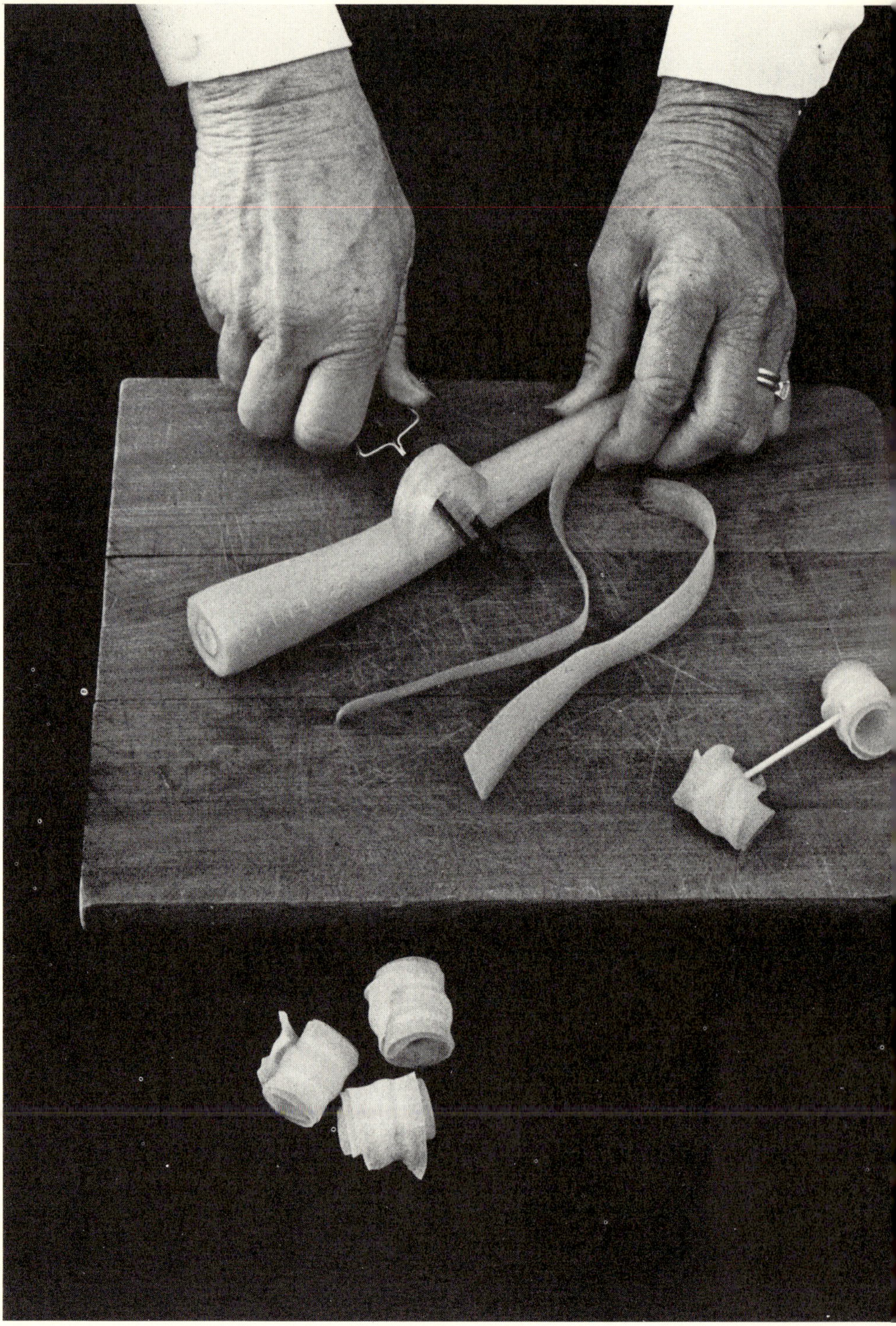

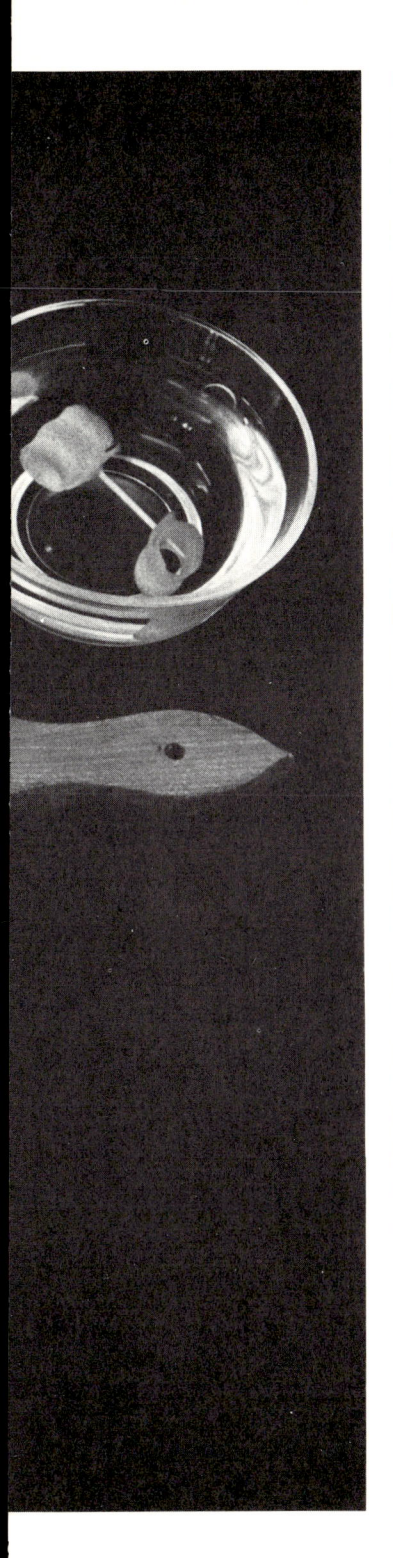

Part 1
Food selection, storage, and preparation

Chapter 2 Fruits

Fruits are produced by the flowers, or flowerlets, of plants. Botanically, tomatoes, squashes, avocados, and olives are fruits, but in cookery, they are more frequently considered vegetables. On the other hand, rhubarb, which is classified botanically as a vegetable, is usually used as a fruit.

Fruits add color, flavor, texture, and nutrients to the menu. Fruits are used raw or cooked, in appetizers, salads, garnishes, and desserts, as well as in between-meal snacks. Today's refrigeration and transportation technology have made many fruits available throughout the year, even though they are not in season locally.

Nutritional value

Fruits are souces of vitamin A (from carotene) and vitamin C (ascorbic acid). They also supply small amounts of iron, calcium, sodium, magnesium, and potassium. All calories in fruits are derived from their sugar or starch (in unripened fruits) content; avocados and olives are the only fruits that contain fat.

The deep yellow fruits—apricots, peaches, papayas, cantaloupes—contain the most vitamin A (carotene); oranges, grapefruits, strawberries, and cantaloupes are the most important food sources of ascorbic acid. In fact, one serving a day of these high–vitamin C fruits is recommended to ensure meeting the daily vitamin C requirement.

The nutritive value of fruits when served is determined by their degree of maturity when harvested and the handling and storage techniques they have had. Unripened fruits that have been harvested contain less ascorbic acid than do those that have been allowed to ripen on the plant. In addition, allowing fruits to remain in produce stands or on kitchen counters speeds up the loss of their nutritive value, especially their vitamin C. For the nutritive value of fruits, see Appendix A.

Effects of preparation on nutrients

Peeling, cooking, standing in air or water, bruising, slicing—all can destroy nutrients. Peeling, for example, removes part of a fruit's minerals, which frequently are concentrated near its skin. And, heat and oxygen (air) easily destroy ascorbic acid. Still, those fruits, like oranges and grapefruits, that contain a fair amount of ascorbic acid will retain more of it than do nonacid fruits.

Effects of cooking and freezing on nutrients

Ascorbic acid[1] and, to some extent, minerals are soluble in water. Therefore, there is some loss of these nutrients when fruit is soaked or cooked in water, unless the liquid is included with the finished product.

Although cooking and canning fruits destroy much of their ascorbic acid, freezing and freezer storage retain most of fruits' nutrients.

Selection

For the best buy in flavor, price, and nutritive value, select fresh fruits during their peak season. At this time, fresh fruits are of better quality and are less expensive than they are at any other time of the year. Plan to use peak-season fruits in your menu frequently, especially berries, peaches, and apricots, which have a short local season. This is also the time to freeze, can, or dehydrate peak-season fruits for later use.

Considerations in selecting fruits

Grade The United States Department of Agriculture (USDA) has set up a fruits and vegetables grading system, based on, among other things, color,

---

1. Carotene is not adversely affected by most cooking methods.

shape, firmness, and bruises. The grades are U.S. Fancy, U.S. No. 1, U.S. No. 2, and U.S. No. 3. Produce wholesalers use the grading system in buying and selling, but fruits and vegetables in markets seldom carry any grade markings.

The fancy grades of fruits are larger, more nearly perfect in color and shape, and more expensive than are the lesser grades of fruits; but, they have no greater nutritive value than do lesser grades that are in good condition. With lesser grades, however, there may be greater waste, so the consumer must consider the cost of the edible portion of the fruit rather than the cost per pound, and choose the quality best for a given recipe. For example, choose a perfect banana for a salad or dessert, when appearance is important. Choose a flavorful and, perhaps, overripe fruit for banana-nut bread, since the banana will be broken up.

When selecting apples, consider the planned use: a variety that is satisfactory when eaten uncooked may not be satisfactory when cooked. A Red Delicious, for example, is excellent raw, but it does not bake well. A Rome Beauty, on the other hand, is a very good cooking apple, and it may be eaten raw if a slightly tart flavor is desired. The green Granny Smith, which is imported from the Southern Hemisphere, is considered to be an excellent eating and cooking apple. Some people feel that pear varieties also should be selected with use in mind. The Bosc pear is preferred for baking and poaching, for instance.

Appearance Fruit that is firm, well colored, and free of bruises should be selected. Always avoid fruit that is soft, bruised, or damaged by insects or handling. Discard any fruit that shows mushy, brown, decayed, or water-soaked spots. Fruit with cracked or broken skins and shriveled fruit should be rejected.

Some fruits, such as cantaloupes, if harvested hard and green will not ripen satisfactorily. Others, like pears, avocados, and, to some extent, peaches and plums, must be harvested green or partially ripened, to prevent excess bruising and transportation damage.[2] Soft, perishable fruits, such as peaches, nectarines, and pears, are bought while they are slightly underripe, and allowed to ripen at room temperature. When ripe, they are refrigerated before using.

Nutritive value Consider nutritive value when selecting a fruit or a fruit product. For example, a cup of orange juice contains 112 milligrams of ascorbic acid and some vitamin A and calcium. An orange drink, on the other

2. Fortunately, these fruits will ripen satisfactorily after harvesting.

hand, may contain sugar, water, flavoring, and only a trace of ascorbic acid. To get the most nutritive value for the money, always read and evaluate all information on a product's label.

Fruits and the consumer dollar

When buying fruits, consider the following questions.

1. What is the local season?
2. Which fruits are grown locally? Local fruits are usually fresher than those that have been shipped in.
3. Which grade is needed for the intended purpose?
4. Will an underripe fruit ripen satisfactorily?
5. What percentage of the fruit is edible, in relation to the size of its seed or core?
6. What is the cost per pound of the edible portion?
7. What is the fruit's nutritive value versus its cost?
8. How much is needed? Purchase ripe fruit for immediate use; purchase less ripe fruit for later use.
9. Are storage facilities at home adequate for the particular fruit?

Fresh versus canned or frozen fruits

Depending on the planned use and the time of the year, in relation to peak-of-season availability, canned or frozen fruits may be a better buy than are fresh fruits. The wise consumer will take time to consider these two points in making up the shopping list, and remember to compare prices in the store. This is particularly important for those who live where growing seasons are short and many fruits are shipped in from other parts of the country or, as in the case of pineapples, from distant parts of the world.

Storage

Fresh fruits

Fruits continue to release ethylene gas after they are harvested. With proper storage, this gas can accelerate the *ripening process*—the process in which flavor and color develop and fruits become mellow. Fruits that have ripened on the plant have the best flavor, but plant-ripened fruits cannot be transported and marketed easily. And, their damage and spoilage can increase consumers' costs.

Storage time and conditions, of course, vary from fruit to fruit. They also will vary depending on the intended use and the fruit's degree of ripeness. For instance, raw apples that are to be eaten from the hand may be kept in a bowl on a table, if family members are going to eat them in two or three days. But softer fruits, like pineapples and melons, have a better flavor if they are stored at cool room temperature and refrigerated just before serving. And, the storage period for softer fruits can be lengthened by refrigerating them.[3] For example, bananas, although their skins will turn brown, will retain their firm texture and creamy color for several days longer in the refrigerator than they do at room temperature.

Fruits may be allowed to ripen at room temperature, then refrigerated until used. (Cantaloupes, which do not ripen well off the vine, are an exception.) A fruit tray, kept out of the sunlight, is a convenient temporary storage place until the fruits are ripe and can be refrigerated.

To store fruits properly, it is important to control moisture. Though some moisture is desirable, too much encourages spoilage. Since fruits continue to ripen and to release carbon dioxide during storage, they must be kept in plastic bags, either perforated or completely open, to allow moisture and gas to escape. Do not wash berries, cherries, grapes, and pineapples before refrigerating them. As a time saver in meal preparation, however, all other fruits can be washed and thoroughly dried.

Table 2-1 summarizes both selection points and storage information for a wide variety of fresh fruits.

Canned and frozen fruits

Canned fruits can spoil on the shelf. To eliminate shelf spoilage, rotate the cans and use the oldest cans first. Once a can has been opened, the fruit may be stored in the refrigerator, covered tightly with plastic wrap or a lid (to prevent evaporation or other damage).

Frozen fruits must be kept in the freezer until shortly before use. Once thawed, use them promptly. Do not refreeze.

3. To store ripe fruits, keep the refrigerator's temperature between 5°C and 10°C (40°F and 50°F).

Table 2-1 *Fruit selection and storage*

Fruits	Characteristics for selection	Storage	Length of storage Raw	Length of storage Cooked
Apples	Firm, well colored	Refrigerate in dry vegetable drawer.	2–3 weeks	1–2 weeks
Apricots	Firm, deep orange or yellow	Refrigerate on shelf or in drawer.	5–10 days	1–2 weeks
Avocados	For use at once: slightly soft when held, with dull-looking skin. For later use: firm or hard. No dark, soft spots in either case	Store at room temperature until ripe (3–5 days). Refrigerate uncovered; wrap cut half in plastic film.	4–7 days	
Bananas	For use at once: firm, yellow with a few brown specks. For later use: plump, well filled, yellow with a green tip	Store at room temperature until ripe (2–3 days). They may be refrigerated then, but flavor is best if they are kept at cool room temperature. Skins turn brown when refrigerated.	3–5 days	
Berries—all types	Fresh appearance, plump, full colored; no shriveled or dull-looking fruit; no mold on fruit nor stains on basket	Refrigerate in market basket in a drawer. Do not wash before storing.	1–3 days	5–7 days
Cherries	Plump, shiny, well colored; stems should be green, not brown	Refrigerate.	1–7 days	5–7 days
Coconuts	Shake vigorously; choose the one that holds the most liquid	Refrigerate whole or in covered container if peeled or cut.	1–2 weeks	
Cranberries	Firm, not shriveled	Refrigerate in market package. May be frozen in original package.	4–8 weeks	4–8 weeks

Figs	Ripe or even slightly overripe; avoid bruised and excessively overripened fruit	Refrigerate.	5–7 days
Grapes—all varieties	Fresh, mature, plump, bright color; fairly loose bunches with firm, green stems (Emperor grapes that have been stored for winter sale have brown stems)	Refrigerate in drawer or in perforated plastic bag. Wash just before using.	3–5 days
Grapefruit	Thin skinned, heavy for their size (hold in hand or weigh on scales to check weight); russet spots are acceptable; avoid thick skins or those with puffy ends	Store at cool room temperature or refrigerate.	1–2 weeks
Kiwis	For use at once: hold and gently add pressure; the fruit should give easily For later use: firm	Store at room temperature or refrigerate. Store at cool room temperature in a plastic bag until ripe.	1–3 weeks 2–3 days 1–2 weeks
Lemons	Thin skinned, heavy for their size	Refrigerate	1 month
Limes	Same as lemons		
Mangoes	Smooth skinned, partially ripened (green fruit may never ripen properly) For use at once: hold and gently add pressure; the fruit should give easily For later use: firm	Store at cool room temperature in a plastic bag until ripe (3–5 days), and then refrigerate.	5–7 days

Table 2-1 Fruit selection and storage *(Continued)*

Fruits	Characteristics for selection	Storage	Length of storage Raw	Length of storage Cooked
Melons	Fruit must be adequately ripe when harvested; press gently at blossom end for a slight softening or springiness, which indicates ripeness; colors vary	Store at room temperature until ripe; refrigerate in drawer or in plastic bag.	3–4 days	
Cantaloupe	Cream or orange color shows through the webbing			
Persian	Same as cantaloupe			
Crenshaw	Smooth skin, golden color			
Casaba	Golden yellow			
Honeydew	Smooth creamy white to yellowish white (greenish white colors indicate that the fruit was picked too soon); velvety or slightly sticky skin.			
Watermelon	Whole: slightly yellow or amber color where fruit rested on ground (avoid greenish white colors); velvety skin (not shiny) Cut: firm red flesh with black or brown seeds; avoid fruit with immature seeds or seeds that have broken away from their cavities; reject fruit that has white streaks running through the red flesh			
Nectarines	Firm, plump, well formed with slight softening along the seed; bright red color over orange or deep yellow	Store at room temperature until ripe (2–3 days), and then refrigerate.	4–7 days	1 week
Oranges	Firm, heavy for their size; choose the smoothest and finest textured skin of the variety	Store at cool room temperature or refrigerate.	2–3 weeks	
Papayas	Firm and about 35 percent ripened in the blossom end, with smooth unbruised skin; with gentle pressure, ripe area will feel slightly soft	Store at room temperature until ripe (2–3 days). Then refrigerate.	3–5 days	

Peaches	For use at once: mature, well colored, slightly soft (ripe peaches bruise extremely easily) For later use: firm, mature, partially ripe	Store at room temperature until ripe (2–4 days); then refrigerate.	5–7 days 5–7 days
Pineapples	Heavy, firm, yellow or golden orange, characteristic ripe odor; buy the largest fruit available	Store at room temperature until ripe (3–7 days), and then refrigerate.	3–6 days
Plums	For use at once: fairly firm to slightly soft, mature, good color for the variety (ripe plums bruise easily) For later use: firm, mature, partially ripe	Store at room temperature until ripe (1–3 days), and then refrigerate.	3–5 days 3–7 days
Pomegranates	Deep color; free from cracks and bruises	Refrigerate.	2–3 weeks
Rhubarb	Firm, crisp, fairly thick stems	Refrigerate in plastic bag or drawer.	1–2 days 4–5 days
Tangerines Mandarin	Heavy for the size, slightly puffy skin, deep orange or yellow, bright luster	Refrigerate.	7–10 days
Tangelo	Heavy for the size, slightly puffy skin; deep color, bright luster		

25

Cooked fruits

Once cooked, fruits must be refrigerated in covered containers to prevent them from drying out. To avoid the growth of molds or undesirable bacteria, do not leave them at room temperature.

Preparation

Fresh fruits

Two factors must be considered in preparing fruit for serving, canning, or freezing: discoloration and osmosis.

Discoloration A number of fruits begin to discolor—turning brown—quite rapidly once they are cut and exposed to the air. Apples, avocados, bananas, pears, and peaches are typical examples.

This discoloration can be prevented by one of the following methods: toss pared fruit with lemon or other citrus fruit juice or with pineapple juice; place pared fruit in a water and ascorbic acid solution (one tablespoon ascorbic acid to one quart water); toss pared fruit with enough sugar to cause the fruit to form its own syrup; or cook the fruit at once.

Osmosis *Osmosis* is the process in which liquid flows through a membrane that will allow passage of some, but not all, substances through it. Such a membrane is called a *semipermeable membrane*. In plants, cell walls form the semipermeable membrane, and water is the liquid.

The process becomes important in preparing fruits (and vegetables) because water from a less concentrated solution will move through a semipermeable membrane toward a more concentrated solution. For example, if fruit is cooked in heavy syrup (concentrated sugar solution), liquid passes from the fruit's cells into the heavy syrup, and the fruit retains its shape. If fruit is cooked in water, the water passes into the fruit's cells, causing them to break and the juice to leak out.

Therefore, certain general rules and procedures should be kept in mind. To maintain the shape in poaching peaches and pears or in coddling apples, the fruit is cooked in a concentrated sugar solution. If these fruits are cooked in water alone, they will be soft and mushy. For fruit sauce, the fruit is cooked without sugar, so it will fall apart easily. Sugar, if needed, should be added at the end of the cooking.

Frozen fruits

Freezing ruptures fruit cells and softens the texture of the frozen product. Frozen fruits to be used in a recipe are allowed to thaw to desired consistency and incorporated. To serve frozen fruits by themselves, partially thaw them; a few remaining ice crystals will improve their texture.

Fruits to be frozen

Fresh fruits may be prepared as for serving, sprinkled with a little sugar or covered with syrup, sealed in airtight containers, and placed in the freezer. Berries, apricots, and peaches will form their own syrup if sprinkled with sugar and left to stand for a few minutes. Blueberries, cranberries, pineapples in wedges or cubes, melon balls, and grapes may be frozen successfully without sugar.

For fruits that discolor rapidly, mix ascorbic-acid powder with sugar. A good mixture is ¼ teaspoon ascorbic acid added to the sugar used for each quart of fruit, or ¾ teaspoon ascorbic acid mixed with each quart of chilled syrup to be used to cover the fruit for freezing.

Dehydrated (dried) fruits

Dried fruits may be used directly from their sealed containers, or they may be rehydrated. In this case, osmosis is a beneficial process, since plain water is drawn into the cells of the dried fruit, and the rehydrated fruit is softer than it was in its dried state. However, additional sugar needed should not be added until the fruit has softened. Fruit may be rehydrated in several ways.

1. Soak moist-packed dehydrated fruits in hot water.
2. Cover the dried fruits with water and cook them very slowly.
3. Or cover the dried fruits with fruit juice or water, and store them in the refrigerator for eight hours.

Dried fruits always must be stored in tightly covered containers and kept in a cool, dry cupboard. Where ants or other insects are a problem, tight closure is important.

Dried fruits may be chopped more easily when sprinkled with a couple of teaspoons of sugar or flour from the recipe. The sugar or flour prevents the fruits from sticking to the knife. Some dried fruit also can be "chopped" with scissors. Frequently dip the scissors into cold water, to prevent the fruits from sticking to the wet surface.

Fruits in gelatin mixtures

Since some fruits will float and others will sink to the bottom of a liquid, a gelatin mixture must be partially jelled before fruits are added. For a layered effect, add some fruits before jelling and others once the mixture is partially jelled.

If hard-frozen fruits are added to gelatin mixtures, they will create pockets of liquid in the finished product, since the gelatin becomes firm before the fruits thaw. Therefore, fruits are defrosted before they are added to the mixture. If desired, the defrosted liquid may be used as part of the recipe liquid.

Fresh or frozen pineapple cannot be used in gelatin mixtures. It contains a substance that breaks down the protein in gelatin and prevents it from jelling. Canned or cooked pineapple, however, may be used successfully, because the substance is deactivated in the heating process.

Cooking methods

Fresh fruit can be served in many ways (Figures 2-1, a-h). Although fresh fruits are both attractive and nutritional, in many cases fruit is cooked, for variety or a particular effect. Fruits will retain more of their flavor if cooked in a covered pan.

Baking

Fruits, such as apples, apricots, peaches, pears, and plums, may be baked whole, pared, or with their skins. They are flavored with appropriate seasonings, and baked in the oven in a covered container. Whole apples may be cored and their cavities filled with fruits, mincemeat, raisins, or nuts before baking.

Fruits also may be pared and sliced, and then topped with a cookie, breadcrumb, cereal, or flour mixture, and baked. Canned fruits may be mixed with brown sugar and curry powder and baked to be served as accompaniments to meat courses.

Broiling

Firm, ripe fruit must be used for broiling. Overripe fruits tend to lose their shape, making them unattractive and hard to serve. Fruits should be watched carefully during broiling. Their high sugar content will cause them to burn very easily.

Broiled fruits are a good edible garnish: serve broiled apricot or peach halves with ham or pork. For a change of pace, top grapefruit halves with brown sugar, broil them, and serve them warm. Fruit can be skewered, brushed with a marinade, broiled, and served with a variety of meats.

Poaching

Poached fruits, such as peaches and pears, should maintain their shape. Therefore, a heavy sugar and water solution (½ cup sugar to 1 cup water) must be used in poaching. If fruits are very firm, the concentration does not have to be as great. Spices may be added to the syrup for flavoring. The fruit is simmered gently in the syrup, until it is tender, cooled in the syrup, and then removed from the syrup before serving. The poaching syrup can be strained to remove any particles of fruit, and stored in a covered container in the refrigerator. The syrup may be reused many times.

Stewing or Boiling

For sauce, prepared fresh fruit is placed in a covered saucepan with a little water. After the mixture comes to a boil, the heat is lowered. Cooking continues until the fruit loses shape and is soft and saucelike. Sugar is added, as desired, and cooking is resumed for about five minutes. Using a heavy-bottom pan will help prevent burning or scorching. Fruit sauce may also be prepared without the addition of water by using a covered container in a microwave oven.

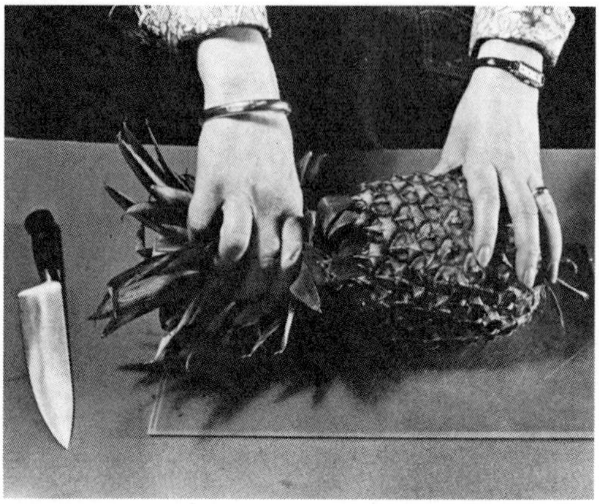

a

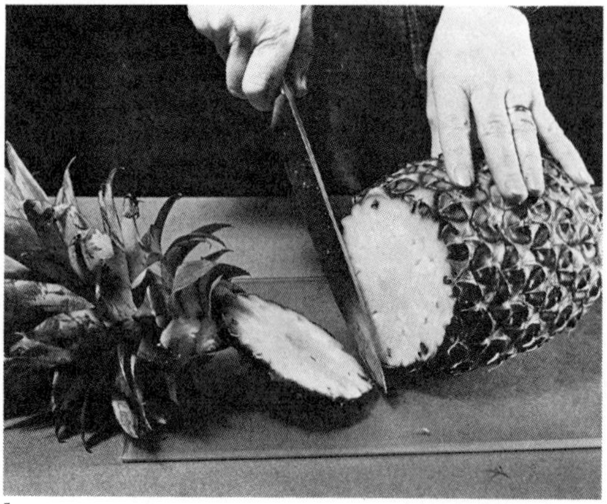

b

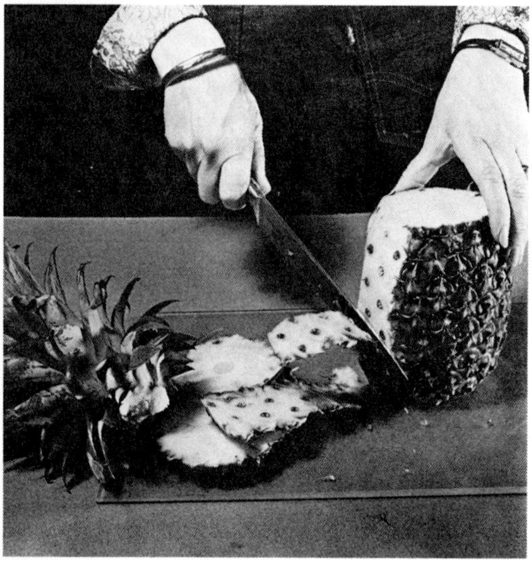

c

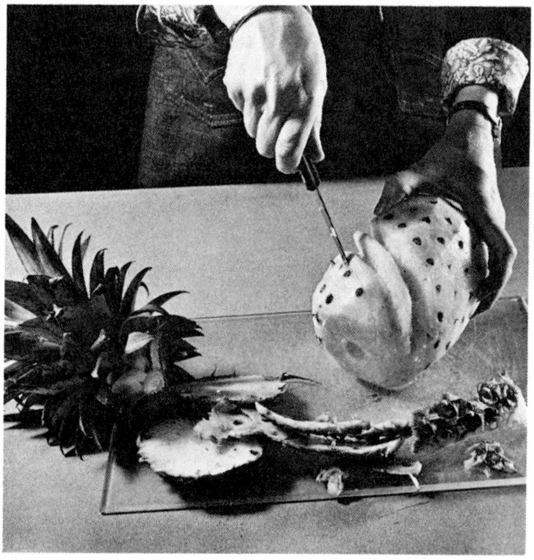

d

Fruits

Figure 2–1 (a) *Twist the pineapple top to remove it, reserving top.* (b) *Slice off top and bottom.* (c) *Remove peel by cutting thin, narrow strips, following the contour of the pineapple.* (d) *Remove eyes by cutting a triangular strip following the diagonal placement of the eyes.* (e) *Slice the fruit in half vertically.* (f) *Cut top of pineapple in half.* (g) *Trim leaves diagonally to retain their points.* (h) *A ready-to-serve pineapple.*

Serving suggestions

Fruits make splendid desserts. They may be served raw, eaten out of hand at a picnic, or eaten with cheese and nuts. They may be served stewed or poached, decorated with a mint leaf or a curl of lemon rind. They may be served in freshly cut pieces or stewed, in a crystal bowl sprinkled with shredded orange peel or coconut, or topped with sour or whipped cream as a beautiful climax to a meal. A fresh, chilled fruit is the king of quick, easy desserts, and it can be served with a variety of cheeses and/or nuts.

Fruit shells, such as those made of melons or pineapples, are attractive serving containers. Lemon, orange, and pineapple shells filled with appropriate ices or sherbets and frozen make easy, special desserts.

Open-faced pies and tarts are hearty desserts after light meals. They are even more appealing if red fruits are glazed with warmed currant jelly, and orange or yellow fruits, with apple jelly or sieved apricot preserves.

Fruit sauces used with puddings that have a high milk content provide additional nutrients, especially if the sugar content is kept down to avoid hidden calories. Upside-down cakes, made with fresh, canned, or frozen fruits, are delicious at any time of the year, and they are particularly suited to Sunday brunch.

In many respects, fruits are one of the most versatile foods we have. They can be served year-round in many forms and recipes.

Chapter 3 Vegetables

Vegetables are the edible parts of a plant—the leaves, the stems, the seeds, the roots. Today, a wide variety of vegetables—fresh, canned, and frozen—is available year-round. Many necessary nutrients may be provided by including raw or cooked vegetables in meals.

Consider color, texture, flavor, and shape when planning vegetable additions to a meal. Notice the variety of shapes of the vegetables shown in Figure 3-1, and think about their different colors, textures, and flavors. Contrast in color and shape makes a plate of food visually more interesting; and contrast in texture and flavor provides variety for the taste buds. Consider, for instance, a plate of chicken supreme with cream sauce, mashed potatoes, and cooked cauliflower. The colors and textures of these foods are much the same, and the food appeals neither to eye nor palate. But, a plate of glazed barbecued chicken, broccoli, and a baked potato (with the skin) with sour cream and chives offers variety in color, shape, and texture. Not only is it more attractive to the diner, it also offers a better range of nutrients since it includes the broccoli and the potato's skin.

Nutritional value

Many vegetables are excellent sources of minerals and vitamins. The dark green and yellow vegetables, such as chard, broccoli, carrots, and winter squash, are especially good sources of nutrients. These vegetables are high in vitamin A, calcium, and iron. Dark green vegetables also are high in riboflavin, while tomatoes, cabbage, and broccoli are good sources of ascorbic acid.

Vegetables contain a high percentage of water and *cellulose* (fiber), so their

Figure 3–1 *Salade Niçoise with perfectly prepared green beans and potatoes, garnished with tomatoes, egg slices, and olives.*

caloric value is relatively low. The seed and root vegetables do contain some carbohydrates—mostly starch; only a few contain a small amount of sugar. However, the calories we commonly assume are in vegetables frequently come mainly from the butter, sour cream, or gravies we use on them.

Legumes, which include peas and lima beans, have some protein content, but it is incomplete. They should be combined with a small amount of meat or other complete protein in the meal. (For additional information, see Chapter 10.)

Appendix A lists the nutritive values of vegetables.

Effects of preparation on nutrients

As with fruits, nutrients may be lost in preparing vegetables for cooking. When vegetables are peeled before they are cooked, more nutrients are lost than when vegetables are cooked in their skins. Even more may be lost when vegetables are prepared long before they are cooked: many nutrients are lost when sliced vegetables are left in water. In general, vegetables served raw or after a minimum of cutting provide more nutrients than do those served thinly sliced and cooked.

Effects of cooking and freezing on nutrients

Some water-soluble nutrients, such as ascorbic acid and the B vitamins, will be lost if vegetables are boiled—particularly if a large amount of water and small pieces of vegetables, with many cut surfaces, are used. Calcium also may leach out of vegetables during cooking.

Fresh vegetables, especially if locally grown and in season, usually provide more nutrients than do canned or frozen vegetables, but the differences are not very important. It is wise to select vegetables on the basis of cost, time, and availability.

Selection

Farm-fresh, field-ripened vegetables are available only to a limited few; the next best—fresh, undamaged vegetables—are in the markets. Wise consumers know how to select, how to prevent damage, and how to store vegetables, to obtain the best nutritive value for their food dollar.

Considerations in selecting vegetables

Grade For top quality, select vegetables that look fresh and free of damage and decay. The top grades of vegetables are more perfect in shape, size, and degree of maturity. They are more expensive, but they have no greater nutritive value than do lesser-grade vegetables of equal freshness.

Again, consider the intended use. If potatoes or other vegetables are to be stuffed and served, select higher-grade items; if they are to be mashed or used in soups or stews, lower-grade vegetables are satisfactory. Less-than-top-quality vegetables may be masked with a sauce or added to a soup or casserole. If vegetables (such as beets or baby carrots) are to be boiled and served whole, select a bunch of same-sized vegetables, to avoid overcooking the smaller ones. And if a vegetable is to be cut and tossed into a salad (such as tomatoes or avocados), it may be less perfect in shape and size than if it is to be filled and served as a salad.

Maturity Select vegetables, whenever possible, in the early stages of maturity for optimum texture and flavor. Most overmature vegetables are tough and have lost flavor. Avoid wilted, spotted, or discolored vegetables.

Nutritive value Since the nutritive value of meals can be improved by choosing and combining vegetables wisely, it is best to plan menus for several days in advance and shop accordingly. Dark green and yellow vegetables are needed daily. And, if ascorbic acid is not provided by citrus fruits, such vegetables as cabbage, tomatoes, peppers, and broccoli should be included in a day's meals.

Occasionally, there will be unexpected vegetables in the market—perhaps they were shipped from a warmer climate. If they are of good quality, fresh, and well priced, it may be possible to substitute them for vegetables on the market list. Out-of-season vegetables generally are shipped by plane, so the vegetables usually have not suffered nutrient loss.

Vegetables and the consumer dollar

When buying vegetables, consider the following questions.

1. What is the local season?
2. Which vegetables are grown locally? Local vegetables usually are fresher than are those that have been shipped in.
3. How much is needed?
4. Are adequate storage facilities available at home?
5. What is the cost per serving, rather than the cost per pound?
6. Compare the cost of fresh, frozen, or canned vegetables. Which is the best buy?
7. What is the vegetable's nutritive value versus its cost?
8. Is it possible to substitute an unexpected high-quality buy for something on the list?

Fresh versus canned or frozen vegetables

Depending on the planned use, the time of the year (peak-season availability), and the time necessary for prepreparation, canned or frozen vegetables may be a better buy than are fresh vegetables. Often, canned or frozen vegetables cost less than fresh ones. The wise consumer will consider these points when making up the market list.

Storage

Proper storage preserves vegetables' nutrients, as well as their appearance and texture. This is especially important if vegetables are served raw; good color and crisp texture add appeal and interest to any meal.

Fresh vegetables

Vegetables are best stored in the refrigerator's hydrator drawer. If they are stored in plastic bags, perforate or partially open the bags, to prevent rapid spoilage. The exceptions are green leafy vegetables. These may be washed, drained, and stored—with paper towels to absorb the excess moisture—in plastic bags. Although this practice shortens the storage time of green leafy vegetables, it is an added convenience in preparing meals.

Store mature potatoes, dry onions, uncut winter squash, and garlic in cool, dry places, in containers that are uncovered. However, the moisture from onions will cause potatoes to deteriorate more rapidly, if onions are stored along with potatoes. Tomatoes may be allowed to ripen at room temperature, then refrigerated until used.

Realistic selection of the quantities to be used and proper storage will result in less waste from spoilage of raw and leftover vegetables. Table 3-1 summarizes both selection points and storage information for a wide variety of fresh vegetables.

Canned and frozen vegetables

As with canned fruits, rotate canned vegetables on the pantry shelf, so that the oldest cans are used first. Once the cans have been opened, store the vegetables in the refrigerator, tightly covered. The acid in canned tomatoes may discolor the can, and, although the contents will not be harmed, it may be desirable to transfer leftover tomatoes to a covered plastic container.

Frozen vegetables should be hard-frozen at purchase, and stored in the

Table 3–1 *Vegetable selection and storage*

Vegetable	Characteristics for selection	Storage	Length of storage Raw	Length of storage Cooked
Artichokes (French)	Tightly closed leaves; compact, heavy for their size; fresh artichokes are crisp and will squeak when leaves are rubbed together	Refrigerate in drawer or plastic bag.	4–5 days	3–4 days
Asparagus	Crisp; firm stalks; tightly closed tips	Refrigerate standing in 1" water or in refrigerator drawer with damp paper towel around butt ends. May be washed and pared (readied for cooking) and stored.	2–3 days	3–4 days
Beans (green)	Young, tender, fresh; crisp pods; velvety feel	Refrigerate in plastic bag. May be washed, prepared to cook, and stored, wrapped in paper towel, in plastic bag.	6–7 days	4–5 days
Beets	Young, fairly small to medium size, smooth, firm	Refrigerate. May be washed, dried, and prepared to cook.	7–10 days	4–5 days
Broccoli	Tender, firm (not woody) stems; bud clusters tightly closed. Clusters may be dark green or purple green, but not yellowish or opened.	Do not wash until ready to use. Refrigerate. Toughest stems may be cut off and discarded.	1–2 days	2–5 days
Brussels sprouts	Small, fresh, compact heads; bright, green, tight-fitting leaves	Do not wash until ready to use. Refrigerate in drawer or unsealed plastic bag.	2–3 days	2–3 days
Cabbage	Firm, compact, crisp heads, heavy for their size; bright color—whether of red or green variety	Refrigerate in drawer. Refrigerate in unsealed plastic bag if shredded.	10–12 days 3–5 days	2–3 days
Cabbage (Chinese)	Small to medium-size heads; fresh crisp leaves	Do not wash until ready to use. Refrigerate in drawer or unsealed plastic bag.	5–7 days	2–3 days
Cabbage (Savoy)	Fresh, crisp leaves in a loose head	Do not wash until ready to use. Refrigerate in drawer or unsealed plastic bag.	5–7 days	2–3 days

Carrots	Small to medium size; well-shaped; crisp; firm; deep orange color	Refrigerate. Remove tops and store in plastic bag. (Carrot sticks, ready to eat, may be stored in plastic bag, wrapped in wet paper towel for 2–3 days.)	7–10 days 2–3 days
Cauliflower	Firm; white or creamy white; compact heads; no yellowed or loose florets	Remove outer leaves and refrigerate in plastic bag.	5–7 days 3–4 days
Celery	Crisp (not woody) stalks; fresh leaves	Refrigerate in plastic bag. (Washed and wrapped with paper towel, celery may be stored in plastic bag for 3–5 days.)	7–12 days 2–3 days
Chard	See Greens		
Collards	See Greens		
Corn	Green husk with both ends free from worms or decay; firm, plump, well-filled kernels	Refrigerate. (Best is 20 min. from field to pot; next best is to keep refrigerated until used.)	5–7 days 4–5 days
Cucumbers	Firm over entire length; green, may have small white (not yellow) tips	Refrigerate. Cut surface should be covered with plastic wrap.	7–10 days —
Eggplant	Firm; bright, shiny color; fresh green top; free from scars or decay spots	Refrigerate.	4–7 days 2–3 days
Garlic	Firm; dry, paperlike skin	Store in cool *dry* place; in cool cupboard or in *tightly closed* jar in refrigerator.	3–4 weeks —
Greens chard, collard, dandelion, kale, mustard	Tender, crisp, young leaves; free from yellow leaves, decay, or insect damage	Refrigerate in plastic bag; may be washed, dried, and wrapped with paper towel in plastic bag.	3–4 days 2–3 days
Leeks	Medium size, with fresh green leaves that are not ragged or wilted	Refrigerate in plastic bag.	3–5 days 2–3 days
Lettuce	*See* Table 4–1, Salad greens selection and storage		

(*Continued*)

Table 3–1 Vegetable selection and storage (Continued)

Vegetable	Characteristics for selection	Storage	Length of storage Raw	Length of storage Cooked
Mushrooms	Fresh, fairly clean, with closed caps (those with exposed gills have been in the market too long and have lost moisture)	May be washed if thoroughly dried. Store in paper bag with paper towel or in plastic bag and place in refrigerator drawer.	7–10 days	2–3 days
Okra	Medium-size (2–4 inch) pods, green color	Refrigerate in plastic bag.	1–2 weeks	2–3 days
Onions, green (Scallion)	Bright, fresh-looking tops with clean 1/4- to 1/2-inch bulbs	Refrigerate in plastic bag.	5–7 days	—
Onions, dry	Firm, with crackly, paper-dry skin; no softness or dampness at the stem end	Store in cool, dry place (not near potatoes, which give off moisture).	2–3 weeks	—
Mild-flavored Strong-flavored	White or red color; elongated or flat Globe shape with white, yellow, or golden brown skins; dry	Peeled onion may be covered with plastic wrap and refrigerated.	3–5 days	2–3 days
Shallots	Large, firm, dry bulb about 3/4" in diameter	Refrigerate in capped jar.	3–4 weeks	—
Parsley	See Table 4-1, Salad greens selection and storage			
Parsnips	Firm; small to medium size	Refrigerate in plastic bag.	5–7 days	2–3 days
Peas	Shiny green, fairly well-filled pods	Refrigerate unshelled peas in plastic bag until ready to use.	5–7 days	2–3 days
Peppers (bell or chili)	Firm, glossy color for the variety; no sign of decay, especially at stem end	Refrigerate in drawer.	7–14 days	2–3 days
Potatoes New	Fairly uniform size; free from blemishes and green spots	Refrigerate in drawer.	5–10 days	2–3 days
Mature,	Well shaped, firm; free from blemishes or any green spots	Store in cool, dry, dark place with good ventilation.	2–3 weeks	2–3 days
Round White, Red, and California Long White	Round White, Red and California Long White, because they have a higher sugar content, hold their shape when cooked and thus are more desirable for casseroles, salads, or boiled potatoes			

Russet and Idaho	Idaho and Russet have a higher starch content and are desirable for baking, frying, or mashing			
Potatoes sweet Yams	Light tan, a dry type, medium size, firm tubers. In the United States a variety of sweet potato, a moister, sweeter type; brownish red or coppery; medium size; firm tubers free from decay	Store in cool, dark, humid place.	1–2 weeks	2–3 days
Spinach	Fresh, crisp, tender leaves; fairly clean	Wash many times to remove all grit. Drain, store in plastic bag with paper towel in refrigerator.	3–5 days	1–2 days
Squash Summer (or soft-shelled) Zucchini, yellow, and so on	Small to medium size; crisp, clean, with no soft spots	Refrigerate in drawer or plastic bag.	2–4 days	2–3 days
Fall and Winter (or hard-shelled: acorn, Hubbard, and so on)	Frequently precut because too large for average consumers; look for crisp, clean, fresh pieces without bruises; well wrapped	Refrigerate cut squash in wrapper or plastic bag. Wash and dry. Peel before cooking.	3–5 days	2–3 days
Tomatoes	Firm and red, ripe; or pale pink to light red to ripen at home; free from blemishes; gently pick up the tomato—its weight on your fingers will indicate whether it is firm or soft (Smaller tomatoes may be a better buy in cost per pound.)	Store ripened tomatoes in refrigerator. Ripen at room temperature *before* refrigerating.	5–14 days (after ripening in refrigerator)	2–3 days
Turnips	Small to medium size; firm and heavy for their size	Refrigerate in drawer.	1–2 weeks	2–3 days
Watercress	*See* Table 4-1, Salad greens selection and storage			

freezer until cooking time. Thawed-and-refrozen vegetables have lost flavor and nutrient content from exposure to the air.

Cooked vegetables

Once vegetables have been cooked, refrigerate them in covered containers to keep them from drying out. Some vegetables, such as green beans, cauliflower, onions, beets, and carrots, may be placed in French dressing and refrigerated for use later in salads.

Preparation

Fresh vegetables

Carefully and quickly wash all vegetables to remove dust, dirt, and insect spray. Some small vegetables—for example, mushrooms—may be washed in a plastic bag with water, and rinsed and drained in a colander, as shown in Figures 3-2 a and b. Almost all vegetables should be washed and dried, whether the vegetable is to be used at once or refrigerated for storage. Some exceptions are Brussels sprouts, potatoes, and onions; do not wash these vegetables until they are to be used.

Time may be saved by prepreparing certain fresh vegetables. Onions, for example, may be finely chopped, as shown in Figures 3-3 a and b, and frozen in a container or plastic bag for later use. Green peppers, although they may be chopped and frozen, do not retain their crispness and are best used in cooked products. If it will be used in a day or two, celery may be cut into uniform pieces (Figure 3-4), tightly wrapped in plastic, and refrigerated.

Other vegetables that are to be served cold may be cooked ahead of time. Examples include baby beets or larger beets for salad, sweet potatoes for pie, and broccoli spears for salad. Artichokes, which require a fairly long cooking time, may be prepared (Figures 3-5 a through c), partially cooked, and chilled rapidly. Later, during meal preparation, they can be cooked until done.

Frozen vegetables

Freezing ruptures vegetables' cells and softens their texture. With the exception of blocks of frozen spinach and corn on the cob, frozen vegetables are

Vegetables

Figure 3-2 (a) *Washing mushrooms in a plastic bag.*

Figure 3-2 (b) *Rinsed and drained mushrooms.*

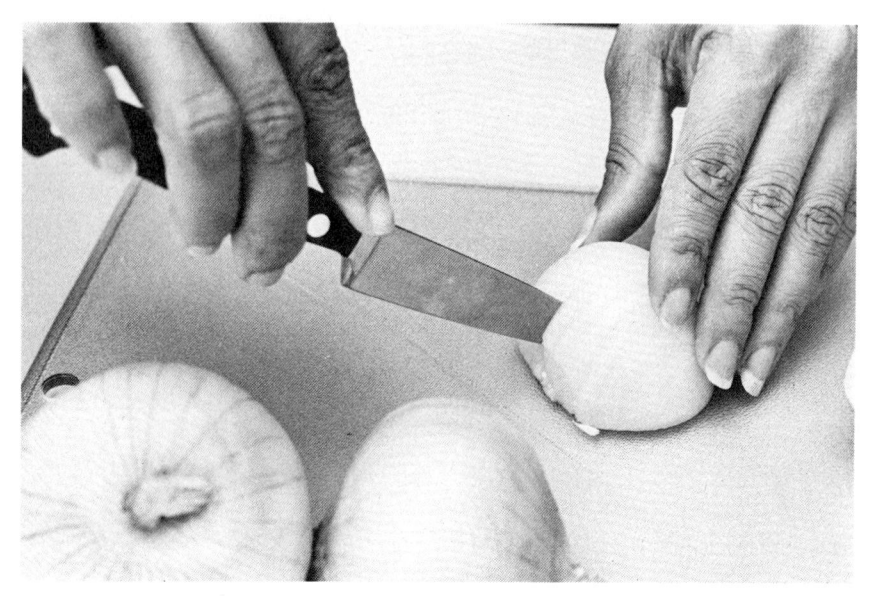

Figure 3-3 (a) *Place cut side of onion on a chopping board and make several vertical cuts.*

Figure 3-3 (b) *Slice onion horizontally to produce finely chopped onion.*

Vegetables

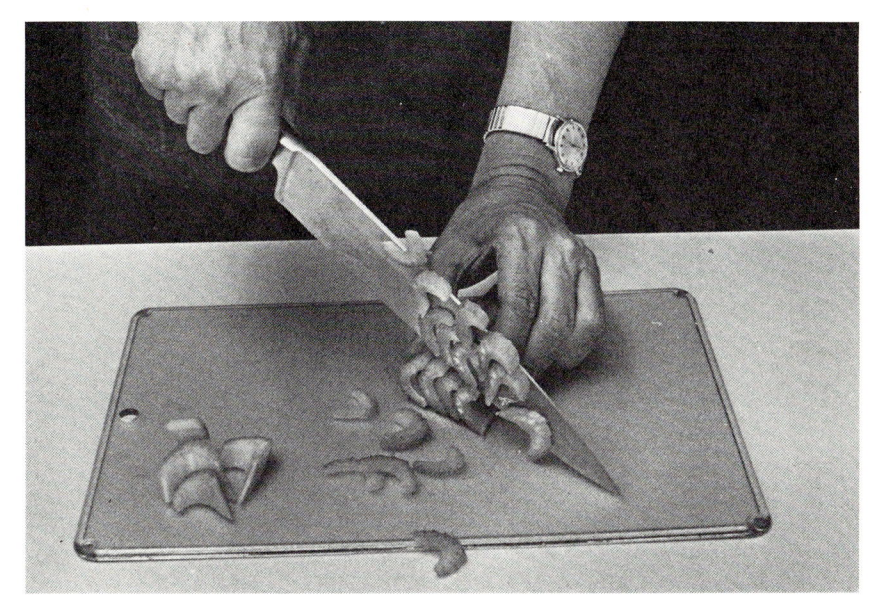

Figure 3–4 *Technique for chopping celery into uniform pieces.*

cooked in a small amount of water, in a covered pan, without thawing. Spinach may be cooked frozen if it is broken apart with a fork during the cooking process. Corn on the cob must be thawed before it is cooked, to avoid overcooking the outside before the frozen cob is heated. The package's instructions for cooking should be followed. One option is to cook a small amount of a frozen vegetable and return the remainder, sealed, to the freezer.

Vegetables to be frozen

Fresh vegetables may be prepared as they are for serving, and then blanched in a large quantity of boiling water for a period of two minutes. Cool them immediately in cold or ice water, seal them in an airtight container, and place them in the freezer. Fresh vegetables may be prepared as for serving and then frozen without blanching if they are to be held for a very short time. Blanching inactivates the substance that causes deterioration during freezer storage.

a

b

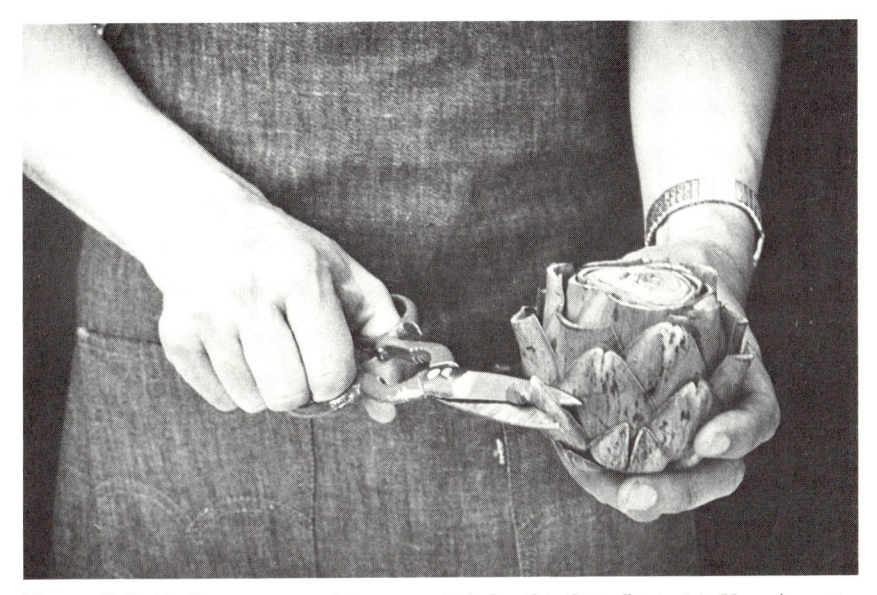

Figure 3-5 (a) *Remove stem of the raw artichoke.* (b) *Cut off top.* (c) *Use scissors to trim the points of the thistle.*

The effect of cooking on vegetables

The method chosen for cooking vegetables may enhance or adversely affect their flavor and color.

Green vegetables

Some green vegetables—broccoli, for example—turn a drab olive color when they are cooked in a small amount of water in a covered pan. As vegetables cook, they release an acid; in a closed container, the acid causes green color to break down. Therefore, to retain the green color, cook green vegetables completely submerged in boiling water in an open pan, even though this method causes greater loss of water soluble nutrients. Spinach is an exception, since its cooking time is very short.

Baking soda should not be added to green vegetables for cooking. It can affect their flavor and texture, and reduce their nutrient content.

White vegetables

Potatoes may turn pink, then brown when air reaches their cut surfaces. This discoloration can be prevented by dropping the cut pieces into salted cold water or by cooking the potatoes at once. To prevent other white vegetables from turning grayish or yellowish, cook them in a covered stainless-steel, enamel, or Teflon-lined pan. Pans made of other materials may react with the minerals in the tap water and cause discoloration.

Red vegetables

To prevent the loss of color, wash beets, cover them completely with boiling water, and cook them with their roots and stems intact. They may also be successfully cooked in a small amount of water if they are peeled and sliced or cut into small pieces. To intensify their red color, an acid may be added, such as vinegar to cooked beets, or tart apples to red cabbage.

Yellow vegetables

Carrots, corn, sweet potatoes, and other yellow vegetables may be cooked in a covered pan in a small amount of water. However, if large pieces of vegetable—such as whole carrots, whole sweet potatoes, or corn on the cob—are being cooked, enough water to cover is needed, to transfer heat.

Strong-flavored vegetables

Onions, cauliflower, Brussels sprouts, rutabagas, and other strong-flavored vegetables, all taste better when cooked completely covered with boiling water in an open pan. However, some people may prefer the heavier flavors obtained by using a smaller quantity of water.

Cooking methods

The general rule is always to cook in as large pieces as possible (to avoid nutrient loss) and just until crisp-tender (to retain color and shape).

Vegetables 49

Overcooking lessens the vegetables' flavor, texture, appearance, and nutritive value. The point of a sharp knife can be used to check degree of doneness. Figure 3-6 shows broccoli spears that are properly cooked, retaining their shape. With proper cooking, the broccoli will retain its color.

Boiling

The most common method used for cooking vegetables is boiling in a small amount of water—just enough to prevent burning. Boil the water before adding the vegetables, and then quickly bring the mixture back up to a simmer or gentle boil. Reduce the heat, cover the pan tightly, and continue cooking just until the vegetables are crisp-tender.

It is not always necessary to add salt to the water. In fact, in areas where the water has a high saline content, salt should *not* be added to the water because it may keep the vegetables from softening. If desired, salt may be added with other seasonings just before the vegetable is served.

Figure 3–6 *Broccoli cooked until crisp-tender, retaining its shape and color.*

At sea level, water boils at 100°C (212°F); at high altitudes, it boils at lower temperatures. Therefore, boil vegetables for a longer time at high altitudes, and add more water as needed. A pressure saucepan, adjusted to the particular altitude, is a convenient piece of equipment for vegetable cookery.

Vegetables that have a high cellulose content—corn on the cob, whole potatoes, and whole beets—are cooked in enough water to cover (to allow adequate heat transfer). The pan may be covered. Green vegetables and strong-flavored vegetables are cooked in water to cover, as well.

Steaming or waterless cooking

Steaming is especially suited to vegetables that cook quickly, or to those that are cut into very small pieces. Almost any heavy pan with a heavy, close-fitting lid may be used, with a controlled-temperature burner.

The nutritive value of steamed vegetables is approximately the same as that of vegetables that have been boiled in a small amount of water in a covered container.

Pressure-cooking

Vegetables to be cooked in a pressure saucepan often are cut into small pieces, to permit uniform cooking. Carefully follow the instructions provided with the pressure saucepan. The pan should be cooled promptly to avoid overcooking the vegetables.

Baking

Vegetables may be baked whole, in their skins, as commonly is done with potatoes or the smaller squashes. Very often, they are baked along with other items for the meal—roast meat, meat loaf—and the oven temperature is determined by the needs of these other items.

Many fresh vegetables (not the green ones) and all frozen vegetables may be baked in casseroles. Cut fresh vegetables into serving-sized pieces and partially thaw or separate frozen vegetables; then place the vegetables in the casserole. A little butter or margarine may be added, along with a very little water and seasonings. The casserole is covered and baked until the vegetables are tender.

Vegetables

Stir-frying

This method uses a large frying pan or an Oriental wok. Heat a small amount of fat in the pan. Add the vegetables, cut diagonally in very thin pieces, and cook, turning constantly, for two to five minutes. Asparagus, onions, green peppers, celery, broccoli florets, zucchini, and shredded cabbage are successfully cooked by this method. If green beans are stir-fried, a spoonful of water may be added and the pan covered for a couple of minutes.

Stir-frying seems to break the rule that vegetables should not be cut into small pieces for cooking. However, since the method uses very little or no liquid and the cooking time is brief, nutrient loss is not great.

Deep-fat frying

In deep-fat frying, the vegetables are cooked in enough oil to cover them. This cooking method requires skill, so always follow certain basic safety rules.

Safety Use a deep kettle, so that the fat or oil will not spatter over its rim. Be sure that the kettle is well balanced, and that there is no danger of its tipping and allowing hot fat to reach the burner. In addition, never leave a kettle of fat that is being heated or that is already hot unattended. If it is necessary to leave the kitchen, turn off the burner and remove the kettle from it.

A wire basket to hold the food is desirable, since it allows food to be quickly and safely immersed and removed from the hot fat. Heat the basket in the fat before adding the pieces of food to it. A thermometer also is a great help. Left in the kettle at one side, it will help the cook adjust the temperature of the fat. Overheated fat ignites easily.

Wet food should not be put into hot fat: water makes hot fat spatter and bubble up, increasing the risk of fire. Drain the food thoroughly and dry it with paper towels if necessary.

Procedure Oils and solid fats (lard or hydrogenated shortening) may be used successfully for deep-fat frying. Oil has a higher *smoke point* (the temperature at which it begins to smoke) than do lard and some solid shortenings. Oil or fat *must* be heated to the correct temperature before the pieces of food are put into it. If the fat is too hot, it will cause the outside of the food to brown before the inside is cooked; if the fat is not hot enough, it will allow the food to absorb fat before it cooks, and the product will be greasy and soggy.

Add the food pieces a few at a time, so as to avoid lowering the fat's

Figure 3–7 *Cutting radishes into attractive forms, to be crisped in ice water.*

Figure 3–8 *To make onion brushes: Cut green onions and place them in ice water to curl.*

Vegetables 53

temperature too much. The thermometer will register any change in temperature, however, and the burner can be adjusted accordingly. When the food is done, the pieces are placed on wire racks or paper towels to allow the extra fat to drain away.

Microwave cooking

This method is effective for cooking small amounts of mild-flavored fresh vegetables—such as asparagus, cut corn, sliced carrots, and winter squash—or for cooking one or two whole potatoes. It is necessary to increase the length of cooking time with the amount of vegetable. The nutritive value of microwave-cooked vegetables is approximately the same as that of vegetables boiled in a small amount of water in a covered container.

Using canned vegetables

The liquid from canned vegetables may be boiled down, to reduce its quantity and to concentrate its flavor and preserve its soluble minerals. The vegetables are then added to the liquid, heated, seasoned, and served. Opened cans of vegetables may be covered and refrigerated for two or three days. Again, it is better to transfer any unused acidic vegetables (tomatoes) to a covered container before refrigerating.

Serving suggestions

Vegetables add texture and color, as well as nutritive value and flavor, to the meal. Since the quality of cooked vegetables deteriorates when they are held at warm temperatures prior to serving, it is best to cook them just before serving. Some vegetables can be partially cooked and refrigerated. Final cooking then is done at mealtime.

Crisp-tender cooked vegetables need little more to be attractively served than a suitable platter.

Raw vegetables, artistically prepared, make most attractive edible garnishes for meat, poultry, fish, other vegetables, and salads. Figures 3-7 to 3-11 show methods of cutting radishes, onions, mushrooms, turnips, and cherry tomatoes for use as garnishes.

Figure 3-9 *To make fluted mushrooms: Rotate mushroom against knife to make a curved, shallow cut. Make second cut (not shown) to remove the thin slices of mushroom.*

Vegetables

Figure 3–10 (a) *To make chrysanthemum turnips: Thinly slice peeled turnips.*

Figure 3–10 (b) *Slice crosswise to complete the chrysanthemum turnip, then place in heavily salted water to form flower.*

a

b

c

Figure 3–11 (a) *To make tomato flowers: First, slice the cherry tomato.* (b) *Continue slicing both sides, to form petals.* (c) *Insert a toothpick to hold two cherry-tomato flowers together.*

Chapter 4 Salads

Salads are served as a first course, as an accompaniment to an entrée, as a main course, or as a dessert. Almost all raw or cooked fruits and vegetables, meats, poultry, eggs, fish, and cheeses may be used in salads; and the variety of combinations is endless. But the first item needed is clean, dry, crisp lettuce or another salad green.[1] To accompany the dry crisp greens, select a combination of foods that enhance and complement the rest of the meal, and top or toss them with just the right dressing. A salad of perfectly prepared vegetables and crisp greens, topped with a vinaigrette dressing (Figure 4-1), will enhance many meals.

Salads also offer an excellent opportunity to use planned-overs—leftover cooked vegetables, meats, and fruits. Yesterday's roast or fried chicken is today's chicken salad; yesterday's roast meat or broiled steak is today's beef salad; yesterday's dilled green beans are today's bean-and-onion ring salad. The creative cook will experiment with whatever foods are available.

Nutritional value

The nutritive value of salad, of course, is as varied as are the foods that go into it. In American menus, salads frequently are the main source of minerals and vitamins, especially vitamins A and C and riboflavin (a B-complex vitamin). Dark green leaves, such as spinach and romaine, are good sources of

---

1. You must dry the greens; salad dressings will not adhere to wet leaves.

Figure 4-1 *Asparagus and butter lettuce salad.*

riboflavin, vitamin A, and minerals. And uncooked vegetables—like cauliflower, zucchini, green pepper, cabbage, carrots, and tomatoes—and most fruits are an easy and excellent way to increase the vitamin and mineral content of a meal.

Frozen and molded gelatin salads are high in calories if they contain sugar and/or fat from whipping cream, sour cream, or mayonnaise. These recipes have limited use when calorie control is important. Appendix A lists the nutritive value of a variety of salad greens and other salad ingredients.

Many raw vegetables used in salads are more desirable if crisped by chilling in cold water. However, if vegetables are allowed to stand in water, they will lose some of their nutrients. So, to reduce the number of cut surfaces (and a greater loss of nutrients), try crisping whole vegetables or large pieces of vegetables. Also, leave the peel on fruits and vegetables whenever possible; this will add color to the salad, as well as retain the nutrients near the peel.

Selection of greens

A salad may complement the rest of the menu; the menu may be built around the salad or the salad may be designed to add the necessary contrast for the menu. Different shades and shapes of green, different textures, and different flavors yield a pleasing contrast. Also, bright fruits, vegetables, and green leaves add color to a meal.

When selecting a salad, consider both the flavor and the texture, to provide contrast and balance with the rest of the meal. For example, in a meal with a spicy entrée, use a bland salad; prepare a sweet salad to accompany a salty entrée; and serve a simple, but elegant, crisp salad with a rich, sauced entrée. Follow a lamb curry, for example, with a salad of tomato, cucumber, and yogurt; serve a fruit salad of cantaloupe, peaches, or pineapple to enhance a ham; contrast chicken with creamed mushrooms with a Caesar salad; or try fried chicken with a molded gelatin salad.

After determining the type of salad needed, be creative. Think about interesting combinations: raw or cooked fruits and vegetables, meat, fish, poultry, and cheese.

For the first course, serve a Caesar salad or a salad of pineapple and papaya, or grapefruit and avocado, or simply butter lettuce garnished with cherry tomatoes, topped with vinaigrette dressing. For the entrée, serve Salade Niçoise or a salad of crab and avocado, chicken and cashews (Figure 4-2), or Swiss cheese or roast beef. Use planned-overs: arrange chicken, turkey, meat, cheese, or ham on top of a tossed salad to make a good lunch or supper entrée.

Considerations in selecting greens

Always choose the freshest, best-colored greens. Not only is it important that the salad look appealing, but the freshest greens also have the highest nutritional content.

Appearance Select fresh, relatively clean greens that are free from insect damage and decay. Any edible greens that are young and tender may be selected. Fruits and vegetables that are to be served whole or in large pieces should be well-colored and free from bruises. If pieces (diced or cut) are used in the salad, lesser grades may be used, but any bruised sections must be removed.

Nutritive value The darker the leaves are, the higher the nutritive value is. Spinach, watercress, and outer leaves of romaine have a higher riboflavin and mineral value than do lighter greens. Dark green leafy vegetables and deep yellow fruits and vegetables are good sources of vitamin A. Cabbage, green peppers, and citrus fruits are excellent sources of vitamin C.

Figure 4-2 *Chicken and cashew salad, garnished with onion brushes.*

Salad and the consumer dollar

Select fruits, vegetables, and salad greens following the guidelines listed in Tables 2-1 and 3-1. Again, use in-season fruits and vegetables. This not only saves money, it also improves the quality of the salad. For example, substitute oranges and red-onion slices for out-of-season tomatoes; substitute spinach and cabbage when lettuce is expensive.

Fresh versus canned or frozen ingredients

Canned fruits and vegetables are convenient additions to a variety of salads. For example, drain canned vegetables and serve them on crisp lettuce, topped with vinaigrette dressing; or, mix drained fruits with sour cream.

Frozen fruits are not very satisfactory in salads; they are too soft when thawed. Usually they are more desirable in a gelatin or frozen salad.

Salads 61

Storage of greens

Store the soft lettuces—butter or Boston, red- or green-leaf, limestone or Bibb—and Belgian endive only for a short time. They are best used in the first few days after purchase. In all cases, the length of storage time and the greens' crispness are related directly to the care given to washing and drying them properly.

Washing

Head (iceberg) lettuce is the easiest of all greens to wash. Remove any damaged outside leaves, and then remove the core (Figure 4-3a) with a sharp knife and run cold water into the head through the cut-core area (Figure 4-3b), or firmly hit the lettuce on the countertop, core side down. Gently pull the head to loosen its leaves, so that the water can get into them and crisp them. Turn the head upside-down to drain.

Loose-leaf greens, such as romaine and red leaf lettuce, require thorough washing to remove sand, dirt, insects, slugs, and small snails. Break away the leaves from the core or center root. Wash, leaf by leaf, under running water

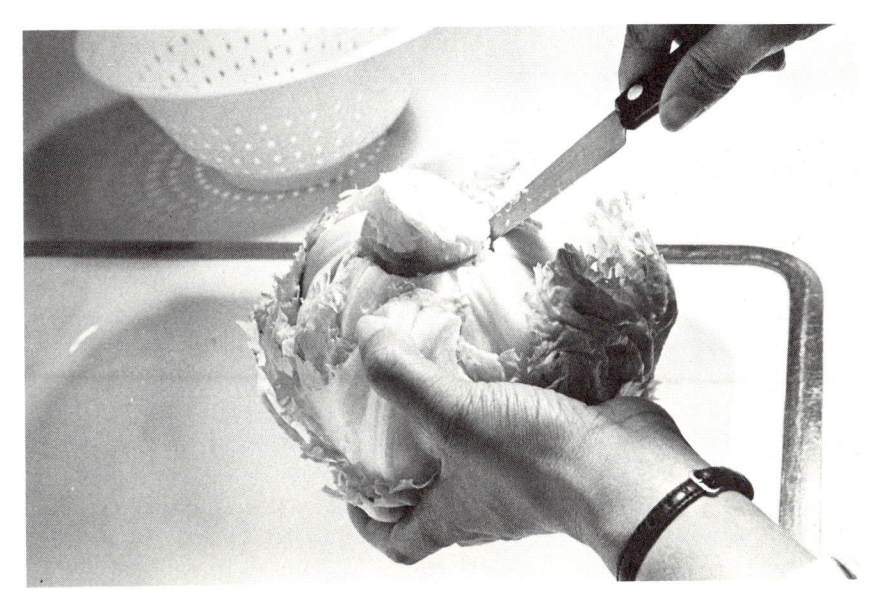

Figure 4-3 (a) *Remove core of iceberg lettuce.*

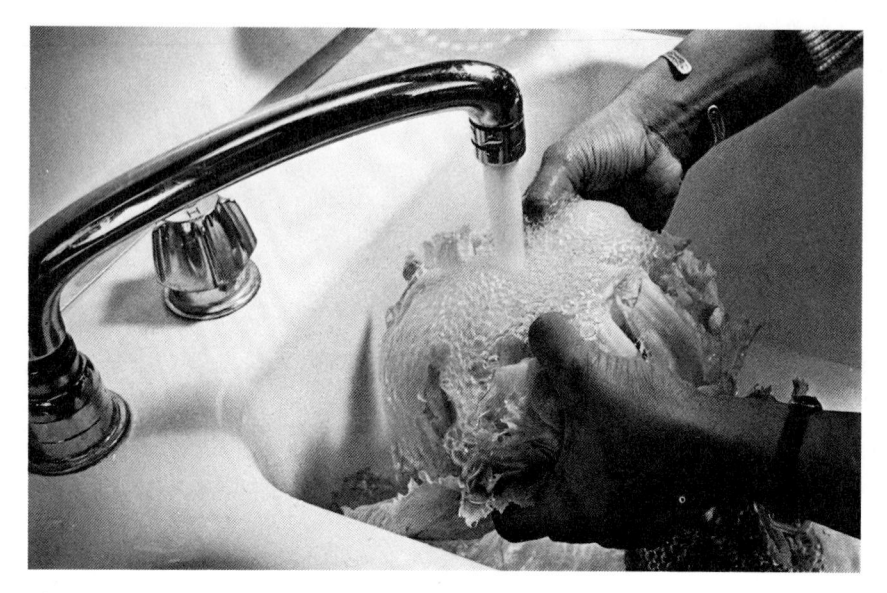

Figure 4–3 (b) *Run water into head and gently loosen leaves.*

or float the leaves in a sink or large container full of water. (When the leaves are removed from the water, sand and grit will settle at the bottom of the sink or container.) This process may have to be repeated two or three times before the leaves are really clean. Washing in *slightly* warm water the first couple of times may relax the leaves so that the sand is more easily removed. Use very cold water for the final wash, and inspect the leaves for insects.

Drying

Salad dressing will not adhere to wet greens. To dry them, first drain the greens. Then, roll them gently in a large cloth or in paper towels, to absorb the water. Or, put the greens into a wire salad basket, go outdoors, and swing the basket around. Or, put the greens into a plastic spinner, set it in the sink or on a tray, and spin the water off the leaves. (One ingenious cook who had to prepare a salad for a large group placed the washed lettuce in three pillowcases, tied the cases closed, and used the spin cycle of her washing machine to dry it.) However you do it, be sure the lettuce is dry: excess moisture hastens spoilage. After the greens are washed, drained, and dried, store them in a cold, moist place—usually the vegetable drawer of the refrigerator.

It may be more convenient, as well as more conducive to better meal management, to prepare and refrigerate the salad greens as soon as they are brought home. They then are ready to use whenever needed. Table 4-1 summarizes selection points and storage information for a wide variety of salad greens.

Preparation

Salad ingredients require draining before they go into a salad. Some ingredients—tomatoes, the juicier fresh fruits, and all canned fruits and vegetables—are best added just before serving.

Salt in salad dressings can affect a salad. Salt causes osmosis (see page 26) of the water in the salad's ingredients. This point is important to remember if such salads as coleslaw and tuna salad are to remain crisp. In many cases, it is wise to omit salt from the dressing and to add it just before the salad is served.

Mixing salads

Most salads are put together just before serving, to prevent the greens from wilting or becoming soggy and to prevent discoloring. However, a few salads improve if left to stand in the refrigerator for an hour or two, allowing their flavors to blend or their dressing to penetrate the ingredients. These include chicken, fish, beef, potato, and macaroni salads. Also, there are certain ingredients that need time to *marinate* (soak). Refrigerate these ingredients in separate containers and combine them in the salad at the last minute to prevent the flavors from blending. A salad tray of several different cooked vegetables—for example, Salade Niçoise—is typical. Any cooked vegetable used in such a salad should be firm but tender.

Avoid overhandling a salad's ingredients. Any salads that need tossing should be tossed gently, only until the ingredients are lightly coated with dressing.

Treat foods that discolor, such as bananas and avocados, with lemon juice or salad dressing, or serve them immediately just after preparation. Special techniques are helpful in this last-minute step (see Figures 4-4 a through h).

Experiment with herbs and unexpected accents: you may end up with a

Table 4-1 Selection and storage of salad greens

Salad greens	Characteristics for selection	Storage	Length of storage Raw	Cooked
Belgian endive	Clean, tightly folded, cream white to light green leaves (blanched by being grown in the dark)	Refrigerate in plastic bag.	1–3 days	—
Bibb or limestone lettuce	Small, loose head with dark outer leaves and creamy white core; no bruises or decay	Refrigerate in plastic bag.	1–3 days	—
Butter lettuce	Smooth, soft, tender, small, loose heads; fresh green, firm leaves; no brown spots or signs of wilting.	Refrigerate in plastic bag.	2–3 days	—
Cabbage	See Table 3-1, Fresh vegetable selection and storage			
Chicory or curly endive	Fresh, young, tender, crisp leaves	Refrigerate in plastic bag.	3–5 days	—
Escarole	Fresh, crisp, tender leaves; leaves are similar to, but more coarsely textured than, curly endive leaves	Refrigerate in plastic bag.	5–7 days	—
Garden lettuce	Young, tender leaves; free from insect damage	Refrigerate in plastic bag.	2–4 days	—
Iceberg lettuce	Fresh-looking, green outer leaves; round, firm (but not hard) head.	Remove core with sharp knife, or hit the lettuce firmly on a countertop, and wash lettuce under running water to force leaves apart. Drain, store in refrigerator on paper towel in plastic bag.	5–10 days	—

Parsley, Chinese	Fresh, tender leaves	Refrigerate in plastic bag.	2–4 days	—
Parsley, curly or flat	Fresh, tender leaves	Refrigerate in plastic bag.	1–2 weeks	—
Red leaf or green leaf lettuce	Medium size loose head, with bronze-red outer leaves, very tender and soft; (no bruised leaves or insect damage); green leaf is similar in shape but coarser in texture	Refrigerate in plastic bag.	3–5 days 5–7 days	— —
Romaine lettuce	Full, closely bunched, crisp, dark green outer leaves	Refrigerate in plastic bag.	5–7 days	—
Spinach	See Table 3-1, Fresh vegetable selection and storage			
Watercress	Fresh, crisp, dark green bunches without yellow leaves	Untie bunch and wash, stand upright in 1″ of water. Cover top loosely with plastic bag. Refrigerate.	2–4 days	—

Figure 4–4 (a) *Cut avocado in half.* (b) *Cut all around the pit.* (c) *Holding each half, firmly twist in opposite directions.* (d) *Separate halves.* (e) *Rap pit sharply with knife, and remove.* (f) *Using a large spoon, loosen avocado from its skin.* (g) *Lift avocado out of its skin.* (h) *Avocado half, ready to be filled and served.*

Salads

e

f

g

h

masterpiece. Use strong-flavored seasonings, such as garlic, onion, or crystallized ginger, carefully, so as not to overshadow the salad's ingredients. Try unusual combinations—onions with oranges, crystallized ginger in chicken salad—and be creative. Even the ever-popular tossed salad, with its crisp, dry greens, can be dull if served too frequently.

Making molded and frozen salads

When these salads are served after the entrée—especially if they are made with fruit—they are excellent desserts.

Gelatin molds When preparing gelatin salads, measure the juices or liquids from the fruits and vegetables, and count them as part of the liquid in the recipe. If the salad is to be served on a very hot day, use less liquid than the recipe calls for, to produce a firmer salad. Thaw frozen fruit before adding it to gelatin; otherwise, the gelatin will jell, the fruit will thaw, and the product will have pockets of water or fruit juice in it. Do not use fresh or frozen pineapple in gelatin molds; the pineapple contains a substance that keeps gelatin from jelling. This substance is deactivated by heating, so canned and cooked pineapple may be used satisfactorily.

Frozen salads Frozen fruit salads, in addition to being a nice change in the meal, are an excellent way to use extra supplies of ripe fruit. Almost any combination of fruits may be mixed with sweetened whipped cream and frozen in ice cube trays or frozen in paper cups. However, mayonnaise or sour cream cannot be used in these mixtures—they do not freeze successfully.

Salad presentation

The amount and the arrangement of the salad should be orderly, creating an attractive, tempting plate. Arrange the salad so that it is easy to eat. Therefore, only partially fill the plate or bowl, leaving enough space to eat or serve the salad without pieces falling onto the table. Serve cold salads, well chilled and on chilled plates when possible, with just the right amount of dressing to complement, not smother, the salad's ingredients.

Salads

Figure 4–5 *Tear chicken into bite-sized pieces to make a salad.*

Size of pieces

With the exception of a wedge of butter or iceberg lettuce, the food in salads should be in a form that can be easily handled with a fork. Figure 4-5 shows cooked chicken being torn into pieces that are suitable for use in a salad. Foods that are soft enough to be cut with a fork—canned peaches, pears, bananas, avocados, papaya, and molded salads—may be presented whole or in large, attractive pieces. All other foods should be cut into pieces that are small enough to be manageable, but not so small that they are mushy and unrecognizable.

Garnishes

Many salads may profit from the addition of an edible garnish. Do not overgarnish. A garnish should complement the salad's color, flavor, and texture. Celery fans and carrot curls, prepared as shown in Figures 4-6 and 4-7 a and b, radish roses or slices, tomato slices, cherry tomatoes, rings of green pepper or onion, slices of mushroom or cucumber, whole or sliced

Figure 4-6 *To make celery fans: Cut the celery as shown, and place it in ice water to form fan.*

hard-cooked eggs, a dash of paprika, or a sprig of watercress are just a few foods that may be used as a garnish.

Salad dressings

There are three main types of salad dressing: French or vinaigrette, mayonnaise, and cooked. Any number of other ingredients are added to these three basic dressings for variation, according to personal preference and to the type of salad to be served.

Originally, olive oil was used in vinaigrette dressing and mayonnaise, but now less-expensive oils, made from corn, soybeans, peanuts, and cottonseed, are widely used. Any of these oils gives satisfactory results. Cider vinegar (made from apples), wine vinegar, or distilled white vinegar is used for the acid. (Lemon or lime juice may be used instead.) White vinegar has a harsher flavor than do the other two vinegars, and some people prefer an acid that

Salads

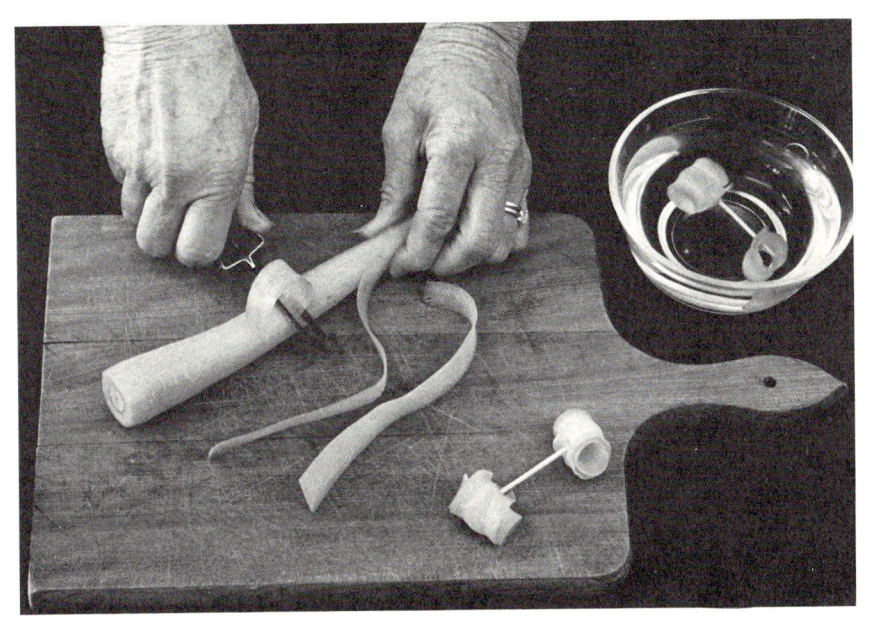

Figure 4–7 (a) *Cut thin strips of carrot.*

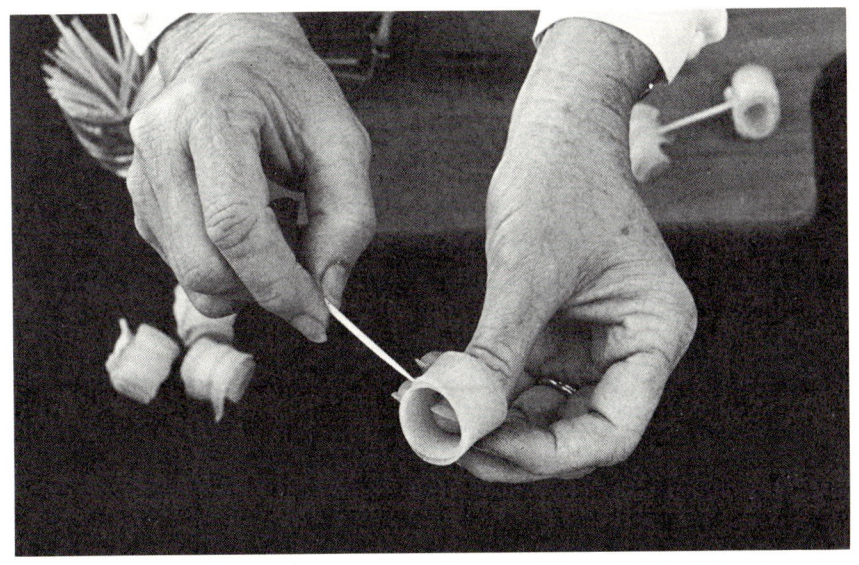

Figure 4–7 (b) *Roll thin strip of carrot and secure with a toothpick. Then, drop strip in water and chill thoroughly.*

has less bite. Flavored vinegars[2] add additional variety to any of the basic dressings.

Because oils tend to become rancid from chemical changes, dressing that contains oil—and those that contain egg—must be refrigerated in tightly covered containers.

Vinaigrette (French) dressing

The basic ingredients are oil and vinegar (or lemon juice) in a ratio of two to four parts oil to one part acid. A ratio of three to one is commonly used. Salt, pepper, and other spices may be added, as desired. Since oil and vinegar will not stay mixed together, homemade vinaigrette dressing is shaken vigorously just before it is poured, to form a temporary emulsion.[3] Commercial vinaigrettes, which must have at least 36 percent by weight of fat, often contain an emulsifying agent to keep the oil and vinegar mixed together. However, most of these products carry labels that direct the user to shake the bottle before pouring.

Ingredients often added to the basic mixture are honey, pickle relish, chopped olives, chili sauce or ketchup, chopped egg, blue or Roquefort cheese, and pimiento.

Mayonnaise

The basic ingredients are oil and vinegar (or lemon juice), which are held in a permanent emulsion by egg yolks or whole eggs. The fat content of commercial mayonnaise must be not less than 65 percent.

Mayonnaise is made with a rotary or electric beater in a bowl with sloping sides, so that the mixture can be beaten properly. Beat the oil into the eggs and seasonings carefully, so that the emulsion will develop without breaking. If it does break, the mixture can be used as the oil and beaten into another egg yolk. A blender also can be used, but the product is not as stiff as is that made with a beater.

As with vinaigrette dressing, many additional ingredients are added to mayonnaise for variation.

---

2. To flavor vinegar, allow herbs or garlic to soak in the vinegar for a week or so.
3. An *emulsion* is a mixture in which the tiny drops of one liquid are suspended in another liquid.

Cooked dressing

This product is similar to mayonnaise but, when made at home, has a much lower fat content. The homemade product consists of flour, egg, vinegar, and seasonings; the flour acts as the thickener. A small amount of butter, milk, or cream may be included, depending on the particular recipe.

Commercial cooked dressing, labeled *salad dressing*, must have a fat content of not less than 30 percent, and, therefore, it contains oil. These dressings also may contain emulsifying agents.

Calorie content of dressings

Vinaigrette and cooked dressing contain between 50 and 60 calories per tablespoon. Mayonnaise, with its higher fat content, contains approximately 100 calories per tablespoon.

Dressings that have a lower calorie content than does mayonnaise may be made at home by using unflavored low or nonfat yogurt as a base. For meat and vegetable salads, a wide variety of ingredients may be added, similar to those mentioned earlier, using water, vinegar, or buttermilk to make the mixture thinner. For fruit salad, honey may be added for sweetness. Also, gelatin may be used for part of the oil in vinaigrette dressing.

Selection of the dressing

For fruit salad, many people prefer a sweet dressing. Sugar or honey may be added to any of the three types of dressing, and sweetened whipped cream often is added to mayonnaise for use with fruit. A vinaigrette dressing made with lemon juice also enhances the flavors of many fruits.

Vegetable and meat salads are served with any of the three dressings, while molded salads invariably are served with mayonnaise. Some people prefer cooked dressing for coleslaw; others prefer mayonnaise.

Some salads have better flavor if the dressing is gently mixed into the ingredients an hour or so before serving, as was mentioned before. Refrigerated, the flavors of the ingredients have time to blend. For all other salads, the dressing is added just before serving. Adding it earlier can cause greens to lose their crispness, making the salad much less appealing. Always take care not to add too much dressing. The result will be an unattractive mass of nearly immersed ingredients. Dressing should just coat the ingredients—no more.

Chapter 5 Eggs

The versatile egg is the original convenience food. The egg may be the sole or main ingredient of the entrée for a quick breakfast, lunch, or supper. It may make an elegant first course or the most elaborate dessert for a formal dinner.

The combination of foods used with eggs seems endless. Each country of the world has its favorite. The creative cook who learns a few techniques and understands the principles of egg cookery has an unlimited opportunity to delight guests. Just mastering the simple French omelet opens the door to herb omelets, Spanish omelets, cheese-and-ham omelets, chicken-liver omelets, flaming strawberry omelets, and many other variations.

Nutritional value

Eggs contain complete protein of high value. In addition to protein, egg whites are a source of riboflavin and a very small amount of calcium. Egg yolks are a source of protein, fat and cholesterol, iron, riboflavin, and vitamin A. The nutritive value of frozen and dried eggs is the same as that of fresh eggs. Appendix A lists the nutritive value of eggs.

Selection

High-quality fresh eggs can be stored commercially under controlled temperatures (just above freezing) and controlled atmospheric conditions (carbon dioxide gas) for up to six months, without deterioration in their cooking qualities. This procedure helps to control the cost and availability of eggs during all seasons. Frozen or dried whole eggs, whites, or yolks, however, are not readily available in large quantities, except for commercial use.

Egg substitutes are found in the dairy or freezer sections of markets. They have similar protein content to whole eggs, less fat with a higher proportion of polyunsaturated fats, more calories, similar vitamin content, higher sodium content, and practically no cholesterol. Egg substitutes also are available in a dried form, which may be stored on the shelf. The dried substitutes contain less cholesterol, less fat, and fewer calories than do fresh eggs, and they may be used successfully for fresh eggs in some recipes.

Considerations in selecting eggs

The freshest eggs are always the best choice. The wise consumer will open the carton and check the eggs. Avoid those eggs with cracked or dirty shells; they are a haven for bacterial growth (see Chapter 1).

Grade Fresh eggs are graded by candling—a process in which the eggs are turned in front of a light. During the candling, the inspector can check for centering of the yolk, clarity, firmness, and any defects in the white, depth of the air cell, and any abnormalities of the shell. The eggs are then graded, according to the USDA standards, AA, A, B, or C. The shell of an AA-grade egg has a satiny appearance; the shell of a C-grade egg has a shiny surface.

Figure 5-1 shows how fresh and not-so-fresh eggs look when broken onto a flat surface. As the photograph shows, the really fresh egg does not spread out very far, and both yolk and white stand up from the surface. A not-so-fresh egg will spread out over a greater area, the white will look thin, and the yolk will be flat.

Size There is a great difference in size between peewee- and small-sized eggs and large- or jumbo-sized eggs. Recipes usually are standardized to use large eggs. In most recipes that call for only a few eggs, large or extra-large may be used. If, however, a recipe calls for many eggs, it is best to measure if either small or extra-large eggs are used. There are approximately two tablespoons white and one tablespoon yolk in a large egg, but there may be variations. In using fresh eggs, measure the amount of white if it seems small; a small quantity of water can be added, if necessary. The measurements also may be used as a guide in measuring yolks or whites that have been stored in the refrigerator from other recipes.

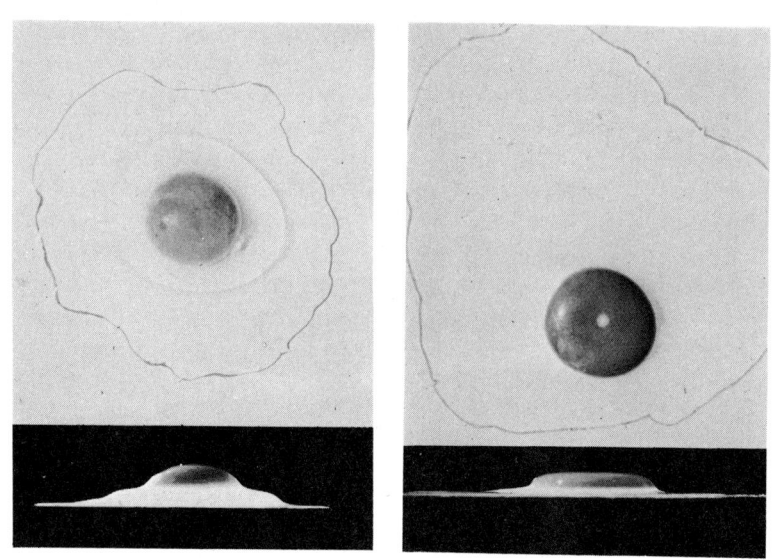

Figure 5–1 *Note different appearances of a fresh versus a not-so-fresh egg when broken onto a flat surface. At left: Grade AA egg, with yolk and white standing up from the surface, covering a comparatively small area. At right: Grade C egg with a thin white, a flat yolk, and the whole egg covering quite a large area.* (Courtesy of USDA)

Nutritive value The nutritive value of eggs is not affected by their grade or size, and fertilized eggs have no greater nutritive value than do unfertilized eggs. Also, the color of the shell and yolk is not an indication of the nutritive value. Shell color is determined by the breed of hen; yolk color is determined by the kind of food the hen eats.

Eggs and the consumer dollar

When buying eggs, consider the following points:

1. Egg prices are lower when hens are laying frequently, or just before that time of year when stored eggs are released in greater quantities.
2. Eggs should be purchased in a market that keeps them under refrigeration. Eggs held at room temperature deteriorate in one *day* as much as do those refrigerated for one *week*.
3. Grade AA is the highest quality, the most expensive, and the best suited

for frying and poaching. Lower grades are suitable for a variety of uses, such as custards, omelets, and baked products.

4. If medium eggs cost seven cents less per dozen than do large eggs, the medium eggs are a better buy, ounce for ounce. Medium eggs are interchangeable with large eggs in recipes that require a small number of eggs.

5. Low-cholesterol egg substitutes may be used successfully in many recipes that call for beaten eggs or egg yolks.

Storage

The grade on the egg carton indicates the condition of the eggs *when they were packaged*. The buyer must always remember that storage conditions affect quality very rapidly. An hour in a warm place—in transport, the market, or the car—will cause as much deterioration in quality as will several days in a refrigerator.

Fresh

Home-refrigerator conditions are not similar to those of commercial cold-storage rooms: unbroken, whole AA-grade eggs may be stored at home, refrigerated, for only two to three weeks. Since their quality will have deteriorated somewhat, making omelets, scrambled eggs, or French toast is a better way to use eggs in the third week than poaching or frying.

Eggs are best stored in the home refrigerator either in a special egg shelf or in the cartons they came in, with the large end up to keep the yolk centered. To help retain quality, take out only those eggs to be used immediately; do not leave the whole carton standing on the counter for any length of time.

Unused egg yolks may be refrigerated for one or two days, if they are covered with a small amount of water to keep the surface from drying out, or placed in a small, closed container. Leftover yolks may be used as garnishes: carefully place them in a small wire strainer and simmer until they are hard-cooked.

Unused egg whites may be refrigerated for five to seven days, in a covered container. Extra whites may be used in meringue shells, angel food cake, or baked Alaska. Table 5-1 summarizes both selection points and storage information for eggs.

Table 5–1 Selection and storage chart for eggs

Form	Characteristics for selection	Storage	Length of storage Raw	Cooked
Fresh, whole	Clean, no cracks; satiny sheen on shell.	Refrigerate, large end up, in carton or on an egg shelf.	2–3 weeks	5–7 days
Yolks		Refrigerate in a small container, covered with water. To freeze, add 1 t. salt or 1 T. sugar (or corn syrup) to each cup of eggs and place in freezer container.	2–3 days	2–3 days
Whites		Refrigerate in covered container. Freeze in covered container.	1–3 weeks 5–6 months	
Egg substitute		Follow instructions on package.		

Eggs

Frozen

Egg whites may be frozen and will keep for five to six months in a freezer section. Use them on thawing; they should not be refrozen. Yolks and whole eggs become thick and gummy if frozen plain, so salt, sugar, or corn syrup is added before freezing. Use 1 tablespoon sugar or corn syrup *or* 1 teaspoon salt for each cup of yolks. If whole, blended eggs are to be frozen, add ½ tablespoon sugar or corn syrup *or* ½ teaspoon salt to each cup before freezing. Thawed, these yolks or whole eggs may be used in making desserts, baking, or scrambling, depending on whether they contain sugar or salt.

Cooked

Once eggs or products that contain eggs—such as cream fillings, custards, and stuffed eggs—are cooked, they must be kept under refrigeration to prevent the growth of undesirable micro-organisms.

Preparation

The temperature and the length of cooking time are the two main considerations in cooking foods that contain eggs. Since the two factors are interrelated, they will be explained together.

Coagulation of eggs

When eggs are cooked, the heat makes their protein *coagulate* (thicken and hold together in a mass). Although coagulation can be useful, it also can create some problems. If an egg dish is cooked too rapidly or over too high a heat, the eggs will coagulate too rapidly. Rapid coagulation may cause the food to *curdle* (separate) as the protein forms small clumps in the mixture. Or, if an egg dish is cooked too long, the protein may form one large, tough curd. The liquid in the food then separates out and forms around the curd, in a condition called *weeping*. Acidic foods tend to make egg dishes coagulate more rapidly than they would otherwise.

The coagulation of eggs is useful in casseroles, meat or fish loaves, and other dishes, since it helps the ingredients hold together. Also, coagulation helps hold cracker crumbs onto fish, veal, and other meats.

Egg-white foams

Air can be beaten into eggs, especially into the whites, so that they can be used as leavening agents for cakes and soufflés. The air expands when it is heated and yields a large-volume product; the egg whites coagulate during cooking and form a structure for the product.

Sugar slows down the foaming action. Therefore, partially beat egg whites before adding any sugar. Add the sugar gradually, beating after each addition. If acid is added to egg whites shortly after they begin to foam, they will produce a more stable foam. Usually, cream of tartar or lemon juice is used for this purpose.

The whites must be beaten with a clean beater, in a clean bowl. Even a small bit of fat from the yolk or other source will interfere with the foaming action. For this reason, plastic bowls are not desirable for preparing foams, because they may retain oil even after washing.

In making egg-white foams, the whites are beaten until stiff (Figure 5-2), to incorporate a great deal of air, but not dry. Then, *fold* the whites into the other ingredients. Never beat whites into a mixture; beating breaks down the air cells. The process is best handled by first folding a fourth or a third of the beaten whites into the product, to thin and lighten it. Then, the remainder

Figure 5–2 *Stiffly beaten meringue will hold peaks.*

Eggs

may be folded in, to allow for minimum blending of the second quantity of whites. This procedure, which is explained in further detail in Chapter 9 (see pages 134–135), retains the maximum amount of beaten-in air and results in a higher-volume product.

Emulsions

Eggs help to form emulsions—they will hold melted margarine, oils, or melted butter suspended in a mixture. This is particularly helpful in preparing mayonnaise, hollandaise sauce, or sauce béarnaise. Acid, in the form of lemon juice or vinegar, added to the egg before the oil is added, will help the emulsion form more readily.

Cooking methods

Since high temperatures and too-rapid cooking produce unsatisfactory products, all egg cookery, regardless of method, must be done with care.

Baking

Baked custards cannot be subjected to too high heat, or they will be watery. Frequently, the filled baking dish is set in a pan of hot water and then placed in the oven for baking. The hot water helps to control the baking temperature. Products such as baked custard, custard pies, and quiches will continue to cook even after they are removed from the oven, because of stored heat. Therefore, they may be removed from the oven before they are quite done.

When soufflés are baked, the oven heat causes incorporated air in the ingredients to expand, and the soufflé rises. Like baked custards, soufflés may be baked successfully in a pan of water. Soufflés tend to collapse readily, so an aluminum band is used to add height to the sides of the baking dish (Figure 5-3). Then, the soufflé will stand above the top of the dish (Figure 5-4) and, even after it deflates, will have a better appearance.

When whole eggs are baked, their tops must be covered with a sauce, bread crumbs, or a lid, to prevent their protein from hardening.

Figure 5-3 *Place an aluminum-foil collar around soufflé dish.*

Figure 5-4 *A baked and deflated soufflé.*

Poaching, hard/soft cooking, and coddling

Since appearance is important, fresh grade-AA eggs are used for each of these cooking methods. The eggs should be cooked in simmering water and removed immediately from the water at the desired degree of doneness.

Poached eggs will coagulate more quickly in water to which vinegar has been added (one tablespoon vinegar to one quart water). To maintain uniform shape, first break the eggs into a small measuring cup, and then gently turn them into the simmering water. When they are done, remove them from the water with a slotted spoon and drain them on a paper towel. Eggs may be poached ahead of serving time, placed in cold water, and refrigerated. Reheat them by placing them in hot water. (Eggs that are cooked in individual poaching cups are *steamed* eggs; steamed eggs are tougher than are poached eggs.)

Soft- and *hard-cooked* eggs may be prepared by two different methods. With the first, place the whole eggs (in their shells) in a pan with enough cold water to cover. Bring the water just to boiling (the water must not boil). Then, turn down the burner so that the water is simmering and continue cooking to the preferred degree of doneness (3 to 5 minutes for soft-cooked eggs, 12 to 14 minutes for hard-cooked eggs). With the second method, use boiling water, adding one teaspoon of salt per quart. Gently and quickly submerge the eggs in the water. Adjust the heat to maintain the water at simmering, and cook the eggs to the desired doneness (4 to 7 minutes for soft-cooked eggs, 15 to 20 minutes for hard-cooked eggs).

To prepare *coddled* eggs, place whole eggs in boiling water. Turn off the heat at once, cover the pan tightly, and allow the eggs to stand one to five minutes before serving. Using another method, place the egg in an egg coddler, top with desired sauce or condiment, secure the top on the coddler cup, place in boiling water, and simmer for 10 minutes.

Occasionally, a greenish ring is found around the yolk of an egg that has been cooked in its shell. This ring is produced by the egg's sulfur and iron combining, and it is most likely to develop if the egg is cooked at too high a temperature or for too long a time or if it is cooled slowly after cooking. To reduce the possibility that this ring will form, remove the eggs from the heat as soon as they are done, and cool them rapidly under cold water.

Frying, scrambling, and making omelets

Moderate controlled temperature is necessary to *fry* a firm, tender egg. Excessive heat will cause the egg white to be tough and crisp. However, many

84

Food selection, storage, and preparation

a

b

c

d

e

Figure 5–5 (a) *Pour eggs into hot pan containing butter that has been heated until it stopped foaming.* (b) *Stir eggs with rubber spatula, for thorough cooking.* (c) *Partially fold the omelet.* (d) *Turn omelet onto a warm plate, completing the folding.* (e) *An omelet served with a broiled tomato.*

people are so accustomed to eating eggs cooked at too high a temperature that they prefer them that way.

For *scrambled* eggs, moderate heat is necessary to keep the butter from browning and to keep the eggs tender. Overcooking will turn them into a dry, hard mass. Stir the eggs occasionally, to allow the uncooked portion to come in contact with the pan. Do not overstir; this causes the eggs to form small, hard pieces.

There are two types of *omelet*: the French variety and the fluffy or soufflé variety. Cook French omelets in a smooth-surfaced pan to prevent the coagulated eggs from sticking. Add butter to the pan, and heat just until the butter stops foaming, before it begins to brown. Then, add the lightly beaten eggs and stir slowly, rotating the pan and using a rubber spatula to allow all of the uncooked egg to come in contact with the pan. Cook quickly over a moderately high heat and, when done, roll the omelet onto a warm plate. Or fill the omelet before rolling it. Figures 5-5 a through e show the steps involved in making a French omelet.

For fluffy or soufflé-type omelets, the egg whites are beaten separately and folded into the beaten yolks. Then, the mixture is cooked on the burner and finished under the broiler or in the oven.

Preparing stirred custards and puddings

Egg mixtures that are stirred during cooking, like soft custards, must be cooked with some caution to avoid coagulation. If a custard is cooked too long

Figure 5-6 *Stuffed and garnished eggs, ready to be served.*

or over too high a heat, the eggs will curdle. Therefore, cook these mixtures in a double boiler over *simmering*, not boiling, water, or use low heat and a heavy-bottom pan, stirring constantly to prevent curdling. If the mixture should curdle, the texture can be improved by quickly placing the pan in cold water and beating the mixture vigorously with a wire whip, or rotary or electric beater.

Some products, such as cream fillings or puddings, often require adding the eggs during the last few minutes of cooking. To do this successfully, the egg must be "tempered" by adding a small amount of the hot mixture to the eggs. After the two are blended together, pour the egg mixture into the pan, and continue cooking until the egg coagulates and thickens the product—usually, within a couple of minutes after the mixture begins to bubble.

Serving suggestions

Serve baked custards warm or cold, with or without sauce or fruit. Soufflés may be enhanced if served with an accompanying sauce; and dessert soufflés are more attractive if topped with a light dusting of powdered sugar. To preserve their height, serve soufflés immediately after cooking, using two serving spoons to separate and serve the individual portions.

Stuffed eggs, made with a pastry tube with a fluted tip, are attractive additions to lunch, dinner, and picnics. They may be garnished with a variety of foods, such as sliced stuffed olives, parsley, capers, ripe olives, pimiento, or dashes of paprika (Figure 5-6).

Appropriate sauces are a desirable and effective addition to omelets. Generally, the type of sauce depends on whether the omelet is served plain or filled and on flavor combinations. Usually, the sauce is spooned across the omelet creating a ribbon effect.

Chapter 6 Milk and milk products

Milk and milk products have been an important part of the human diet for several thousand years. And, they continue to provide a substantial amount of protein for people in many parts of the world. In the United States, cows are the chief source of milk; in other countries, goats, sheep, and yaks also provide significant amounts of milk.

Nutritional value

Milk contains high-quality protein, carbohydrates, fat, minerals, and vitamins. It is especially important in the American diet as a source of protein, calcium, riboflavin (one of the B vitamins), and vitamin A. The nutritive value of cultured milk products, such as yogurt, buttermilk, and sour cream, is the same as the form of milk from which they are made, plus any added ingredients.[1]

The different products made from milk—cream, butter, cheese, and milk desserts—have varying amounts of the nutrients found in whole milk. Appendix A lists the nutritive value of a variety of milk and milk products.

Kinds of dairy products

Milk

The safety of the milk supply is ensured by systematic local and state inspection and testing of dairy herds, along with sanitary handling and safe storage.

1. For example, the fruits that frequently are added to yogurt.

Milk and milk products

Because milk is an excellent substance for the rapid growth of micro-organisms, it is pasteurized. In the United States, most milk is pasteurized by heating it to 71°C (161°F), holding at that temperature for 15 seconds, and then cooling rapidly. In some European countries, milk is pasteurized by heating to 63°C (145°F) and holding at that temperature for 30 minutes before cooling. However, many people prefer the flavor of milk pasteurized by the faster process.

The following list shows the different forms of milk that are available.

1. *Homogenized* milk is pasteurized whole milk that has been forced by high pressure through small openings, to break the fat into small particles. Once broken down, the fat stays in suspension in the milk and will not rise to the surface.

2. *Nonfat* milk is milk from which almost all fat has been *skimmed* (removed). It contains less than 0.5 percent fat.

3. *Low-fat* milk is partially skimmed milk that contains about 2 percent fat.

4. *Fortified* milk is milk to which vitamins have been added. Much of the fluid milk sold in the United States is fortified with 400 I.U. (international unit) vitamin D per quart, because vitamin D may be inadequate in the American diet. Nonfat milk, which has had its Vitamin A removed by processing, frequently has 2,000 I.U. vitamin A added per quart. Some brands of dry nonfat milk powder also have vitamin A added. Carefully read labels on cartons and packages to determine the amount of fortification, if any.

5. *Evaporated* milk is milk that has had about 60 percent of its water content removed. Then, it is homogenized, canned, sealed, and sterilized. Evaporated milk can be made from whole or skim milk and will be labeled accordingly.

6. *Condensed* milk is milk that has had sugar added to it before it was evaporated and reduced to two-fifths its original volume.

7. *Dried* milk—whole or nonfat—has had 95 to 98 percent of its water removed. Dried whole milk, because of its fat content, does not keep as well as does the nonfat type, and once the vacuum-sealed cans of whole milk have been opened, they must be refrigerated. This form is not usually available in the market.

8. *Buttermilk* is pasteurized skim milk to which bacteria have been added, making it slightly acid and, thus, slightly thick. Sometimes, small particles of butter also are added to buttermilk.

9. *Chocolate* milk is whole milk plus sugar and chocolate.

10. *Chocolate-flavored* milk is whole milk plus sugar and cocoa.

11. *Chocolate drink* or *low-fat chocolate* is skimmed milk to which nonfat milk solids, sugar, and chocolate have been added.

12. *Yogurt* is made from whole, low-fat, or nonfat milk and is labeled accordingly. Acid-forming bacteria are added to the milk, making it thicker and semifirm. Dry milk solids also may be added.

Cream

Cream is the fat that is removed from whole milk. These are the different kinds of cream.

1. *Whipping* cream is the heaviest form, with 34 to 40 percent fat in the *heavy* type and 30 to 36 percent fat in the *light*.
2. *Coffee* cream has 18 percent fat.
3. *Half-and-half* is a mixture of milk and cream that has 10.5 percent fat.
4. *Sour* cream is an 18 percent cream to which bacteria have been added, to sour it.
5. *Whipped-cream products* are available in pressurized cans. They may be mixtures of cream and other substances or of milk solids and nonmilk fats, or they may be made entirely from nondairy products. Read the labels to ascertain their contents.

Butter and margarine

Butter and margarine have the same nutritional value. Both are used extensively and interchangeably in preparing cooked products and at the table.

Butter is cream that has been *churned* (agitated) to make all the fat particles lump together. Once formed, the butter is washed with water. Usually, butter is salted after washing, although *sweet* (unsalted) butter is available as well. Depending on the degree of yellowness wanted in the final product, food coloring or carotene may be added. The fat content of butter must be at least 80 percent.

Margarine is made by processing vegetable oils in skim milk to obtain a flavor similar to that of butter. The amount of saturated or polyunsaturated fatty acids in margarine is determined by the kind of oil used and the method of processing. Cottonseed and coconut oils contain a very high percentage of saturated fatty acids; corn, safflower, and soybean oil contain a high percentage of polyunsaturated fatty acids.

Several margarine companies now use a process that allows much of the liquid oil to be held in a soft, solid mass. This oil is used to make margarine with a higher polyunsaturated fat content. These products are of special importance to people who must follow diets that are low in cholesterol and saturated fatty acids.

Cheese

Many types of cheese are available—both domestic and imported—and all make a valuable contribution to the nutrients in the daily diet. Some common forms of cheese are natural, processed, processed cheese foods, processed cheese spreads, and imitation cheese. Cheeses are frequently served as appetizers or desserts (Figures 6-1 a and b).

1. *Natural* cheese is made from the whole or skimmed milk of cows, sheep, and goats. The milk is coagulated with lactic-acid bacteria or *rennin* (an enzyme). The *curd* (solid mass after the liquid whey has been removed) may be *cured* (aged) or left *uncured*, depending on the type of cheese being made. Other bacteria, molds, moisture, controlled temperature, and time may be involved in producing the finished cheese. A variety of natural cheeses are listed in Table 6-1, which also gives serving suggestions.
2. *Processed* cheese is a mixture of aged and fresh natural cheeses that are ground up and heated to a temperature high enough to pasteurize them and to prevent further aging. Sometimes, an emulsifier and additional seasonings are added, and the mixture then is poured into molds, wrapped, and packaged.
3. *Processed cheese foods* are similar to processed cheese, but they contain more moisture and less fat.
4. *Processed cheese spreads* have a higher moisture content and less fat than do processed cheese foods. These spreads frequently are sold in bottles, tubes, or vacuum containers.

Selection

The form or type of milk (or milk product) selected will depend on individual preference, intended use, budgetary considerations, and, in some cases, diet

Figure 6–1 (a) *Pepper cheese with crackers, grapes, and vegetables.*

restrictions. Whole milk and butter, with their higher fat content, may be neither necessary nor desirable.

The least expensive form of milk is dry nonfat milk powder, which may be *reconstituted* (mixed with water) and substituted for fluid milk in most recipes—with little or no discernable change in the product. Many people find the flavor of reconstituted milk as a beverage more acceptable if it is chilled for several hours before use. It also may be reconstituted and mixed with an equal amount of fresh milk.

Milk and milk products

Figure 6–1 (b) *Gourmandise cheese with cherries and ginger snaps and pepper cheese with grapes and crackers.*

Storage

Milk

To prevent spoilage and destruction of riboflavin, promptly refrigerate fresh milk in its original container. Close the container tightly, since milk readily absorbs flavors from other foods. Fluid milk usually may be held in its container, refrigerated, up to one week after the date stamped on the carton. (If milk has been poured from the container or bottle and has not been used, it should be returned to the refrigerator in a separate container.) Milk may be frozen and kept for several months, but the flavor may change and the fat may separate.

The cultured forms of milk, such as yogurt and buttermilk, may be refrigerated for up to two weeks. Evaporated and condensed milk may be refrigerated after opening—in the original cans—and held up to a week. Unopened

Table 6–1 *Types of cheeses*

Type	Description	Serving suggestions
SOFT, UNCURED OR UNRIPENED		
Cottage cheese	Soft with small or large curds; creamed or uncreamed	With fruits or vegetables
Farmer cheese or pot cheese	Very dry, like some cottage cheese, but formed into a block and wrapped in foil	With fruits, vegetables, desserts
Ricotta	Soft curd with salt added	In cooking
Cream cheese	Soft and smooth; mild flavor	In cheesecakes, dips, sandwiches
Neufchatel (American variety)	Soft, creamy, with lower fat content than cream cheese	In cheesecakes, dips, sandwiches
Mozzarella	Semihard, rubbery; mild flavor	In cooking, especially pizza.
SOFT, CURED OR RIPENED		
Camembert	Soft to liquid interior with a thin, edible crust; delicate characteristic flavor that becomes more distinctive as the cheese ages	With crackers or French bread, or with fruits such as apples or pears
Brie	Soft interior with a thin, edible crust; delicate characteristic flavor	With crackers or French bread, or with fruits such as apples or pears
Gourmandise (cherry or walnut)	Soft, creamy cheese; delicately flavored with cherries or walnuts	With hard rolls, wheatmeal crackers, gingersnaps, apples, cherries, or walnuts

SOFT TO FIRM, CURED OR RIPENED

Roquefort	Soft to firm; white with characteristic blue mold veining	In salads and salad dressings, or with crackers and assorted fruits
Port Salut	Soft to firm; slightly rubbery texture; very distinctive pungent flavor	With crackers and fruit, especially apples and pears
Tilsit	Soft to firm; mild and mellow flavor; caraway seeds sometimes added	With rye bread or rye crackers, or with fruit
Blue	Soft to firm; creamy white with characteristic blue mold veining	In salads or salad dressings, in gelatin-based molds, or with crackers and assorted fruits
Monterey Jack	Soft to firm; mild	In cooking; in sandwiches, with crackers or bread, or with assorted fruits.
Muenster	Soft to firm; with a distinctive flavor	In sandwiches, or with crackers or bread.

SEMIHARD

Gruyere	Semihard; with gas holes; nutty flavor	With crackers or bread, or in fondue.
Swiss	Semihard; with large gas holes; sweet-nutty flavor	In cooking; with crackers, or bread, in sandwiches, and with fruit.
Cheddar	Semihard; smooth; mild to sharp flavor	With crackers or bread, with sandwiches, in soufflés, with fruit and apple pies

HARD

Parmesan	Very hard; well aged; with a distinct flavor	In cooking, grated

cans may be held at cool room temperature for up to a year. Nonfat dry milk may be stored at cool room temperature for several months. The flavor may deteriorate slightly if an open box of milk is stored for an extended period of time. Dry whole milk must be refrigerated after the container is opened, because its fat will become rancid.

Cream

Like milk, cream should be refrigerated in its closed container. Sterilized whipping cream may be held in the refrigerator for several weeks.

Butter and margarine

Because of their fat content, both butter and margarine should be kept carefully wrapped in the coldest section of the refrigerator. If a softer consistency is desired for table use, remove the needed amount and let it stand at room temperature for a short time before the meal. These table spreads may be stored in the refrigerator for several weeks, or wrapped in moisture-proof paper and frozen.

Cheese

Uncured soft cheeses, such as cottage and farmer cheeses, should be kept in the refrigerator in a covered container, to prevent formation of molds. For best flavor, they should be used promptly.

Cured cheeses must be completely covered, sealed with plastic wrap, and stored in the refrigerator to keep them from drying out and, also, to prevent mold from forming on them. If mold should develop, carefully trim it off and discard it. Cheese may be frozen, but many varieties will show a slight texture or flavor change. Bits and pieces of cheese may be grated, mixed, sealed, and refrigerated or frozen for later use in omelets, casseroles, and other dishes.

Preparation

Milk

Three problems commonly are encountered in milk cookery: scum formation (on the top of heated milk), scorching or burning, and curdling.

Milk and milk products

Scum formation Heating milk, even at low temperatures, will cause a thin film, or scum, to form on the top of the milk, and this scum will stick to the sides of the pan. As heating continues, pressure builds up and suddenly the scum will break, allowing the milk to boil up and over the sides of the pan. Beating the milk with a wire whip or rotary beater, to form a foam on the surface, helps to prevent scum formation, and stirring the milk frequently during heating will prevent it from boiling up and over.

Scorching or burning As milk is heated, its protein coagulates and collects on the bottom of the pan. When milk or milk products are cooked over direct heat, the layer of coagulated protein may burn or scorch. Therefore, always stir frequently and cook milk and milk products in a heavy-bottom pan over low heat or in a double boiler. Special care is needed when adding cornstarch or flour to milk and then cooking the mixture, as for puddings and pastry fillings. The cornstarch and milk mixture will burn even faster than will plain milk. (Over 1,000 feet altitude, double boiler cooking is not satisfactory.)

Curdling If an acidic food is added to milk or a milk product, the milk's protein will coagulate and curdle the mixture. Therefore, if a recipe calls for the addition of an acidic food, slowly add a small amount of the food (heated) to the milk mixture and stir thoroughly. Then, repeat the process until all the acidic food has been incorporated.

Curdling also may result from the lactic acid in old milk, and heating hastens the process.

In addition, cooking a milk mixture at too high a temperature or for too long a time may cause curdling. Temperatures and cooking times for such products as stirred custards must be watched carefully.

Whipping cream

Cream will whip more easily and to a more desirable consistency if the cream, beater or whip, and bowl are well chilled before whipping. Since whipped cream will deflate if it is served on or combined with warm foods, the custard-gelatin mixture used to make molded desserts, such as that shown in Figure 6-2, must be chilled, but not jelled, before the whipped cream is folded in.

Figure 6–2 *Chestnut Chinoiserie.*

Milk products

Sour cream curdles very quickly when it is heated. Therefore, add it at the end of the heating period, just before the food is served. Never heat sour cream to boiling. Also, sour cream and yogurt will become thin if overstirred.

Butter

1. Butter, when hot enough for sauteéing, will begin to stop foaming.
2. Butter, because of the milk it contains, will burn easily.
3. Clarified butter, liquid and milk solids removed, can be heated to a higher temperature without browning. To make clarified butter, cut butter into pieces and place in saucepan over medium heat. Heat until butter is melted and foam forms. Remove foam with a spoon. Gently pour clear liquid into container, leaving the milk residue in the saucepan.
4. Butter mixed with oil may be heated to a higher temperature before burning.

Cheese

When cheese is melted, a low temperature and a short time are used: overheating or overcooking will make the cheese tough, stringy, and rubbery. Grated and finely chopped cheese will melt quickly. Processed and cured cheeses melt more easily and are less likely to be stringy than are uncured young cheeses.

Except for cottage cheese, cheeses taste better if served at room temperature. A good general rule is to remove the needed amount of cheese from the refrigerator 30 minutes before it is to be served.

Frozen milk desserts

Frozen desserts with high milk or cream content are basically of two types: those that are *stir-frozen* (agitated during freezing), which includes sherbets, ice milks, and ice creams; and those that are *still-frozen* (without agitation), such as parfaits, bombes, and mousses. Table 6-2 shows a variety of these desserts, with their usual ingredients and serving suggestions.

A desirable frozen-milk dessert has small ice crystals, evenly distributed throughout the mixture, so that the product is smooth on the tongue. The formation of these small crystals is affected by the ingredients, the freezing method, and the rate and amount of agitation used for the product.

Frozen desserts may be made from a variety of milk products—whipping cream, half-and-half, whole milk, dry whole or nonfat milk, or from combinations of these ingredients. The fat content of the product helps to produce the desired smooth texture and also contributes to the rich taste. Eggs may be added for increased richness, and gelatin or cooked cornstarch mixtures may be used to prevent the formation of large crystals in storage.

At home, prepare frozen milk desserts by freezing them in a special ice cream freezer, immersed in rock salt and ice using one part salt to eight parts ice. Still-frozen desserts may be frozen in a refrigerator tray, according to recipe directions. These desserts are best if frozen as quickly as possible, so that large crystals do not form. Depending on the ingredients, some of the still-frozen products can be stirred when partly frozen, to encourage formation of small crystals.

Table 6-2 *Frozen milk desserts*

Type	Ingredients	Serving suggestions
SHERBET	Milk, sugar, fruit or fruit flavoring; may contain gelatin or egg white for firmness	Before or with entrée, with fruit salad or for dessert
ICE CREAM		
French or frozen custard	Cream, eggs, and sugar cooked to a custard as the base; may contain flavorings and other ingredients; the richest type, with highest butterfat content	Dessert
Philadelphia	Cream, sugar, and flavorings; may contain other ingredients	Dessert
American, or plain	Made like French but may contain gelatin, stabilizers, or other ingredients; must have at least 10% milk fat	Dessert
MOUSSE	Based on whipped cream and flavoring; may have beaten egg whites or gelatin; very rich	Dessert
PARFAIT	A true parfait contains beaten egg whites mixed with sugar syrup, into which stiffly beaten whipped cream is folded before freezing (the name is also used for a dessert made by layering softened ice cream and fruit or sauces in a tall glass and freezing before serving).	Dessert
BOMBE	Ice cream frozen with a center of different color and different flavor of ice cream, mousse, or sherbet; often made in a melon or cylindrical mold	Dessert

Table 6-3 *Other frozen desserts*

Type	Ingredients	Serving suggestions
Water ice or ice	Water, sugar, and fruit flavoring	Before entrée; or for dessert
Frappe	Similar to sherbet but served mushy, in a chilled dish	As an appetizer; as an accompaniment to entrée; or for dessert
Ice milk	Similar to plain ice cream but with lower fat content; may have more sugar than plain ice cream and thus an equally high calorie content	Dessert

Homemade frozen milk desserts are best eaten promptly, since they do not store well. If they must be held for a short time, they should be carefully covered, to protect the flavor. Do not allow them to thaw, lest large crystals and undesirable texture result.

Several other types of frozen dessert are made—some with milk and some without milk. Table 6-3 lists these products, their ingredients, and serving suggestions.

Chapter 7 Breads

Bread, in one form or another, is a mainstay in the diet, yet it is one of the most enjoyable and tantalizing of foods. Think of breakfast and the aroma of freshly baked cinnamon rolls or muffins. Think of hot pancakes and coffee over a campfire. Any meal can be enhanced with one of the breads shown in Figure 7-1.

Nutritional value

The exact nutritional value of a particular bread will depend on its ingredients, as listed in Appendix A. Breads made from whole-wheat or enriched flours contribute a significant amount of nutrients, and they are almost a necessity in the American diet if the average person is to obtain adequate amounts of the B vitamins, especially thiamin. Eggs, milk, and dry milk solids increase the nutritional value of breads, including their protein content.

Ingredients

Although the combination of ingredients may vary, most breads contain flour, fat, liquid, egg, and a leavening agent.

Wheat flour

Most flour is made from wheat by a *milling* process, which involves grinding, sifting, and separating. Wheat is described in two ways: the time of year it is

Breads 103

Figure 7-1 *A selection of home-baked breads, to add appeal and nutrition to meals.*

sown and the hardness (or softness) of its kernel. *Winter* wheat is planted in early fall and harvested in early summer; *spring* wheat is sown in spring for late-summer harvesting. And, depending on the variety of plant, wheat will produce either a *hard* or *soft* kernel.

Hard wheat has more protein than does soft wheat, and it will form more gluten. *Gluten* is an elastic substance, that develops when the protein in flour combines with the water or other liquid in a mixture. Gluten is important because it determines shape and height of the flour-based product and contributes to its firmness.

The following list describes the different kinds of flour.

1. *Hard-wheat* flour has the ability to form strong gluten. It is used in bread and is available primarily for commercial use.
2. *Soft-wheat* flour, often called *cake* flour, is a very fine flour that is used for making cakes, both commercially and in the home.
3. *All-purpose* or *general-purpose* flour is a mixture of hard and soft flours that is used for baking and other home cookery.
4. *Self-rising* flour contains salt and baking powder. It is used mostly in the South where hot breads are served with most meals and quick preparation is important.

5. *Instantized* or *instant-blending* flour is processed in such a way that it will not pack or stick together. It is easy to measure and does not have to be sifted. It is best used to thicken sauces and gravies; if quickly and thoroughly stirred into a hot mixture, it will not develop lumps. Recipes for other products must be adjusted to use this type of flour, and a resulting baked product may not always be satisfactory.

6. *Enriched* flour is white flour to which iron, thiamin, riboflavin, and niacin have been added, to replace some of the nutrients removed in the milling process.

7. *Whole-wheat* or *graham* flour contains all the natural nutrients of the wheat kernel. It does not keep as well as does white flour. All-whole-wheat dough does not form as much gluten as does wheat flour with the bran removed, so if used in bread making, a small compact loaf results. To produce greater volume in baked products, whole-wheat flour usually is mixed with white flour.

Other wheat products

Wheat germ—a small, tan flake—contains many of the nutrients of the wheat kernel, and it is used to increase the nutritional value of baked products and other foods. Because of its fat content, refrigerate it in a tightly closed container if it is to be held several weeks.

Cracked wheat is wheat kernels that have been cracked into small particles, not milled like flour. It has a coarse texture, and usually is softened with water and mixed with flour to make bread.

Other flours

Flour also is made from rye and soybeans. *Rye* flour contains some protein, but it does not form gluten as does wheat flour. It will make a very compact loaf of bread (pumpernickel, for example), so it often is mixed with wheat flour for a larger, lighter loaf. *Soy* flour most often is used as a concentrated protein source that is added to foods to increase their nutritional value.

Cornmeal

Cornmeal, made from white or from yellow corn, is a grainy substance that is coarser than flour. It produces no gluten and must be mixed with wheat flour to create a product that will hold together without crumbling.

Fat

Fat adds flavor to breads and *shortens* (tenderizes) the gluten; the amount of fat used in making breads influences both their tenderness and texture. Oils or solid fats—lard from hogs or hydrogenated shortening[1]—may be used interchangeably, but the texture will differ. Biscuits made with solid fat have a desirable, flaky interior; those made with oil have a fine, tender crumb.

Liquid

Liquid is used to moisten the protein, to develop the gluten, to help in the formation of steam for leavening the product, and to activate any chemical leaveners to form carbon dioxide for leavening.

Whole milk, reconstituted dry-milk solids, evaporated milk, buttermilk, cream, and sour cream, all are used in breads, and all add to their nutritional value. In addition, water and fruit juices also may be used.

Eggs

Eggs help to develop the structure of the bread by their coagulation during baking. And, when used as a whipped foam, they trap air and aid in leavening the product. They also add flavor, color, and nutritional value.

Leaveners

The function of the leavener—air, steam, or carbon dioxide—is to make the baked product light and airy. Most products have more than one leavener: beaten eggs incorporate air; water produces steam; chemical agents, such as baking powder, produce carbon dioxide. Many quick breads contain all three types of leavener.

Steam can produce dramatic results, as in popovers, Yorkshire pudding, and cream puffs. To make these products, the mixture is beaten to produce the gluten necessary for the framework—a framework to support the large, thin, hollow shells.

---

1. *Hydrogenation* is a process in which hydrogen is added to the fatty-acid molecule in the oil, to solidify it. This process also results in a saturated fatty acid.

In food, carbon dioxide, the gas that acts as a leavener, can be developed in three ways. Baking powder, which will release carbon dioxide when it is moistened by the liquid in the mixture, may be used.[2] The mixture may contain an acidic liquid, such as buttermilk or sour milk, which combines with baking soda, forming the carbon dioxide. Or, yeast may be incorporated into the mixture to produce gas.

The first two methods are used for foods that are baked immediately after they are mixed; the third requires a different technique. Yeast is available in both a dry and a compressed, slightly moist form, and it is a live microorganism. Time, moisture, and warm temperature allow the yeast to react with the sugar to release the carbon-dioxide gas.

Preparation

Flour

Lighten flour by stirring it and spooning it gently into a measuring cup. Once it is measured, put the flour into a sifter and place the dry ingredients on top of the flour, to allow proper mixing during sifting.

Do not sift whole-wheat flour and cornmeal; simply stir and spoon them into a measuring cup. Add other dry ingredients and stir the dry mixture well, to ensure even distribution.

Other ingredients

Fat and eggs usually can be handled more easily if they are at room temperature. Liquids should be cold or warm, whatever the recipe directs. When melted fat is called for in muffins, cornbread, and yeast breads, the same quantity of oil may be substituted for convenience.

Mixing methods

Flour mixtures generally are considered to be batters or doughs, depending on the amount of liquid in them. A *batter* uses enough liquid so that the

---

2. At high altitudes, it may be advisable to use slightly less baking powder.

Breads

mixture can be stirred or beaten; a *dough* uses less liquid and is too thick to be beaten.

Thick batters and soft doughs

These mixtures, used for pancakes, muffins, coffee cakes, and biscuits, must not be overmixed. Stir the ingredients only until the dry elements are moistened; the mixture will have visible particles of flour and a lumpy texture. If overmixed, too much gluten will form; although the mixture will look smooth and shiny, the product will be very coarse textured and tough.

Thick batters usually are spooned into muffin tins. Soft doughs may be dropped onto a cookie sheet, or kneaded lightly and then rolled out quickly and cut for baking.

Thin batters

Batters for griddlecakes and waffles are stirred only until the ingredients are well mixed, as in muffins, to prevent the overdevelopment of gluten.

A crepe mixture is a thin batter that is well mixed with a wire whip, beater, or blender. The batter may be refrigerated before cooking, and the crepes may be baked, stacked, and refrigerated or frozen before filling. To freeze crepes, wrap them tightly (air tight) in aluminum foil. Warm frozen crepes in an oven before they are folded over the filling (see Figures 7-2 a and b).

Batters for popovers and Yorkshire puddings are thin, and they contain more eggs than do crepe batters. Popovers will have a higher volume if placed on the lower shelf of a very hot, preheated oven.

Yeast doughs

Because yeast doughs must have time to develop carbon dioxide, a different procedure is used. Too high temperatures will kill yeast, so use lukewarm, not hot, liquid. Follow the recipe's directions for combining ingredients. After kneading (Figure 7-3), shape the dough into a round ball, set it in a greased bowl, and turn it, lightly coating the surface with the grease. Then, set the bowl in a warm (27°C to 29°C [80°F to 85°F]) place so that the dough will rise until it has doubled in bulk. Sufficient warmth for rising may be provided by setting the bowl near the top of the range, an oven pilot light, an electric

Figure 7-2 (a) *A gratinée dish filled with crepes. Note the filled crepe being rolled.*

Figure 7-2 (b) *Crepes garnished and ready to serve.*

Breads

Figure 7-3 *Kneading yeast bread.*

heating pad, or a radiator. Dough in a glass or pottery bowl also may be placed in an oven that has been preheated for ten minutes and then turned off. A pan of water is placed on the bottom rack to provide moisture. When the dough has doubled, punch it down, shape it, and allow it to rise again or prepare it for baking, depending on the type of dough and the product being made.

Yeast dough tends to rise more rapidly at high altitudes than it does at lower elevations. Therefore, watch the dough carefully and allow it to rise only to double its bulk.

Baking

Accurate control of oven temperatures is less critical in baking breads than for other baked products, such as cakes. Oven temperatures used for quick breads range from 204.4°C to 232°C (400°F to 450°F); those used for yeast breads range from 176.7°C to 190.6°C (350°F to 375°F).

Most recipes suggest preheating the oven, but to conserve energy, the oven

Figure 7-4 *Yeast bread served on a cutting board.*

may be turned on when the bread goes in the oven. In either case, place the pan in the center of the oven, for even distribution of heat. If you are cooking several loaves, place the pans so that they are not directly above one another, to allow free circulation of hot air around them. In order to get the best circulation, it may be best to hold some pans until a first batch has been baked.

For popovers and Yorkshire pudding, preheat the oven (unless it is an oven that comes up to temperature quickly), since the high temperature is necessary to allow the product to expand while the batter is soft. Place the pan on the bottom rack, to allow for quick production of steam in the mixture. Once the batter has expanded, reduce the oven temperature and continue baking until the popovers or pudding are thoroughly cooked, being sure not to overbrown. It also is possible to bake satisfactory popovers at a constant high temperature.

Muffins, biscuits, and rolls are ready to remove from the oven when they are golden brown on the outside. Quick bread loaves, such as apricot and banana nut, are tested for doneness by inserting a long toothpick, a small bamboo skewer, or a cake tester into the center. If the toothpick has no uncooked dough clinging to it on removal, the loaves are done.

Breads

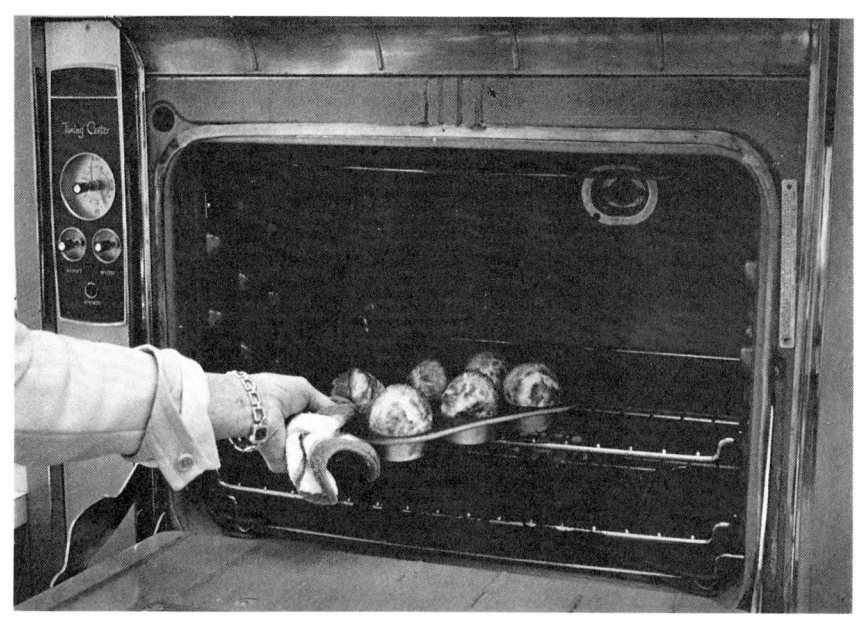

Figure 7–5 (a) *Muffins turned in the pan to keep them warm and to prevent them from becoming soggy.*

Figure 7–5 (b) *Muffins served in a napkin.*

Yeast bread is done when it has a golden brown crust and gives a hollow sound when tapped. Alternatively, the loaf may be tipped from the pan and thumped on the bottom. If the loaf sounds hollow, it is done; if not, return it to the pan and continue baking. When the loaf is done, serve it cooled or partially cooled (Figure 7-4).

Baked breads that are not to be served immediately must be removed from the pan and cooled on a wire rack. Those quick breads to be held and served warm are best if partially removed or turned in the pan, to keep trapped steam from making them soggy. They will retain heat and a dry crust if served wrapped in a napkin (Figure 7-5 a and b).

Storage

Quick breads are best eaten soon after they are baked; most of them do not keep well. However, they may be reheated for a few moments—cut and toasted, or buttered and broiled—for a later meal.

Quick breads, yeast loaves, and other breads that are to be stored may be baked, thoroughly wrapped, and frozen. If you frequently need small amounts of bread, slice the loaf before freezing it.

Rolls can be wrapped in aluminum foil or freezer wrap and frozen, then thawed, placed in a paper bag, and heated. Or, the frozen rolls may be placed on a baking sheet and reheated in a hot oven.

Refrigerating bread retards the growth of mold, but refrigeration makes the bread grow stale more rapidly than does room-temperature storage.

Chapter 8 Pies, tarts, and turnovers

Pastries are the delight and specialty of many cooks, who use them as appetizers, entrées, and desserts. A meat-filled pastry needs little more than a green salad to provide a nutritious, simple meal. However, calorie counters should remember the high calorie content of pastries—from both the large amount of fat used in them, and the sugar in many of the fillings.

There are several types of pastry: standard, cookie-dough, crumb, and hard-meringue. The type used should complement the planned filling. All four types are used for pies and *tarts* (small, individual-serving pies), but turnovers, discussed at the end of this chapter, usually are made with standard pastry. Cookie-dough pastry often is used for *flans*, a pie made in a special pan with fluted sides and, often, a removable bottom (Figure 8-1 a and b).

The nutritive value of different pastries varies, depending on the ingredients. Appendix A lists the nutritive value of a variety of standard pastry shells and pies with different fillings.

Pie pans

Pie pans are made of tin, aluminum, and glass. Casseroles of oven-proof ware or glass are used for deep-dish dessert pies and for main-dish meat or poultry pies. Glass pie pans and metal pans with a dull finish are considered best, because both types allow better baking of the bottom crust. Lower oven temperature is used with a glass pan.

The standard size for pie pans is nine inches, and recipes usually are written for this size. Larger pie pans are available, and pastry recipes may

Figure 8-1 (a) *Remove rim from the flan pan.*

Figure 8-1 (b) *Attractively glazed apple flan.*

have to be increased to accommodate such pans. The number of tart shells a pastry recipe will yield depends on the size of the pans.

Standard pastry

Often it is said that making successful pastry depends on using a "light hand"—that is, the ingredients should be combined with a minimum of handling and no delay. The phrase applies particularly to standard pastry.

This type of pastry uses flour, usually all-purpose flour, as the main ingredient. Fat, which may be lard, oil, or a hydrogenated fat, is added to the flour to make the pastry tender. The type of fat will affect both the flavor and the texture of the pastry. Solid fat makes a tender, flaky crust; an oil crust may be tender but not flaky. For flavor, salt is added. And water, the fourth ingredient, is used to hold the mixture together.

Mixing

The procedure used to mix standard pastry sounds simple; success largely depends on the technique and skill of the pastry maker. First, mix the flour and salt, then add the fat. Solid fat is cut into the dry mixture with a pastry blender (Figure 8-2a) or with two knives held so that they work like scissors (Figure 8-2b). To obtain the best result, combine the fat and dry ingredients into a coarse mixture with many large (½ inch) pieces of fat coated with flour. (If the mixture is finely cut, the pastry may be tender but not flaky.) If oil is used, it is stirred lightly into the dry ingredients.

After fat and dry ingredients are combined, add cold water, briefly stirring and tossing with a fork (Figure 8-3). Overmixing at this stage will yield tough pastry, so care should be taken with this step. Add only a little water at a time, and move the moistened ingredients to one side of the bowl as they hold together. Stir very quickly, with light movements of the fork. Once the mixture holds together, set it aside for 5 or 10 minutes before you roll it. During this time, the moisture will disperse evenly through the mixture, making the pastry easier to handle.

A tender pastry that is not as flaky as in the method above may be mixed by combining the oil with water or by mixing hot water with the fat, before stirring the oil or fat into the flour and salt. The doughs from these methods are more easily rolled if thoroughly chilled.

Figure 8–2 (a) *Cut fat into flour-salt mixture with pastry blender.*

Figure 8–2 (b) *Cut fat into flour-salt mixture with two knives scissor-fashion.*

Pies, tarts, and turnovers

Figure 8–3 *Gradually add cold water; stir and toss the fat-flour mixture to moisten.*

Forming

Avoid overhandling this pastry. Overhandling develops the gluten in the flour and makes a tough product. The mixture only needs to be formed into a ball, and rolled out with a rolling pin to ⅛ inch in thickness. A pastry sock may be used on the pin. A floured pastry board, a cloth, or waxed paper may be used for the rolling surface. Roll the pastry from the center out into a circle, with light, quick movements, until it is two inches larger than the top of the pan to be used. Fold the circle of pastry in half, then over into quarters, and place the point in the center of the pan (Figure 8-4). Next, carefully unfold the pastry, so it does not stretch. Stretching will cause the pastry to shrink during baking. Unfold it from the center out, to prevent air from being trapped beneath it, and firmly press the pastry into the pan. Be especially careful at the junction of the bottom and the sides of the pan.

Trimming

Trim the pastry with kitchen scissors or a knife (Figures 8-5 a and b). For a single-crust pie, leave ⅓ inch to ½ inch pastry beyond the pan's edge, for

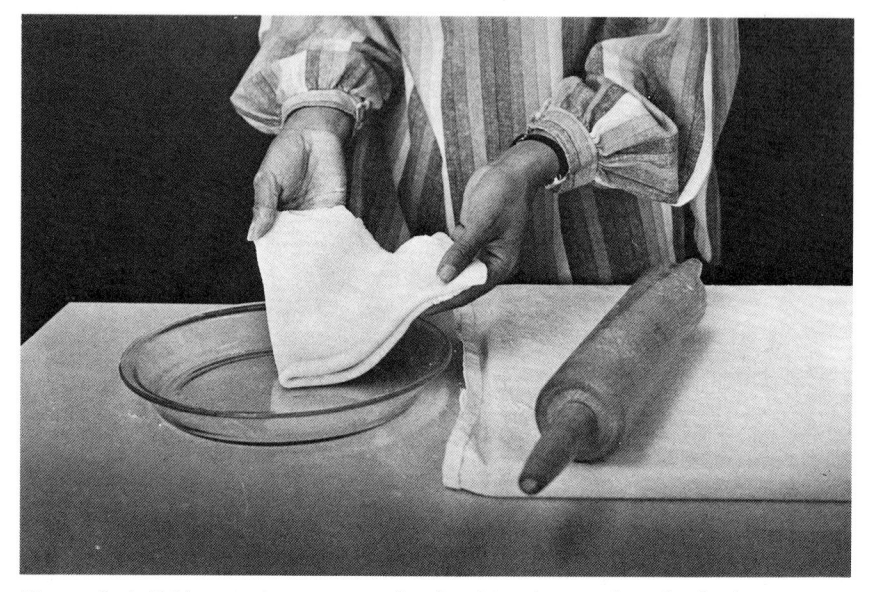

Figure 8–4 *Fold pastry in quarters to be placed in pie pan, the point in the center.*

fluting. To flute, fold the extra crust under and shape the crust edge with the first finger of one hand while holding the crust against the thumb and first finger of the other hand. Or, twist the pastry between thumb and forefinger (Figure 8-6).

For a lattice-topped pie, trim the bottom crust, leaving ⅓ inch to ½ inch beyond the pan's edge. The lattice strips are placed in position and woven from one edge of the pan, across the filling, to the opposite edge. The edge of the bottom crust is folded over the lattice ends and fluted.

For a double-crust pie, trim off the bottom crust at the pan's edge. After the pie is filled, carefully lay the top crust, rolled ⅓ inch to ½ inch larger than the pie pan, over the pan. Seal the two crusts together by pressing them firmly with the tines of a fork, or flute them after the upper crust is folded under the bottom crust edge. Slash the top crust with a sharp knife or prick it with a fork, in six or seven places. And, make a vent near the center of the pie, to allow steam to escape during baking.

Baking

Unfilled pastry shell Just before the shell is baked a circle of oiled waxed paper may be placed firmly on the bottom of the pastry. Rice or dry beans

Pies, tarts, and turnovers 119

Figure 8–5 (a) *Trim pastry with scissors for a fluted or a lattice-topped pie.*

Figure 8–5 (b) *Trim pastry with a knife for the bottom of a double-crust pie.*

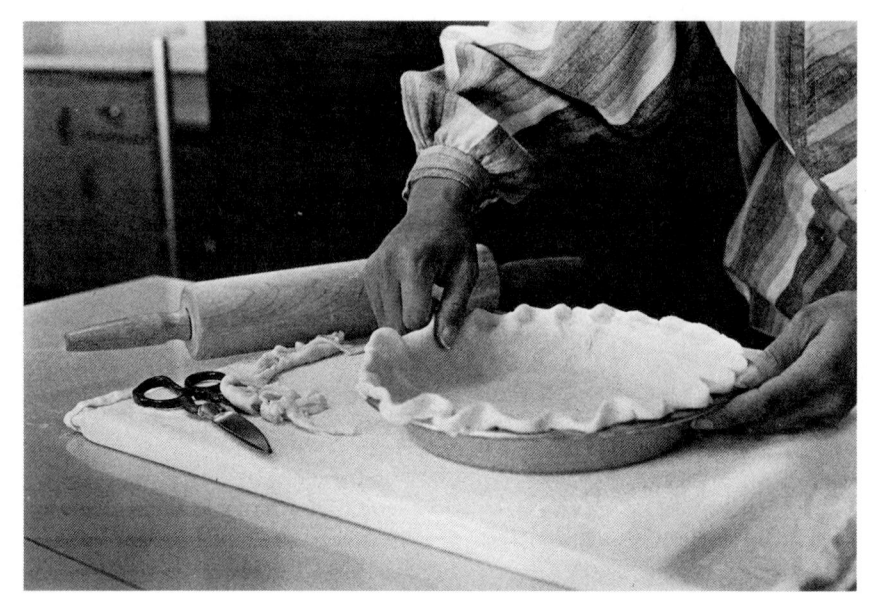

Figure 8–6 *Flute pastry by twisting it between thumb and forefinger.*

then may be put on top of the paper, to hold it in place. After the shell has baked in the oven for 10 minutes, remove the paper with the rice or beans and continue baking for 5 minutes, or until the shell is golden brown. Another alternative is to use a sharp-tined fork to prick many small holes in the bottom and sides of the crust before it is baked.

Filled pastry shell It is a real challenge to bake a custard-, meat-, or fruit-filled pie without a soggy bottom crust. Different methods for dealing with this problem are: use a minimum of water in mixing the pastry; preheat the filling; coat the inside of the bottom pastry with partially beaten egg white and partially bake the shell in a very hot oven (218°C [425°F]), for 3 to 5 minutes; or start baking in a very hot oven (218°C [425°F]) for about 10 minutes with the *pie* in the lower third of the oven and then lower temperature to 176°C(350°F).

Double-crust and lattice-topped pies are baked until they are golden brown. Both should be well filled, so that the top pastry is raised enough to brown properly. Brushing the top crust (avoiding the edges) with milk or a slightly beaten egg, or sprinkling it with a little sugar will further help it to brown. If the fluted edges begin to overbrown, foil strips may be used to cover the edges until the pie is done.

Cookie-dough pastry

Mixing

The ingredients for this pastry are flour, butter, egg or cream cheese, and, possibly, sugar (depending on the planned filling). Mix the ingredients as you would those for standard pastry, using the egg to provide the moisture. Mixing may be done with a pastry blender or an electric mixer. The mixture is not as likely to be overmixed as is standard pastry, and it yields a tender type of pastry.

Forming

This type of pastry is formed into a ball and rolled into a circle that is 1½ inches to 2 inches larger than the pan. Although cookie-dough pastry does not toughen as quickly as does standard pastry, it will tear very easily. To move it from the board without tearing it, lightly place the rolling pin on the pastry and gently roll the pastry around the pin (Figure 8-7 a and b). Then, lift the pin, lay the crust on the pan, and unroll it. If the pastry tears it may be easily repaired by pressing it together with the fingers (Figure 8-8).

Trimming and baking

Trim as you would trim standard pastry. If a flan pan is used place the pastry into position in the standard manner, but cut off the excess with the pressure of your hands or by rolling the pin against the sharp edge of the pan.

Flute and prick as for standard pastry. The shell may be partially baked before filling, but usually the shell is baked, and then filled. Cookie-dough pastry is used for single-crust pies, flans, and tarts.

Crumb crust

Crush cereal, flakes, crackers, or dry cookies in a plastic bag, with a rolling pin or a bottle. Then, mix the crumbs with seasonings and melted margarine

Figure 8–7 (a) *Gently roll pastry around the rolling pin.*

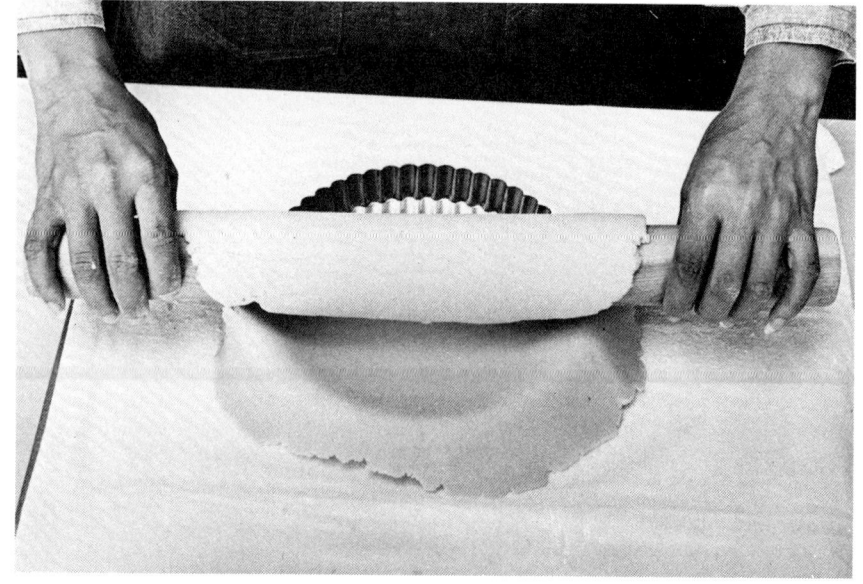

Figure 8–7 (b) *Unroll pastry and place it in the flan pan.*

Pies, tarts, and turnovers

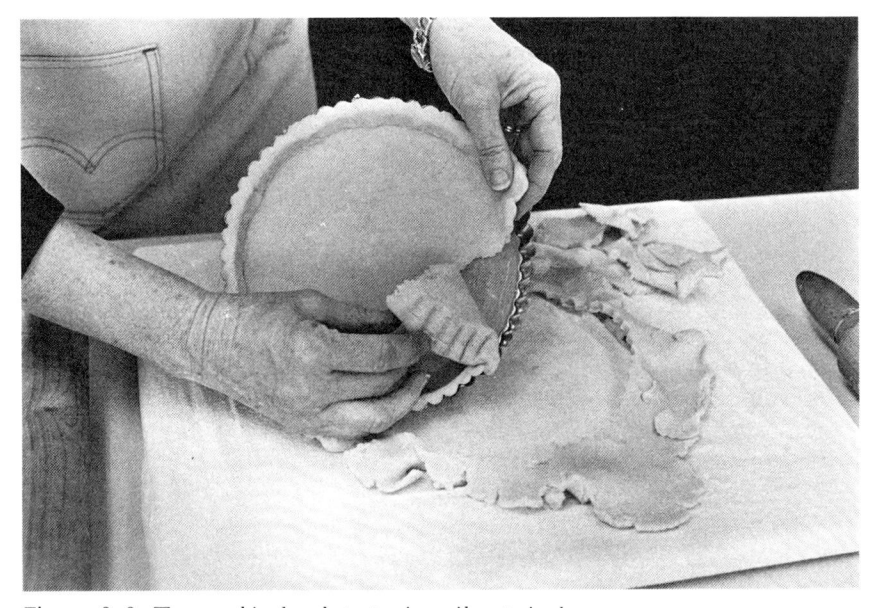

Figure 8–8 *Torn cookie-dough pastry is easily repaired.*

or butter. When the fat and crumbs are well combined, press the mixture onto the bottom and sides of a pie pan, with the back of a spoon. Firm, heavy pressure is needed, so that the crust will hold its shape when the pie is cut.

This crust is used only for single-crust pies, and the edge is left flat. Depending on the flavor desired, crumb crusts may be baked before they are filled in a 190.6°C (375°F) oven for six to eight minutes, or filled without baking. Coconut crusts are tastier if baked before filling. All crumb crusts should be thoroughly chilled before baking, to allow the fat to become very firm and retain shape.

Hard-meringue shells

Mixing

Beat egg whites until they froth, and add an acid (cream of tartar, vinegar, or lemon juice). Continue beating, gradually adding sugar. Beat until stiff peaks stand up straight when the beater is withdrawn from the mixture.

It is important to dissolve the sugar completely. Extra-fine granulated sugar produces the best results. Lemon juice or vinegar will add some liquid to the mixture; cream of tartar will not. If the meringue is grainy at the end of the beating period, add a very small amount of water (no more than one tablespoon for four egg whites) and beat it in to help to dissolve the sugar.

Forming and baking

The foam is transferred with a spoon or rubber spatula to the bottom and sides of the pie pan, and carefully shaped. Or, it may be placed on a greased sheet of brown paper, which has been placed on a cookie sheet for baking, and shaped into a circle (Figure 8-9).

Meringue shells are baked at low temperatures (107°C to 163°C [225°F to 325°F]), so that the meringue will dry all the way through without browning.

Prepared mixes and shells

Commercially prepared pastry mixes are available, and it is best to follow directions on the container for good results. Most of these mixes contain additives to keep the fat from becoming rancid, and the flavor of the pastry may be a little different from that of the home-prepared product. Ready-to-use frozen pie shells also are available. It may be useful to compare the cost and quality of these shells (and of the prepared mixes) to the cost and preparation time for products made at home, especially if a food budget is being followed.

Fillings

Meat, poultry, cheese, vegetables, fruits, eggs, and nuts are only some of the foods used in making fillings. Fresh, frozen, partially cooked, completely cooked, or dried foods may be used. In all cases, however, moisture must be controlled to avoid either a soggy, doughy crust or a dry, tasteless one.

All fillings that contain eggs, milk, poultry, or meat must be refrigerated if not served immediately. They are excellent media for rapid growth of micro-organisms. If the filling is prepared ahead of time, to be put into the pie shell

Figure 8-9 *Using two spoons, shape individual meringues into small circles on greased paper.*

later, it must be refrigerated directly after it is prepared. Also, refrigerate finished, baked pies that contain these ingredients, if they are not to be served soon after baking.

Fruit fillings

Fresh, frozen, or canned fruits are used with flour, cornstarch, or tapioca, as thickeners, for pie fillings. The amount of thickener needed for uncooked fruit and berries is difficult to estimate, because the amount of juice that will be produced during baking is not known. Many people prefer to use tapioca for fruit pies, because cornstarch and flour produce a fairly firm filling. The goal in all cases is to use just enough thickener to keep the juices from being runny, but not enough to make a rigid, stiff filling.

Fruit and berry fillings tend to boil up and over the sides of the pan, and the thickener helps to prevent this exasperating problem. Reducing the amount of sugar in the recipe also may help and will reduce the total calories at the same time.

Fresh fruit and unbaked pastry Gently, but thoroughly, pack the raw fruit into the unbaked standard pastry shell. Keep the fruit slightly higher toward and around the center, so that the pie will be completely filled after it is baked. Mix together the required amount of thickener, sugar, and other dry ingredients, and sprinkle them over the fruit as you layer it into the crust.

These pies usually are started in a 218°C (425°F) oven for 10 minutes. Then, the oven temperature is reduced to 176.7°C (350°F) for the remainder of the baking time. The higher temperature at the beginning helps to keep the bottom crust from absorbing the filling's liquid and becoming soggy.

Frozen or canned fruit and unbaked pastry Cornstarch, flour, or tapioca may be used to thicken the drained juices of frozen, thawed, or cooked fruits and berries. Allow not more than one cup of juice (less juice is preferred by many) for each two cups of drained fruit in the filling.

Preheating the juices and thickener and pouring the hot mixture over the drained fruit helps the fruit—especially frozen fruit—to retain its shape and flavor. Starting with a warm or hot filling will hasten the thickening of the juices and helps to prevent the bottom pastry from absorbing liquid and becoming soggy. Bake as you would a fresh fruit pie or a berry pie.

Fruit for baked shells The fruit—fresh, frozen, or canned—is thickened, cooled, and placed in the pie shell. Often, only a bottom crust is used, and an attractive arrangement of fruit is laid over the top and glazed. Figure 8-10a shows a flan shell filled with very dry, well-seasoned applesauce being topped with raw apple slices. In Figure 8-10b, a glaze is being brushed onto the apple slices. A fruit glaze may be prepared by heating and, sometimes, thinning jelly or preserves. Currant jelly is used for red fruit; apple jelly or sieved apricot preserves, for orange or yellow fruit. You also can glaze raw fruits and use them to top cream pies.

Baked tart shells often are filled with well-flavored applesauce, cranberry-raisin mixture, other fruit combinations, or lemon or orange *curd* (a filling made with eggs). These fillings may be prepared ahead of time and refrigerated for several days. Then, the tart shells are filled immediately or up to two hours before serving time. These tarts are very attractive, quickly prepared desserts for family or festive meals.

Pies, tarts, and turnovers 127

Figure 8–10 (a) *Arrange apples attractively over applesauce in an unbaked cookie-dough shell.*

Figure 8–10 (b) *Glaze baked apple flan.*

Custard filling

This type of filling probably causes more trouble than does any other, because the crust absorbs liquid during baking and becomes soggy. There are several procedures for dealing with this problem.

1. Increase the egg in the recipe, so custard thickens sooner.
2. Coat the pie shell with slightly beaten egg white and partially bake before it is filled.
3. Bake the pie near the bottom of the oven instead of in the center, so that more heat reaches the crust. Like any other custard, custard pies must be baked with care. Using too high a temperature or baking too long will make the custard separate.

The one sure way to avoid a soggy bottom crust is to bake the custard by itself in a buttered pie pan that is the same size or slightly smaller than the pan used for the shell. Set the pan of custard in a shallow pan of water for baking, and, when it is done, remove it from the oven and let it cool a little. Then, very carefully loosen the custard and slide it from its pan into the pie shell. This operation takes skill, and the edges of the custard may be broken in the process. If the edges do break, a garnish of fruit, whipped cream, or toasted coconut can be used as a decorative camouflage.

Squash, pumpkin, sweet potato, and pecan pies also are made with a custard base. Ingredients vary, but care must be taken to prevent a soggy bottom crust in all of them.

Cooked-pudding fillings

Cream These fillings are basically cooked puddings. Whatever the flavor—chocolate, vanilla, banana, butterscotch, or coconut cream—the basic ingredients are liquid (usually milk), eggs, and a thickener.

Heat the liquid and quickly add the thickener, thoroughly mixed with the sugar. Stir well. Cook the mixture, over boiling water or over controlled heat until it boils or bubbles, stirring constantly. Remove the pan from the burner. Then, either quickly beat in the beaten eggs or egg yolks with a wire beater or add part of the hot mixture to the beaten eggs and quickly stir the warmed egg mixture into the rest of the hot pudding. Be careful not to scramble the eggs. Return the combined mixture to the heat and cook until it bubbles for a couple of minutes, in order to coagulate the eggs.

If cooking the mixture over boiling water, cook for five minutes, to be sure it is done. Whether the mixture is cooked over water or over controlled heat, it must be slowly and thoroughly stirred, so that all areas of the pan bottom are reached.

Lemon Lemon filling is a cooked pudding, but the acidic lemon juice is added at the end—after the mixture is thoroughly cooked. If it is added sooner, the mixture may not thicken properly. The lemon juice will make the filling look thin, but if the pudding has been prepared correctly the filling will be soft but firm.

In all these cream- or pudding-type pies, the fillings, when cut, should be soft yet firm—not rigid and stiff. They may shift a little in the shell, but they should not run into the pan when a slice is removed.

Meat and poultry fillings

These fillings—which often combine cooked, diced, or cubed meat or poultry with partially cooked fresh or uncooked frozen vegetables—are basically a very thick stew covered with crust. Mix the ingredients with a well-seasoned brown or white sauce, and pour them into a baking dish. Use no more than one cup of sauce to two cups of meat mixture. If ground meat is used in the recipe, it may be necessary to remove any excess fat or liquid. Then, lay a crust of standard pastry over the top, slash it, and vent it. The pie is baked and served hot.

Sometimes, a crust made with a little vinegar is used for meat or poultry pies. And, a *cobbler dough*—a muffin-type of topping—also is used. For serving, the meat mixture is poured over the topping, like a heavy gravy. Meat pies, served with a salad and a light dessert, make a very satisfactory meal. And, leftover odds and ends may be used to great advantage in the fillings.

Toppings

Soft meringues that contain only egg whites and sugar are used on many cream pies, including lemon. Beat the foam only until peaks bend over when the beater is lifted. Then, spread the meringue on the *hot* filling, meeting the crust around the sides, and bake in a moderate (176.7°C [350°F]) oven until the meringue is lightly browned. If meringue is spread on a cold pie, it may *weep* (produce a thin layer of water underneath). Baking in a too-hot oven also can make the meringue weep.

Sometimes caramel-colored beads of moisture appear on the cooled meringue after it is baked. These beads indicate that the sugar was not thoroughly dissolved in the foam when beaten. The problem can be avoided by starting to add the sugar to the egg whites early in the beating process. This will lengthen the time needed to beat the foam, but it will ensure that the sugar is properly dissolved.

Whipped cream—flavored or plain—also is used to decorate the top of pies. The pie must be chilled first, however, to prevent the cream from deflating when it is spread.

Turnovers

Turnovers usually are filled with fruit, meat, or poultry fillings that are not likely to seep through the crust during baking. Standard pastry, which holds its shape, is used. Small turnovers may be served as canapés and larger ones, as part of the main course or as dessert, depending on the filling.

Roll out the pastry to a ⅛-inch thickness, and cut it into the size squares or rounds desired. Spoon the filling onto it, just off-center, and fold the pastry over into a triangle or half-circle, so that the edges meet at the sides. A very little water may be brushed between the pastry edges, to make them hold together; the tines of a fork are used to seal the two crusts. Prick the top with a fork before baking, and bake as you would a pie with standard pastry crust. Turnovers may be served hot from the oven or cold.

Chapter 9 Cakes and frostings

Cakes frequently are used to celebrate special occasions, and a special cake very well may be associated with a happy experience. The expert and the novice can use their skills and creativity to produce a masterpiece. Génoise cakes are delicate, delicious, and difficult to make; carrot cakes also are delicious, but they are not at all difficult to make. And, many delightful baked products use packaged cakes as their bases.

Nutritional value

Most cakes contain a substantial amount of sugar and fat, so their calorie content is high. Their nutritional value depends on their particular ingredients. In most cases, however, cakes represent little more than extra calories and are best avoided, except on special occasions. See Appendix A for the nutritive values of a variety of cakes and frostings.

Ingredients

Basically, there are two kinds of cake: shortened and unshortened. *Shortened* cakes contain butter or some other fat and, usually, a chemical leavener, such as baking powder or baking soda.[1] *Unshortened* cakes contain no fat and,

---

1. Baking soda is not a leavening agent in itself. It is combined in a product with an acid, such as sour milk or molasses, to produce the leavening effect.

usually, no chemical leavener; true unshortened cakes depend on air and steam for leavening.

Different cakes use different proportions of ingredients. The ingredients in any cake are carefully balanced for the best results, and, therefore, they must be measured with more care and accuracy than is needed in making any other food product. Best results can be expected if all ingredients are at room temperature before they are mixed, and if they are mixed properly.

Flour

The flour provides the structure or framework of the cake. Cake flour is more finely ground, is smoother, and develops less gluten than does all-purpose flour. Cakes made with cake flour generally are larger and have a more velvety texture than do those made from all-purpose flour. It is best to use only cake flour for cakes, but if all-purpose flour must be used, reduce the amount by 2 tablespoons per cup.

Liquid

The liquid in cake batters moistens the proteins and starch, and dissolves the sugar, salt, and chemical leavener. Too little liquid makes a stiff, dry cake; too much liquid, a very moist but small product.

Frequently, the liquid in a cake is whole milk, but buttermilk, sour milk, evaporated milk, or fruit juices are used as well. Also, dry-milk solids may be reconstituted with water and used successfully in cake recipes.

Fat

Fat makes a cake tender. Butter, margarine, lard, vegetable shortening, and oil, all are used. Although butter gives a desirable flavor, hydrogenated fats will produce a cake with a fine-grained texture and good volume. Creaming the fat with sugar adds air to the cake.

Sugar

Sugar contributes to the tenderness of a cake as well as to the cake's flavor. But, sugar can cause problems, so care must be taken to measure it accurately.

Cakes and frostings

Honey and corn syrup also are used to sweeten cakes, but they produce cakes with different qualities than those in which granulated sugar is used. Some sweetness is added by using mashed or cooked fruit, as is done in applesauce and banana cakes. In all these cases, recipes should be followed exactly.

Eggs

Eggs serve several purposes in cakes: their coagulation during baking helps to form the framework of the cake; and they add both color and flavor to the finished product. Unless otherwise stated, most recipes are written for medium or large eggs. If small or extra-large eggs must be used, or the recipe calls for a large number of eggs, the eggs should be measured. One large egg usually contains two tablespoons white and one tablespoon yolk, but there may be some variation. When in doubt, measure.

Air is added to the mixture when eggs are beaten before they are added to the other ingredients. Egg foams are the leavening agent in angel food and sponge cakes.

Leaveners

As mentioned above, air is beaten into eggs to provide leavening for unshortened cakes. Steam, which is formed from the liquid ingredients that includes the moisture in eggs, also may serve as a leavener. Chemical agents, such as baking powder and baking soda (mixed with sour milk or fruit juice), also may be used in cakes. When combined with the liquid in the ingredients, these chemical leaveners form the carbon dioxide that leavens the cake.

Altitude and cake making

Because water boils at a lower temperature at higher altitudes, steam forms sooner in a baked product prepared at higher elevations. The rate at which gas expands also is affected by altitude. The result is that cake recipes developed for use at sea level yield unsatisfactory products if used over 3,000 feet above sea level. Adjustments must be made according to the particular altitude and best results are obtained by following recipes that have been worked out for such use.

Many comprehensive cookbooks include cake recipes that may be used at higher elevations, and cake-mix packages usually carry instructions for use at high altitudes. The Bibliography includes some helpful publications for the cook.

Mixing methods

The method in which the ingredients are combined will determine the quality of the cake, especially its texture. Therefore, use the method of mixing specified in the recipe. There is some difference in the formulation of recipes intended to be mixed by the different methods.

Shortened cakes

Conventional method The extra creaming and mixing required in this method result in a more tender, finer-textured, delicate cake than do the two following methods. This method is the one frequently used for special cakes.

Cream the fat with either a wooden spoon or an electric mixer, and then gradually add the sugar. Beat the mixture until it is light and fluffy from the air incorporated into it. Add the eggs next, beating them in. Sift together the dry ingredients, and add them *alternately* with the liquid. Usually the flour mixture is added in three parts; the liquid, in two. Begin with the flour and end with the flour.

Sometimes the eggs are separated, and only the yolks are added to the fat-sugar mixture. In such recipes, the whites—beaten stiff but not dry—are added last, carefully *folded* into the batter so as not to break down the air in them.

Occasionally, the solids and liquids in a batter separate during mixing, giving the batter a curdled appearance. Although this change is not desirable, it does not seem to have a major effect on the finished product.

Muffin method The muffin method is the fastest way to combine the ingredients, and it is often used for cakes that are to be served warm or with a sauce. These cakes do not keep as well as those made by the conventional method; they tend to dry out more rapidly.

Sift together the dry ingredients, as for muffins, and then combine the eggs, liquid, and melted fat. Add all the liquid ingredients, at one time, to the dry, and beat the mixture until it is smooth and well blended.

One-bowl method In some recipes, all the ingredients are brought to room temperature, placed in a bowl, and beaten. In others, two steps are involved: the dry ingredients, fat, and part of the milk are combined, and then the eggs and remaining liquid are added. The whole mixture is beaten to combine all the ingredients.

Chiffon cakes

These cakes have a high egg content. Sift together the dry ingredients into a bowl, and then shape them, so that there is a well in the center of the bowl. Pour the liquid, egg yolks, oil, and flavoring into the well, and stir the whole to mix. Fold in the stiffly beaten egg whites last.

Unshortened cakes

Angel food cake This cake requires only three basic ingredients: egg whites, sugar, and flour. In addition, small amounts of salt, cream of tartar, and flavoring are used.

Using an electric, rotary, or wire beater, beat the egg whites, which have been brought to room temperature, until they are foamy. Then, beat in the salt, cream of tartar, and flavoring. Gradually add part of the sugar, and continue beating until the foam forms peaks that just bend over. Mix the remaining sugar and the flour, and sift the mixture over the surface of the bowl, in small amounts, folding the mixture very carefully into the whites, to retain the air in the foam.

A rubber spatula works well for folding in. Cut down through the batter; then, at the bottom of the bowl, turn the spatula so that it parallels the bottom. At the opposite side of the bowl, bring the spatula straight up the side and out of the mixture, holding it so that the batter gently falls off it. Rotate the bowl as you fold and continue folding until the sugar-flour mixture has been incorporated. If an electric mixer is used, it should be set on low speed, to mix in the flour-sugar mixture in small portions. In either case, the batter should not be overmixed.

Sponge cake The basic ingredients for sponge cake are eggs, sugar, and flour. Lemon juice replaces the cream of tartar used in angel food cakes, and flavorings may be added.

When whole eggs are used, beat them until they begin to foam. Add the lemon juice and any other liquid required, and beat the mixture until it becomes stiff. Sift the dry ingredients over the top, in small amounts, carefully folding in as you would in preparing an angel food cake.

Some sponge cake recipes call for separating the eggs. In this case, part of the sugar is beaten into the egg yolks until the mixture forms a ribbon when the beater or whip is lifted. The liquid and then the flour are beaten in separately. The egg whites are beaten stiff but not dry, using the remainder of the sugar, and are folded in last.

Cake mixes

Both shortened and unshortened cakes are available in dry-mix form, to which various other ingredients are added according to directions on the box. These cakes are easy to prepare and the results are satisfactory. In addition, cake mixes may be used as base recipes for a wide variety of cakes (Table 9-1). Directions for these variations usually are given on the box. Also, these mixes may be combined with commercially made pudding mixes for still other cake variations (Figure 9-1). The following general instructions apply to most

Figure 9-1 *A specialty cake made with both prepared cake and pudding mixes.*

Cakes and frostings

cake mixes and variations and can be used in combining ingredients for the cakes in Table 9-1.

1. Preheat oven to 176.7°C (350°F). Grease and flour pan (except for Almond Cake).
2. Place the ingredients with the exception of those listed under "Other ingredients with special instructions" in a large bowl and beat well to combine.
3. Follow the special-ingredients instructions.
4. Pour the batter into the prepared 9 × 5 or 7 × 11 inch pan and bake 25 to 30 minutes or until the cake tests done.

The cost of a dry-mix cake versus a homemade cake will vary with the locality, the kind of store, the season of the year, and many other factors. Time also is an element that should be considered, since dry-mix cakes can be prepared very quickly, with a minimum of equipment.

Cake pans

Selection

Consider the shape, size, and the pan's material. Using a large, shallow pan results in a large cake that has a flatter top than has a cake baked in a deep pan. Cake batter baked in a deep pan sets around the outside edges, and the batter in the center rises up to form a hump, which often cracks. A square pan has more area than does a round pan of the same size, and if its corners are sharp, the cake will overbrown and become dry in the corners. Follow the recipe's recommendations for pan size.

Because pan materials react differently to heat, the material the pan is made of will affect the length of time needed to bake the cake. A dull-finished or dark-colored pan absorbs heat rapidly, so that a cake may bake in less time than it will in a shiny pan, which reflects the heat. A glass pan transmits radiant heat, so that the outside of the cake may overbrown. For this reason, a lower oven temperature—3.9°C (25°F) lower than that in the recipe—is recommended if baking in a glass pan. Ungreased tube pans are used for angel food, sponge, and chiffon cakes, because the tube allows for better distribution of heat and also gives support to the batter during baking. This distribution results in more uniform cooking. When a smaller amount of batter is prepared, it may be baked successfully in a loaf pan.

Table 9–1 Cake mixes and variations

Cake	½ of 18.5 oz. pkg. cake mix*	½ of 3¾ oz. pkg. instant pudding or flavored gelatin**	Oil	Liquid	Eggs	Flavoring	Other ingredients with special instructions
Almond Cake	Yellow	Vanilla	¼ C.	½ C. buttermilk	2	½ T. lemon peel, grated	2 T. butter ⅓ C. almonds, sliced ½ T. sugar Butter bottom and sides of pan; press almonds onto bottom and sides and sprinkle with sugar.
Banana Cake	Banana	Vanilla	⅓ C.	½ C. buttermilk	2	1 med.-size banana, mashed	¼ C. chocolate syrup Add chocolate to batter and swirl through batter to marble, just before pouring into prepared pan.
Butterscotch Cake	Yellow	Butterscotch	¼ C.	½ C. strong coffee	2	½ t. each cinnamon, nutmeg, and allspice	½ C. raisins Fold raisins into batter before pouring into prepared pan.
Chocolate Cake	Chocolate	Chocolate	⅓ C.	½ C. water	2	1 t. vanilla	None
Chocolate Maraschino Cake	Chocolate	Chocolate	⅓ C.	½ C. water	2	1 t. vanilla	¼ C. maraschino cherries, drained and chopped ½ C. nuts, chopped Fold into mixture, before pouring into prepared pan.
Cinnamon Cake	Yellow	Vanilla	⅓ C.	½ C. water	2	None	1½ T. sugar 1 t. cinnamon Combine ingredients. Pour ⅓ of the batter into the prepared pan, and sprinkle with ½ of the sugar and

Cinnamon Swirl Cake	Yellow	Vanilla	¼ C.	½ C. sour cream	2	1 t. vanilla	⅓ C. brown sugar 1½ t. cinnamon ½ C. chopped nuts Combine ingredients. Pour ⅓ of the batter into the prepared pan, and sprinkle with ⅓ the sugar-cinnamon mixture. Draw knife through to marble, repeat, and top with remaining mixture. cinnamon mixture, pour in ⅓ more of the batter, add remaining sugar and cinnamon, top with remaining batter.
Lemon Cake	Yellow	Lemon-flavored gelatin	⅓ C.	⅓ C. water	2	None	1 lemon, juice of 1 C. powdered sugar Combine lemon juice and powdered sugar; frost hot cake.
Peanut butter Cake	Yellow	None	None	⅔ C. water	1	1 T. peanut butter ½ C. peanuts	½ C. peanuts, chopped ⅓ C. brown sugar 2 T. butter 2 T. peanut butter 2 T. milk Combine ingredients and spread over cooled cake, broil 3–5 minutes. (Watch carefully as it will burn easily.)
Sesame Cake or Poppyseed Cake	Yellow	Vanilla	½ C.	½ C. water	2	1 t. vanilla	1 T. sesame seeds or 1 T. poppy seeds (Figure 9-1) Fold into mixture before pouring into prepared pan.

*Approximately 2 C. cake mix
**Approximately ⅓ C. instant pudding

Preparation

Pans must be prepared *before* the batter is mixed, so that there is no delay in getting the batter into the pans and getting the pans into the oven. If batter is allowed to stand after mixing, the carbon dioxide from the chemical leavening agent or the air in the recipe may escape.

For shortened cakes, cut a piece of waxed paper to fit the bottom of the pan. Then grease the bottom of the pan and lay the piece of waxed paper over the grease. The waxed paper will help remove the cake from the pan. If the waxed paper is not used, grease only the *bottom* of the pan. Do not grease the sides, or the batter will not have support as it rises. Or, both bottom and sides of the pan can be greased and floured, as Figure 9-2 shows.

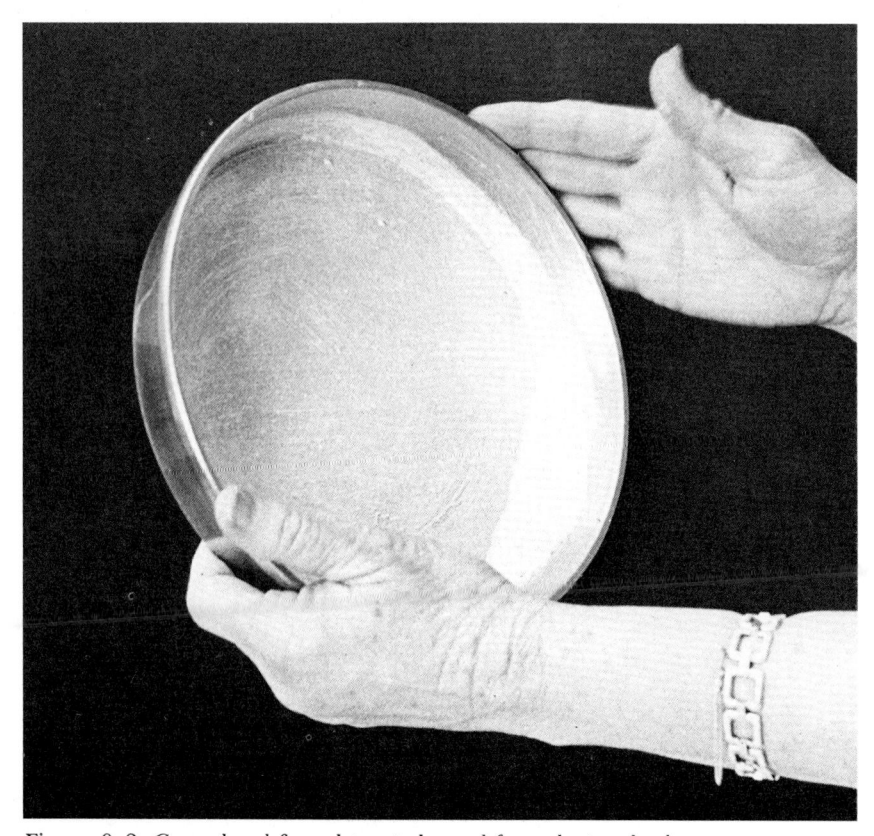

Figure 9–2 *Greased and floured pan to be used for a shortened cake.*

Cakes and frostings

Figure 9–3 *For best results, fill cake pan only two-thirds full.*

Pans should be filled no more than two-thirds full (Figure 9-3). After filling, sharply rap the pan on a flat surface to eliminate any large air bubbles.

For angel food, sponge, and chiffon cakes, pour the batter into an ungreased tube pan. Then, using an ordinary table knife, cut through the batter several times to break up any large air bubbles.

Baking

Oven temperature

Oven temperature is vital, and it may be wise to use an oven thermometer periodically to check the accuracy of the oven temperature control. If the thermometer shows a different temperature, it may be necessary to adjust the control up or down to obtain the correct temperature. Table 9-2 gives a general guide for selecting the proper oven temperature for the different types of cake. Remember that the length of time needed for baking will vary with the quantity of batter and the size and shape of the pan used. If a glass pan is used, the oven is set at a lower temperature.

Table 9-2 *General guide for baking times*

Shortened cakes		
Layers	Cupcakes	Loaf
190°C (375°F)	190°C (375°F)	176°C (350°F)
Unshortened cakes		
Angel food cake	Sponge cake	Chiffon cake
163–176°C (325–350°F)	163–176°C (325–350°F)	163°C (325°F)

Pan location

Place the pan in the oven so that air will circulate around it, again for even distribution of heat. Preferably, put a rack in the center of the oven, and place the pan in the center of the rack. If more than one cake is baked at the same time, stagger them on the racks so that they are not under one another and so that the air can circulate around them. Pans should not touch each other nor the sides of the oven.

Testing

It is good practice to set a timer for the shortest baking time given in the recipe and to test the cake when the timer goes off. A cake is done when the top springs back after being touched lightly with a fingertip; or when a toothpick or cake tester is inserted in its center and comes out clean; or when the cake begins to shrink from the sides of the pan. If the cake is not done when the timer goes off, continue baking. To avoid a dry cake, do not overbake.

Once the cake is done, take it from the oven and place it on a wire cake rack to cool for 10 minutes before it is removed from the pan. A hot cake is fragile, and, if removed from the pan when it first comes from the oven, it may break—as it cools, it becomes firmer. But, do not leave the cake in the pan too long; it may become soggy and stick to the pan.

When the 10 minutes are up, loosen the sides of the cake from the pan with a metal spatula, in a sawing motion. Place a wire rack over the pan, and invert the pan. Once the cake is out, immediately remove the piece of waxed paper (if used). Then, reverse the cake onto another rack, so that it will cool right side up.

Angel food cakes that have been baked in pans without cooling supports on the sides may be placed in an inverted position over the neck of a large soda bottle and allowed to remain in the pan until they are entirely cooled.

Desirable characteristics

Shortened cakes should have good volume and should be delicately browned, with a soft surface that shows no trace of sugar. The top should be rounded, unless it is a layer cake, which should have a flat top. The cake should be light in weight, with a fine, even grain of velvety, tender texture; and both the flavor and aroma should be pleasing.

A properly prepared and baked angel food cake should be very high and tender. It should be delicately browned; the inside should be moist, with a delicate flavor. A good chiffon cake should be high—its texture even, moist, and tender.

Making good cakes takes practice, combined with careful attention to the recipe's instructions for measuring, mixing, and baking in the correct pan. Table 9-3 lists both the desirable and undesirable characteristics of homemade cakes. In addition, the table lists some possible causes of the undesirable characteristics. In addition, further details are given in the books listed in the Bibliography, and the interested reader may wish to check this point in these references.

Fillings and frostings

Cakes often are filled and frosted to add to their appeal and decorative effect, or to turn a simple cake into a dramatic dessert, as shown in Figure 9-4. In the photograph, a plain sponge cake has been filled with mocha filling, rolled, and covered with a chocolate cream frosting to make an eye-catching finish to a meal. However, all these additions contain many calories.

Fillings

A cake may be filled with the same mixture—cooked or uncooked—used to frost it or with a different mixture. Cream fillings that contain milk and eggs

Table 9-3 *Evaluation of cakes*

Characteristics	Desirable characteristics	Undesirable characteristics	Possible causes of undesirable characteristics
Texture	Fine Velvety Moist	Coarse Grainy Dry	Improper measuring, overmixing, incorrect oven temperature
Volume and weight	Large increase in volume	Small increase in volume	Incorrect measurement of sugar, fat, or liquid, incorrect baking
Color	Golden brown for all except dark cakes such as chocolate, spice, and so on	Too brown Too light	Oven temperature too high or too low, baking time too long or too short, pan too small or too large

Cakes and frostings 145

Figure 9–4 *Bûche de Noël Sponge Roll with Mocha (coffee) Filling and with Chocolate Frosting.*

or whipped-cream fillings may be made with a wide variety of flavorings. These filled cakes must be refrigerated. Other fillings may be made from fruits or jams and jellies.

Frostings

Glazes, frostings, and icings are all similar, differing primarily in their thicknesses. *Glazes* are thin mixtures that are poured, spread, or painted over warm or cool cakes; *frostings* and *icings*[2] are thicker sugar mixtures and must be spread on a cooled cake. All three may be cooked or uncooked.

Uncooked These frostings are the quickest to prepare, and the fastest one of all is confectioners' sugar. Lay a paper-lace doily on top of the cake and

---

2. *Frostings* and *icings* are frequently used interchangeably, although *icings* may indicate a thin coating.

sprinkle the doily with sifted, very smooth confectioners' sugar. Then, very carefully remove the doily, leaving a sugar pattern on the cake.

Most uncooked frostings, spread on the cooled cake, are mixtures of fat, confectioners' sugar, liquid, and flavoring. Whole egg or egg yolk also may be included, and cream cheese, as well as butter, may be used. All frostings that contain confectioners' sugar should be beaten until they are very smooth and thinned to spreading consistency.

Cooked Some frostings are placed on the cake before it is baked and cooked at the same time; others are spread on a warm cake, and the cake is then broiled for a few minutes.

One type of boiled frosting is made by combining egg whites, sugar, and corn syrup or cream of tartar in the top of a double boiler. As the mixture cooks over boiling water, it is beaten with a rotary beater until it forms peaks when the beater is removed.

Other recipes direct that the sugar, water, and corn syrup or cream of tartar be made into a syrup first. The egg whites are beaten and the hot syrup slowly poured over them, as beating continues. This frosting must be beaten until it is thick enough to spread. The use of a candy thermometer to check temperatures is recommended for this frosting.

To make fudge-type frostings, bring the sugar mixture to a boil, making sure the sugar is dissolved. Cover pan to allow steam to wash sides of pan to prevent undesirable crystals from forming. Again, a candy thermometer is helpful to check the temperature. Remove the mixture from the heat, allow to cool, and beat until it is thick enough to spread.

The most desirable characteristic of all cooked frostings is a very smooth texture. However, weather and humidity affect these products, and problems can develop in preparing them. Sometimes, a boiled frosting will not thicken and may have to be salvaged with sifted confectioners' sugar, added in small amounts until the frosting is thick enough to spread. Other times, the frosting may harden before it can be spread, and a small amount of hot water will have to be added to thin it.

Spreading fillings and frostings

Brush all loose crumbs from the cake, so that the surface is smooth. If the cake is to be cut horizontally into layers for filling, place toothpicks around the sides to serve as cutting guides (Figure 9-5). Cut a small vertical notch in

Cakes and frostings 147

Figure 9-5 *Split cake in half. Insert toothpicks at intervals around the edge, for a guideline. Cut two notches, top and bottom, for matching top and bottom after filling.*

the top and bottom, so that the two sections can be matched after the filling is spread.

To protect the serving plate, lay overlapping sheets of waxed paper on it, and place the cake or bottom layer on the waxed paper. For a layer cake, spread the frosting or filling on the bottom layer, and then put the top layer into position. Frost the sides next and the top last. For a whole cake, again frost the sides first and the top last. Use a spatula for frosting, dipping it in hot water to keep it slick if the frosting or filling sticks to it. However, do not allow the excess water to run into the frosting and make it runny.

Once the cake is frosted, leave it on the waxed paper until the frosting is set firmly. Then, carefully remove and discard the paper.

Chapter 10 Grains, pastas, and legumes

Grains, or cereals, and legumes make great contributions to the human diet, and they are of major importance in countries where meat is scarce or too expensive for the budgets of many people. In wheat-producing countries, bread is the staff of life; in many rice-producing countries, particularly in the Far East, rice takes the place of wheat as the mainstay in the diet.

Grains are the dried seeds of grasses. We use the seeds of wheat, rice, corn, oats, and barley for food. Other grains are made into flours—rye flour, for example, as was mentioned in Chapter 7. Grains or the coarsely milled meals made from them are used in breakfast cereals, breads, and pastas.

Legumes are plants whose seeds grow in pods, such as lentils, peas, and beans. Many of these pods—with the seeds inside them—are eaten at the immature stage, as fresh vegetables; the mature seeds also are dried for use in other products. Dried legumes form the basis for many main dishes and are increasingly important because of their protein content and low cost (in comparison to meat).

Nutritional value

The nutritional content of cereals and legumes varies according to the kind and method of processing they have received. Cereals and legumes provide vitamins—especially the B vitamins—minerals, and carbohydrates. They also supply protein—plant protein—which is best used with some animal protein foods to obtain a more usable combination of the essential amino acids. Figure 10-1 shows a combination of wheat, oat, rice and corn cereals served as a breakfast cereal.

Grains, pastas, and legumes 149

Figure 10-1 *Granola, a combination of wheat, oat, rice, and corn cereals.*

It is wise to read the labels on all cereal-product containers, because nutrients are removed from some of them during the refining process. In some cases, thiamin, niacin, riboflavin, and iron are added, and the label indicates the specific nutrient content of the final product. Appendix A lists the nutritive values of a variety of grains, pastas, and legumes.

Consumers may wish to compare the cost of ready-to-eat breakfast cereals with the amount of nutrients obtained. Some of these products carry very high prices and a comparatively large amount of added sugar. The empty calories are seldom needed, and whole-grain cereals, cooked at home, usually provide better nutritive value at lower cost.

Cereals and cereal products

Grains have three main parts: the protective covering, or *bran*, which contains a little protein and minerals; the *endosperm*, which contains mostly starch and some protein; and the *germ*, which contains fat, vitamins, protein, and minerals. Often, the germ is removed during processing, because its fat content becomes rancid and shortens the *shelf life* (length of storage time) of the product.

Wheat

As was explained in Chapter 7, most of the wheat grown is made into flours, but many breakfast cereals also are made from wheat. Ready-to-eat wheat cereals are more highly processed than are those that require cooking.

Bulgur Bulgur is made by cooking whole wheat and drying it. Part of the bran then is removed and the remainder is cracked into a coarse product. The product often is cooked and served as a breakfast cereal or as an accompanying dish to the entrée, as is tabooleh (Figure 10-2)—its distinctive nutlike flavor making it compatible with many meat and poultry dishes. Often, simply adding hot water and letting the bulgur stand for 15 minutes will rehydrate and heat it.

Farina This product is made by removing most of the bran and germ from the wheat and grinding the remainder. Farina is served as a hot, cooked breakfast cereal or as an accompaniment with the entrée, as in gnocchi. To cook, add the required amount of farina to boiling salted water, and stir to keep lumps from forming.

Wheat germ The germ of the wheat kernel is flattened into flakes, which may be used in a variety of foods, such as breads, doughs, and meat loaves, to add nutritive value.

Pasta Commercially made pasta products include spaghetti, linguine, macaroni, shells, bows, and many other forms. All are made from the same basic mixture, which uses a flour made from durum wheat. This flour has a high gluten content that helps the pasta hold its shape when it is cooked. A few forms of pasta, including egg noodles, contain egg, and the label on their packages will include egg in the ingredient list. Some forms of pasta may be made at home; others require special machinery to achieve their shape.

All pastas are best cooked in a large quantity of rapidly boiling salted water to the *al dente* stage—cooked but still firm to the bite. A teaspoon of oil stirred into the water will keep pasta from sticking together. Pasta may be used as the base for entrées or simply seasoned with butter and/or cheese, parsley or basil, or garlic and oil dressing and served as a first course (Figure 10-3). Pastas increase in size during cooking, so follow the package's directions for the quantity needed.

Figure 10–2 *Tabooleh, made with bulgur and garnished with tomatoes and parsley.*

Figure 10-3 *Fettucine, to be served as a first course.*

Rice

This grain often is classified according to its length, as long-grain, medium-grain, or short-grain.

1. *Long-grain* rice is considered to be the highest quality rice, and, generally, it is more expensive than the other types. Its kernels stay separate when cooked correctly, and the product is fluffy.
2. *Short-grain* rice tends to stick together when cooked.
3. The *medium-grain* variety has properties of the other two types and may be selected for use in recipes in which the product is to be molded, since the product will hold its shape when removed from the mold (Figures 10-4 a and b).

There are several basic kinds of rice.

1. *Brown rice* is rice from which all the bran is not removed. It contains more vitamins and minerals than does *polished white rice,* unless the polished rice has been enriched with these nutrients in processing. Cooking time for brown rice is longer than that required for white rice.

Grains, pastas, and legumes 153

Figure 10–4 (a) *Soon after cooking, pack rice into a buttered mold.*

Figure 10–4 (b) *Unmold rice ring immediately after packing, or reheat in the mold and unmold at a later time.*

2. *Converted* or *parboiled* rice is rice that has been partially cooked (or parboiled), dried, and enriched. It requires approximately the same time to cook as does regular rice.
3. *Wild rice* is a grass seed, not a true rice. It has a long brownish grain and a very distinctive flavor. Often regarded as a delicacy, it is expensive because of the cost of harvesting and the limited supply.

Most rice should not be washed before cooking; washing will remove some of the enriched coating. Rice should be cooked in only enough boiling, salted water to be absorbed by the rice in the process: a general rule is to allow two cups of water for each cup of rice. This procedure holds the nutrients in the product. Rice may be pan-fried in butter, with or without onions, until the kernels are partially cooked and lose their translucent appearance. Liquid and other ingredients are added, the pan covered, and the rice cooked until it is done. One cup of raw rice yields about three cups of cooked rice.

Corn

Cereals, meals, hominy, and grits are made from corn, and each is used in a variety of ways. Corn cereals are available in ready-to-eat products, and hot corn cereal can be prepared by cooking white or yellow cornmeal in water. Cornmeal may or may not be enriched; check the container label for this information. Hot corn cereals are prepared by adding the meal gradually to boiling water, stirring constantly to prevent lumps from forming.

Hominy is the corn kernel from which the hull and germ have been removed; *grits* are small pieces of hominy. Hominy usually is purchased canned; it is heated and used as a vegetable. To prepare grits, add them gradually to boiling water while stirring to keep the mixture smooth. Grits are served as a hot cereal or as an accompaniment to an entrée.

Oats

Oatmeal is processed by removing the hull and rolling the *groats* (inner portion) into flakes. *Regular* oatmeal is a comparatively thick flake, which requires a longer cooking time than does the *quick-cooking* or *instant* product, which has a thinner flake. Oatmeal usually is served as a hot breakfast cereal, but it also may be used in a variety of baked products, from meatloaf to cookies. When used for hot cereal, regular and quick types are prepared like the hot corn cereals.

Barley

Both hulls and bran are removed from the grain to produce *pearl* barley. This product often is used to thicken soups slightly, since it contains a large amount of starch, but it also may be cooked and served for breakfast or for a light supper dish. It is sometimes sautéed in butter or ham fat before it is cooked in water.

Dried legumes

Legumes frequently are dried for easy storage and must be rehydrated before they are cooked and incorporated into recipes. Lentils and peas are more easily rehydrated than are beans. Carefully sort dried legumes before they are cooked. Remove any damaged seeds and small stones or other foreign matter, such as bits of seed pod or stem.

Lentils

These distinctively flavored seeds are used primarily in soups and stews, but they also may be served as a vegetable. They may be cooked until tender; or, to help retain their shape, boiled for two minutes, left to soak for half an hour, and then cooked until just tender.

Peas

Dried split peas have long been used in making soup, and black-eyed peas, combined with rice, is a regional dish in this country. Chickpeas, or *garbanzos*, once eaten primarily in the Middle East, have become more popular in America and are used in salads and soups. Cook dried peas as you would cook lentils: place them in boiling water for 2 minutes, soak for 30 minutes, and cook until tender.

Beans

Dried beans are available in a wide variety of colors and sizes: brown red, speckled, white, light tan, pink, red, black; and oval, kidney shaped, plump, and slender. Common varieties are kidney, pinto, cranberry, navy, lima, and black.

Dried beans resist softening, and they must be cooked long enough to become thoroughly rehydrated and tender. They may be soaked overnight in cold water, or boiled for two minutes in water to cover and left to stand for an hour before cooking. They also may be cooked in a pressure cooker, according to the directions provided with the pan.

Dried soybeans are increasingly important as a source of plant protein. They may be cooked like other dried beans, or allowed to sprout. To sprout, place them in a cool place and leave them for four or five days. During this time, sprinkle them with cool water several times a day, to encourage the sprouts to form. Once they have fully sprouted, place them in a covered container and refrigerate until they are used. Raw bean sprouts may be added to sandwiches, salads, soups, and stews; cooked bean sprouts may be served as a vegetable.

Other soybean products are used to add nutritive value to prepared foods or to substitute for meat. Soy flour may be blended with other flours for use in some recipes; a meal-like soy substance may be added to soups and casseroles for greater nutritive value with no added fat. A dry soy product has been developed that can be shaped to resemble sliced meat, and it also is available as small bits—similar to bacon bits—for use in salads, soups, and other dishes.

In most cases, the soy product costs less than the animal product does, so it is more economical. When ground meat is mixed with the extender form, the flavor is altered slightly, but shrinkage is reduced and the product is moist and tender. This type of soy product, often called *TVP* (textured vegetable protein), is particularly useful for low-fat and low-budget meals.

Selection and storage

Select cereals, cereal products, and dried legumes according to the planned use. Some of these foods are packaged in thin plastic or cellophane; check these packages to be sure that they have no holes. Avoid any bag with a hole, since it may have been contaminated.

All these foods are best stored in a cool, dry place, in tightly covered containers to protect their quality and to prevent insect infestation. Glass jars with screw-on lids are excellent for this purpose. Ready-to-eat breakfast cereals, since they have a tendency to lose their crispness, may be wrapped in plastic bags with tightly fastened tops.

Wheat germ, whole-wheat flour, and other whole-grain products cannot be stored for long periods of time, because the fat in the germ may cause them to become rancid. Dried legumes have a long shelf life.

Chapter 11 Finfish and shellfish

Although a great many varieties of fish are available in markets in this country, many kinds are available only locally and are not well known to consumers in other sections of the country. As a result, most people are familiar with only a few fish. Shellfish, since they are more widely distributed, are better known.

Fish, often called *finfish* to distinguish them from shellfish, have a skeleton, firm solid flesh, scales, and fins. *Shellfish* have no bones so their bodies are very soft, and they have hard shells for protection. *Mollusks*—clams, oysters, and scallops—have shells that are joined and held together with a strong muscle. *Crustaceans*—crabs, lobsters, and shrimp—have shells made in sections, like their bodies, and they all have legs.

Nutritional value

Fish and shellfish are excellent sources of complete protein, and most are low in fat content. Those that have higher fat content contain vitamin A; and some fish livers, especially cod, contain significant amounts of vitamin D. Finfish contain a higher percentage of polyunsaturated fatty acids than they do saturated fatty acids; they also contain a very small amount of cholesterol. Shellfish contain a high percentage of cholesterol, even though they contain very little fat.

Fish vary in mineral content, but shrimp and oysters have high calcium content. Saltwater fish are an important source of iodine; freshwater fish contain no iodine.

Fish flour, which is made from dehydrated whole fish, is an excellent high-quality protein and, probably, will become a more important source of protein in the United States and other countries as acceptable recipes using it are developed. The other nutritive contents of fish and shellfish are shown in Appendix A.

Retail forms

The Department of the Interior has established an inspection and grading system for use by the fishing industry. Fish and shellfish taken from polluted waters can be very hazardous: they contain harmful micro-organisms. Oysters, clams, and some fish are eaten uncooked or cooked at temperatures that are not high enough to kill the micro-organisms. The inspection system is voluntary, but it is used by many states and fish processors.

Finfish

Fish may be purchased in several forms.

1. *whole*: as they come from the water, called "*round fish*"
2. *drawn*: their interior organs removed; their head, fins, and tail left on
3. *dressed*: drawn; their head, fins, and tail removed
4. *filleted*: sliced lengthwise from the side; nearly boneless
5. *steaks*: sliced crosswise; bones included
6. *sticks*: serving-sized squares or rectangular pieces cut from steaks or fillets

In some parts of the United States, the supply of raw fish is limited, and many kinds of fish are available only in the frozen form. Frozen fish is available both cooked and uncooked, and frequently it is found in the frozen-and-thawed form that permits purchase of smaller amounts. Fish also is canned or dried, and these forms are available in all sections of the country.

Shellfish

Crab Blue crabs are found only along the Atlantic and Gulf coasts. Dungeness crabs come from the Pacific, and the large, long-legged king crabs come from the northern Pacific.

In season, crabs are available whole—alive or cooked—but the majority of the supply is canned or frozen. Whole crabs and crab meat—frozen or frozen-thawed—are found in many markets.

Lobsters Many people feel that the most desirable lobster comes only from the cold North Atlantic, and lobsters from Maine are considered choice. These lobsters have meat throughout most of their bodies. Spiny, or rock, lobsters, another type, come from warmer waters in several parts of the world, and their meat is almost entirely in the tail. In many markets, the tails are the only part found.

Frozen lobster tails and whole, live lobsters are available in many parts of the United States. Live lobsters are shipped by air, and they are always expensive.

Shrimp Shrimp are caught in waters off the southern United States and in warm waters off South America and Far Eastern countries. They are sold raw or cooked; in the shell, whole or headless; or peeled and cleaned. Frozen and canned shrimp also are available. The size of shrimp varies from extremely small to very large, approximately two to three ounces each.

Clams Different varieties are obtained in the coastal waters around the United States. Sizes and shapes vary, and shells may be hard or soft. Live clams can be purchased in the shell or *shucked* (removed from the shell). Frozen and canned clams—whole or chopped—also may be purchased.

Oysters Oysters are another coastal-water shellfish. Atlantic Ocean oysters are smaller than are those from the Pacific, and many people feel that Atlantic oysters served raw on the half-shell are a great delicacy. Pacific oysters have a slightly different flavor and texture than does the Atlantic variety. Both varieties are sold alive in the shell, or shucked and frozen; and canned oysters also may be found in markets.

Scallops Bay scallops, caught in shallow bays or inlets, are pinkish beige, small, and tender. Sea scallops, from deeper waters, are larger—usually about 1¼ inch in diameter—and white. The bay variety is considered the more desirable by many. The muscle that controls the two shells of the scallop is the only part that is eaten in the United States.

Selection

The wisest rule for selecting fresh fish or shellfish is easily remembered: if in any doubt about its freshness, do not buy. Fish in markets may be fresh or

Finfish and shellfish

frozen and thawed, and it may not be properly identified. Fresh whole clams, oysters, crabs, and lobsters must be alive when cooked, which means they must be very fresh at the time of purchase. If doubtful about freshness, investigate frozen products; and if in doubt about the frozen products, change the meal plan.

Finfish

All fresh forms of high-quality finfish have firm flesh and no unpleasant odor of any kind. In whole fish, eyes are clear and bright, and the scales are tight on the body. The flesh will spring back into place if pressure is applied with a finger and then suddenly removed. There is no slime on any part of the fish. Fresh fish will float if placed in water.

A good-quality frozen finfish should be hard-frozen and should not show signs of damage or discoloration from freezing. Look for frozen juices in the bottom of the carton: they indicate that the package has thawed partially and has been refrozen. This also could be a result of too long a trip from market freezer to home freezer. A good-quality frozen fish has very little, if any, odor.

Unfortunately, many buyers are unaware that most fish in the market have been frozen and thawed, because they are seldom so identified. The quality of this fish frequently is poor. Frozen-and-thawed fish should be used within one or two days, or refrozen at once. And refreezing, which may be done safely if ice crystals are still present, will cause a loss of quality.

Shellfish

Fresh whole clams, oysters, crabs, and lobsters must be alive when they are cooked. The shells of good clams and oysters are tightly closed; soft-shelled clams may open their shells very slightly, but the shells will snap shut if touched. Live lobsters—kept in tanks of water, or in wet seaweed or in wet paper—move their legs and claws readily, not slowly and laboriously. Fresh raw shrimp, called *green shrimp*, are a greenish-gray color. The shells are hard and firm, and there is no unpleasant odor. Shellfish that have deteriorated often have a sharp, ammonialike odor.

Amount to buy

As a rule, about 3 to 4 ounces are needed for each serving of fish. Usually, however, a small, whole lobster is considered to be an adequate size for one serving, and servings from larger lobsters will vary greatly. In areas where mostly frozen fish is available, it may be difficult to purchase small quantities, unless the market has frozen-and-thawed fish.

Storage

Raw fish and shellfish deteriorate very rapidly, even in modern refrigerators, and they cannot be held safely for long. Further, they provide excellent conditions for bacterial growth. It always is best to cook them the day that they are purchased, but under good refrigeration really fresh fish may be held for two days. If it must be held for a longer period, wrap properly and freeze.

Frozen fish that has been completely thawed before it was sold is best cooked the day that it is purchased; refreezing at home is undesirable. Frozen fish that has thawed only slightly—and still has many ice crystals—can be refrozen, but its quality will not be as good as that of fish that has been held hard-frozen.

Cooked fish and opened cans of fish may be tightly wrapped or covered, and held in the refrigerator for a day or two. The length of storage time is determined by the following:

1. the freshness of the fish
2. the degree of temperature reached out of refrigeration
3. the length of time held at that temperature
4. the wrapping used for storage
5. the temperature inside the refrigerator.

Storage times may be shorter or longer than indicated above (see Chapter 1).

Preparation

Most fish is purchased ready to cook. It is best to thaw frozen fish before cooking, so that the outside does not overcook. Frozen fish may be thawed in the refrigerator slowly or, more quickly, under cold running water.

Clam shells must be scrubbed with a brush to remove sand; discard those that have cracked shells or shells that stay open. Clams may be placed in a large pan (or pail) of salt water and sprinkled with cornmeal several hours before they are used, to *purge* (clean the stomachs of) the clams.

Shrimp must be shelled, and unless very small, deveined. *Deveining* is the removal of the intestinal tract—the black line along the curved outside. Using the point of a paring knife or the end of a toothpick, cut or gently scrape along the black line, holding the shrimp under running water. The force of the running water will loosen and wash away the vein.

Cooking methods

Fish dries out and toughens easily during cooking. Best results are obtained by careful temperature control and the shortest possible cooking time. To retain the shape of the fish—whole or section—use extreme care in handling during cooking and in transferring the fish from pan to platter.

Whichever cooking method is used, it is very important to know when the fish is done. To test doneness, use a toothpick or cooking fork to prick the thickest part of the fish. If it is done, the fish will *just begin* to flake apart. Another test of doneness involves piercing the thickest part of the body with a very sharp-tined fork: if the fork slides easily through the meat, the fish is done.

A meat thermometer, inserted in the thickest part, may be used in cooking large, whole fish. When the thermometer registers 60°C (140°F), the fish is done.

Broiling

This method is used for fillets, steaks, and sticks, and for scallops. It also may be used for a whole fish that has been split along the backbone, so that the halves will lie flat. Place the pieces, or the whole fish, on a greased broiler pan or rack. If the skin was not removed, position the skin side against the rack or pan. If desired, a small amount of melted fat may be poured on, and seasonings may be sprinkled over the pieces.

The length of time needed for broiling and the distance from the heat vary with the size and thickness of the fish. Place smaller pieces closer to the heat than thicker ones are placed. The pieces may or may not be turned during broiling: turning makes it very difficult to retain the shape of a whole split fish.

Baking

Steaks and thick fillets may be baked in a greased pan. Brush melted fat over the tops of the pieces and add seasonings. Baste the pieces during cooking.

Fish often are baked whole—stuffed or unstuffed. As with poultry, the stuffing may be held in with skewers, and the fish is basted with melted fat or pan liquid during cooking. Moving a whole baked fish from the pan to the serving dish is a delicate process. Sometimes, two large spatulas are helpful, and, for a large fish, even two people.

Frying

Whether pan-fried or oven-fried, the fish or shellfish usually is dipped in milk and flour or in beaten egg and crumbs or in a batter before it is fried. These coatings help to keep the fish from drying out and also give it a crisp, brown crust.

The temperature used in deep-fat frying or pan-frying must be high enough to cook the inside of the fish by the time the outside is brown. The temperature of deep fat used is 187.8°C (370°F); an oven temperature of 204.4°C (400°F) often is used. Usually, the burner will need adjustments during pan-frying, according to the size and thickness of the pieces being cooked.

Steaming and boiling

Finfish Often, a fish that is to be served whole on a platter is steamed or boiled. To keep it from breaking apart during cooking or when it is removed from the pan, tie the fish in cheesecloth or wrap it in heavy foil before cooking.

To steam finfish, place the wrapped fish on a rack or steamer tray in a heavy pan and cook over boiling water. To boil, bring the water to a boil, and then put the fish on a rack and into the pan, covering it with the water. When the water returns to boiling, lower the burner temperature and simmer the fish until done. In either case, remove the fish from the rack with a spatula and unwrap it very carefully. Then, roll it from the wrapping onto a serving dish.

The time required for these two methods varies with the size of the fish and its temperature at the beginning of cooking. For both methods, fresh, frozen, or frozen-and-thawed fish may be used.

Finfish and shellfish

Shellfish Lobster, crab, and green shrimp are submerged in boiling water and simmered until done. The shells of all three turn bright red during cooking. Clams are steamed until shells open, and the cooking takes a very short time, from 3 to 10 minutes.

Poaching

Fillets may be rolled or folded for ease in handling. Figures 11-1 a and b show fillets that have been made smaller in this way.

Poach fish fillets in a cup or less of liquid. Use a covered pan on the burner, or cover the fish with a piece of waxed paper and bake it in a hot oven. The poaching liquid may be reduced and made into a sauce, to be served with the fish: after removing the fish, rapidly boil the liquid so that most of it evaporates, concentrating the flavor.

Preparing chowders and soups

Many kinds of finfish and shellfish are used in chowders and soups. Chowders often have milk as a main ingredient; soups frequently do not, although

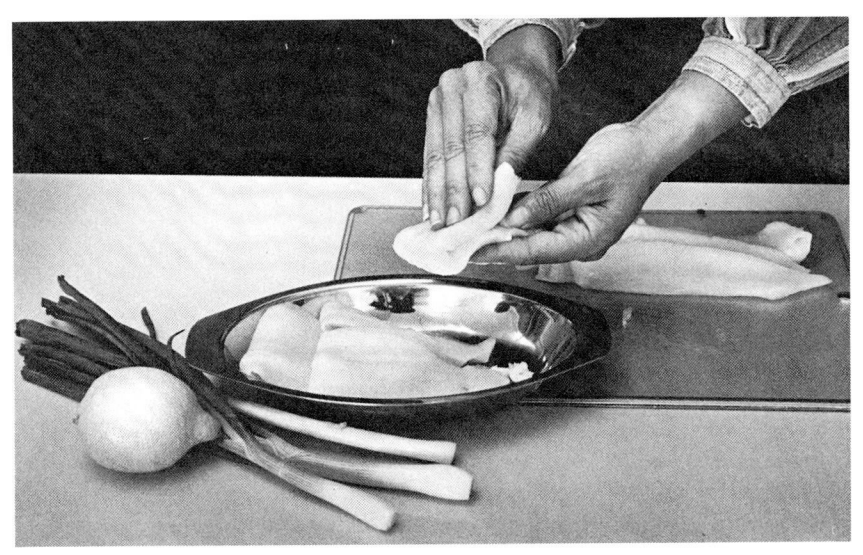

Figure 11–1 (a) *Fold fish fillet so that the inside of the muscle is on the outside.*

Figure 11-1 (b) *Roll fish fillet around a shrimp.*

oyster stew is a thin, milk-based soup. In making chowders and soups, add the pieces of raw fish or steamed shellfish near the end of cooking—as in preparing stews or creoles—so that they will not become tough.

Serving suggestions

If the skin is to be removed before the fish is served, do it after the fish is cooked, while it is hot (Figures 11-2 a through d). In many instances, however, the skin is left on and removed by the diners. Whole fish usually are deboned by the server as portions are separated from the whole. Deep-fried fish must be served immediately to retain its crispness.

The soft texture and the mild, bland flavor of fish is enhanced with sauces and crisp garnishes. Try any of the following: parsley, lettuce, watercress, lemons, olives, cucumbers, tomatoes, sliced cooked eggs, toasted almonds, and sour-cream dill, hollandaise, and rémoulade sauces.

Figure 11–2 (a) *Partially unwrap poached fish and place it on the platter.* (b) *Roll the wrapping from under fish.*

c

d

Figure 11-2 (c) *Remove skin from cooked fish.* (d) *Garnish fish with lemon slices and tartar sauce–filled cucumber cups.*

Chapter 12 Poultry

The demand for poultry has grown in the past twenty years, and, today, raising poultry is big business. Birds are raised indoors in huge sheds, under artificial lights; and they are fed with food mixed by computer. At market age, they are trucked to processing plants that use assembly-line equipment to prepare the birds for the retail market.

In the United States, chicken and turkey are the most popular poultry, but ducks, geese, pigeons, and *squab* (young pigeons) also are raised for market. Rock Cornish hens, small birds developed by crossbreeding, have grown more popular in recent years and are now widely available.

Nutritional value

All types of poultry are excellent sources of high-quality, complete protein, and they also contain significant amounts of niacin and iron. In fact, poultry meat is considered to be nutritionally very similar to that of other meats and is a desirable alternative to red meats in the daily menu.

The fat content of poultry varies with the age and kind of bird. Young birds have less fat than do older birds, which develop a layer of fat under the skin and around the abdominal organs; white meat has less fat than does dark meat; and chickens have less fat than do ducks, turkeys, and geese. In fact, geese over a year old are likely to have such strong-flavored fat that they do not taste good. Appendix A lists the nutritive value of various types of poultry.

Nutritional content also depends on the cooking method. A roasted bird, for example, may lose fat during cooking; some melted fat drains into the pan and some may be absorbed in the stuffing. Fried chicken, on the other hand, will not lose much fat during frying, and if it is dipped in batter or another mixture before it is fried, the coating may absorb the fat, increasing the fat content. Chicken stews and soups, from which some or all of the fat is removed before serving, may have little or no fat. And, if the skin has been removed before cooking, almost all fat has been removed as well.

Provided that low cooking temperatures are used, cooking does not significantly alter the nutritional value of poultry. Correct freezing also does not affect nutrients, and frozen chickens, turkeys and ducks commonly are available.

Inspection and grading

By law, all poultry sold in markets in the United States must be inspected under federal or state inspection systems. Birds are inspected alive and at several processing stages. Food products, like canned chicken and chicken or turkey pies, must be prepared under federal inspection, and their labels must show all the ingredients (listed by their proportion in the product), the net weight, the product's name, the packer's name and address, and the official plant and inspection mark. The USDA uses a round inspection mark on all poultry.

Poultry grading is not required by law, but the USDA has issued grade standards for packers who wish to use them. Birds are checked for shape, amount of meat and fat, bruises or torn skin, and bone structure. Graded birds carry a mark shaped like a shield.

Grade-A birds are full fleshed and meaty: they have no crooked bones, no tears in the skin, and no bruises, and they look attractive. Grade-B birds are a little less meaty: their skin may have a few small rips, and they look slightly less attractive than do Grade-A birds. Grade-C birds are poorly covered with meat: they look skimpy, and, sometimes, have an uneven shape. Usually, Grade-C birds are used for prepared products; only Grades A and B are found in retail markets.

Retail poultry forms

Most poultry is marketed after it has been *eviscerated* (internal organs removed) and the inedible parts have been removed. It is ready for cooking, fresh or frozen. Geese, Rock Cornish hens, and ducks usually are left whole; chickens and turkeys may be cut into halves, quarters, or smaller pieces.

Chicken and turkey are labeled according to age, and the label suggests the cooking method. Chickens labeled *fryer, broiler,* or *roaster* are young, tender birds, and are cooked as the labels imply. A *stewing hen* or *fowl* is an older bird, best stewed or boiled, to make the meat tender. *Capons*—young, very meaty birds—and Rock Cornish hens are usually roasted.

Turkeys range in weight from 4 pounds to well over 40 pounds. In recent years, breeding improvements have produced turkeys with a large amount of breast meat, even in small birds. Young turkeys, sometimes called *fryer-roasters*, can be fried, roasted, or broiled. Turkeys labeled *young hen* or *young tom* (male) generally are roasted—with or without stuffing.

Fresh turkeys usually are available only at certain times of the year; whole frozen birds and smaller sections are on hand in markets year-round. Whole birds may or may not be stuffed. Turkey meat is available in boneless rolls of all-white or all-dark or light-and-dark meat; it also is available as ground turkey. Canned chicken and turkey and other prepared products may be purchased in all seasons.

Selection

Select poultry according to the planned use: fryer-roasters for frying or roasting; stewing hens for soup, stew, or salad; whole turkeys, ducks, or geese for roasting, and so on. Certain exceptions will be explained later.

Grade

Grade-A poultry is probably more desirable if the bird is to be roasted whole and carved at the table, where an attractive appearance enhances the meal. If the bird is to be served in smaller sections, appearance may be less important and Grade-B poultry will probably be quite satisfactory. If the meat is to be removed from the bones as for chicken salad, a Grade-B bird will be adequate. Further, if the price of a Grade-B bird were less than that of a Grade-A bird, the former would be a better buy for the purpose.

Amount to buy

When poultry is purchased whole or in sections, the bone, skin, and fat are included. Bone is inedible waste, and fat and skin also may be waste. Therefore, a good general guide is: one pound of chicken or turkey serves one or two, and one pound of goose or duck serves approximately one. Usually, larger birds have a greater proportion of meat to bone: half of a 24-pound turkey will have more meat than will a whole turkey that weighs 12 pounds.

Also, consider seasonal variations in supply and market competition when selecting poultry. At times, two large broilers may be a better buy than a roasting or stewing chicken. At any time of year, it is more economical to buy a whole chicken than it is to buy a cut-up one. Figures 12-1 a through q show the techniques to use in cutting up poultry.

The prepared, ready-to-roast turkey rolls and breasts vary slightly in price around the year, but they always are expensive. On the other hand, they have little or no waste, so they may be a good purchase for certain meals.

Storage

Poultry is an excellent medium for the growth of micro-organisms and—raw or cooked—must always be handled carefully. Proper refrigeration is extremely important at all times.

Raw

Raw poultry must be kept refrigerated at all times, either in the plastic market wrap or in a plastic bag, if the market wrap has been removed. If included, the *giblets* (heart, liver, and gizzard) are packed in the abdominal cavity or under the loose neck skin. Remove them, and wrap and refrigerate them separately. Since poultry often drips, place the bird in a shallow container to protect other refrigerated foods.

Properly refrigerated, fresh raw poultry may be kept one to two days. To keep it longer, seal it in an airtight, moisture-proof freezer wrap and freeze it rapidly. Frozen raw poultry may be held hard-frozen for 9 to 12 months.

Cooked

If poultry is not to be eaten directly after it is cooked, wrap it carefully and refrigerate. Leftover poultry also should be refrigerated as soon as possible after the meal. It may be kept in the coldest part of the refrigerator for two to five days.

Stuffed, roasted birds present an additional hazard. Even in modern refrigerators, considerable time is needed to chill the inside and the stuffing of a large bird. If any micro-organisms are present, they can multiply during this time and cause illness after a later meal. Therefore, remove the stuffing and refrigerate it in a separate closed container.

Do not refrigerate creamed chicken or products that contain chicken livers for longer than two days. Cooked poultry used for a picnic should be refrigerated until it is thoroughly chilled before it is packed in the picnic cooler. Never take cooked poultry to a picnic site without a cooler.

Cooked chicken and turkey may be carefully wrapped, frozen, and held for four to six months. The flavor usually is better if it is frozen in a sauce.

Preparation

A moist, tender, flavorful product is the goal. Poultry is a high-protein food, and improper cooking can make it tough and dry. Cook tender, young poultry by a dry-heat method, but cook older, less tender birds by a moist-heat method or by a combination of moist and dry methods, to prevent drying and toughening.

Frozen birds

Frozen poultry may be thawed in its original wrapping in the refrigerator (in a shallow container) or under cold water, in a deep pan or bowl. Although it also can be thawed at room temperature, this procedure is unwise: the bird may be forgotten or overlooked and become too warm, allowing micro-organisms to multiply. Refrigerator thawing is generally considered easier and safer.

Thawing time varies with size of the bird or number of frozen-together sections. A 3-pound chicken will take about one and one half to two hours to thaw in cold water; a 12-pound turkey may take about six hours. Thawing may be hastened by loosening the legs and wings as they thaw, or by loosening and pulling apart the cut pieces.

Frozen ready-to-cook poultry may be cooked without thawing. And, if the poultry was stuffed before it was frozen, it *must* be cooked without thawing. Do not allow it to thaw at all, and carefully follow the directions on the wrapper. The length of time needed for cooking frozen poultry—stuffed or unstuffed—will vary with the size of the bird.

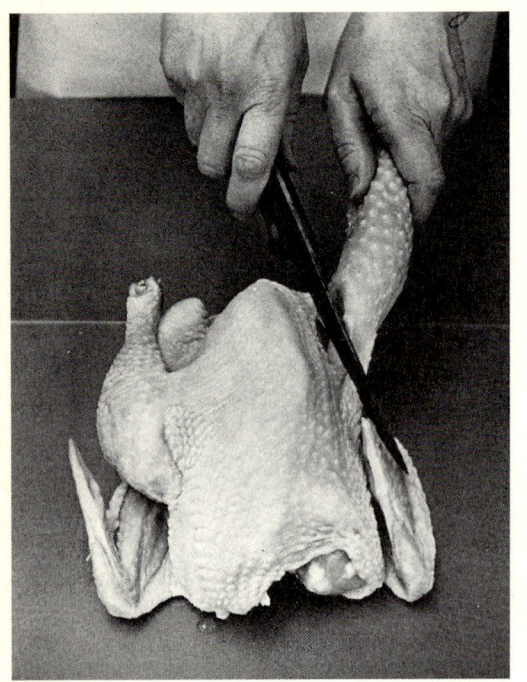

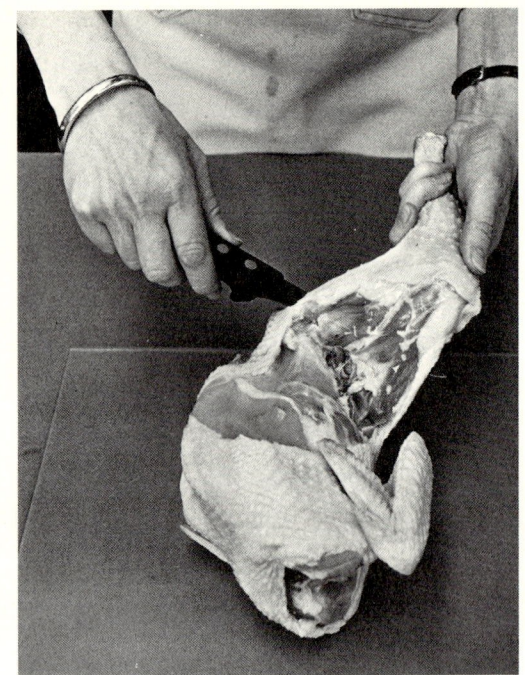

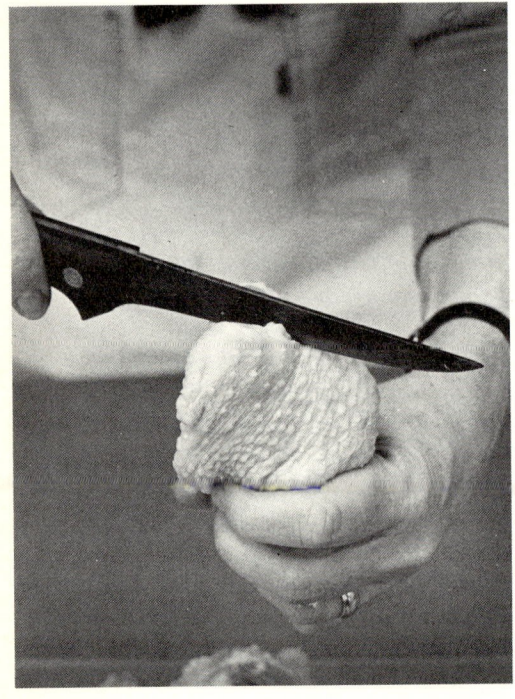

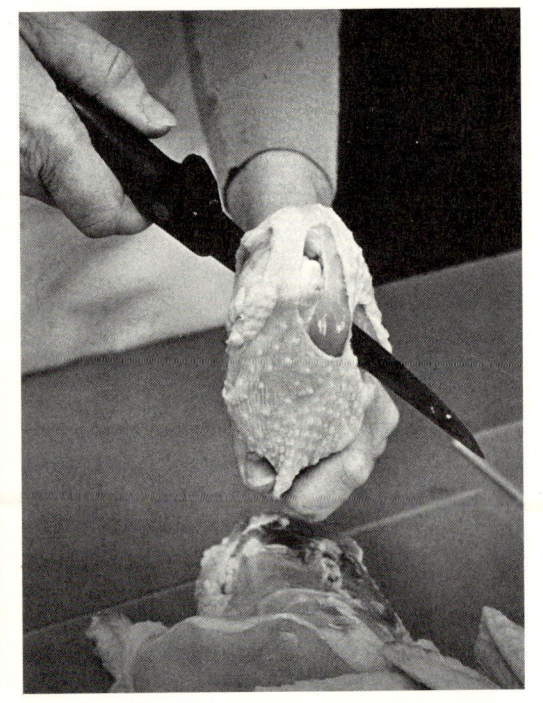

a

b

c

d

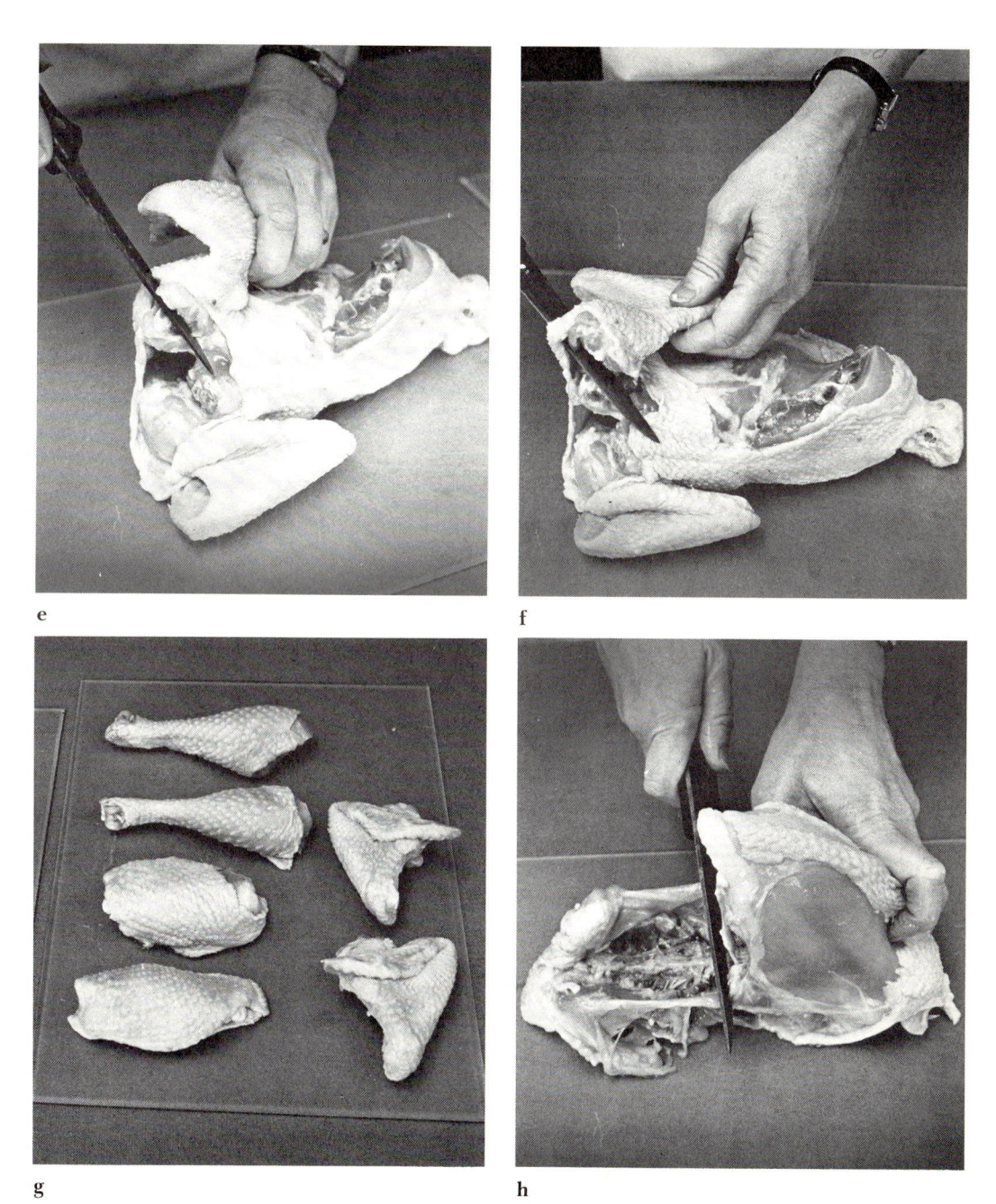

Figure 12–1 (a) *Cut through skin of leg.* (b) *Cut from underneath side through the joint, to separate.* (c) *Bend leg and cut down to the joint.* (d) *Reverse knife and cut up through joint to separate it into thigh and drumstick.* (e) *Cut to joint of wing.* (f) *Reverse knife and separate wing from body of chicken.* (g) *Drumsticks, thighs, and wings shown removed.* (h) *Cut from bottom of breast through membrane, to center back.*

i

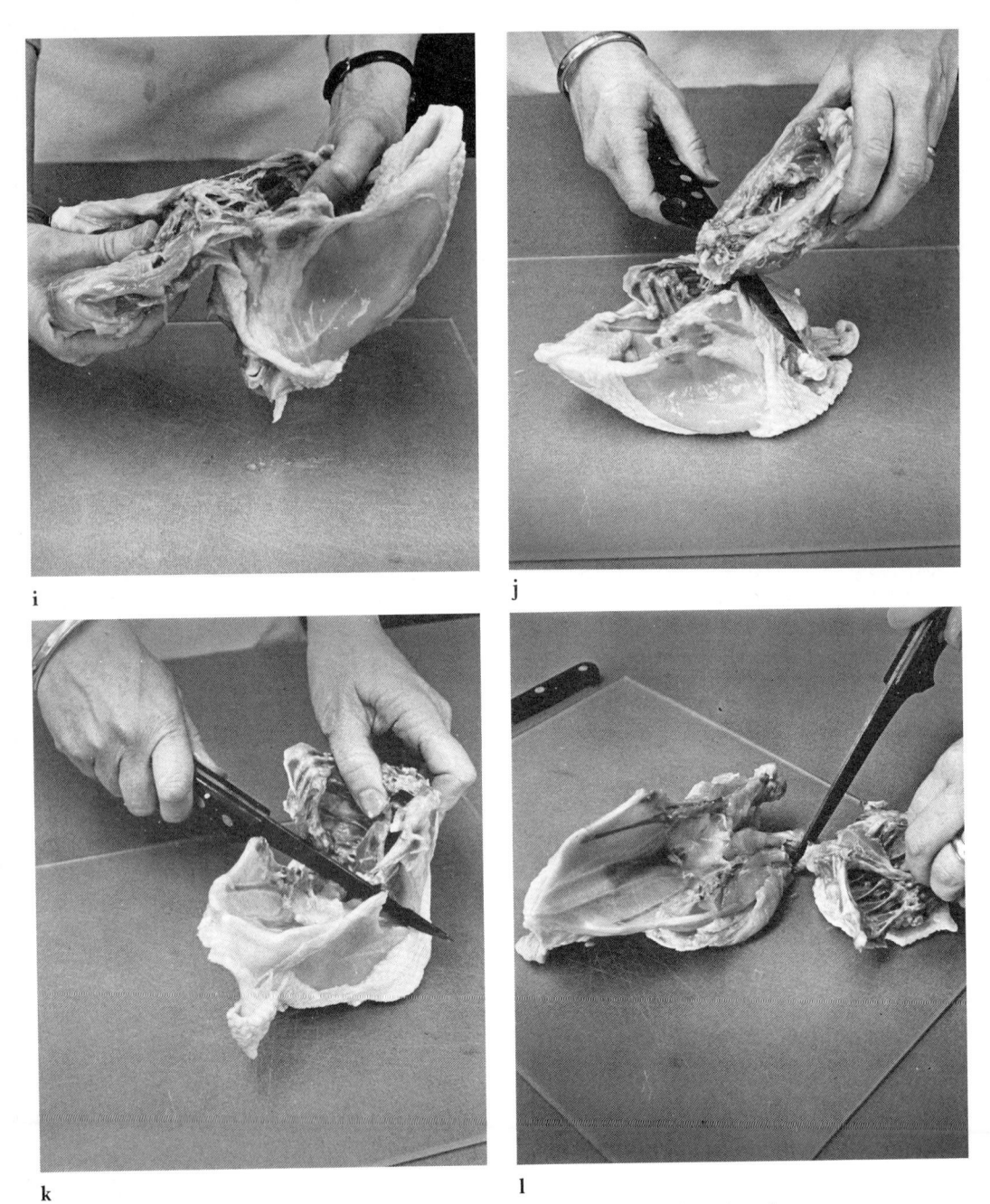

j

k

l

Figure 12–1 (i) *Bend lower back to separate it more easily from breast.* (j) *Using the knife, cut through to separate completely the lower back from the breast.* (k) *Cut through ribs to separate upper back from breast.* (l) *With the point of the knife, separate the joint that holds the back to the breast.*

m

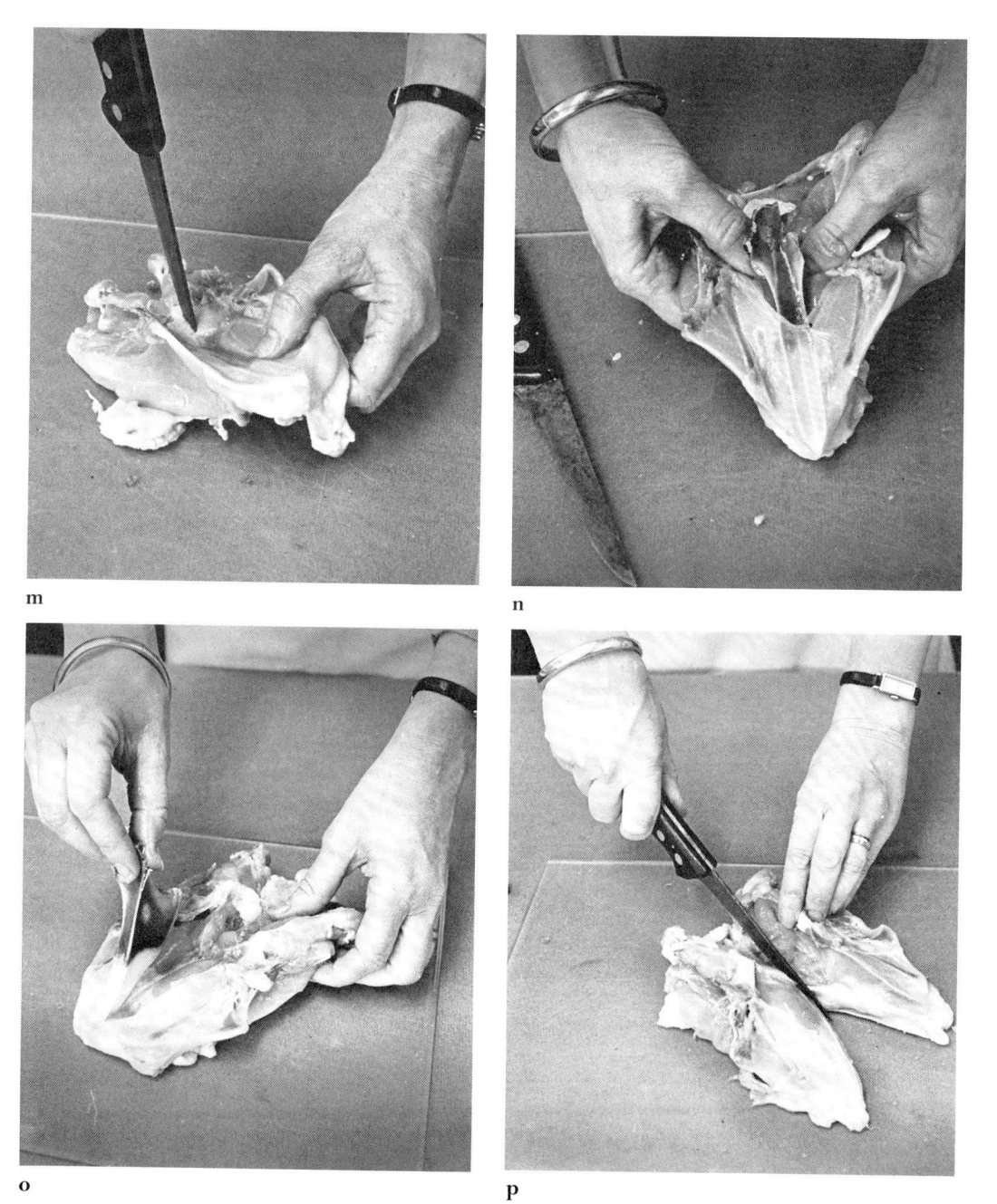

n

o

p

Figure 12–1 (m) *Place point of the knife at top of the keel bone and cut through membrane. Using both hands, bend parts backward to expose the keel bone.* (n) *Place thumbs on either side of bone to release it from the tissue.* (o) *Complete removal by pulling.* (p) *Cut through the remaining skin and tissue to separate the breast into two pieces.*

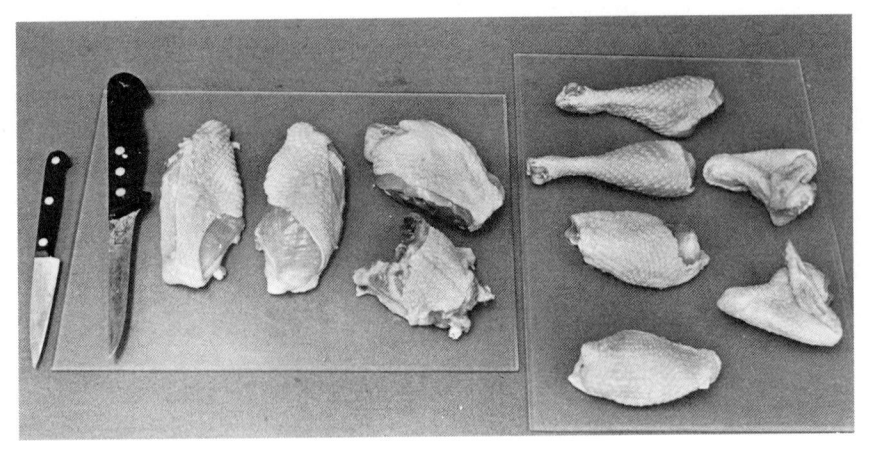

Figure 12–1 (q) *Complete cut-up chicken.*

Raw poultry

Usually, raw poultry is cooked as soon as it is prepared. If this is not possible or if the meal must be delayed, wrap the poultry and return it to the refrigerator. The only exception is a bird that has been stuffed: once it is stuffed, the poultry must be cooked without delay to prevent the growth of micro-organisms. An alternate method is to cook the stuffing separately in a casserole and during cooking, spoon juices from the roasting bird over dressing, for additional flavor. This procedure has additional advantages: the unstuffed bird bakes in less time and the stuffing is easy to serve.

Kitchen sanitation

After poultry has been handled or prepared, thoroughly clean the counter so that other food will not be contaminated by any micro-organisms from poultry. If a chopping board is used, scrub it thoroughly, along with any implements or utensils used. (Further details on this aspect of sanitation were explained in Chapter 1, in the section on *Salmonella* bacteria.)

Dry-heat cooking methods

Roasting

If stuffing is used, pack it lightly into the abdominal cavity with a spoon or cup. The stuffing will absorb juice from the bird during cooking and will expand, so leave some room around it. Then, *truss* (tie the legs together with the tail with a string), or force the leg ends under the band of skin at the bottom of the stuffed cavity, to hold the stuffing in place and to keep the bird in compact shape. Fold back the loose neck skin and fasten it with a *skewer*

Poultry

(long metal pin) or with a long string; bend back the wing tips behind the top of the wing at the shoulders. Figures 12-2 a through d show the complete trussing procedure. A meat thermometer, if used, is inserted into the center of the inner thigh muscle.

Place the bird on a rack, breast side up in a roasting pan, and roast, uncovered, at 163°C (325°F). If the bird is not stuffed, it may be roasted at 205°C (400°F) for the first 15 minutes, turning every 5 minutes, and the heat then reduced to 190°C (375°F). Total roasting time varies with the size of the bird, as Table 12-1 shows.

Since chickens and turkeys tend to dry out during roasting, they are *basted* (moistened) with the liquid that collects in the pan or with seasoned fat. Use a long-handled spoon or a basting syringe. A small bird may be turned during cooking, as well as basted.

The skin is apt to brown long before the bird is done. Place a thin cloth (dipped in oil or liquid fat) or a tent-shaped sheet of foil over the bird to slow down the browning process. When the bird is about half done, cut the trussing string so that the inside and muscles of the legs can cook.

During roasting, use a sharp fork to prick the duck or goose in the lower breast section, thighs, and back, so that some of the extra fat can drain out. Ducks and geese may be roasted at 176.7°C (350°F).

Poultry is done when the thermometer registers between 82.1°C and 85°C (180°F and 185°F) or when the drumstick moves easily and the leg joint at the body feels loose.

Broiling

This method is used for halves or smaller pieces of chicken and small turkeys. Lay the pieces—coated with butter or fat, and seasoned—on the broiler pan or rack. Locate the rack or pan four to five inches from the heat. Frequently baste the pieces with fat to keep them from drying out. After about 25 minutes, turn the pieces, baste them, and broil them for another 25 to 30 minutes or until tender. To check for doneness, pierce the thickest section with a fork.

Barbecuing

The procedure is the same as for broiling, but the sections are cooked on a grill. Many barbecue sauces have an unpleasant flavor if burned, so brush on most barbecue sauces during the last few minutes of cooking.

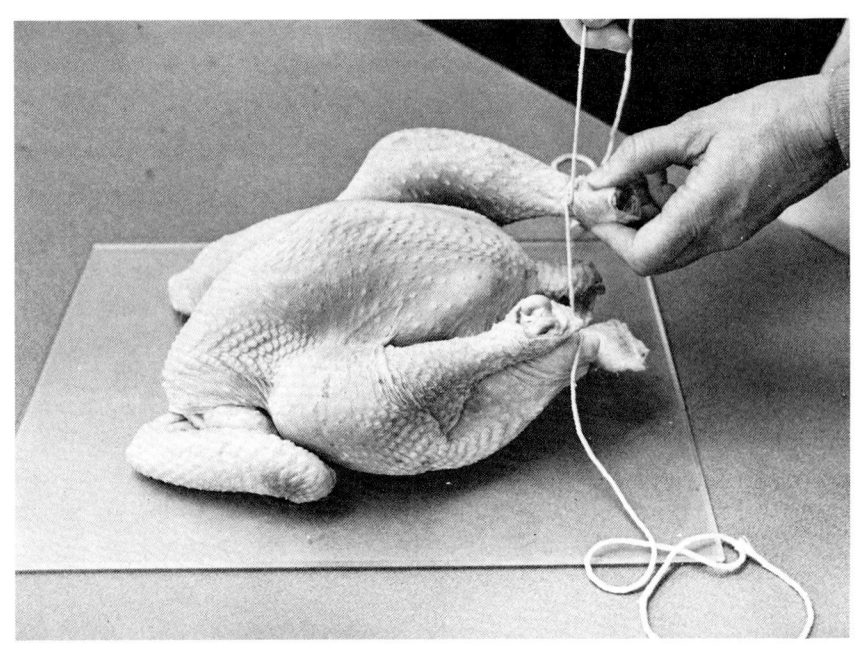

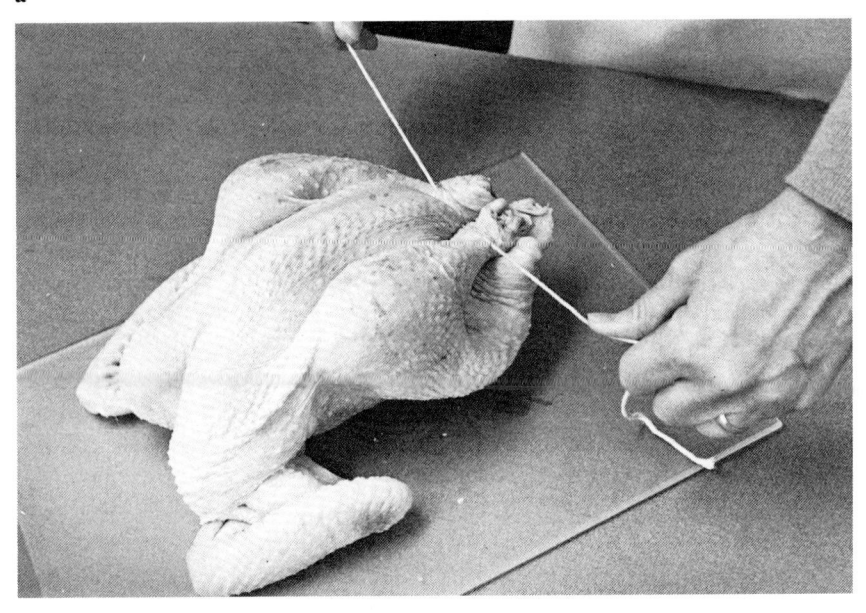

a

b

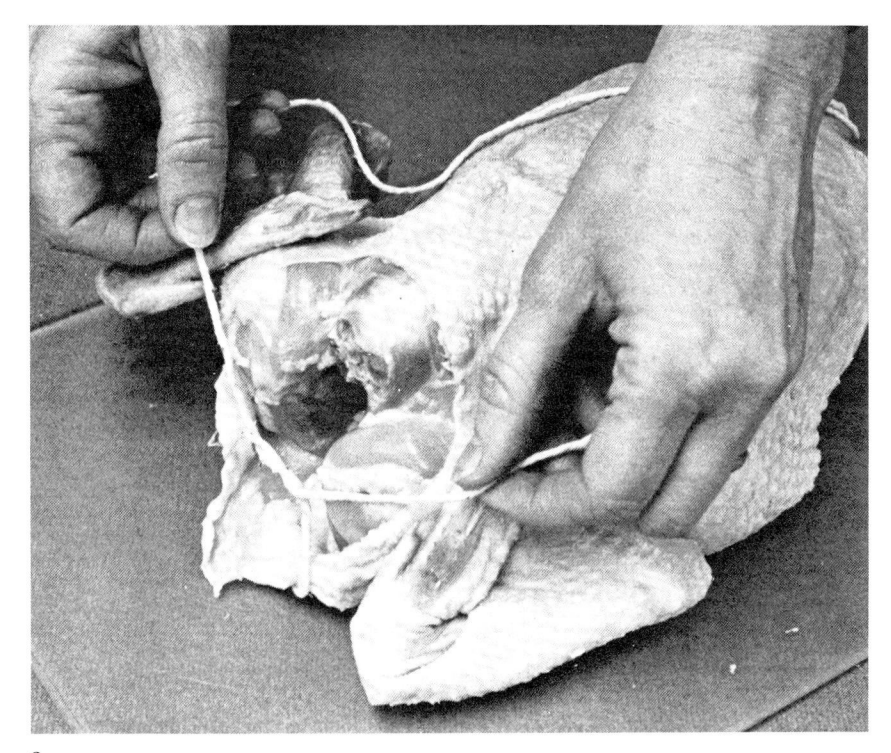

c

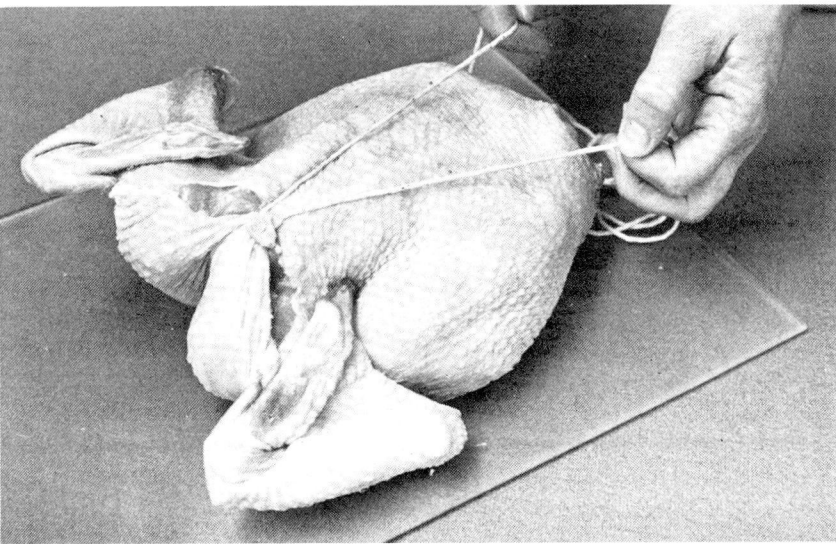

d

Figure 12-2 (a) *Tie center of cord around tail; wrap one side of cord around one lower leg joint.* (b) *Wrap other side of cord around the other lower leg joint; pull securely together and tie.* (c) *Pull cord on each side of the breast; turn bird; wrap and tie neck skin.* (d) *Pull skin toward back and secure cord around tail and leg joints.*

Table 12-1 *Roasting guide for poultry*

Kind	Ready-to-cook wt.[a] (in pounds)	Approx. roasting time (in hours) at 325° (stuffed)[b]	Internal temperature when done (in °F)
Chickens			
(fryers, broilers,	1½ to 2½	1 to 2	
or roasters)	2½ to 4½	2 to 3½	
Ducks	4 to 6	2 to 3	
Geese	6 to 8	3 to 3½	
	8 to 12	3½ to 4½	
Turkeys	6 to 8	3 to 3½	180 to 185 in
	8 to 12	3½ to 4½	center of thigh
	12 to 16	4½ to 5½	muscle
	16 to 20	5½ to 6½	
	20 to 24	6½ to 7	

FROM: *Family Fare: A Guide to Good Nutrition*, Home and Garden Bulletin, no. 1, rev. July 1974. Washington, D.C.: U.S. Department of Agriculture.

[a] Weight of giblets and neck included.

[b] Unstuffed poultry may take slightly less time than stuffed poultry. Cooking time is based on chilled poultry or poultry that has just been thawed—temperature not above 40°F. Frozen unstuffed poultry will take longer. Do not use this guide for commercially stuffed poultry; follow package directions.

Frying

Young chicken often is pan-fried or fried in deep fat after it is coated with seasoned flour or bread crumbs, or dipped in a batter. For pan-frying, use a heavy fry pan with about ½ inch fat in it. Heat the fat and place pieces in pan, leaving room around them. As they brown, turn them with tongs. During frying, watch the pieces to see that they do not overbrown. Regulate the heat so that the pieces cook thoroughly yet brown slowly, or tightly cover the pieces once they are brown, and cook them until tender. The process takes between 35 and 60 minutes. An alternative method is to brown the pieces rapidly in a fry pan on the burner, and then move the pan to a 176.7°C (350°F) oven, to bake until the pieces are well done. In either method, test fried chicken for doneness as for broiled chicken.

Stir-frying small pieces of boneless chicken is a very quick method. High temperature, constant stirring, and short cooking time are needed. Cashew Chicken (Figure 12-3) is an example of a stir-fried chicken dish.

Poultry 183

Figure 12–3 *Cashew Chicken.*

Oven-frying

Prepare the pieces as for frying. Place them in a shallow pan with room between them and baste with fat. Put the pan in a 190.6°C (375°F) oven, and bake the pieces until they are brown and tender. With this method, less fat is used than in pan-frying.

Moist-heat cooking methods

These methods are used for older birds, such as stewing hens and fowl. As is the case with red meat, the liquid and length of cooking tenderize the poultry.

Fricasseeing

This method is the same as stewing for red meats. After the chicken pieces are browned in hot fat in a deep, heavy pan, add a small amount of liquid and cover pan: gently simmer the pieces until tender. Serve with a gravy made from the liquid.

Stewing or steaming

To stew, place the chicken—whole or in pieces—in a deep pan with enough water to cover; add seasonings. Then, simmer until the bird is tender.

To steam, set the chicken on a rack over boiling water. Use a deep pan and cover the pan. Steam until the bird is tender. Using either method, periodically check the level of the water or liquid, since some may evaporate. As a liquid, use either water or vegetable juice or a combination of the two for both stewing and steaming. Another method is to seal the chicken or turkey in foil or in a baking bag, and to bake it. The bird steams in its own juices. Stewed or steamed chicken meat usually is used for salads, sandwiches, or creamed dishes.

Turkey giblets also are stewed in water to cover, with seasonings, until they are tender.

Figure 12–4 *Roast turkey garnished with parsley and orange slices.*

Poaching

Boned, skinned chicken breasts brushed with melted butter may be poached in a shallow pan, covered with waxed paper, in a 204.4°C (400°F) oven, for 6 to 10 minutes. The meat cooks in its own juices. Test for doneness by gently pressing a finger on it: if the meat springs back, it is done; if the fingerprint remains on the meat, continue cooking.

Serving suggestions

Roasted whole chicken or turkey, often carved at the table, may be garnished, as shown in Figure 12-4, with parsley sprigs, curly endive, or an assortment of cooked, raw, or spiced vegetables or fruits around the edge of the platter. Duck often is garnished with very thin slices of orange and lemon; goose, with drained stewed prunes or tart apple slices poached in a little orange juice and water. Cranberries or balls of cranberry stuffing are a traditional garnish for turkey and chicken.

Chapter 13 Meat

Meat, the edible part of mammals, has long been considered the starting point in planning certain meals. The most frequently used meats are beef, veal, pork, and lamb. After the kind and cut of meat and the way it is to be prepared have been determined, the rest of the menu can be selected quickly, according to personal preference and good nutrition rules.

Nutritional value

Meat provides high-quality protein and calcium, phosphorus, iron, fat, and B vitamins, but the amount of each nutrient will vary in different meats and in different cuts. Protein and B-vitamin content is highest in the *muscle*, the lean part of the meat. The fat, either in layers or *marbled* (speckled) through the lean, may have very little vitamin-A content. Liver is an excellent source of iron, vitamin A, and niacin (a B-complex vitamin).

The nutritional value of meat also depends on whether it is beef, veal, lamb, or pork. Pork contains more thiamin (another B-complex vitamin) than do the other meats. The calorie content also depends on the kind and cut of meat and on whether or not the fat was removed before the meat was cooked and eaten. Appendix A lists the nutritive values of a variety of meats.

Except for thiamin, the nutrients in meat are not affected significantly by cooking when *low* temperatures are used. High temperatures will cause the meat to shrink excessively. When meat is cooked with liquid, nutrients from the meat dissolve into the liquid. Therefore, the liquid should be used for soups, stews, or gravies, not discarded. The nutrients in meat are not affected by freezing, provided the meat is correctly wrapped and is not held beyond its proper storage time.

Kinds of meat

Beef

Beef is the most popular meat in the United States, and the major part of the market supply comes from steers, which carry more meat in proportion to bone than do cows or heifers.

A good beef *carcass* (body of the animal after it has been slaughtered) has a layer of creamy white, firm fat around the outside and fat marbled through its lean portion. Although fat adds flavor to meat, too much fat is not considered desirable; thus efforts are being made to develop cattle that carry less fat. Until late 1974, most steers raised for the market were fed grain for several months before they were slaughtered. At that time, however, younger animals, fed primarily on grass and not held as long in confined areas, called *grass-fed* beef, became available. These steers carry less fat and are less tender; thus their quality is different than that of grain-fed cattle.

Veal

Veal comes from young (less than three months old) beef animals. Four- to eight-week-old animals are considered best for veal. Because these animals are so young, a veal carcass contains a large proportion of connective tissue and next to no fat.

Pork

Young hogs, preferably 7 to 12 months old, are the source of most pork on the market. The best carcasses carry firm, marbled, lean meat with layers of firm white fat around the outside.

Lamb and mutton

Both these meats come from sheep. Young lambs, under 14 months old, are marketed as lamb; meat from older sheep, as mutton. Very little mutton is marketed in the United States. Both meats have varying amounts of fat marbled through the meat, but lamb generally is considered to be a low-fat meat.

Cured meats

Bacon, ham, salt pork, corned beef, and smoked shoulder are meats that have been cured or treated. Originally, curing was done by salting or smoking to preserve the meat. Today, chemical procedures that hasten the process frequently are used.

Variety meats

Certain other parts of the animal are called *variety meats*. Liver, heart, tongue, kidneys, and brains are variety meats, as are *sweetbreads* (glands from young cattle and lambs) and *tripe* (stomach lining from beef). These meats are both high in nutritive value and low in waste. At their comparatively low cost, they can and should be used in many meals.

Sausage

Sausage is meat—usually pork or pork combined with beef and/or other meat and poultry—that has been ground or chopped with seasonings. The resulting mixture may be stuffed into a casing to hold it together, and the casing may be left on the sausage. Sausages may contain as much as 50 percent fat.

Sausages also may contain other foods to *extend* (increase the yield of) the meat content: cereals, dry-milk solids, and soy flour commonly are used. Extended sausages must carry labels that state their specific content. In addition, other ingredients also may be put into the mixture to cure it.

Some sausages are cooked before they are sold, including bologna, knockwurst, frankfurters, and salami; others are sold uncooked, for example, pork sausages in link or bulk form. Still other types are sold dried, including pepperoni, thuringer, and kinds of salami.

Luncheon meats

These meat products, often called *cold cuts*, for the most part are made like sausages from ground or chopped meat, and they also may contain as much as 50 percent fat. Extenders are commonly used in them, as are ingredients like pickles, olives, and pimiento. Usually, these products are formed into rolls or loaves and sold by the pound—sliced or unsliced.

Inspection and grading

All meat that is shipped interstate must be inspected by USDA agents. Animals are inspected before they are slaughtered, and carcasses are inspected at several stages in the meat-packing plants. If the meat is wholesome and safe for human consumption, the agent marks the carcass with the official inspection stamp. Diseased animals or carcasses cannot be processed or sold. For meat to be sold within states, states are required by law to have an inspection service equal to the federal program. If a state does not meet this requirement, its meat-packing plants are subject to federal inspection.

Although hog carcasses are subjected to federal or state inspection, *trichinae*, which are found in hogs, cannot be detected during inspection. A disease, *trichinosis*, is caused by ingesting the *trichinae* of infected pork. If a person swallows live *trichinae*, he or she may be infected with the disease. Therefore, thoroughly cook all fresh pork and fresh pork products: an internal temperature of at least 76°C (170°F) is required to kill any *trichinae* that might be in them.

The USDA also has established a quality grading system for beef, veal, calf, and lamb carcasses. Meat packers may choose to have their own grading systems or to use the USDA's system. If they choose the latter, they pay for the grader to check the carcass, to decide on its quality, and to run a roller stamp that leaves a purplish red mark down the side of the carcass. This mark may be visible on retail meat, depending on the cut of meat. A list of the federal grades is shown in Table 13-1. Pork is not graded in this program.

Most retail markets carry Choice, Good, or Standard meat. Prime grade usually is available only to the restaurant trade; lower-grade meats are used in making sausages and luncheon meats.

Choice grade is more tender and has fat marbled through it. Good grade is not as tender nor as marbled as is Choice; it is equally as nutritious, however, and is a good buy. Standard grade meat, although it is fairly tender and lean with little fat, often is not found in markets. Some meat packers use their own names to indicate grade: Armour uses Star, Quality, and Banquet; Swift uses Premium, Select, and Swift.

Table 13-1 *USDA quality grades for meat*

Beef	Veal and calf	Lamb	Yearling mutton[a]	Mutton
Prime	Prime	Prime	Prime	—
Choice	Choice	Choice	Choice	Choice
Good	Good	Good	Good	Good
Standard	Standard	Utility	Utility	Utility
Commercial	Utility	Cull	Cull	Cull
Utility				
Cutter				
Canner				

[a] An animal over one and under two years old

Cuts

Carcasses are cut into sections by meat packers for distribution to wholesalers. Figure 13-1 shows the wholesale and retail cuts of a beef carcass; hog, veal, and sheep carcasses are cut in much the same way. However, since the animals vary widely in weight and size, the weight and size of the wholesale and retail cuts will vary as well. And, the proportion of bone and fat to meat is great but, again, will vary with the size and weight of the carcass.

Cut and degree of tenderness

Tenderness, which depends on muscle and connective-tissue content, varies with the cut. The muscles and connective tissues of an animal's legs, shoulders, and underside are well developed from constant use. Therefore, cuts from these sections—chuck, fore shank, brisket, plate, flank, and round—are not tender. The tender cuts come from the top of the animal along the backbone—the rib, short loin, and loin end sections, short loin being the most tender.

Ground beef

Different names are used for ground and packaged beef by the retailer. These include: hamburger, ground beef, ground chuck, ground round, ground sirloin, and chopped sirloin. The amount of fat contained in each grind varies, and, since up to 30 percent fat is allowed, the buyer must read

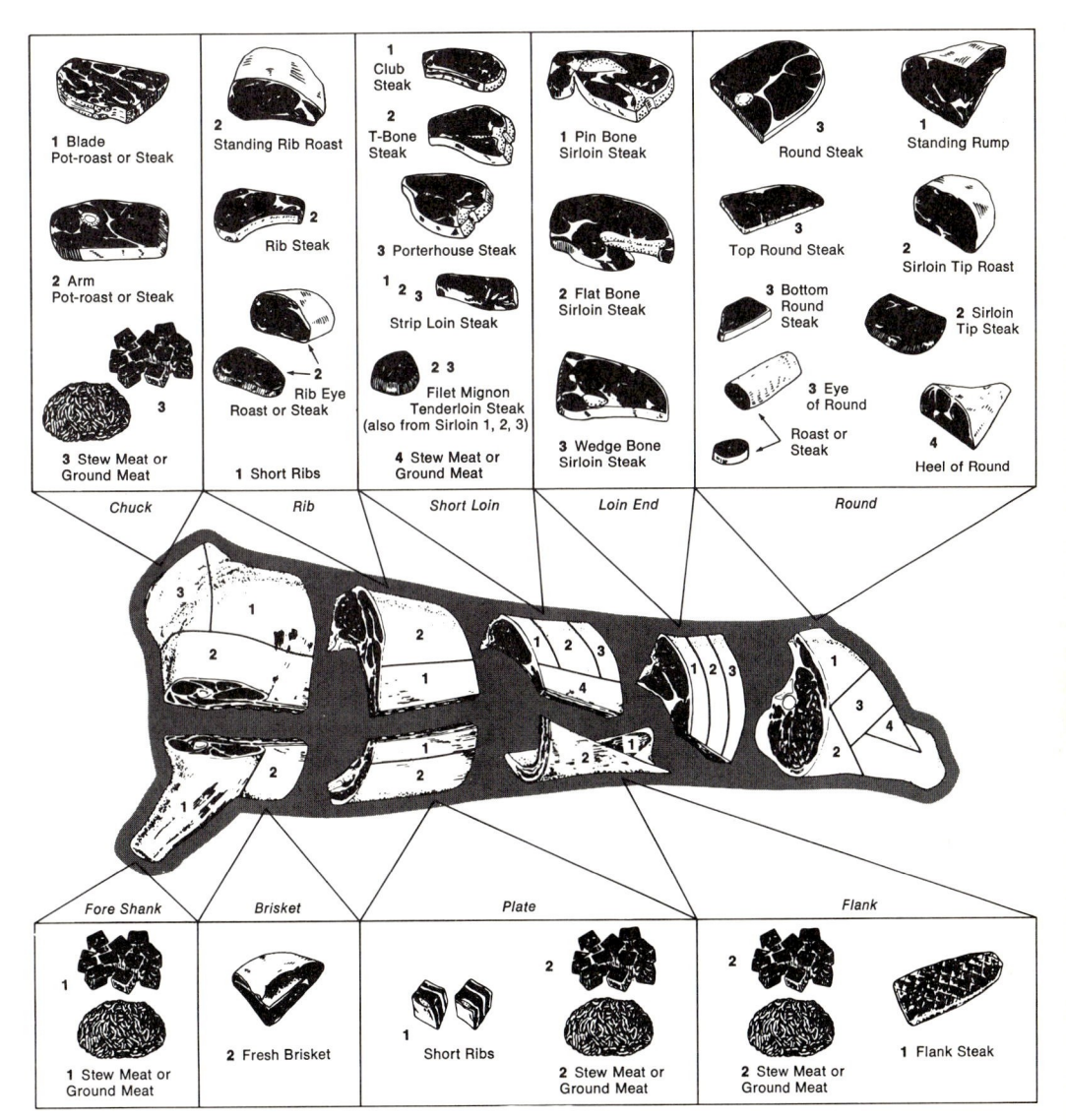

Figure 13-1 *The wholesale and retail cuts made from a beef carcass.* (From *How to Buy Beef Steaks,* Home and Garden Bulletin, no. 145, USDA, 1968)

the labels. Markets may voluntarily post charts or label the meat to indicate the proportion of fat in it.

Selection

Quality

Quality may or may not be important when buying meat, depending on the type of meal planned and the particular use to be made of the meat.

High-quality beef is bright red, finely textured, and marbled with fat that should be firm and creamy white. Lower-grade beef is dark colored, coarsely textured, and has little or no fat marbled in the lean.

High-quality veal is light gray pink with a fine grain. Its small amount of fat is grayish or pinkish white and firm. Lower-grade veal is pale or very dark, but the texture remains fairly fine.

High-quality pork is grayish pink with finely-grained lean and fairly firm, white fat. Lower-grade pork is dark in color with coarse grain and it may have a large amount of soft fat.

High-quality lamb is pinkish red and finely textured. Its fat is firm and pinkish or white. In the lower grades, lamb has a darker red lean, with a fairly fine texture and a heavy layer of fat.

Variety meats deteriorate more rapidly than do other meats and, when purchased, they must look fresh, smell fresh, and feel firm. If there is any doubt about their freshness, it is wise not to buy.

Amount to buy

Amount of meat purchased for a given use depends on budget, family/personal preferences, and the cut being considered. As a general rule: one pound of lean or ground meat will serve three or four; one pound of fairly bony meat will serve two or three; and one pound of very bony meat will serve one or two. This rule will vary according to the cut of meat, the amount of bone and waste, and the serving size, but it does provide a guideline at the market. Look at the two chuck roasts in Figures 13-2 a and b. Although the two roasts have the same per pound price, the second photograph shows that the top roast has a smaller percentage of bone and fat waste than does the other roast. The consumer would pay less per ounce of edible lean meat if the roast at the top were chosen.

Meat

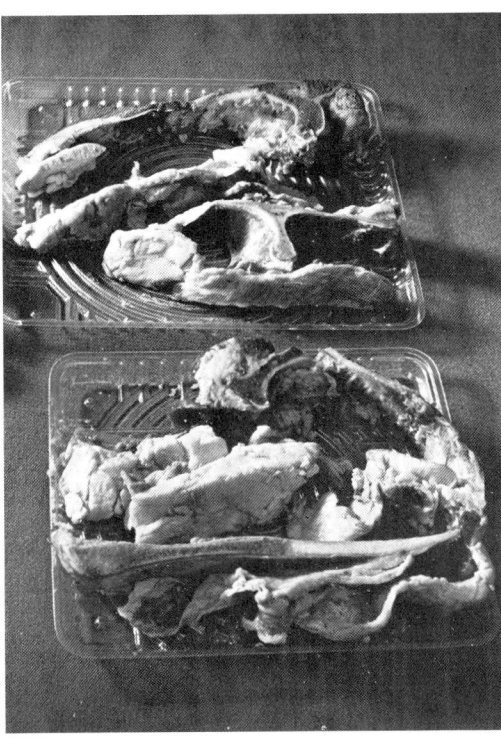

Figure 13-2 (a) *Two chuck roasts that cost the same per pound.* (b) *The waste in the two chuck roasts after the edible meat has been removed.*

A large roast or ham, usually is intended for more than one meal. If the roast has little or no bone, expect to get three or four servings to the pound; if the roast has more bone, two or three servings to the pound. Even when cooking for two, a larger roast is both convenient and economical when planned for use in several meals.

Nutritional value and cost

Meat is expensive, so its nutritional value and cost probably are more important considerations in purchasing than is its quality. Pound for pound of

Figure 13–3 *Tournedos and Beef Sauté.*

edible meat, less expensive cuts provide nutrition equal to that of more tender and costly cuts. Figure 13–3 shows a very expensive filet of beef (tournedos) and a much less expensive lean ground meat (sautéed beef) prepared in the same manner and yielding approximately the same nutritive value. Additionally, if low-fat or other special diets must be followed, the less tender cuts certainly will be better buys, because of their low fat content.

Variety meats, which have little waste and high nutritional value, usually are less expensive than other meats. Calves' liver, though more expensive, has nutritive value similar to that of beef liver.

Soybean products

Special soybean-based protein products are now available. These may be added to meat to extend the nutritional content of the prepared food. These products, usually in flour or small-chip form, can be mixed with ground meat and used in any recipe that calls for ground meat. (For further information, see Chapter 10.)

Other considerations in selection

Cost per serving usually is a better guideline than is cost per pound. Cuts that have not been properly trimmed of fat or those that contain a high proportion of bone to edible meat may cost less per pound than do well-trimmed, less-bony cuts, but the number of servings may be smaller. In this case, a cut with a higher price per pound may be a better value, if it serves more people. Bones are not necessarily a total waste: they may be removed from the meat and frozen for later use in making soup stock or gravy. Here, however, freezer space and the cost of electricity to run the freezer also must be considered.

The consumer's wisest course is to buy the cut and grade that is correct for the use intended, in the quantity sufficient for that use. Chuck or round is satisfactory for pot roast, for example; shank or plate, for stew. Flank or top round may be marinated, broiled, and thinly sliced for a more economical steak than T-bone or sirloin.

One exception to this general rule may be to buy a large roast at a lower price and have the butcher cut it into meal-sized sections. A large chuck roast, for instance, can be cut into a steak, a pot roast, and, perhaps, some stew beef; a pork loin, into an easily served boneless roast and ribs for barbecuing. In this case, the consumer pays for the bones and may wish to take them home to freeze them for later use. Figure 13–4 shows a boneless pork roast and the bones to be steam-baked, ready for broiling with a barbecue sauce.

Convenience meats and meat dishes

Precise comparisons between meals that are prepared at home and those that are bought partially prepared are difficult to make, but meat in convenience form is likely to be much more expensive than is the home-prepared meat. The cost of frozen ready-to-use beef patties is likely to be higher than is that of fresh ground beef.

In some cases, time available may warrant using the partially prepared foods, but the wise consumer will consider nutritive value and cost, as well as time. Once cooking skills are acquired, similar meals may be prepared for the same, or less, time and cost. Examples would be stir-fried flank steak, broiled beef patties, and sautéed liver, all with accompanying frozen vegetables.

Figure 13-4 *Pork and bones.*

Refrigerator storage

Fresh meat

The length of time fresh meat can be kept safely in the coldest part of the refrigerator or meat-keeping compartment varies. Meat may be refrigerated for one or two days in the plastic wrapping from the market. Meat wrapped in butcher paper must be rewrapped in plastic or aluminum foil before refrigerating. If the meat is freshly cut when purchased and it is properly wrapped and refrigerated, ground meat, cubed meat, and variety meats can be kept for one or two days. Steaks, chops, cutlets, and roasts may be kept for three to five days. Bacon, ham, and corned beef may be kept for one or two weeks.

Cooked meat

Most cooked meats may be refrigerated, tightly wrapped in plastic or foil, in the coldest part of the refrigerator or meat-keeping compartment for one to four days. Cooked variety meats will keep for one or two days. If cooked meat must be held for a longer time, wrap it in airtight, moisture-proof freezer paper or foil, and freeze it.

Freezer storage

Fresh meat

Raw meats, carefully wrapped in freezer paper, plastic freezer bags, or foil, can be frozen and held for varying periods of time. Uncooked pork and veal can be held for four to six months; beef, up to one year. Cured meats, such as ham, bacon, and some luncheon meats, are best if not held longer than one or two months, because their salt content may keep them from freezing properly.

Depending on the supply on hand and freezer space, it may be possible to make good meat buys when prices are low or when special sales are held. These extra meat purchases can be wrapped for the freezer in meal-sized portions, in cubes for stew, or in other convenient forms. A large roast can be cut into smaller pieces according to family preferences. Ground beef may be made into patties (layered between paper or packed in sandwich bags), stacked, and wrapped for freezing; the patties are ready for use in a quick meal or for quick thawing to make a meat loaf.

Cooked meat

The quality and taste of home-prepared frozen meats varies greatly. Meats frozen in a sauce or gravy retain their flavor well, but a prebroiled steak—frozen and thawed—may be disappointing unless it is sliced and combined with other ingredients, as in a beef salad or sandwich.

Preparation

The tender cuts of meat, such as steak, chops, and rib roasts, as a rule do not require prepreparation before they are cooked. Meats that are not as tender can be improved in flavor and texture by following certain procedures.

Tenderizing

Less tender cuts of meat may be tenderized before they are cooked in three ways: mechanically, by enzyme action, or by marination.

Mechanical means Cuts of meat can be run through a mechanical cutter to break up the connective tissue; usually the meat is cut once in each direction. Pieces of meat also may be scored with a knife (in both directions), but this process usually cuts only the surface tissues. In a third method, pieces of meat may be put on a chopping block or cutting board and pounded with a wooden or metal mallet (Figure 13–5a) or with the edge of a very heavy saucer or plate. The mallets used for tenderizing have either a smooth base or a base with cutter blades.

Enzyme action Enzymes will tenderize fairly thin cuts of meat, such as steaks and chops; the process is not satisfactory for roasts. The enzyme causes the protein of the muscle and connective tissue to break down, but the action occurs primarily on the surface of the meat and does not penetrate deeply. Figure 13–5b shows tenderizing by enzyme action.

Commercial mixtures—containing enzymes from such fruits as papaya and pineapple—are available for tenderizing meat at home. Moisten one side of the meat with water, and sprinkle on the tenderizer. Use a sharp fork to pierce the meat on both sides at ½-inch intervals. The enzyme begins to work as the meat is heated. Do not use too much: overtenderizing makes the meat mushy in texture.

Marinating Pieces of meat may be *marinated* (soaked) in a mixture of wine vinegar and oil to tenderize them. The length of time needed will vary with the thickness of the meat, and the marinade will affect the flavor. Figure 13–5c shows a marinade being poured over beef cubes for flavor and partial tenderizing. The cubes will be cooked in the baking bag to tenderize them further with moist heat.

Frozen meats

Frozen meats or meat dishes are best thawed in the refrigerator. They may be taken from the freezer the day before use and placed on a refrigerator shelf. Also, they may be thawed at room temperature, but the food must be cooked as soon as it is thawed to prevent the growth of harmful bacteria.

Frozen meats and meat dishes also may be cooked or heated while frozen, but they will need a third to a half again as long a time as do thawed dishes to finish cooking.

Cooking methods

Using the correct cooking method and the correct temperature for the particular cut of meat is the secret to preparing a satisfactory product. The wrong method or the wrong temperature can make an excellent cut of meat tough and/or unpalatable, and it cannot make a less tender cut more acceptable.

Always cook pork to the well-done stage (76°C [170°F] internal temperature) to destroy any trichinae that may be present.

Tender cuts of meat or those that are tenderized before cooking (steaks and chops) may be cooked by a *dry-heat* method, such as roasting, broiling, pan-broiling, or barbecuing. They also may be pan-fried. The less tender cuts must be cooked by a *moist-heat* method, such as braising or stewing, which combine slow cooking and moisture to break down the tough connective tissue in the meat.

The choice of cooking method involves consideration of moisture, fat content, and thickness of the meat. For example, a very thick pork chop is a tender cut of meat, but it would be dry if pan-fried long enough to reach the necessary degree of doneness; pan-braising would be a better method. Veal, which has little fat, should seldom be broiled; again, braising is a better method. Veal also may be pounded until it is very thin, coated with eggs and crumbs to protect the protein from the intense heat, and pan-fried quickly, as is done in preparing Wienerschnitzel.

Dry-heat methods

Roasting Roasting is baking in an oven. The method is used for cooking tender cuts of meat without adding liquid during the cooking period. Sometimes, strips of bacon or fat are laid on top of a veal roast before it is roasted, because veal does not have a protective layer of fat.

Place the meat, fat side up in a pan, on a rack in a 163°C (325°F) oven.[1] Do not cover the pan. Insert a meat thermometer in the middle of the largest muscle—but not in fat or resting against a bone. This is the most reliable way

---

1. Pork may be roasted at this temperature or at 176.7°C (350°F).

a

b

c

Figure 13–5 (a) *Mechanical tenderizing.* (b) *Tenderizing with an enzyme.* (c) *Pour marinade over meat in a plastic bag.*

to determine the degree of doneness. If the roast is frozen when placed in the oven, put the thermometer into position after the meat has thawed a little.

Roasting time depends on the initial temperature of the meat, the oven temperature, and the size and composition of the roast. Preferences for rare, medium, or well-done meat must be considered. Beef may be roasted to any degree of doneness; veal usually is cooked to the well-done stage; and most people in the United States prefer lamb well done as well. Pork, of course, also is cooked to the well-done stage. Some examples of approximate roasting times for different cuts and kinds of meat are listed in Table 13–2. At high altitudes, longer roasting times may be needed for meat to reach the desired degree of doneness.

All roasts should be removed from the oven and allowed to stand at room temperature for 20 minutes or so before carving. During this interval, the juices cool and gel a little, making the meat easier to carve. Also, the inside of the roast will continue to cook from the heat present there.

Broiling Broiling is a method used for tender cuts of meat, such as steak, lamb chops, ham slices, and bacon. If less tender steaks are tenderized before they are cooked, they also may be broiled.

Before the meat is broiled, slash the fat at intervals to keep it from curling (Figure 13–6). When the broiler is heated, place the meat on a broiler pan or greased rack, with a pan under it to catch the drippings. The thickness of the meat determines the distance between the rack or pan and the burner or flame. A thick steak may be placed four to five inches from the heat (Figure 13–7), while a thin steak may be placed only two inches from it.

The door of an electric oven must be open during broiling, but the door of a gas oven may be closed. Cook the meat until it is brown and half done, then turn it, season it, and allow it to cook until the desired degree of doneness is reached. Turning is best done with tongs; if a fork is used, it should be inserted into the fat at the edge of the meat—not into the meat itself—to prevent the juice from running out.

The length of time needed for broiling varies with the thickness of the meat and the desired degree of doneness. Table 13–3 shows a range of times used for a variety of meats. To test for doneness, make a small cut with a sharp knife in the center of the meat, and check the meat's color.

Pan-broiling The tender cuts of meat listed for broiling also may be pan-broiled over a burner in a heavy fry pan. Lightly grease the pan or sprinkle it with salt, to keep the meat from sticking. Or, a nonstick, plastic-coated iron pan may be used. Do not cover the pan at any time.

Table 13-2 *Timetable for roasting meats*

Kind and cut	Ready-to-cook (wt., pounds)	Approx. time[a] (in hrs.) at 163°C (325°F)	Internal temp. of meat when done
BEEF			
Standing ribs, rare	6–8	2½–3	60°C (140°F)
medium	6–8	3–3½	71°C (160°F)
well done	6–8	3⅔–5	77°C (170°F)
Rolled rump, rare	5	2¼	60°C (140°F)
medium	5	3	71°C (160°F)
well done	5	3¼	77°C (170°F)
Sirloin tip, rare	3	1½	60°C (140°F)
medium	3	2	71°C (160°F)
well done	3	2½	77°C (170°F)
VEAL			
Leg	5–8	2½–3½	77°C (170°F)
Loin	5	3	77°C (170°F)
Shoulder	6	3½	77°C (170°F)
LAMB			
Leg (whole)	6–7	2¼–4	82°C (180°F)
Shoulder	3–6	2½–3¼	82°C (180°F)
Rolled shoulder	3–5	2½–3	82°C (180°F)
FRESH PORK			
Loin, center cut	3–5	2–3½	77°C (170°F)
Shoulder, picnic	5–8	3–4	77°C (170°F)
Ham, whole	12–16	5½–6	77°C (170°F)
Ham, boneless, rolled	10–14	4⅔–5½	77°C (170°F)
Spareribs	3–4	2	—
CURED PORK			
Cook-before-eating			
Ham, whole	10–14	3½–4¼	71°C (160°F)
Ham, half	5–7	2–2½	71°C (160°F)
Picnic shoulder	6	3½	77°C (170°F)
Fully cooked[b]			
Ham, whole	12–16	3½–4	60°C (140°F)
Ham, half	5–7	2	60°C (140°F)

Figures from *Family Fare: A Guide to Good Nutrition*, Home and Garden Bulletin, no. 1, rev. July 1974. Washington, D.C.: U.S. Department of Agriculture.

[a] Time is for meat at refrigerator temperature.

[b] Can also be served without heating, if desired.

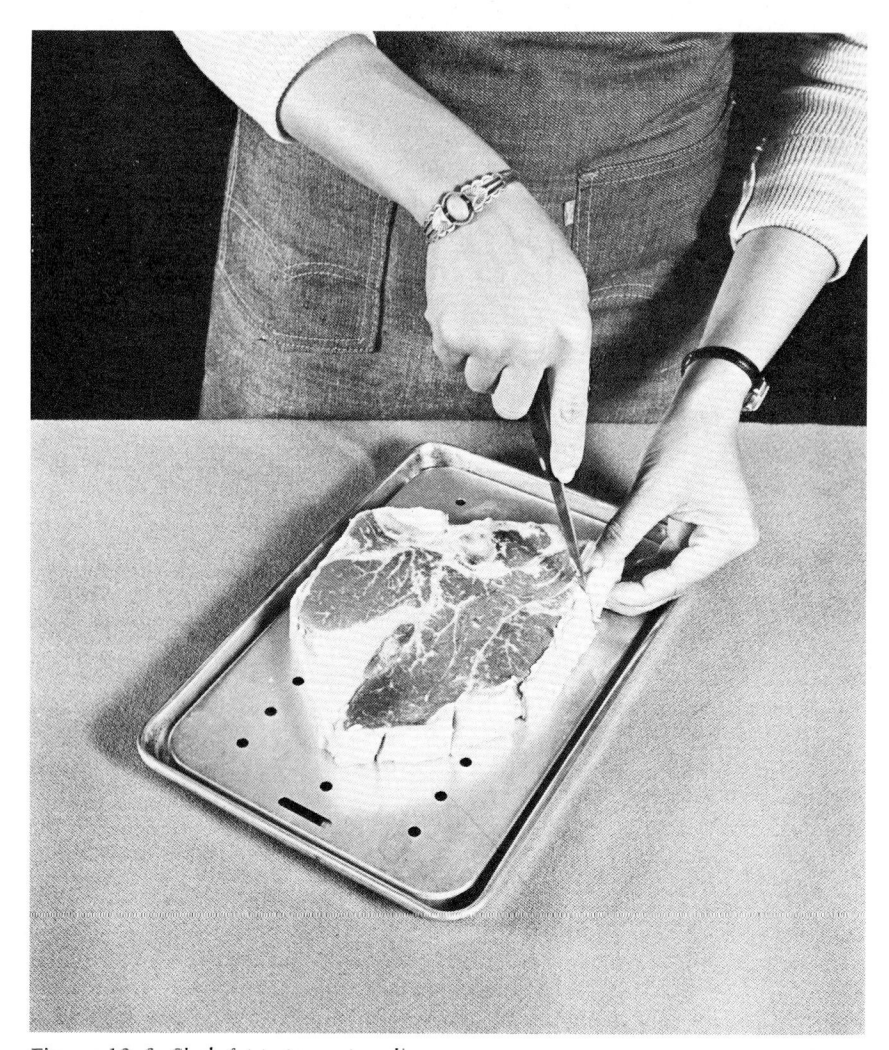

Figure 13-6 *Slash fat to prevent curling.*

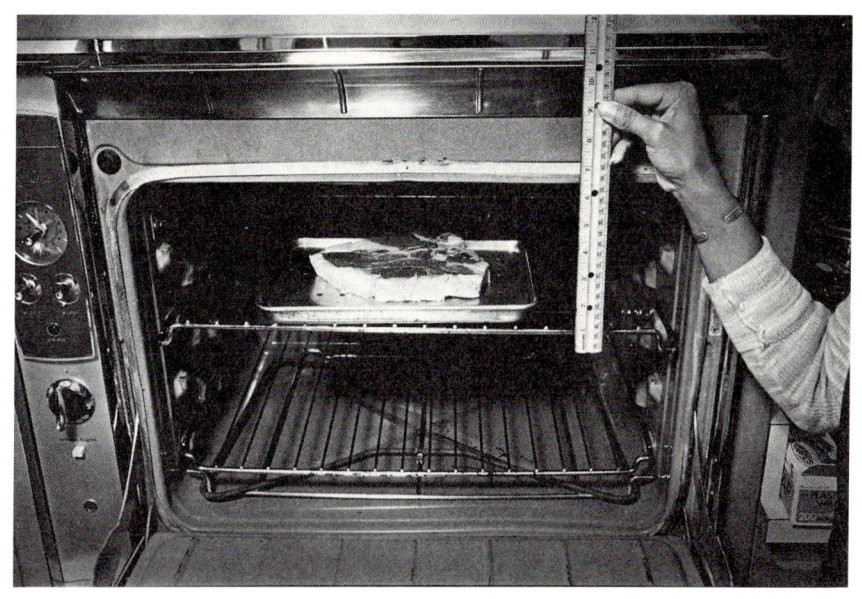

Figure 13–7 *Measure distance from the heating element, for broiling.*

Place the meat in the hot pan and quickly brown on each side. Then, turn down the burner and allow the meat to cook to the desired degree of doneness. Pour off any fat that accumulates, and test for doneness in the same way as for broiled meats.

Barbecuing This method is similar to broiling but charcoal and a brazier are used instead of a range. The charcoal's temperature can be judged by holding the hand over the hot coals at about the height at which the meat will be and counting, "One thousand one, one thousand two, one thousand three," and so on. The number of seconds the hand can be held at that level will indicate the fire's heat: one or two seconds is a very hot fire, three or four seconds is a moderate fire, and five or six seconds is a slow fire.

A very hot fire is desirable for thin steak or hamburger, or when a very rare-cooked steak is preferred. A moderate fire is used for a very thick cut of meat, such as a London broil or kebabs. A slow fire could be used for pork spareribs, unless the ribs were steamed to precook them. Lay the meat on the rack or grill and cook until half done; then, turn and cook until the meat is done. Test as you would a steak.

Table 13-3 *Timetable for broiling meats*

Kind and cut of meat	Approx. thickness (in inches)	Degree of doneness	Approx. total cooking time[a] (in minutes)
Beef steaks	1	Rare	10–15
(Club, porterhouse, rib,	1	Medium	15–20
sirloin, T-bone, tender-	1	Well done	20–30
loin)	1½	Rare	15–20
	1½	Medium	20–25
	1½	Well done	25–40
Hamburgers	¾	Rare	8
	¾	Medium	12
	¾	Well done	14
Lamb chops	1	Medium	12
(Loin, rib, shoulder)	1	Well done	14
	1½	Medium	18
	1½	Well done	22
Cured ham slices	¾	Well done	13–14
(Cook-before-eating)	1	Well done	18–20

Figures from *Family Fare: A Guide to Good Nutrition*, Home and Garden Bulletin, no. 1, rev. July 1974. Washington, D.C.: U.S. Department of Agriculture.

[a] Meat at refrigerator temperature at start of broiling.

Pan-frying This method also uses an uncovered, heavy fry pan. Tender cuts of meat that are broiled or pan-broiled may be pan-fried. Liver also may be pan-fried. Sometimes, as is done with veal cutlets, the meat is dipped into beaten egg and crumbs or flour before it is fried. Heat a small quantity of fat in the pan, put the meat into it, and cook until it is done on both sides. Again, do not cover the pan at any time.

Moist-heat methods

In the moist-heat methods, a small or large quantity of liquid may be used and cooking time also may be long or short. In Figure 13–8a, for example, beef cubes and vegetables are being wrapped in foil and, in Figure 13–8b, tightly sealed. They will be cooked slowly, and the foil will hold the juices in, so that the moisture will help to tenderize the meat.

At high altitudes, it may be necessary to watch meat carefully that is being braised or stewed, since more liquid may be needed during cooking.

Meat

Figure 13–8 (a) *Place meat and vegetables on foil for wrapping.*

Figure 13–8 (b) *Wrap meat and vegetables securely for baking.*

Braising This method combines dry and moist heat but is considered to be a moist-heat method, because most of the cooking is done with liquid. Braising is used for less tender cuts of meat, for meat that has little fat, and for heart, sweetbreads, and brains.

Brown the meat in a small amount of fat in a heavy fry pan. Sometimes it is dipped in flour before it is browned. Then, a small amount of liquid is added to the pan, the pan is covered, and the meat allowed to cook or steam slowly, either on the burner or in the oven.

Larger pieces of meat, such as chuck roasts, may be sealed in aluminum foil or plastic oven bags, or put in a tightly covered pan with seasoning. They are then cooked in the oven, with or without more liquid.

Cook braised meat until it is well done and fork-tender. The length of time required varies according to size and cut. Chops will need approximately one half to three quarters of an hour. A two- to three-pound chuck steak may require two to two and one half hours, while a three- to five-pound pot roast would need about three and one half to four hours.

Stewing This method involves simmering the meat in liquid. Stewing is done in a covered pan or an automatic slow-cooker. Less tender cuts of meat that need long, slow moist heat to tenderize, such as cubes of beef or lamb, are used for stewing.

Place the meat in liquid to cover, and cook at a low temperature, until it is fork-tender. The liquid may be water, bouillon, tomato juice, wine, the water in which a vegetable has been cooked, or a combination of any or all of these. Vegetables may be added to the meat for flavoring, as well. Add vegetables to be served with the meat near the end of the cooking time, so that they will not be overcooked.

Stewing also is used to remove excess curing salt from cured meats, such as corned beef or dry cured hams. Sweetbreads, brains, tongue, heart, and kidneys also may be stewed.

Microwave cooking This method must be used with care, because the meat will cook much faster than it will with conventional methods. Results are not always satisfactory, since the meat may cook unevenly. Follow the directions provided with the oven exactly.

Some meats will not develop an attractive brown on the outside in a microwave oven, although some of these ovens do have a browning element, which gives a brown appearance to the meat.

Table 13-4 gives a short summary of the different cooking methods for tender, less tender, tenderized, and tough meats.

Table 13-4 *Summary of cooking methods for meat*

Method	Kind of meat and cut	Source of heat	Additional ingredients
DRY HEAT			
Roasting	Tender cuts—beef, lamb, pork, veal, mutton	Oven	Bacon strips sometimes used with veal
Broiling	Tender steaks, chops (not pork), ham slices, bacon	Broiler	Not usually
Pan-broiling	Same as for broiling	Burner, heavy pan, no cover; drain fat often	Not usually
Barbecuing	Same as for broiling	Charcoal, brazier	Barbecue sauce or other sauce
Pan-frying	Same as for broiling	Burner, heavy pan, no cover	Fat melted in pan
MOIST HEAT			
Braising	Less tender cuts—all meats	Burner or oven, covered pan	Small amount of liquid for simmering
Stewing	Same as for braising; meat often in small pieces	Burner, covered pan	Usually liquid to cover meat; vegetables
MICROWAVE COOKING			
Moist or dry	All meats; may not be satisfactory	Electromagnetic waves	As required by recipe and method

Serving suggestions

Roasts and steaks may be carved in the kitchen or placed on a platter and taken to the table to be carved there. A good carving surface—a plastic or wooden insert on a serving tray or platter—a thin, very sharp carving knife, and a suitable fork are desirable.

Most roasts should be sliced across the grain; chuck roasts are carved into large pieces. Beef rib roasts are placed with meat side on serving tray, and sliced horizontally toward the bones. Very thick steaks and flank steaks are carved in diagonal slices. Thin steaks are cut into serving-sized portions. Rack of lamb and pork rib roast are placed with the bones perpendicular to the serving platter, and sliced vertically between ribs. Leg of lamb and whole ham are placed on the serving platter or tray with the shank bone to the carver's right. Two or three slices are cut from the bony side, and then the roast is turned up so that it rests firmly on the tray and cut toward the bone to remove the slices. Another method for carving a leg of lamb is to grasp the shank bone and rotate the roast as slices are cut from the surface, parallel to the bone.

Gravies and sauces can be prepared using the drippings of the cooked meat. After removing the meat from the pan, pour off all drippings and most of the fat. (The amount of fat left for use is determined by the thickness and quantity of gravy or sauce desired.) Then make a roux by combining the melted fat (or substitute butter) and flour and cooking for two or more minutes. To make a browner gravy or sauce, brown the flour before mixing with the fat, or lightly brown the flour by increasing the cooking time; browned flour has slightly less thickening power. The amount of fat, flour, and liquid used depends on the thickness desired and the quantity needed. One or two tablespoons each of fat and flour are needed for each cup of

Figure 13-9 *Broiled meat loaf filled with Brussels sprouts.*

liquid. After the roux is made, quickly stir in the liquid (meat droppings and/or water, milk, or cream)—a wire whisk is helpful. Cook the mixture for about five minutes, constantly stirring to prevent lumps from forming.

Meats cooked by moist-heat methods also may be served in the kitchen or at the table. A large, deep container is needed for table service if the meat is to be served in its cooking liquid. Or, the meat may be removed from the pot, and placed on a platter, surrounded by perfectly cooked vegetables, and the cooking liquid reduced to a slightly thickened sauce and served in a sauce boat.

Often, meats are garnished with vegetables or fruit for presentation. Inexpensive meats may be cooked and presented in a very attractive manner, which adds to the overall enjoyment of the meal. For example, look at the meat loaf pictured in Figure 13–9. A ground-meat mixture was packed in a ring mold to shape it, unmolded, brushed with a barbecue sauce, and broiled. Just before serving, the center was filled with an appropriate vegetable.

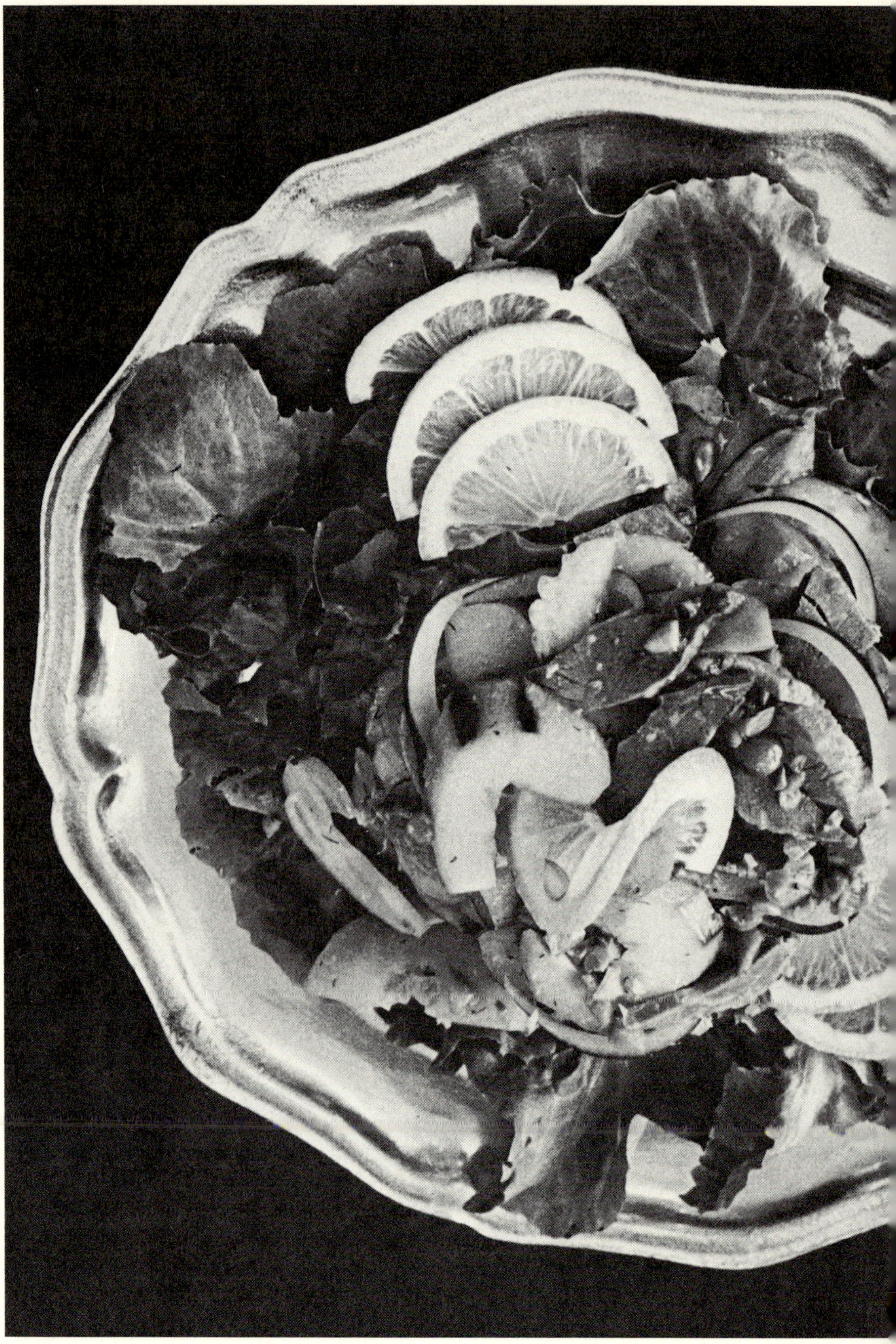

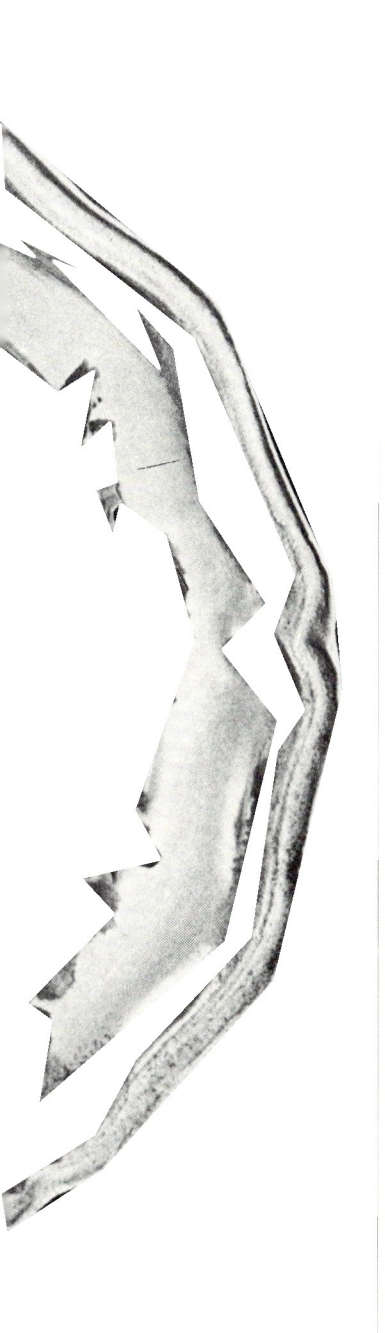

Part 2
Nutrition and menu management

Chapter 14 Nutrition

All people must eat to live—their well-being depends on air to breathe, water to drink, and an adequate supply of nutrients for each cell . . . and these nutrients are derived from food. Almost all foods supply more than one nutrient, but there is no single food that contains all the nutrients to provide adequately for the body's needs. All nutrients must be available in the body—in suitable amounts—for each of its millions of cells to be formed and maintained and to function normally because their uses are interrelated.

The nutrients needed are carbohydrates, fats, protein, minerals, and vitamins. Water also is essential. And plant fiber plays an important role. The purpose of this chapter is to provide a general, brief survey of the nutritional elements, their uses in the body, food sources, amounts required, and the problems associated with deficiencies or excesses. Absorption and distribution of these nutrients in the body also are discussed briefly. More detailed information on the subject may be found in references in the Bibliography or in any nutrition book that is based on sound, scientific studies and facts.

Recommended dietary allowances

The amount of each nutrient that should be included in the diet will vary with an individual's age, physical condition, activity, state of health, and so on. To help in planning a diet to meet nutritional needs, a committee of the Food and Nutrition Board (FNB) of the National Academy of Science–National Research Council has established a list of recommended amounts for each nutrient. These recommendations are called *Recommended Dietary Allowances* (RDA). In the recommendation, as indicated by note a in Table 14–1, is the

Table 14-1 *Food and Nutrition Board, National Academy of Sciences–National Research Council Recommended Daily Dietary Allowances,*[a] *revised 1974. Designed for the maintenance of good nutrition of practically all healthy people in the United States*

	Age (years)	Weight (kg) (lb)	Height (cm) (in.)	Energy (kcal)[b]	Protein (g)	Vitamin A activity (RE)[c]	Vitamin A activity (IU)	Vitamin D (IU)	Vitamin E activity (IU)
Infants	0.0–0.5	6 14	60 24	kg × 117	kg × 2.2	420[d]	1400	400	4
	0.5–1.0	9 20	71 28	kg × 108	kg × 2.0	400	2000	400	5
Children	1–3	13 28	86 34	1300	23	400	2000	400	7
	4–6	20 44	110 44	1800	30	500	2500	400	9
	7–10	30 66	135 54	2400	36	700	3300	400	10
Males	11–14	44 97	158 63	2800	44	1000	5000	400	12
	15–18	61 134	172 69	3000	54	1000	5000	400	15
	19–22	67 147	172 69	3000	54	1000	5000	400	15
	23–50	70 154	172 69	2700	56	1000	5000		15
	51+	70 154	172 69	2400	56	1000	5000		15
Females	11–14	44 97	155 62	2400	44	800	4000	400	12
	15–18	54 119	162 65	2100	48	800	4000	400	12
	19–22	58 128	162 65	2100	46	800	4000	400	12
	23–50	58 128	162 65	2000	46	800	4000		12
	51+	58 128	162 65	1800	46	800	4000		12
Pregnant				+300	+30	1000	5000	400	15
Lactating				+500	+20	1200	6000	400	15

SOURCE: Food and Nutrition Board, *Recommended Dietary Allowances*, 8th ed. (Washington, D.C.: National Academy of Sciences, 1974).

[a] The allowances are intended to provide for individual variations among most normal persons as they live in the United States under usual environmental stresses. Diets should be based on a variety of common foods in order to provide other nutrients for which human requirements have been less well defined.

[b] Kilojoules (k J) = 4.2 × kcal.

[c] Retinol equivalents.

[d] Assumed to be all as retinol in milk during the first 6 months of life. All subsequent intakes are assumed to be half as retinol and half as beta-carotene when calculated from international units. As retinol equivalents, three fourths are as retinol and one fourth as beta-carotene.

	Water-soluble vitamins							Minerals				
Ascorbic acid (mg)	Folacin[f] (μg)	Niacin[g] (mg)	Riboflavin (mg)	Thiamin (mg)	Vitamin B$_6$ (mg)	Vitamin B$_{12}$ (μg)	Calcium (mg)	Phosphorus (mg)	Iodine (μg)	Iron (mg)	Magnesium (mg)	Zinc (mg)
35	50	5	0.4	0.3	0.3	0.3	360	240	35	10	60	3
35	50	8	0.6	0.5	0.4	0.3	540	400	45	15	70	5
40	100	9	0.8	0.7	0.6	1.0	800	800	60	15	150	10
40	200	12	1.1	0.9	0.9	1.5	800	800	80	10	200	10
40	300	16	1.2	1.2	1.2	2.0	800	800	110	10	250	10
45	400	18	1.5	1.4	1.6	3.0	1200	1200	130	18	350	15
45	400	20	1.8	1.5	2.0	3.0	1200	1200	150	18	400	15
45	400	20	1.8	1.5	2.0	3.0	800	800	140	10	350	15
45	400	18	1.6	1.4	1.0	3.0	800	800	130	10	350	15
45	400	16	1.5	1.2	2.0	3.0	800	800	110	10	350	15
45	400	16	1.3	1.2	1.6	3.0	1200	1200	115	18	300	15
45	400	14	1.4	1.1	2.0	3.0	1200	1200	115	18	300	15
45	400	14	1.4	1.1	2.0	3.0	800	800	100	18	300	15
45	400	13	1.2	1.0	2.0	3.0	800	800	100	18	300	15
45	400	12	1.1	1.0	2.0	3.0	800	800	80	10	300	15
60	800	+2	+0.3	+0.3	2.3	4.0	1200	1200	125	18+[h]	450	20
80	600	+4	+0.5	+0.3	2.5	4.0	1200	1200	150	18	450	25

[e] Total vitamin E activity, estimated to be 80 per cent as alpha-tocopherol and 20 per cent other tocopherols.

[f] The folacin allowances refer to dietary sources as determined by *Lactobacillus casei* assay. Pure forms of folacin may be effective in doses less than one fourth of the recommended dietary allowance.

[g] Although allowances are expressed as niacin, it is recognized that on the average 1 mg of niacin is derived from each 60 mg of dietary tryptophan.

[h] This increased requirement cannot be met by ordinary diets; therefore, the use of supplemental iron is recommended.

statement: "The allowances are intended to provide for individual variations among most normal persons as they live in the United States under usual environmental stresses. Diets should be based on a variety of common foods in order to provide other nutrients for which human requirements have been less well defined."[1] At intervals, the information from research is reviewed, and the RDA is revised according to current findings.

Carbohydrates

Plants take water, nitrogen, and minerals from the soil, and carbon dioxide from the air. With these elements, the energy of the sun, and the aid of *chlorophyll* (the leaves' green coloring), they manufacture carbohydrates. This process is called *photosynthesis*. Carbohydrates are used for the structure of the plant; they also are stored in the plant's stem, roots, and fruits or seeds. Carbohydrates from plants are the main source of human energy. These carbohydrates contain carbon, hydrogen, and oxygen and may be in the form of starches, sugars, or celluloses. The starches and sugars are broken down into simple sugars and, finally, into glucose, which is circulated by the blood to the cells. The celluloses (or fibers) are not easily digested and are useful mainly as bulk for elimination.

Food sources

The following foods are our primary sources of carbohydrates:

1. cereal or whole-grain products (also may supply some protein, fat, minerals and vitamins)
2. bread, macaroni, rice, breakfast cereals, spaghetti, cakes, and cookies
3. many fruits and vegetables (also may supply some minerals and vitamins)
4. white potatoes, sweet potatoes, peas, and lima beans
5. milk (also an important source of protein, minerals, and vitamins)
6. sugar, honey, and molasses[2]

---

1. Food and Nutrition Board, *Recommended Dietary Allowances*, 8th ed. (Washington, D.C.: National Academy of Sciences, 1974).
2. Molasses also has a very small amount of iron.

RDA

Since the body can use fats and proteins as well as carbohydrates for energy, it is difficult to establish a definite requirement for carbohydrates. The FNB suggests that at least 100 grams of carbohydrates be included in the diet each day for efficient metabolism. The number of grams of carbohydrates found in various foods is given in Appendix A.

Uses in the body

The main function of carbohydrates is to provide energy. One gram of carbohydrate, when *oxidized* (burned), will yield four calories. A *calorie* is the amount of heat or energy required to raise the temperature of a gram of water one Celsius degree. Carbohydrate as glucose always must be available to provide the energy necessary for the functioning of the brain and the nerve tissues. In addition, a small amount of carbohydrate is necessary for complete oxidation of fat by the cells of the body. Without carbohydrates, fats cannot be completely *metabolized* (broken down) for use in the body.

Energy requirements take priority over tissue building. So, if carbohydrate is available for energy needs, protein intake will be available for tissue building; otherwise, as much of the protein as necessary, along with any fat in the diet, will be used for energy needs.

Carbohydrates also help to regulate the gastrointestinal tract. *Lactose*, a sugar (carbohydrate) in milk, promotes the growth of desirable bacteria in the small intestines, and cellulose provides roughage, which aids in normal elimination.

Related problems

The incidence of dental *caries* (tooth decay) may be increased by the presence of fermentable sugars near the teeth. These carbohydrates, such as candy, dates, and raisins, which cling to the teeth, are most harmful. Excess calories not needed for energy are converted into body fat. Concentrated carbohydrate foods, especially those including fat—candies, cookies, and cakes— may contribute to excess calorie intake. For example, one cookie or one ounce of fudge may contribute 100 calories; an extra 100 calories a day will result in a 10-pound weight gain over a year's time. (In Chapter 18 weight regulation is discussed.)

Fats

Fats contain carbon, hydrogen, and oxygen, as do carbohydrates, but in different proportions that increase the calories in each gram.

Fats are broken down into fatty acids and glycerol for use in the body. The fatty acids may be saturated or unsaturated, depending on the structure of their molecule. The unsaturated fatty acid, linoleic, is essential and must be included in the diet.

Food sources

Butter, margarine, cream, mayonnaise, vegetable oil, and meat fats are the most readily recognized high-fat foods. Corn and safflower oils contain a large proportion of polyunsaturated fatty acids; animal fats and coconut oil contain a higher percentage of saturated fatty acids. Other foods, such as pastries, some cakes, nuts, olives, avocados, cheeses, and some kinds of meats also have high fat content. Appendix A lists the fat content of some foods.

RDA

Currently, it is recommended that calories from fat should not exceed 35 percent of the calorie intake. Polyunsaturated fats frequently are recommended because of the apparent association of saturated fats and cholesterol and the deposit in the arteries of substances that may lead to coronary heart disease.

Uses in the body

Fats provide energy. One gram of fat provides nine calories, as compared to the four calories in a gram of carbohydrate or protein. Fats also may carry fat-soluble vitamins.

A moderate deposit of fat is needed to support and protect such organs as the kidneys and to insulate the body, reducing the loss of heat. Fats leave the stomach more slowly than do carbohydrates or protein, thus they help to delay hunger. They also enhance the flavor of foods, as is the case with butter, sour cream, and whipped cream.

Related problems

Deficiency and excess Prolonged, extremely low fat intake, such as might be found in an unwise weight-control program, may lead to deficiency of the essential fatty acid, linoleic acid, which may result in a related skin problem. Further, such diets might not provide an adequate amount of the fat-soluble vitamins. Fat eaten in excess of the body's caloric needs will be converted to body fat and stored, resulting in weight gain.

Cholesterol Cholesterol is a fatlike substance and is considered here because of its possible relationship with atherosclerosis. Risk factors — lack of exercise, overeating, heredity, smoking, high blood pressure, emotional strain, and cholesterol level in the blood—also are involved. Dietary factors that influence the level of cholesterol in the blood are the intake of saturated fats and of cholesterol. Research on the problem is continuing.

Cholesterol is *synthesized* (made) in the body, mainly by the liver. In normal conditions, the body maintains a balance by producing only as much cholesterol as is needed if the diet does not provide it. However, there is some evidence that for certain "high-risk" people (potential coronary patients), the total intake of cholesterol is not matched by a decrease in the body's production, and high levels of cholesterol may circulate in the blood. In these people, total intake of cholesterol and fats may have to be controlled.

Cholesterol is essential to many tissues of the body and is also a *precursor* (a substance from which the body can synthesize another needed compound) of vitamin D. A form of cholesterol found in the skin may be changed to vitamin D when exposed to the ultraviolet rays of the sun.

Liver, sweetbreads, brains, oysters and other shellfish, and egg yolk contain a substantial amount of cholesterol. There is also cholesterol, as well as saturated fatty acids, in cream, butter, and animal fat.

Proteins

Proteins contain carbon, hydrogen, oxygen, and nitrogen; some also may contain sulfur, phosphorus and/or iron. Proteins are broken down into amino acids for use by the body. There are 22 amino acids, and 8 of these (9 for infants) are known as *essential amino acids*— those that the body cannot synthesize. The others also are needed by the body, but they may be synthesized from parts of other amino acids, carbohydrates, or fats.

Each type of protein is a combination of specific amino acids in varying quantities, formed in sequence or arrangements as indicated by the heritage or the genetic code for each cell. Each tissue—glands, bone, blood, hair, and so on—contains proteins that are unique to the tissue. In fact, each protein is unique in its make up and arrangement of amino acids.

Since the body does not store amino acids or the substances needed for the synthesis of amino acids, all the essential amino acids and the precursors for the nonessential amino acids must be available to the cells at the same time for use by the specific tissues. If all necessary amino acids are not available, those that are available are *deaminized* (broken down), and the amino group, which contains the nitrogen, will be excreted in the urine. The remainder of the protein molecule will be used for energy or will be stored as body fat; it will not be used for tissue growth. One gram of protein will yield four calories.

Food sources

The patterns, or combinations, of amino acids in foods influence the total amount of protein needed. Scientific studies have determined the relative quality of protein foods. The efficiency of a protein food may depend on the quantity as well as the quality of its protein.

Generally, animal protein foods are better utilized by the body than are plant protein foods. A plant protein food mixed either with a small amount of animal protein (cereal with milk) or with other vegetable or plant protein food (corn with wheat or soybean) will more nearly match the quality of animal protein food. Eggs, milk, all meats, fish, and poultry are sources of high-quality animal protein. The plant foods that contain protein are dried beans— especially soybeans— peas, lentil, nuts, cereals, and grains. Refer to Appendix A for the protein content of various foods.

RDA

The RDA for males 19 to 22 years old is 54 grams; for females of the same ages, 46 grams. An increase of 30 grams during pregnancy and of 20 grams during lactation is recommended. Refer back to Table 14–1 for the recommended amounts for other age groups.

A liberal intake of protein is especially important in growth periods and in times of stress. It also is important when a large percentage of the dietary protein is composed of plant protein (incomplete) foods.

Uses in the body

Almost all tissues in the body have a limited life span; they constantly are being replaced or renewed. Some cells are replaced daily, while others may not be replaced for years; blood cells are replaced about every three months, while the life of a bone cell is about five years.

The building of new tissues, especially important during the rapid growth periods of pregnancy, infancy, and childhood, requires an adequate supply of proteins. Protein is important for tissue growth (as when muscles are being enlarged at the beginning of athletic training periods) and for tissue replacement (as a result of burns, surgery, or bone fractures).

Many essential body compounds, such as enzymes, antibodies, hormones, and sperm cells, are synthesized from protein. The exchange of fluids between the tissue cells and the body fluids also is influenced by the concentration of protein in the fluids.

If enough carbohydrates and fats are not available to satisfy the need for energy, the nitrogen will be removed from the amino acids. The remainder of the protein molecule will be used for energy and will not be available for other uses. Any excess intake of protein will be converted and deposited as body fat.

Related problems

A sufficient intake of protein during pregnancy, infancy, and childhood is especially critical. Severe protein deficiencies during pregnancy and the first few months of life affect the growth— including the brain growth—of the child. A low intake of protein usually results in inadequate intake of other nutrients, especially the minerals calcium and iron and the B vitamins thiamin, riboflavin, and niacin.

Minerals

About 60 minerals have been identified in the human body, but only about a third of them have been established by research as essential to human beings. There are 7 minerals, called the *macronutrients*, that are needed in comparatively high amounts; there are 14, the *micronutrients*, that are needed in very small amounts. These mineral elements are listed in Table 14–2. Even though

Table 14-2 *Essential mineral elements*

Macronutrients	Micronutrients
Calcium	Iron
Phosphorus	Iodine
Magnesium	Fluorine
Potassium	Zinc
Sodium	Cobalt
Chlorine	Copper
Sulfur	Chromium
	Manganese
	Molybdenum
	Nickel
	Selenium
	Silicon
	Tin
	Vanadium

a mineral might appear in the most minute amount, they all are essential for one or more functions in the human body.

Minerals can be a part of the body's structure — the bones, teeth, muscles, and blood, for example — or they can be a part of the many body compounds that regulate the body's functions— enzymes[3] and hormones,[4] for example.

The concentration of minerals in the fluids inside and surrounding the cells influences the flow of fluids through cell walls, the process called *osmosis*. The fluids carry substances, including nutrients and waste materials, through the cell walls (membranes). The transmission of nerve impulses and the contraction and relaxation of muscles also are dependent on the presence and concentration of various minerals in the body's fluids.

Most of these minerals, which are so very necessary for normal body functioning, are relatively abundant in foods and, since many are needed in such small amounts, frequently no particular recognition or attention is given to a special selection of foods to supply them in the diet. However, a few, such as iron, calcium, magnesium, iodine, fluorine, and zinc, may require special selection in order to meet the body's needs.

---

3. *Enzymes* are substances produced by many different body cells. They act as *catalysts* (activators) to initiate chemical reactions in a large number of metabolic processes.

4. *Hormones* are substances produced by different organs of the body, and each hormone regulates a specific activity in the body.

Calcium and phosphorus

Calcium and phosphorus are needed throughout life to build and maintain all the bony structures in the body. Special attention must be given to provide an adequate supply of calcium during periods of rapid growth — infancy, childhood, the teen-age years—and in pregnancy and lactation.

Food sources Milk is the best source of calcium. It also supplies phosphorus and, often, is fortified with vitamin D, both of which contribute to well-formed bones and teeth. Hard cheeses and dark green vegetables also are excellent sources of calcium; other vegetables, fruits, and grains contain smaller amounts. Meats, fish, poultry, eggs, nuts, and legumes are excellent sources of phosphorus; grains also contain phosphorus.

RDA The recommendation for calcium is 800 milligrams for both adult males and females. An increased amount is needed during the growth periods of childhood and pregnancy and during lactation.

Phosphorus is found in so many foods in such sufficient amounts that no special attention to it is necessary in planning the daily diet. The RDA for phosphorus is 800 milligrams for an adult, the same as for calcium. Again, Table 14–1 lists the requirements for the different age groups.

Uses in the body Both calcium and phosphorus, along with other minerals, vitamins, and protein, are necessary for the proper formation of bones and teeth. In addition, calcium in the blood is essential for blood to clot. And, with magnesium, potassium, and sodium, calcium is necessary for the normal contraction and relaxation of muscles.

Phosphorus, in addition to being a structural part of the bones and teeth, also is a part of every living cell of the body and some enzymes and vitamins. Substances in the body that contain phosphorus influence or control many bodily functions, such as the release of energy and the absorption, transportation, and metabolism of other nutrients.

Related problems Of the minerals needed for strong bones and teeth, calcium and fluorine are the ones most likely to be in short supply in the American diet. Inadequate intake of these two minerals, especially during rapid growth periods, can result in the stunting of growth, poor bones and teeth, and malformation of bones.

Since phosphorus is so easily obtained in adequate amounts, a dietary deficiency is unlikely.

Magnesium

Most of the magnesium found in the body is stored in the bones and soft tissues. When needed, it is withdrawn from storage and used for the body processes.

Food sources and RDA Magnesium is found in many foods: meat, fish, milk, poultry, grains, and green vegetables. A magnesium deficiency is not common, because the average diet usually provides it in adequate amounts. The daily recommendation for adult females is 300 milligrams, and for adult males, 350 milligrams. This amount is easily obtained in daily diets.

Uses in the body and related problems Magnesium is a catalyst for many enzyme reactions in the body, including the production and release of energy from the glucose in the cells. Magnesium, along with other minerals in the fluids surrounding the cells and muscles, influences transfer of nerve impulses and the relaxation and contraction of muscles. Magnesium has a relaxing effect; calcium, a stimulating effect—causing the muscles to contract.

Deficiency is not common but may be found in a long-term alcoholic, in persons on inadequate diets, or in persons who have suffered long-term nausea, vomiting, and diarrhea.

Potassium

This mineral is closely related to sodium and chlorine in regulating the normal water balance in the body.

Food sources and RDA Many foods provide potassium—apricots, bananas, oranges, grapefruit, meats, poultry, fish, vegetables, and grains. No recommendation has been set, but potassium is readily available in so many foods that the average diet provides it in adequate amounts.

Uses in the body Like magnesium, potassium is a catalyst in many of the body's reactions, including the production of energy. The concentration of potassium, along with the concentration of sodium, is most important in the flow of substances through the membrane, or walls, of the cells in the body. Potassium also is important for the transmission of nerve impulses and for the relaxation of muscles.

Related problems A potassium deficiency is unlikely to occur. Infants with diarrhea, persons using certain diuretics, or persons following certain fad diets may develop a deficiency. An excess intake of sodium or an inadequate intake of magnesium—both of which cause loss of potassium from within the cells—also can result in a potassium deficiency. Weakness in the muscles, including those of the heart and respiratory system, may result from a lack of potassium.

Sodium

Unlike other minerals, sodium, which is common table salt, causes more problems from excess intake than it does from an inadequate supply.

Food sources and RDA This mineral is added to many foods during processing, in meal preparation, or at the table. Most foods contain sodium, and no RDA has been set for the mineral.

Uses in the body Sodium is involved primarily with maintaining the balance of fluids inside and outside the cells and the body's fluid volume. Since these fluids carry nutrients and other substances into or out of the cells, a proper equilibrium of fluids is important. Sodium also is a factor in the absorption of glucose, in the transmission of nerve impulses, and in the relaxation of muscles.

Related problems Prolonged vomiting and diarrhea, and excessive perspiration, may cause a loss of sodium. A low sodium level in the fluid surrounding the cells will cause partial dehydration of the cells. Also, too much sodium in the fluids surrounding the cells will interfere with the synthesis of protein.

Chlorine

Most of the chlorine in the diet comes from salt, which is sodium chloride. A deficiency of chlorine, therefore, would be unusual, and no RDA has been set. Chlorine is part of the hydrochloric acid used to maintain normal acidity in the stomach.

Sulfur

Sulfur is a part of some of the B vitamins and of many of the amino acids, especially those in the hair and nails. It also is important in the transfer of energy and the formation of certain connective tissues. The amount needed daily, which has not been set, is readily met by the average diet.

Iron

For reasons that are not fully understood, the body is very inefficient at absorbing iron from foods. Therefore, foods that are good iron sources must be included in the diet every day.

Food sources The best sources of iron are liver, oysters, clams, egg yolks, molasses, dry beans, dark green vegetables, whole-grain and enriched cereals and breads, and beef. In addition, some iron may be obtained when foods are cooked in iron pans.

RDA The iron recommendation for females 11 to 50 years old is 18 milligrams daily. Males 11 to 18 years old also need 18 milligrams daily, and 10 milligrams after age 19. Table 14–1 lists the daily recommendations for other age groups.

Uses in the body Iron is part of the hemoglobin in the red blood cell, myoglobin in the muscle, and a number of enzymes. Without iron, the blood could not transport oxygen from the lungs to the tissue cells to be used in the oxidation processes; nor could the blood transport carbon dioxide back to be released by the lungs before beginning the cycle again.

Once iron is absorbed (only about 10 percent of the iron in food is absorbed) from the food into the body, it may be stored in the liver, spleen, and bone marrow if it is not used immediately. The iron that is released when red blood cells disintegrate at the end of their life span (about three months) can be recycled. Only a small amount of iron is lost from the body each day, although there is some increased loss for females during menstruation.

Related problems An insufficient intake of iron is a common nutritional problem in the United States as well as in most of the world, especially among infants, growing children, and young females who have high iron needs due to menstrual losses or pregnancy. An adequate intake of iron prior to and during pregnancy is necessary if the infant is to have adequate iron for the first three to six months of its life, when the diet is mostly milk (a low-iron food). Iron deficiency also is found in those who donate blood too frequently

Nutrition

and in those who have lost excessive amounts of blood because of surgery, wounds, or abnormal menstruation.

An inadequate amount of iron results in a less than normal amount of hemoglobin and/or red blood cells in the blood. This condition is called *nutritional anemia*, and it is treated by eliminating the cause, when appropriate, and by a diet that includes iron-rich foods as well as adequate amounts of ascorbic acid and protein. Under some situations, a physician may prescribe iron by injection or oral therapy.

Iodine

Obtaining an adequate amount of iodine is a worldwide problem, even though only a minute quantity is needed daily. In many parts of the world, the soil contains no iodine, so plants grown in those areas also lack the mineral.

Food sources and RDA The most effective source of iodine is iodized salt; and dry seaweeds and seafood are good food sources. The daily recommendation is based somewhat on individual weight. For a male 19 to 22 years old, the recommendation is 140 micrograms, and for a female in the same age group, 100 micrograms, with an increase of 25 micrograms during pregnancy. Table 14-1 shows daily recommendations for other age groups.

Uses in the body and related problems Iodine is a vital micronutritient needed by an extremely important gland, the thyroid. This gland produces a hormone, *thyroxine*, that influences the *basal metabolic rate* (rate of oxidation in the body's cells). Adequate intake of iodine is highly important for females before and during the child-bearing years. The infant born of a mother whose diet has been severely deficient in iodine may suffer from *cretinism*, a condition characterized by retarded physical and mental growth. *Endemic* (simple) *goiter*, which is an enlargement of the thyroid gland, results from insufficient intake of iodine.

Fluorine

So little fluorine is found in foods that the most reliable source is considered to be addition of 1 part per million (p.p.m) of fluoride to the water supply. Controlled studies have shown that this amount will reduce the incidence of dental caries in children, especially if the fluorine is available when the teeth are being formed. There also is indication that women who ingest fluorine throughout life may be less subject to *osteoporosis* (deterioration of the bones).

No recommendation has been set for fluorine, but the use of the quantity discussed above is considered beneficial for all ages. Other ways to supply it include the application of fluorine directly to the teeth by a dentist, the use of a fluoride toothpaste, and the use of fluoride tablets. These other methods are thought to be less effective than fluoridation of drinking water.

Zinc

Only recently, with additional scientific knowledge, has zinc been added to the list of nutrients included in the RDA.

Food sources and RDA Oysters, beef, lamb, chicken legs, and other dark-colored meats are the best sources of zinc; cereal grains, vegetables, and milk, the next best sources. An adequate zinc intake may be obtained from a mixed diet that contains sufficient amounts of animal protein. An intake of 14 milligrams of zinc is recommended for both the adult male and female, with an increase for the female during pregnancy and lactation.

Uses in the body and related problems Zinc is a part of the enzymes involved in many metabolic processes. Its involvement in protein synthesis also indicates its importance in the development of the fetus during pregnancy and in wound healing.

There is a rapid turnover of zinc in the body. Loss of appetite and failure to grow are the deficiency symptoms. Excessive intake is unlikely to occur, except possibly from an intake of acidic foods that have been canned in zinc containers.

Other mineral elements

The minerals cobalt, copper, chromium, manganese, molybdenum, nickel, selenium, silicon, tin, and vanadium have been established as essential to normal reproduction, growth, and/or functioning of the body for human beings and/or animals. Estimates of the amounts of each mineral that are needed have been made, but recommendations have not been set. The quantities needed are so small and the minerals are present in such a wide variety of foods that there rarely is a problem.

Unusually large amounts of some of these minerals may cause adverse effects, but an intake of quantities large enough to be toxic usually is the result of an unusual circumstance and a long period of time.

Vitamins

Vitamins are needed in very small quantities for growth and maintenance, and each vitamin has special functions in the metabolic processes of the body. Vitamins act as catalysts to cause or speed up many chemical reactions that occur in the body.

Vitamins traditionally have been grouped into two classes: fat soluble and water soluble. The *fat-soluble* vitamins include vitamins A, D, E, and K. The *water-soluble* vitamins include the B-complex group (thiamin, riboflavin, niacin, pyridoxine, pantothenic acid, biotin, folic acid, and cobalamin, or vitamin B_{12}) and vitamin C (ascorbic acid).

A well-balanced mixture of foods, as suggested by the Basic Four Food Groups (Chapter 15), will supply all necessary vitamins, as well as other nutrients, to the normal adult. Vitamin supplements may be prescribed by physicians for infants, growing children, women during pregnancy and lactation, and people with certain illnesses.

Particular caution is needed when vitamin supplements containing therapeutic amounts are used. More research is needed to determine the effect of taking large amounts of various vitamins over a period of time. It is known that an excessive intake of vitamins A and D can be toxic and should be avoided. Also, it is especially important for the pregnant mother to avoid excessive doses of vitamin D, which might affect her developing baby.

Vitamin A

This vitamin has several forms, but the general term *vitamin A* is used here to include all forms except the carotenoids. The *carotenoids* are compounds the body can convert into vitamin A, and they sometimes are called *provitamin A*.

Food sources Vitamin A is found in animal foods that contain fat, such as butter, cream, liver, egg yolk, fish, and especially fish-liver oils. *Carotene*, one of the carotenoids, is found in the bright yellow and dark green fruits and vegetables—sweet potatoes, carrots, butternut and Hubbard squashes, apricots, cantaloupes, spinach, broccoli, and beet greens. Margarine and nonfat milk—fluid and dry—usually are fortified with vitamin A, as their labels will indicate.

Vitamin A is fairly stable to heat, so normal cooking methods do not destroy it. However, oxidation, which causes fats and oils to become rancid, does destroy the vitamin.

RDA Vitamin A is measured in *International Units* (I.U.) because this method was used to measure its biological value in food before the vitamin was isolated from food. It is now known that 1 I.U. is equal to 0.3 microgram (1,000 mcg = 1 mg) vitamin A.

The RDA for a normal, healthy adult is 5,000 I.U. daily. This amount is assumed to be provided partially by plant sources (carotene). All carotene in plant food cannot be completely absorbed and converted to vitamin A in the body.

Uses in the body Vitamin A is necessary to maintain the normal condition of mucous membranes, for growth, for normal bone and tooth formation, and for reproduction, but its exact role in these processes is not known.

All the body's passages—mouth, nose, respiratory and digestive tracts, and the genitourinary system—are lined with epithelial tissue, which normally is moist and flexible. Vitamin A is involved in keeping this tissue in healthy condition. It also is involved in maintaining healthy skin.

Vitamin A also is extremely important in maintaining healthy eye structure and proper vision in low lighting or at night. In night driving, for example, good vision and the eyes' ability to adapt to changes in lighting are vital, lest the headlights of an oncoming car blind a driver.

Related problems If vitamin A is lacking in the diet, the epithelial tissues gradually dry and become scaly, making them more vulnerable to infections. The skin becomes rough, dry, and scaly. An inability to see in dim light appears early in a deficiency situation. Over time, the structures of the eye are damaged and blindness can develop.

Large doses of vitamin A can be harmful, as was mentioned earlier.

Vitamin D

This vitamin remains somewhat mysterious, in that researchers have not yet determined how it functions in the body. However, the fact that it is vitally important in several processes has been established.

Food sources Fish-liver oils and fortified milk are the best sources of vitamin D; salmon, sardines, herring, and tuna contain smaller amounts. Fortified milk is the most common source, since most fluid milk contains 400 I.U. vitamin D per quart. Check the labels on containers of dry and evaporated milk to determine the fortification.

A *precursor* (provitamin) of vitamin D, which is a derivative of cholesterol, is present in the human skin. The ultraviolet light of the sun, or of an ultraviolet lamp, converts this precursor into vitamin D, which then passes into the blood stream.

Vitamin D is a stable compound, so normal cooking methods do not destroy it.

RDA For children, teenagers, young adults, and pregnant and lactating women, the daily recommendation is 400 I.U. One I.U. vitamin D equals 0.025 microgram vitamin D.

Uses in the body Vitamin D is necessary for the body's absorption and utilization of calcium and phosphorus to build bones and teeth. Obviously, adequate amounts of these two minerals also must be available in the body for the process to take place. These three nutrients are most important during rapid growth periods.

Related problems *Rickets*, a deficiency disorder resulting from lack of vitamin D, still is found in this country. Inadequate intake of the vitamin prevents the normal growth and development of good bones and teeth in children. Children, pregnant and lactating females, and old people with low vitamin-D intake who are not exposed to the sun may show indications of mild vitamin-D deficiency.

Excessive amounts of vitamin D can cause toxic reactions; excessive exposure to the sun will cause sunburn, not a toxic reaction. It is advisable to look at the day's total intake of vitamin D, especially when fortified foods or vitamin supplements are used for young children and pregnant women. The indiscriminate addition of vitamin D to foods is prohibited; milk, an excellent source of calcium and phosphorus, is the food that is allowed to be fortified with the vitamin.

Vitamin E

Vitamin E is important in commercial food processing, where it is used as a preservative in foods that contain fat. Labels on foods to which it has been added may call it *vitamin E* or *tocopherol*, its chemical name.

Food sources and RDA Polyunsaturated vegetable oils, such as those made from corn, cottonseed, and soybeans, the margarine and mayonnaise made from these oils, and wheat germ are the best food sources of vitamin E. Whole grains, cereals, and some vegetables also have small amounts. Very little vitamin E is destroyed by normal cooking methods.

The RDA for vitamin E is 15 I.U. for the adult male and 12 I.U. for the adult female, with an increase to 15 I.U. during pregnancy and lactation. One I.U. equals 0.55 milligram vitamin E.

Uses in the body and related problems Vitamin E is an *antioxidant*—its chemical structure is such that it combines with available oxygen, so the oxygen is not free to react with other substances. As an antioxidant, this vitamin is useful in preventing damage to certain substances within the cells. Also, an adequate supply of vitamin E will help to prevent oxidation of vitamins A and C and the polyunsaturated fatty acids, so that these nutrients are available for use by the body. Vitamin E also is necessary for the normal composition of the blood, especially the red blood cells.

Infants are born with a low tissue concentration of vitamin E. If a baby is fed a homemade formula based on evaporated milk, it may develop a form of anemia related to vitamin-E deficiency. However, human milk contains adequate amounts of the vitamin, so breast-fed babies do not develop this problem.

Vitamin K

Vitamin K actually is a group of related compounds that have similar chemical structures. Some of these compounds are natural; some are synthesized.

Food sources and RDA Green vegetables—especially spinach and kale—cabbage, egg yolks, and liver are good sources of vitamin K. This vitamin is stable to heat but may be destroyed by light.

Vitamin K can be synthesized by bacteria in the intestinal tract. The average diet, therefore supplies an adequate amount to supplement the amount synthesized. A small amount of the vitamin is stored in the liver.

No recommendation has been set for vitamin K, because there is little information about the amount synthesized in the body and the amount taken in in the daily diet.

Uses in the body and related problems Vitamin K is essential for normal coagulation of the blood; without an adequate supply of vitamin K, the blood would not clot and hemorrhage could occur.

Prolonged diarrhea or the intake of antibiotics may decrease the amount of vitamin K in the body. A new-born infant does not have an adequate amount of vitamin K, and bacteria do not develop in the intestinal tract for several days. Therefore, this vitamin frequently is administered to infants soon after they are born.

Thiamin (vitamin B₁)

As was mentioned earlier, the B-complex vitamins are thiamin (vitamin B₁), riboflavin (vitamin B₂), niacin (nicotinic acid), pyridoxine (vitamin B₆), pantothenic acid, biotin, folic acid (folacin), and cobalamin (vitamin B₁₂).

Food sources The best sources of thiamin are whole-grain and enriched breads and cereals, dried beans and lentils, flour, nuts, and pork.

Thiamin may be destroyed during storage or by heating, and, since it is a water-soluble vitamin, using large amounts of water in cooking will deplete the thiamin in the food. Freezing has little or no effect on the thiamin content of foods.

RDA The amount of thiamin needed daily is influenced by many factors: weight, activity, the calories needed for activity, and dietary habits. The larger the caloric need, the greater is the need for thiamin. If the caloric need is met by large amounts of carbohydrates, thiamin need will be greater than if the same number of calories is furnished by fats and proteins. A high alcoholic intake also increases the need for thiamin.

Thiamin is not stored in the body to any great extent, so it must be supplied in the diet each day. Any thiamin taken in and not needed is excreted in the urine.

Even though the daily requirement is based on total calories, and especially carbohydrate intake, it is recommended that the intake be not less than 1.5 milligrams for the male 19 to 22 years old or 1.1 milligrams for the same aged female. Table 14–1 lists daily recommendations for other age groups.

Uses in the body Thiamin is necessary in the individual cells for oxidation of carbohydrates. It is a part of a coenzyme[5] that is involved in carbohydrate metabolism.

---

5. A coenzyme works with an enzyme, acting as a catalyst for a specific reaction to take place. Many coenzymes have a vitamin as part of their structure.

The health of nerve tissues depends on an adequate supply of thiamin in order to break down the glucose that is essential to the tissues' functions. Thiamin also is known to take part in other nutrient interactions, and research is continuing to determine the exact role it plays.

Related problems *Beri-beri* is a deficiency disorder that results from inadequate thiamin intake. It can be fatal. It is not often found in the United States except in alcoholics. A mild deficiency, not enough to cause beri-beri, is frequently seen in American people who eliminate almost all bread and cereal from their diet, either as a result of poor eating habits or because they adhere to an unsound weight-reduction diet. These persons may suffer from a loss of appetite, general fatigue, and apathy.

Riboflavin (vitamin B$_2$)

Riboflavin deficiency has been found in recent years in the United States and in many other parts of the world. In this country, individuals who did not include milk in their daily diet were among those with the deficiency.

Food sources The best sources of riboflavin are milk and milk products, liver, eggs, legumes, meats, and dark green vegetables.

Riboflavin is stable to heat and acid, but it is fairly soluble in water, so that some of it is lost in ordinary cooking methods. Riboflavin is very easily destroyed by light. Milk that is packaged in dark-colored plasticized containers or in amber bottles will retain more riboflavin than will milk in clear glass containers.

RDA The body does not store riboflavin to any great extent, so a daily supply of the vitamin is needed. The RDA is related to body size, metabolic rate, rate of growth, caloric expenditure, and protein intake.

For males 19 to 22 years old, the daily recommendation is 1.8 milligrams; for females in the same age group, 1.4 milligrams is recommended, with an increase to 1.7 milligrams during pregnancy and to 1.9 milligrams during lactation.

Uses in the body Riboflavin works with enzymes in metabolizing nutrients in the cells. It functions specifically in the transfer of hydrogen from one substance to another in the metabolic process, especially with amino acids or protein. Riboflavin also takes part in many biochemical reactions in the body,

Nutrition 237

in oxidation of carbohydrates, and in conversion of the amino acid, tryptophan, to the vitamin niacin. It is essential for the growth and repair of body tissues, as well as for the production of energy.

Related problems The symptoms of riboflavin deficiency are cracks at the corners of the mouth, cracks and soreness of the lips, or sore throat and mouth. The skin may be greasy and scaly on various parts of the body, especially around the nose and other facial parts, as well as on the scrotum. The eyes become sensitive to light, and dimness of vision and burning or watering develops.

Niacin (nicotinic acid)

Niacin is the name for all the chemical forms of nicotinic acid and its related compound, nicatinamide. The essential amino acid, tryptophan, is a provitamin, or precursor, of niacin. Other B vitamins, thiamin, riboflavin, and pyridoxine, are all necessary for the conversion of tryptophan to niacin.

Food sources Since niacin can be formed in the body from its precursor, tryptophan, foods that contain tryptophan and/or niacin are important in the diet. Most protein from meat, fish, poultry, milk, and eggs—all of which contain tryptophan—is a good source of niacin. Brewer's yeast, enriched and whole-grain breads and cereals, whole wheat, wheat germ, and soybeans also are good sources of niacin.

Niacin is stable to heat, light, and oxidation, so very little of it is lost in ordinary cooking.

RDA The niacin recommendation is based on the caloric requirement and also on the source of the calories. The average diet that meets the protein recommendation also will meet the niacin recommendation. The minimum recommended allowance for niacin, including those on less than 2,000 calories' intake, is 20 milligrams for males 19 to 22 years old and 14 milligrams for the same age female, with an increase during pregnancy of 2 milligrams and of 4 milligrams during lactation. Table 14-1 lists daily recommendations for other age groups.

Uses in the body and related problems Niacin is essential to all cells. It is a part of the coenzymes that are needed for release of energy from carbohydrates, fats, and proteins.

Prolonged niacin deficiency results in *pellagra*, a disease that affects the skin (especially the areas exposed to the sun), the nervous system, and the digestive tract.

Pyridoxine (vitamin B$_6$)

The names *pyridoxine* and *vitamin B$_6$* are used to represent the chemically related forms pyridoxine, pyridoxal, and pyridoxamine, all of which are utilized by the body.

Food sources and RDA Meats—especially liver—fish, fruits, vegetables, egg yolks, and whole-grain cereals are good sources of vitamin B$_6$. Pyridoxine, the form of the vitamin found in vegetable foods, is more stable than are the other two forms, which are found in animal foods and may be destroyed by heat and air. All three forms, however, may be destroyed by light.

The daily requirement for vitamin B$_6$ is based on the protein content of the diet. The RDA for the adult male and adult female is 2.0 milligrams with an increase advised during pregnancy and lactation.

Uses in the body and related problems Vitamin B$_6$ is essential in protein metabolism in the breakdown and formation of amino acids. It also is required in the conversion of trytophan to niacin.

A deficiency is rare, but irritability, insomnia, and skin problems may be symptoms of a deficiency.

Pantothenic acid

Almost all foods contain pantothenic acid, and deficiency is not likely to occur. Liver, egg yolks, wheat bran, and broccoli are excellent sources. Pantothenic acid is stable to moist heat but easily destroyed by dry heat, so foods processed by dry heat are poor sources of the nutrient.

No RDA has been set, because the exact amount needed is not known. However, the average diet appears to provide an adequate amount of the vitamin.

The release of energy from carbohydrates, fats, and proteins requires a coenzyme that contains pantothenic acid. It also is necessary for many other of the body's processes.

Biotin

Many foods contain biotin; liver, milk, and egg yolks are good sources. The amount needed daily has not been established, but the average diet seems to supply an adequate amount. Biotin also is synthesized in the intestines.

Biotin, as a co-enzyme, is essential in metabolism of carbohydrates, fats, and proteins. It plays a role in the oxidation of glucose, the synthesis of fatty acids, and in the deaminization of some amino acids.

Folic acid (folacin)

Folic acid is another nutrient that is not well understood. Researchers have established some information about it, and it is known to be essential to several body processes.

Food sources and RDA Folic acid is widely available in many foods, including dark green vegetables, liver, yeast, wheat germ, nuts, and such fruits as bananas and oranges.

Folic acid is unstable to heat. Therefore, foods that are stored at room temperature for extended periods of time or that are subjected to long cooking will lose significant amounts of the vitamin.

The daily recommendation for adults of both sexes is 400 micrograms (0.4 milligram). During the last three months of pregnancy, the recommendation is doubled, to ensure adequate supplies for both the mother and the developing infant.

Uses in the body Folacin coenzymes are essential in a number of enzyme reactions in the cells, especially in the synthesis of certain amino acids and in the formation of nucleic acids. Thus, folacin is necessary for cell growth and reproduction and for the formation and maturation of red blood cells in the bone marrow.

Related problems The folacin requirement is so small that most healthy adults easily meet their needs. However, certain illnesses can lead to folacin deficiency, which, in turn, can lead to *macrocytic anemia*, an anemia in which the red blood cells fail to mature.

Folacin deficiency has been observed in pregnant women and in formula-fed infants who have received no vitamin supplements. Deficiencies also have been noted in alcoholics and in elderly persons who follow poor diets or have poor intestinal absorption.

Vitamin B_{12} (cobalamin)

Vitamin B_{12} is a comparatively new addition to the B-complex vitamins; it was discovered in 1948. All the details of the way the vitamin works are not yet known.

Food sources and RDA All animal protein foods contain cobalamin; plant foods contain none. Liver and organ meats, muscle meats, fish, poultry, and eggs are good sources of the vitamin.

Cobalamin is not very stable to heat or light, so some of the vitamin may be lost in normal cooking. Pasteurization destroys some of the cobalamin in milk, and even more is lost in the processing of evaporated milk.

The RDA for vitamin B_{12} is very small: 3.0 micrograms for the normal, healthy adult, an amount easily met by the average American diet. During pregnancy and lactation, the recommendation is increased.

Uses in the body and related problems It is known that cobalamin is required for the formation of blood cells and in the metabolism of nutrients needed by the nervous system.

Pernicious anemia is a disorder that develops in individuals who have stomachs that are unable to secrete a substance that is necessary to the absorption of vitamin B_{12}. These persons are given B_{12} by injection to control the disorder.

Persons who follow strict vegetarian diets may develop a cobalamin deficiency, which may be indicated by nervous disorders. However, these individuals do not have pernicious anemia.

Ascorbic acid (vitamin C)

Although ascorbic acid was not positively identified until the late 1920s, oranges and lemons were known as the cure for scurvy two hundred years ago. *Scurvy*, the vitamin-C deficiency disease, was widespread among crews of sailing ships. On long voyages, fresh fruits and vegetables were unobtainable, and the disease frequently disabled or killed sailors. In the middle of the eighteenth century, an English navy doctor, experimenting to find a cure, discovered that lemons and oranges cured the disease.

Food sources Fresh or frozen citrus fruits and juices, strawberries, and cantaloupe are excellent sources of vitamin C. Kale, turnip greens, green peppers, broccoli, Brussels sprouts, and raw cabbage also are good sources. One serving of orange juice, grapefruit, cantaloupe, broccoli, or green pepper each day will supply the recommended amount of ascorbic acid.

The ascorbic acid content of fruits and vegetables is affected by their degree of ripeness when harvested. A tomato harvested while green and allowed to ripen off the vine will contain less ascorbic acid than will a similar tomato allowed to ripen on the vine.

Ascorbic acid is the most unstable of all vitamins. It is highly soluble in water and easily oxidized. Oxidation is hastened by heat and by an enzyme action that starts when raw fruits or vegetables are cut or bruised. There is less destruction of vitamin C when foods are protected from air, refrigerated, or are acidic in content.

Storage time and temperature and the method of preparation and cooking, all affect the final ascorbic acid content of the food. Heat, oxygen, and water, all increase its destruction.

RDA The FNB recommends 45 milligrams per day for adults, 60 milligrams per day during pregnancy, and 80 milligrams per day during lactation.

Uses in the body Ascorbic acid is essential for the production and maintenance to *collagen*—a protein that is important in connective tissues. Collagen is the substance that cements cells together, so vitamin C is important for the strength of blood vessels and other tissues. Ascorbic acid is important in the metabolism of some of the amino acids and in the body's use of iron, calcium, and folic acid. Ascorbic acid appears to have a protective role against some infections but is not a guarantee against infection. It is essential for wound healing and in surgical or injury situations.

Related problems The vitamin-deficiency disease *scurvy* is not common in the United States. Children and adults who have borderline intake of ascorbic acid develop symptoms, such as gums that bleed easily, small *hemorrhages* (bruises or black-and-blue-marks) under the skin, and fleeting pains in the muscles and joints.

Water

Sources and requirements

All fluids—water, juices, and other liquids—are the primary sources; and almost all foods supply some water. In addition, water also is formed during the metabolic processes.

It is estimated that from 4 to 6 cups (1 to 1½ liters) of water should be consumed daily under normal conditions. High temperatures and/or dry environmental conditions, elevated body temperature due to fever, or excessive physical activity may increase the amount needed.

Uses and related problems

Water is an essential part of and surrounds each cell of the body. Water gives shape or form to the cells; it is the substance in which the chemical changes take place. It is used in the digestion and metabolism of the nutrients and is necessary for removal and excretion of waste products. In addition, water aids in the regulation of the body's temperature.

Water is lost from the body through the skin, lungs, urine, and feces. Excessive loss or abnormal retention of water will interfere with the normal functioning of the cells. Excessive water loss may result from diarrhea—especially in infants—nausea, or very heavy perspiration. A severe loss of water may be fatal.

Digestion and absorption

Digestion is the term used to describe the very complex mechanical and chemical processes by which food is changed into substances that can be used by the body's cells. *Absorption* is the transfer of the digested substances into the body's circulatory systems.

Digestion

Food is broken into very small pieces by chewing and, at the same time, is mixed with saliva in the mouth. It then passes into the stomach, where it is churned and mixed with gastric juices, and, finally into the small intestines, where it is mixed with additional digestive juices that contain enzymes. These digestive enzymes break the larger molecules of foods into smaller molecules of nutrients, such as simple sugars, fatty acids, glycerol, amino acids, minerals, vitamins, and water, that can pass through the intestinal walls into the circulatory system.

Absorption and transportation

The molecules of nutrients pass through the *intestinal mucosa* (lining of the intestines) to enter the circulatory system, which transports these substances throughout the body. Some nutrients may undergo further change in the cells of the mucosa.

The circulatory system is composed of two subsystems: the blood system and the lymphatic system. Some nutrients, mostly fats and fat-soluble substances, go into the lymphatic system and do not go through the liver. The *lymphatic system* delivers the fats to the general circulatory system and then on to the fluids surrounding each cell of the body. The other nutrients pass into the *blood stream* and are carried to the liver and from there into the general circulatory system.

The nutrients needed by each cell are absorbed by the cell; the waste products are passed out of the cell into the circulatory system. The blood stream then carries the waste products to either the lungs or the kidneys, from which the waste products are excreted.

Metabolism

The chemical and physiological processes by which the nutrients delivered to the cells are converted into substances useful to the tissues and into energy are known as *metabolism*. All of the internal body processes require energy, as does the digestion of foods and physical activity. As all the body's activities increase, the energy needs increase; and the metabolic rate must increase to meet these needs. The energy needed to sustain normal functions when the body is in a state of complete rest is called *basal metabolism*. The total energy needed is that for basal metabolism, the digestion of foods, and physical activity.

Nutritional summary

All nutrients are needed all the time, since their uses are interrelated. To ensure an adequate daily nutritional intake, it is best to eat a wide variety of foods. Since most foods supply more than one nutrient, the proper selection makes all the nutrients available to the body.

Food labeling

As was mentioned earlier, labels on food containers must include a variety of information about the contents. The information must be stated in easy-to-understand language, and it may not be false or misleading.

Ingredient listing

Some foods are produced to *standards of identity*—they are made of certain amounts of certain ingredients, as established by the Food and Drug Administration (FDA). The labels on such foods do not have to state the ingredients, since no substances other than those listed in their standards are included. However, some standards allow the addition of other optional ingredients, which must be listed on the label if they are used. If chemical preservatives or artificial flavorings or colorings are used in a food, the label must so state, but the specific names of these substances do not have to be given. If a product does not meet the standard of identity, it must be labeled *imitation*. Mayonnaise, butter, ice cream, and macaroni products are examples of foods that are produced under standards of identity.

Labels for all other foods for which standards of identity have not been

```
          NUTRITION
         INFORMATION
         (PER SERVING)
      SERVING SIZE = 1 OZ.
    SERVINGS PER CONTAINER = 12

  CALORIES                      110
  PROTEIN                       2 GRAMS
  CARBOHYDRATE                  24 GRAMS
  FAT                           0 GRAM
      PERCENTAGE OF U.S. RECOMMENDED
         DAILY ALLOWANCES (U.S. RDA)*
         PROTEIN                2
         THIAMIN                8
         NIACIN                 2
      *Contains less than 2 percent of U.S.
       RDA for Vitamin A, Vitamin C,
          Riboflavin, Calcium and Iron.
```

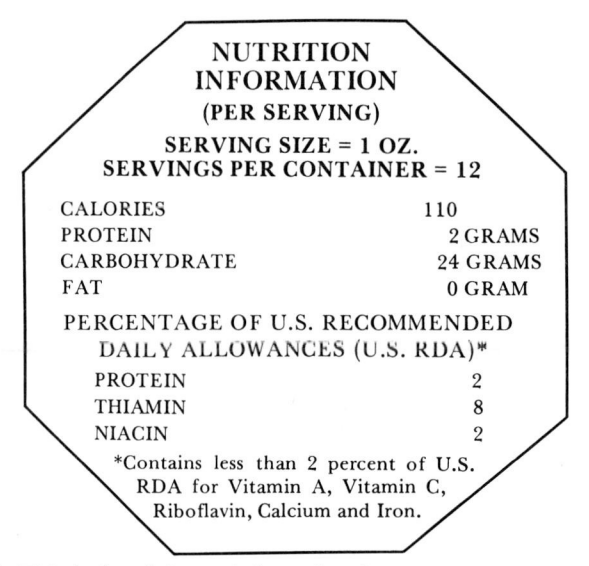

Figure 14–1 *This is the minimum information that must appear on a nutrition label.* (Source: U.S. Government Printing Office, no. 1712-00179)

established must include a list of all ingredients, if they are made of two or more. These ingredients must be listed in descending order of their amounts—the food contains the largest quantity of the first ingredient in the list and the least amount of the last ingredient named.

Nutritional labeling

When a food producer provides nutritional information on a product, the information always must be printed on the label in a certain way, as shown in Figure 14–1. Polyunsaturated and saturated fats, cholesterol, sodium, and other nutrients also may be listed, in the format shown in Figure 14–2.

NUTRITION INFORMATION
(PER SERVING)
SERVING SIZE = 8 OZ.
SERVINGS PER CONTAINER = 1

CALORIES............ 560	FAT (PERCENT OF
PROTEIN............. 23 GM	CALORIES 53%)......... 33 GM
CARBOHYDRATE....... 43 GM	POLYUNSAT-
	URATED*............ 2 GM
	SATURATED.......... 9 GM
	CHOLESTEROL*
	(20 MG/100 GM)........ 40 MG
	SODIUM (365 MG/
	100 GM)............. 830 MG

PERCENTAGE OF U.S. RECOMMENDED DAILY ALLOWANCES (U.S. RDA)

PROTEIN.................35	RIBOFLAVIN.............. 15
VITAMIN A...............35	NIACIN................... 25
VITAMIN C	CALCIUM................. 2
(ASCORBIC ACID).........10	IRON..................... 25
THIAMIN (VITAMIN	
B$_1$).......................15	

*Information on fat and cholesterol content is provided for individuals who, on the advice of a physician, are modifying their total dietary intake of fat and cholesterol.

Figure 14–2 *A label may include optional listings for cholesterol, fats, and sodium.* (Source: U.S. Government Printing Office, no. 1712-00179)

Table 14-3 *U.S. Recommended Dietary Allowances (U.S. RDA)*

Nutrient	Adults and children 4 years or older	Under 4 years	Pregnant or lactating women
REQUIRED LABEL LISTINGS			
Protein	45 or 65 gm.[a]	20 or 28 gm.[a]	45 or 65 gm.[a]
Vitamin A	5,000 I.U.	2,500 I.U.	8,000 I.U.
Vitamin C (ascorbic acid)	60 mg.	40 mg.	60 mg.
Thiamin (vitamin B_1)	1.5 mg.	0.7 mg.	1.7 mg.
Riboflavin (vitamin B_2)	1.7 mg.	0.8 mg.	2.0 mg.
Niacin	20 mg.	9.0 mg.	20 mg.
Calcium	1.0 gm.	0.8 gm.	1.3 gm.
Iron	18 mg.	10 mg.	18 mg.
OPTIONAL LABEL LISTINGS			
Vitamin D	400 I.U.	400 I.U.	400 I.U.
Vitamin E	30 I.U.	10 I.U.	30 I.U.
Vitamin B_6	2.0 mg.	0.7 mg.	2.5 mg.
Folic acid (folacin)	0.4 mg.	0.2 mg.	0.8 mg.
Vitamin B_{12}	6.0 mcg.	3.0 mcg.	8.0 mcg.
Phosphorus	1.0 gm.	0.8 gm.	1.3 gm.
Iodine	150 mcg.	70 mcg.	150 mcg.
Magnesium	400 mg.	200 mg.	450 mg.
Zinc	15 mg.	8 mg.	15 mg.
Copper	2 mg.	1 mg.	2 mg.
Biotin	0.3 mg.	0.15 mg.	0.3 mg.
Pantothenic acid	10 mg.	5 mg.	10 mg.

[a] Forty-five or twenty grams if protein quality equals or is greater than that of milk protein; 65 or 28 grams if protein quality is less than that of milk protein.

On such labels, the specific nutrients are listed as percentages of the U.S. RDA. The U.S. RDA, shown in Table 14-3, is not the same as the NAS-NRC RDA shown in Table 14-1; they are standards established as a basis for nutritional labeling. The figures are based on the needs of healthy people and include extra amounts to allow for variations among individuals. Therefore, the exact amounts listed are not needed by many people.

The figure for a nutrient stated on a food label is read as a percentage. For example, in Figure 14-2, the "25" shown for iron represents 25 percent, or one quarter, of the amount of iron needed by an individual under the U.S. RDA.

Nutritional labeling helps the consumer to select foods for their nutritive value. For example, the label on one frozen meat casserole lists meat first, then potatoes, and indicates a content of 20 grams protein per serving. The label on another meat casserole lists potatoes first, meat second, and indicates a per serving protein content of 15 grams. The first casserole, with more meat than potatoes and 5 more grams protein per serving, is a better nutritional selection. Having determined that fact, the consumer needs only to calculate the cost advantage to make an informed selection.

A second example involves fruit beverages. The label on one can lists water, sugar, and vitamin C (ascorbic acid), and the nutritional information shows the amount of calories and carbohydrates and the percentage of vitamin C. The label on another lists the fruit juice and vitamin C; calories, carbohydrates, vitamin C, other vitamins, and minerals are listed in the nutritional information. Clearly the contents of the second beverage can provide more nutritive value, and its cost can be calculated accordingly.

Additive labeling

The FDA has established a list of substances that are considered to be safe for use in foods. Referred to as the *GRAS list* ("Generally Recognized as Safe"), it includes substances used to increase nutritional content, to preserve the food and prevent it from spoiling, and to make the food product more desirable in one way or another. More than a thousand substances are given on the GRAS list, and Table 14-4 lists some of them and the foods in which they are used.

Table 14-4 *Some intentional additives and foods containing them*

Additive	Food usage
NUTRIENTS	
Vitamin A	Margarine
Vitamin B (thiamin)	Flour, cornmeal, cereals
Vitamin B_2 (riboflavin)	Flour, cornmeal, cereals
Vitamin C (ascorbic acid)	Canned fruits and juices, jams
Vitamin D	Milk
Niacin (nicotinic acid)	Flour, cornmeal, cereals
Calcium	Cereals, canned fruits
Iron	Cereals, canned fruits
Phosphorus	Chocolate-milk powder, cereals
Potassium iodide	Iodized salt
FLAVORINGS	
Anise oil	Licorice candies
Citrus oil	Soft drinks, ice cream
Cloves	Spice cakes, cookies
Acetaldehyde	Coffee-flavored candies
Allyl caproate	Pineapple jellies, puddings
Allyl isothiocyanate	Garlic-seasoned mixes
Amyl acetate	Banana candies, puddings
FLAVOR ENHANCERS	
Disodium inosinate	Soup mixes, canned vegetables
Ethyl maltol	Soft drinks, jams
Monosodium glutamate (MSG)	Processed foods, sauces
ANTIOXIDANTS	
Ascorbic acid	Canned fruits, packaged meats
Butylated hydroxyanisole (BHA)	Cereals, canned fruits and vegetables
Phosphoric acid	Fruit-drink mixes
BACTERIOSTATS AND FUNGISTATS	
Benzoic acid	Breads, pastries
Calcium propionate	Breads
Potassium propionate	Cheese
Sorbic acid	Processed cheeses, pastries
Sulfur dioxide	Dried fruits and vegetables
ANTICAKING AGENTS	
Calcium phosphate	Baking powder, seasonings
Calcium silicate	Salt, baking powder
Sodium silico aluminate	Salt

Table 14–4 (continued)

Additive	Food usage
EMULSIFYING AGENTS	
Lecithin	Candies, peanut butter
Propylene glycol monostearate	Candies, pancake mix
THICKENERS	
Acetylated monoglycerides	Pie fillings, puddings
Ammonium carrageenan	Cheeses, salad dressings
Cellulose derivatives (methocel, HEC, and so on)	Ice creams, cheeses, salad dressings
Gum arabic	Packaged soups, salad dressings
Gum tragacanth	Packaged soups, salad dressings
Sodium alginate	Jellies, packaged soups
MOISTURE RETAINERS	
Glycerine	Dried fruits, pastries
Glycerol lactopalminate	Dessert mixes, prepared dips
Mannitol	Dried fruits, candies
ACIDITY CONTROLLERS	
Calcium carbonate	Canned vegetables, wines
Citric acid	Fruit-drink mixes, soups, jellies
Lactic acid	Butter, chocolate candies
Malic acid	Canned fruits and vegetables
Phosphoric acid	Carbonated soft drinks
Tartaric acid	Jellies, jams, candies
NATURAL COLORANTS	
Annatto (yellow)	Butter, margarine, soft drinks
Cochineal (red)	Meat products, candies, pastries
Saffron (yellow)	Meat products, rice mixes
Turmeric (yellow)	Salad dressings, meat products
SYNTHETIC COLORANTS	
FD&C 1 (blue)	Soft drinks, candies
FD&C 5 (yellow)	Soft drinks, candies
COLOR ENHANCERS	
Sodium erythrobate	Packaged meats, ground meat
Sodium nitrate	Packaged meats

Chapter 15 Meal patterns and menu planning

The food an individual eats affects his or her life at all times. Mental alertness, physical efficiency, and even personality depend, in varying degrees, on the health and condition of the body. In turn, the body's condition depends on the nutrients obtained from food.

The kind and variety of foods eaten are based on a number of factors seldom recognized by most people: availability, tradition and custom, habit, dislikes, personal preference, special or self-chosen diets, season of the year, money, and many other factors.

Factors affecting food selection

Availability

All kinds of food grown in this country and abroad are rapidly transported either fresh, frozen, or canned—to all sections of the United States. Tomatoes from Texas are available in New England, and Idaho potatoes are sold in Florida. Pineapples from Hawaii commonly are found in markets all over the country, as are cheeses from Europe and kiwi fruit from Australia. This availability is a comparatively new development, dating roughly from the end of World War II. It is affecting food selection as more people become accustomed to newly introduced foods, particularly those from abroad.

Family traditions and customs

Individual eating patterns are established during infancy, before children are old enough to make decisions. If a family originally came from another country, they may have continued to eat many of the foods that were customary in that country. Thus, people of Italian descent often are used to many pasta dishes, and those of Oriental descent may continue to emphasize the use of rice.

Similarly, the family's eating pattern may be established by religious belief, which may require that some foods not be eaten and/or eaten only in certain combinations. Other families are accustomed to eating certain foods on festive occasions, religious holidays, or on other days that were customarily feast days in the country in which their ancestors lived. Still other families are used to eating large meals, as was the custom when people did heavy work in factories or on farms. Whatever a family's eating pattern, a child born into the family becomes accustomed to it and his or her own pattern is established.

Regional customs, too, are interwoven with customary family eating patterns. In the South, for instance, most people are used to having a hot bread at many meals, while New Englanders regularly serve brown bread containing raisins with baked beans. People in the Southwest, close to Mexico, regard chili and tamales as usual food, and those who live in California and the Northwest emphasize the fruits and vegetables grown there. These regional patterns also are reflected in the child's, and later the adult's, eating pattern.

Habit

Once an individual's eating pattern is established, he or she habitually continues to eat much the same variety and combinations of food. In time, food habits may change as a person hears about and tries new foods, travels, moves, or is otherwise exposed to different foods or other eating patterns. But food habits, like all other habits, are slow to change, and many people hold all their lives to the eating habits formed in childhood.

Likes, dislikes, and preferences

Most people eat the foods they recognize and know they like, no matter where they live. Often a child will develop a so-called dislike, perhaps picked up from another child or a family member who refused to eat a certain food. The dislike may be permanent, or it may be temporary, if in later years the individual tries the food and decides it is good. In other cases, an individual may find the flavor or texture of a certain food unpleasant, for reasons that are not understood. He or she may learn to like the food in time, or it may remain a permanent dislike.

A preference for certain foods also can be temporary. Peanut butter and jelly sandwiches, for example, may be a favorite food at one age, only to be replaced a few years later by another food or food combination. Some people prefer a certain food throughout life, simply because the taste or texture seems particularly pleasing to them.

Further, a food that is preferred by one person may repulse another, who will avoid it at all costs. Foods that are highly regarded or prized by members of one culture may be considered inedible by members of other groups. In Japan, for instance, raw fish is served consistently and taken for granted by most Japanese people; in this country, fish almost always is cooked before it is eaten, and many people would hesitate to try it raw.

Diets

A great many people are obliged to follow diets prescribed by their doctors because of an illness or a physical problem, such as an allergy. Their food selections may be limited in one way or another, or they may emphasize only certain kinds of food or certain cooking methods.

Other people may elect to follow diets that are currently popular among their friends or that are widely discussed in books, newspapers, and magazines. These diets may be based on only a few foods or on certain kinds or combinations of foods. Many such diets are nutritionally unsound and can lead quite rapidly to deficiencies, particularly if followed by young people, children whose bodies are still growing and building bone and muscle, or by pregnant women.

Season

Although the time of year no longer restricts the distribution of foods as it did a hundred years ago, people still tend to eat according to season. We eat heavier meals in the colder months, lighter meals with more fresh fruits and vegetables, in the summer. Similarly, hot foods are more popular in winter, while cold foods are preferred in summer.

Economics

Budgetary limitations may hamper individuals and families when they select foods. In some cases, equipment and storage space may not be adequate for handling all types of foods and/or personal or family income may be restricted. The latter situation often holds true for young adults who are just starting on their own, for retired persons, and for those who have lost their employment as a result of sudden shifts in the national economy.

The meal manager-cook

The individual who plans and prepares meals probably exerts the most influence, directly or indirectly, on the types and variety of foods selected and prepared. Not only are the manager-cook's knowledge and skill involved, but also his or her energy, interest, and enthusiasm.

If the manager-cook has other responsibilities, available time may affect planning, purchasing, and preparing meals. Also, equipment and available storage space, can influence not only the manager-cook's selection of foods, but also the cooking methods used. Often, these two factors require a good deal of ingenuity and improvisation on the manager-cook's part, and knowledge and skill in this area are invaluable.

Other factors

Psychological aspects may be involved in food selection and eating habits, and they may have a very strong effect on the types or amounts of foods eaten. Conversely, they may cause individuals to refuse to eat. Food and food habits are receiving increasing attention and study from psychologists.

Individual life styles and daily schedules also affect food selection. Some families or groups seldom sit down for a meal together, either because their schedules do not coincide, or because they are accustomed to eating out or to eating snacks throughout the day in place of meals. Erratic eating patterns have become increasingly common in recent years, and nutritional intake, in many of these cases, frequently is insufficient for good health—especially among children and young adults. Many older persons, for lack of income or interest, also are eating nutritionally inadequate diets.

Meal patterns

Using a variety of foods will make meals more interesting and enjoyable and will allow greater flexibility and creativity in planning. However, the first aim always must be to provide adequate nutrients daily for all persons for whom the food is prepared. Good nutrition is essential if children and young people are to build strong bones and teeth. In addition, good nutrition provides better resistance to disease, prolongs the years of activity and vitality, and delays the aging process.

Nutritional guides

Over the years, the USDA has developed basic guides to help in planning meals. At one time, a Basic Seven grouping of foods, as shown in Table 15–1, was recommended, with required amounts of each group stated. This grouping separates fruits and vegetables according to their nutrient content, and it includes fat. It later was thought to be too complicated, and a Basic Four grouping (Table 15–2) replaced the Basic Seven. The Basic Four puts all vegetables and fruits in one group and omits fats. In recent years, partly in connection with the concern over the amount of fat in the American diet and its apparent relationship to atherosclerosis, there has been renewed interest in the Basic Seven grouping. Both groupings present some problems, but either one provides help in planning nutritionally sound meals. Refer to Chapter 14 and Table 14–1 (showing the RDA) for additional information about the nutrients in food.

Table 15–1 *The Basic Seven food groups*

Daily quantity	Group
Children, 3–4 C. Adults, 2 C.	Milk and milk products
1 serving	Fruits and vegetables Green and yellow vegetables
1 serving	Citrus fruits or raw cabbage
2 servings	Potatoes, other vegetables, and fruits
1 serving; 1 egg (at least 4 per week)	Meat, poultry, fish, and eggs
3 servings	Bread, flour, and cereal (enriched or whole grain)
Equivalent of 2 T.	Butter or fortified margarine

Table 15-2 *The Basic Four food groups*

Group	Daily quantity	One serving represents
Milk and cheese	Children under 9, 2–3 C. Children 9–12, 3 C. or more Teenagers, 4 C. or more Adults, 2 C. or more Pregnancy, 3 C. or more Lactation, 4 C. or more	1 C. milk (whole or fortified nonfat) 1 C. yogurt 1 oz. Cheddar or Swiss cheese 1¼ C. cottage cheese or 1½ C. ice cream
Meat, poultry, fish, and eggs	2 or more servings	3 oz. lean, boneless fish, poultry, or meat 2 to 3 eggs 4 T. peanut butter or 1–1½ C. cooked dry beans or legumes, when used with partial servings of animal-protein food
Fruits and vegetables	4 or more servings a. 1 serving of citrus fruit or another fruit or vegetable that is a good source of ascorbic acid, or 2 servings of a fair source b. 1 serving, at least every other day, of a good source of vitamin A (dark green or dark yellow vegetable) c. 2 servings of other fruits or vegetables	½ medium-size grapefruit ½ (4½ inches in diameter) cantaloupe 1 medium-size orange ½–¾ C. orange juice ½ C. broccoli or green pepper ⅔ C. strawberries or ¾ C. raw cabbage 1 medium-size apple, banana, or potato ½–¾ C. of all other fruits and vegetables
Breads and cereals	4 or more servings	1 slice whole-grain or enriched bread 1 oz. ready-to-eat cereal ½–¾ C. cooked cereal, cornmeal, grits, macaroni, noodles, rice, or spaghetti

Developing a meal pattern that is custom tailored to the individual, family, or group simplifies the problem of managing meals. The pattern must be flexible enough to meet nutritional requirements, eating habits, and daily schedules. Therefore, it must be worked out with those points in mind, as well as the limitations of money, time, skill, equipment, and interest.

Nutritional requirements

Table 15-3 lists the number of servings and the amount per serving needed daily from each food group. Since each of the foods in each group contains different amounts and combinations of nutrients, using a variety of foods is important, to be sure that all the nutrients are supplied. Other vitamins and minerals are not listed because they are supplied in adequate amounts if the Basic Four is used as a meal-planning guide.

Fats also are omitted from the chart. However, varying amounts of fat are supplied by the milk and meat groups and by vegetable oils used in margarine, salad dressing, and food preparation.

A record can be kept of all foods eaten for several days including the times of day and the individuals who ate them. This record then can serve as the foundation for custom-tailoring a workable meal pattern. Basic nutritional needs can be crosschecked with the information in Table 15-2 and deficiencies corrected, in line with personal preferences, amounts eaten at different times, caloric requirements, and varying daily schedules. Snacks can be planned to fill gaps in the amounts of specific nutrients or to provide extra amounts needed by growing children or very active individuals.

Caloric requirements

When considering meal patterns, the caloric requirements of the individuals concerned also must be taken into account, to ensure that their intake of food

Table 15-3 *Nutrients found in each food group*

Number of servings daily	Food group	Nutrients furnished
MILK AND CHEESE		
Children under 9, 2-3 C.	**Milk** Whole	Calcium Phosphorus
Children 9-12, 3 C. or more	Low-fat Nonfat	Riboflavin Animal protein
Teenagers, 4 C. or more	Yogurt Buttermilk	Vitamin A (whole or fortified) Vitamin D (if fortified)
Adults, 2 C. or more	**Cheeses** Cottage	
Pregnancy, 3 C. or more	Cream Semihard or Cheddar types	
Lactation, 4 C. or more		

Table 15-3 (continued)

Number of servings daily	Food group	Nutrients furnished
MEAT GROUP		
2 or more servings	Meat Variety (liver, kidney) Fish Eggs Poultry	Animal protein B vitamins Iodine (seafood) Iron (especially liver) Vitamins A and D (fish and eggs)
	Dried beans Legumes Nuts	Plant protein Thiamin Niacin
FRUITS AND VEGETABLES		
4 servings [at least 1 serving of (a) and (b) each day]	a. Citrus (oranges and grapefruit), cantaloupe, strawberries, raw cabbage, green pepper, broccoli, Brussels sprouts	Ascorbic acid (Vitamin C) Other vitamins Minerals
	b. Dark green vegetables, leafy vegetables, broccoli, asparagus	Minerals (calcium and iron) Vitamin A Varying amounts of ascorbic acid
	Deep yellow fruits and vegetables	Vitamin A Other vitamins and some minerals in smaller amounts
	c. Root vegetables, corn, peas, and so on, and all fruits	Carbohydrates Minerals Vitamins
	d. Other fruits and vegetables	Vitamins and minerals in varying amounts
CEREAL GROUP		
4 or more servings	Whole grain or enriched	Carbohydrates Thiamin Riboflavin Niacin Minerals, including iron Plant protein in small amounts
	Unenriched	Carbohydrates Very small amounts of B vitamins and plant protein

will not only meet their nutritional needs but also will be in line with maintaining or correcting weight. The calorie content of foods is given in Appendix A.

Tailoring the pattern

Once eating habits and nutritional needs, including calories, are known, a pattern can be made. Tables 15-4 through 15-6 show three patterns and menus as examples, although many others can be developed. The goal is to arrive at a pattern that will work for the family or group and be flexible enough to meet nutritional needs. The breakfast menu in Pattern I may or may not include approximately a quarter of the daily protein and caloric requirement. Chart 15-1 may be used to doublecheck the nutritional planning; if the plan falls short, it must be readjusted until it is sound.

Menu planning

With the custom-tailored meal pattern as a basis, the manager-cook can proceed to plan specific menus keeping a number of aspects in mind.

Individual situations

As mentioned earlier, the individual situation of the manager-cook is probably the key factor in meal preparation. The amounts of time and

Table 15-4 *Meal Pattern I and possible menus*

Meals	Pattern I	Menu for I
Breakfast	Cereal	Oatmeal
	Beverage	Milk
Lunch	Protein	Ground-beef patty
	Fruit	Peaches
	Beverage	Milk
Dinner	Salad	Tossed vegetable salad with tomatoes and mushrooms
	Protein	Cheese-stuffed chicken breast
	Vegetable	Broccoli
	Bread or pasta	Dilled rice
	Beverage	Tea

Meal patterns and menu planning

Table 15-5 *Meal Pattern II and possible menus*

Meals	Pattern II	Menu for II
Breakfast	Fruit	Orange juice
	Protein	Bacon and eggs
	Bread	Whole-wheat toast
	Beverage	Coffee
Lunch	Soup or salad	Almond bisque
	Protein	Chicken salad
	Dessert	Fresh pineapple and strawberries
	Beverage	Milk and coffee
Dinner	Salad	Coleslaw salad
	Protein	Meat loaf
	2 vegetables	Broccoli and baked potato
	Bread or pasta	Whole-wheat roll
	Dessert	Apple crisp
	Beverage	Milk and coffee

energy, the variety of equipment, the available storage space, the manner in which the meal is to be served, all place certain limits on the work. In addition, the manager-cook's degree of skill, interest, enthusiasm, and imagination also will influence decisions about food.

If the manager-cook works outside the home, less time will be available for meal preparation. Therefore, it may be necessary to plan meals according to the time available or to use many prepared or partially prepared foods. If

Table 15-6 *Meal Pattern III and possible menus*

Meals	Pattern III	Menu for III
Breakfast	Bread	Sweet rolls
	Beverage	Coffee
Snack	Beverage	Milk shake
Lunch	Protein	Tuna salad with celery and tomatoes
	Bread	Whole-wheat roll
	Beverage	Milk
Snack	Fruit or Vegetable	Orange
Dinner	Salad	Bulgur and parsley salad (Tabooleh salad)
	Protein	Broiled steak
	Vegetable	Sliced tomatoes and onions
	Beverage	Milk

Chart 15-1 *Nutritional check of meal pattern and menus*

Food group	Number of servings for nutritional adequacy (daily)	Pattern	Break-fast	Snack	Lunch	Snack	Dinner	Snack	TOTAL
Milk or Milk Products	2 (for adults)								
Meat or High Protein	2 or more								
Fruits and vegetables	1 of (a) for vitamin C 1 of (b) for vitamins A and C 2 others (See Table 15-3)								
Cereals and grains	4 or more								

freezer space is available, the cook may prefer to prepare extra quantities of some dishes, freeze them, and use them in later meals.

The amount of energy the manager-cook has must be considered: other demands on energy may be such that meals must be kept very simple. Available equipment and storage also may dictate simple meals, although as skill increases, ways to improvise with equipment are learned. An enthusiastic and interested manager-cook will enjoy planning and preparing food and improvising will be a challenge.

The amount of money the meal manager-cook has for food is a further very important factor. For some individuals, it imposes definite limitations—retired persons on limited incomes are good examples. For other people, cost of food is of lesser significance.

In addition, the serving method will influence or dictate the type of food to be prepared. An at-home luncheon may be very different from a brown-bag lunch; forms of foods for a casual setting may not be appropriate for a formal setting. The manager-cook must consider the individual serving situation to establish the framework for managing and carrying out food plans.

Preparation methods

For variety, include foods prepared by different methods in a meal. Several fried foods or several foods with sauce at the same meal are monotonous. Also, different cooking methods use different equipment, allowing the manager-cook easier time control for proper preparation.

The cook's skill, available equipment, as well as the situation near serving time, must be considered when selecting preparation methods. Proper planning will avoid last-minute problems as the meal is being assembled.

Staying quality

The staying quality, or the *satiety value*, of foods is important in planning meals. Fats and meats are digested more slowly than are other foods, and they stay in the stomach for a longer time. Therefore, they keep the individual from feeling hunger for a longer period—they have a higher satiety value.

Use a high-satiety food at breakfast to avoid the so-called 11 o'clock slump, when people have run low on energy from inadequate food at the day's beginning. For weight control, this may require a readjustment of the calorie content of other meals for certain individuals. A breakfast of fruit, meat, bread, and beverage may contain fewer calories than do doughnuts and coffee.

Flavor

Certain foods seem to go naturally together; others definitely do not. Apple pie and cheese, sweet potatoes and pineapple, fish and lemon, all are foods whose flavors complement one another. Although cheese can be eaten with lemon pie, and sweet potatoes can be served with fish and brown bread, their flavors do not agree, and the combination gives each food less appeal. Using some strong-flavored foods in a meal is desirable, for contrast. A meal of only mild-flavored foods is dull, and many strong flavors will conflict with each other in an unpleasant way. Thinking of the way flavors of different foods will interact will help in working out pleasing combinations.

Contrasts in flavor do much to improve the quality of meals. Highly seasoned foods contrast well with bland foods, as is the case when Spanish or Mexican foods—hot with pepper—are complemented in a meal with bland Monterey Jack cheese, avocado, or a dessert custard. Sweet-sour contrasts add interest to meal flavors; thus fish is served with lemon, and pork is served with or followed by apple, cherry, or rhubarb.

Texture

Soft or smooth foods need contrast with crisp, crunchy ones: soup with crackers or a salad or other raw food, for example. Avoid using the same-textured foods at a meal: cream sauce, hollandaise sauce, Roquefort dressing, and whipped cream in the same meal would be boring, because all these foods have similar texture. Changing the hollandaise sauce to a lemon slice, the Roquefort to French dressing, and/or deleting the whipped cream would improve the texture, as well as the color, of the meal.

Color and shape

Using foods of different colors and shapes adds greatly to a meal's interest and eye appeal. A plate that holds roast-pork slices, cauliflower, and mashed potatoes is very uninteresting—the colors are too similar. Instead, serving sweet potatoes and broccoli or roasted potatoes and green beans with the roast pork would add color to the plate, as well as a variety of shapes.

And, shape is equally important for interest and appearance. In the example given above, cauliflower and mashed potato are similar in color and in shape. The shapes of the suggested substitutions are different, as are their textures, so those vegetables would be even more desirable. In this example, nutritional values of the substituted vegetables are good but would have to be considered with other foods planned for the day.

Temperature

Hot foods should be served hot; cold foods should be served cold. Foods intended to be hot or cold, if served lukewarm have little appeal because of changes in flavor and, often, in texture. Temperature contrast in a meal may be achieved by including one cold food with a hot meal, or one hot food with a cold meal. Soup, salad, or dessert often will furnish this contrast.

Problem areas

The manager-cook should be aware of certain considerations in planning meals:

1. the calorie content of meals
2. the nutritive value of a manufactured food
3. special dietary requirements of any diners

Sugars and alcoholic beverages furnish only calories. And, desserts may be a problem for some, because they too can contain so many calories. To reduce the calorie content of meals, plan a dessert that incorporates fresh fruit and/or milk, with little or no sugar or fat.

Manufactured, imitation, and fabricated foods may or may not furnish nutritive value similar to that of the natural food. The manager-cook must *read the labels* and understand exactly what is purchased.

Special dietary considerations may be necessary for certain members of a group or family. Nutritional value is of utmost importance to the small child or pregnant woman. Short-term illness may require the substitution of appealing, easily digested foods that are high in protein and liquid content. Long-term problems, such as overweight or underweight and diabetes or heart disorders, may require careful planning, so that individual needs may be met from the general meal. In some cases, the meal may need to be

Figure 15–1 *Casual table setting: red and white mat and napkin; daisy and strawberry arrangement; red goblet, white dinnerware, and stainless steel flatware.*

Figure 15–2 *Formal table setting: linen table covering; flower arrangement of roses and gypsophila; sterling silver bowl and flatware; fine china and crystal.*

planned separately, with the advice of a physician, dietitian, or a professional nutrition counselor.

Serving suggestions

The arrangement of the prepared food on the serving dish contributes greatly to appeal and interest. Chops placed on a platter in an orderly fashion, perhaps with a garnish for additional color, are more attractive than if they are simply stacked on the platter in a heap. Take the time to think of appealing arrangements; although at first it is an additional chore, after a few weeks it will become semiautomatic.

A pleasant atmosphere is of utmost importance to the enjoyment of the meal. A very casual table presentation (Figure 15-1) may well be as desirable as a more formal setting (Figure 15-2).

<blockquote>
Orange Onion Salad
Chicken Kiev
Broccoli   Dill Rice
Melon Balls
</blockquote>

The meal could be served with brass and yellow table appointments. The salad, served on butter lettuce, has orange slices, the pale green of the lettuce, and red onion rings. The Chicken Kiev could be served on a round tray with watercress; the broccoli, with a garnish of twisted lemon slices. And the melon balls—honeydew, cantaloupe, and casaba—could be garnished with mint leaves and served in a brass compote or grapefruit shell.

Planning visually pleasing meals can add to the creative expression, pleasure, and satisfaction of the manager-cook, who is faced with the task hundreds of times. And, it can create an enjoyable experience for the diners as well.

Chapter 16 Organization and management of meals

Meal organization and management begins with the selection and arrangement of kitchen equipment and appliances. The organization and management of food buying follows. The production of the necessary meals in the most efficient manner—with the least time and energy—is accomplished only with the realization that excellent meals do not just happen—they are the result of careful preplanning, trial and error, and practice. With practice, the amount of time needed for planning and preparation will decrease, and the whole process will become more automatic as the manager-cook becomes more knowledgeable and efficient.

Kitchen equipment

Large kitchen equipment—range, refrigerator, freezer, and sink—is not considered in this book because of the many factors involved in selection. Information about these items may be found in several of the books listed in the Bibliography. Pots and pans, tools, and the microwave oven will be discussed here.

The number and types of small equipment needed will be determined by the number of people for whom cooking is regularly done, the kinds and quantities of foods prepared, the available storage space, the personal preferences of the manager-cook, the available money, and, perhaps, the type and frequency of entertaining done.

Inexpensive tools and utensils rarely are satisfactory for long use; they tend to break or become distorted after a comparatively short time. Experienced cooks always advise purchasing high-quality small equipment, which will stand up for a long time, perform properly, and be of great help in obtaining successful products. The new manager-cook may have to start with a minimum number of high-quality items because of budgetary limitations and then add items as funds become available; this procedure prevents the need to replace inferior items.

Materials used

The most common materials used for the different types of pans, pots, bowls, and kitchen tools are shown in Table 16–1. No one material is suitable for all purposes and usually the manager-cook's personal preference determines the selection.

Enamelware (iron or steel with a porcelain enamel coating) is not listed in the table. Although it is used for pans and casseroles, it is not always satisfactory. The heavier ware, with a thick coating, gives better performance than do most lighter grades. All enamelware must be handled very carefully, since it chips easily. Protect it from high and low temperatures, and do not clean it with an abrasive. Remove sticky foods by soaking or boiling a baking soda and water solution in pans.

Different types of pans—particularly useful for frying and baking—are available with nonstick linings. Little fat is needed for frying, and baked products do not stick to the pans. However, heat-resistant plastic or wooden tools must be used for stirring foods in most nonstick pans, because metal will scratch the linings.

Pans

Straight or tapered sides, rounded bottom corners, and straight-cut or rolled rims are desirable. Pans with these features perform well and are easy to clean. Top-of-range pans should have flat bottoms (to sit evenly on the burner) and heavy, tight-fitting covers with heat-resistant knobs. Heavy-gauge aluminum pans or stainless steel pans with aluminum-coated bottoms (to distribute heat evenly) perform well for making cream sauces and cream-pie fillings.

Pan handles should be comfortable in the hand and, preferably, be made of material that will stay cool. A handle that is too heavy will throw a pan off balance, and it is likely to tip over on the burner. Handles may be spot-welded, riveted, or screwed to the pan. If fastened with screws, check that the screws can be tightened when the handle works loose with use.

Table 16–1 *Materials used for kitchen utensils and tools*

Material	Use	Heat conduction	Cost	Durability	Significant points
Copper	Pans, pan bottoms, and cores	Best	High	Good	Must be lined with tin or stainless steel and eventually may need relining; very heavy; must be polished often with commercial cleanser or vinegar-salt paste to remove tarnish.
Aluminum	Pressed, cast, stamped; pans, molds, utensils, and trays.	Good	Varies	Good	Light gauges will dent and may not distribute heat evenly; may allow food to burn on; pits and stains may develop after use; darkens, but this is not harmful to foods. To remove darkening, boil a solution of 2 T cream of tartar to each 1 qt water in the pan. Do not use steel wool on polished-aluminum pans. Hand washing recommended because dishwashers darken the metal. Some types of cast-aluminum pans may be heavy.
Cast iron	Pans	Slow to heat but holds heat well.	Moderate	Good	Heavy; will rust if not properly washed and thoroughly dried. To season new pans, coat them with salt-free oil and heat. Abrasives and detergents may be used, but seasoning must be maintained.
Stainless steel	Pans, tools, and bowls.	Poor; better used with copper or aluminum cores or bottoms.	High	Excellent	Resists corrosion and discoloration from foods but may eventually pit; will discolor permanently if used on very high heat or boiled dry; easy to care for; wiping dry avoids water spotting. Saucepans without special bottoms frequently have hot spots.

Glass	Pans, bowls, and casseroles	Slow to heat but holds heat well.	Varies	Depends on care	Some types may crack from sudden change in temperature or sudden shock. Will not stain, pit, or corrode. Abrasives cannot be used on some types; others may be easy to clean. Allow use of lower oven temperatures. Pans used on burners have hot spots.
Glass ceramic	Pans and casseroles	Same as glass	Varies	Same as glass	May be heavy and will break if it is dropped; easily cleaned. Soak in baking soda and water to remove sticky foods.
Wood	Spoons, cutting boards, and chopping blocks.		Varies	Depends on care	Cannot be soaked in water; must be dried well after use. Boards and blocks used to prepare meat and poultry require thorough cleaning after use. Mineral oil may be used to oil some pieces.
Plastics	Measurers and bowls		Varies	Varies	Some types cannot be exposed to heat; others are heat-resistant. Inexpensive grades may distort, dent, or break with use. Most will be scratched by abrasives. Plastics are easy to care for; good grades last well.

Knives

Always buy the best knife the budget will allow. An inexpensive steel knife usually will not hold its sharpness, and a dull knife is dangerous and frustrating. Knives with blades made of good-quality carbon steel or high-carbon stainless or vanadium steel are expensive, but their performance and durability warrant the expense. Different types of knives are needed for different food preparation techniques: the right knife for each task will save the cook much time and exasperation. Properly cared for, good knives will last indefinitely and always perform well.

Knife construction is very important. The blade should extend the full length of the handle, so that the two pieces of the handle fit smoothly over it. The handle sections should be riveted together, so that the blade extension between them holds the blade firmly in position. Large knives also should have a finger guard.

A good sharpening stone is required to maintain the cutting edge of knife blades. To avoid an accidental cut and to protect the sharp blades, store knives separately, not with other kitchen tools. The safest practice is to wash and dry a knife after each use, and then return it to its storage place, out of the way but ready for use when needed.

Measurers

Measuring cups and spoons must have accurate markings to ensure correct ingredient proportions. Stainless steel or glass measurers are satisfactory; plastic measurers are likely to become distorted or bent.

Turning and stirring tools

These tools—spatulas, spoons, scrapers, and so on—take very heavy use, and must be strong and well made. Heat-resistant handles that are well fastened to the metal are best. Stainless steel, although more expensive, is considered to be the best material for these implements.

Beating and blending tools

Good-quality stainless steel whisks with securely fastened wires may be used for a variety of tasks, including whipping egg foams, thin batters, and sauces and gravies. Some people prefer a stainless steel rotary egg beater for beating egg foams and thin batters.

Miscellaneous tools

Sifters, strainers, egg slicers, graters, and many other tools may be required and can be purchased over time, depending on the quantity and types of foods prepared frequently. In all cases, however, check the materials and construction of each tool.

Small electrical appliances, such as blenders and mixers, can be very useful. However, be sure there is a real need for them: these are too expensive to be left idle on a shelf.

A list of basic kitchen pans and tools (and items to be added) is given in Appendix C. The number and kind needed will vary according to personal preference and, ultimately will be determined by the individual situation.

Microwave ovens

These ovens use the radiation from short electromagnetic waves to cook food. Microwaves cause water molecules in food to move so rapidly that heat is generated and the food is cooked.

A microwave oven is primarily a supplement to the usual cooking methods; it does not replace the conventional oven. In addition, some foods when cooked by microwave do not have the same desirable characteristics as they do when cooked by conventional methods, so different standards for judging their quality may be needed. And since microwaves cook food more rapidly than conventional methods do, different sequences in meal preparation often must be worked out.

Uses Many foods are prepared successfully by microwave cooking. In fact, fresh apples, asparagus, corn, green peas, and winter squash, and frozen vegetables, if properly prepared, may be more desirable when cooked by microwave than when cooked by another method. Meats, poultry, seafood, sauces, and gravies also can be cooked successfully. Their texture and flavor may be satisfactory, but the products may not have the same appearance as those cooked by conventional methods. The brown color may be missing. Therefore, different characteristics may be used for evaluating foods cooked by microwaves. Otherwise, coloring agents, such as soy sauce and caramelized syrup, may be used to create a satisfactory appearance, or the food may be browned by a conventional burner or oven.

Some foods develop undesirable flavor, texture, and toughness if cooked in a microwave oven. For example, toasting bread is more satisfactorily done by conventional methods. And angel food cake tends to be tough unless great care is taken.

Safety In using a microwave oven, the main precautions to take involve checking the door seal regularly and following the instructions in the manufacturer's manual. In addition, the FDA has suggested the following tips.[1]

1. Follow the manufacturer's manual for recommended operating procedures.
2. Examine the oven before use, for evidence of shipping damage.
3. Never insert metal objects (wire, for example) through the door grill or around the door.
4. Never tamper with the safety locks in any way.
5. Never operate an empty oven.
6. Have the oven serviced regularly by a qualified serviceman for signs of wear, damage, or tampering.
7. On models made before October 1971, switch off the oven before opening the door. Stay an arm's length away from the front of the oven while it is on.

Advantages and disadvantages The manager-cook's schedule and personal preference determine the advisability of purchasing a microwave oven. Time may or may not be a factor. Although foods cook faster in a microwave oven than they do with conventional methods, cooking time does increase as the volume of food increases. Also, since successful cooking may involve special attention, in some cases more time is involved in microwave cooking than is involved in conventional-method cooking. For example, if several foods are being cooked at the same time in a microwave oven, it may be necessary to move them about during cooking, to allow the microwaves to penetrate the foods enough to cook them. In some cases, this additional time could be a disadvantage for the manager-cook. However, performance varies among the different models available, and the oven programming determines the amount of attention that the different foods require.

1. "Facts About Microwave Radiation," FDA 72–8017, rev. ed. (Washington, D.C.: Food and Drug Administration, September 1971).

Consideration also must be given to the containers used in these ovens. The substance from which a container is made, its color, size, and shape—all affect the microwaves' penetration of the food. Metal containers are not desirable: they deflect the microwaves. Clear glass is satisfactory: the microwaves easily can pass through the glass. China, plastic, and earthenware also may be used, although the thickness of some earthenware may slow down the cooking process.

Kitchen arrangement

The exact arrangement of all equipment in a kitchen is a highly individual matter, based on the number of individuals who regularly use the kitchen, the amount of space and money available, the life style and habits of the group concerned, and the personal preferences of the manager-cook. However, there are several basic guidelines, and the first rule is to locate equipment in the area in which it is first used.

The kitchen often is considered to have three main work centers: preparation area, cooking area and cleaning area. Many kitchens also have areas for planning and for eating. Ideally, each area has sufficient storage space for the equipment and foods or other supplies used in the area, and the kitchen has additional storage space for items used less frequently. However, in today's smaller houses and apartments, many compromises must be worked out for individual situations, since space allotted for the kitchen may be minimal.

Preparation area

This section of the kitchen includes:

1. counters, cupboards, and, perhaps, the refrigerator and freezer
2. measuring and mixing equipment, bowls, and possibly, baking pans
3. frequently used foods, such as flour, sugar, and other baking supplies

Ideally the preparation area also will be near the sink, so that knives, chopping boards, vegetable scrapers, and colanders will be stored near the place of use.

Cooking area

The range is the central feature in this area with counter space and storage areas nearby. The storage areas provide room for:

1. Fry pans, griddles, and other top-of-range pans
2. cooking tools, wooden spoons, forks, and tongs
3. oils, salt, and other seasonings (these also may be stored in the mixing area)

Some cooks find a teakettle of water on the range saves steps and time, especially if pans are not stored near the sink.

Cleaning area

Sink, counters, and dishwasher (if present) are the main items here. Store soap, detergents, cleansers, and dishtowels near the sink. Since dishes are washed here steps may be saved if they are stored near this area. In some situations they are conveniently stored in the dining area.

Planning area

If the kitchen space permits, a planning area is very convenient. Keep cookbooks, food magazines, paper for notes for marketing lists, and other materials in this area.

Reorganization of work areas

Many kitchens can be improved by a simple relocation of utensils and equipment. One way to check the efficiency of the kitchen is to draw a model of the kitchen on a large piece of cardboard, putting thumbtacks in the board at each work center. Then, plan a quick, easy menu and think through the entire sequence of preparation for each food. As you think through the sequence, use a long piece of string and catch it behind the tack in each center as the sequence moves you to and from a center—from sink to stove, or from preparation area to cooking area. The string will crisscross back and forth, tracing your trips as you prepare the food.

When the process is complete, leave the string in place and consider whether or not some of the trips back and forth could be eliminated if certain foods or equipment were stored in different locations. If you feel that this is the case, relocate those items in the new places, and then repeat the preparation process in your mind, using another piece of string for the board. When you have worked the meal through again, remove the string and measure it against the first string. A shorter second string means that time and steps have been saved. Often, these simple relocations can save many steps and much time, especially when you consider the number of meals prepared each day, week, month, and year.

Food buying

The manager-cook also, in a very real sense, is a buyer who may spend a very substantial amount of money for food over the months and years. Depending on his or her knowledge and skill, a varying percentage of this sum may represent a poor investment or a total loss. A great many manager-cooks could save significant amounts of money in a few years, without sacrificing good nutrition or meal quality, by consistently practicing wise selection and using all the food that has been purchased.

Basic knowledge needed

In order to arrive at this happy state of affairs, the manager-cook needs serveral types of information, which must be turned into knowledge that is used constantly and kept current by addition of new information and details as sources change. The information should include a knowledge of the following:

1. *Basic nutrition and food sources of the nutrients.* The manager-buyer who knows the nutritional value of foods will choose the most economical source of a nutrient on a given shopping day. For example, grapefruits and oranges will be a wise choice for a source of vitamin C in one season, but at other seasons strawberries or cantaloupe will be a better choice. The informed manager will know that vegetables lose nutrients more rapidly when they are cut into many small pieces and held for a time and probably will not buy a cellophane bag of shredded cabbage for coleslaw. This manager will purchase a good fresh cabbage and prepare the coleslaw at home, just before serving time—providing better nutrition for less money.

2. *Forms of food and their costs.* The manager-buyer who knows that green beans are available fresh (whole), frozen and canned (whole and straight- and French-cut), can select the best type of green beans at the best price for the intended use. This buyer also will be sure to use the amount purchased.
3. *Labels.* The wise manager-buyer will read labels on all containers for information on grade, weight, measure, servings, ingredients, and the packer or distributor. (For additional information, see the section on food labeling in Chapter 14.) He or she will check the nutritional label, if available, and also will know that ingredients are listed in the order of their predominance by weight in the product and understand the nutritional and cost differences indicated by this order of listing.
4. *Usual and seasonal fluctuations in costs of foods.* The food buyer who knows that prices of different foods vary according to season and to supply and demand can know whether an advertised special really is a bargain or is just intended to draw people into the store. This buyer will know the difference between well-priced lean stewing beef and low-priced fatty stewing beef. This buyer also will know to stock up when a brand of canned food that has been satisfactory is on special, but will remember to use caution if the special is a brand of unknown quality.

Knowledge of alternatives

While this range of information is being assembled, a full understanding of certain alternatives should be recognized. Once the manager-buyer is aware of these alternatives and the options they offer, choices based on the individual situation can be made for the wisest use of time, energy, and money. Because the alternatives involve choice, they can be thought of in terms of *which*: *which* store to use; *which* day and time to shop; *which* grade, form, and quantity of food to buy; or, indeed, *which food* to purchase.

Store The number and kind of food store vary with community size, but many food buyers have several different types of store within a reasonable distance.

1. *Supermarkets* stock hundreds of food items. They may be owned by a huge national chain, a local-area chain, or one individual.
2. *Discount food stores* emphasize low prices.
3. *Neighborhood convenience stores* carry small stocks of a limited range of foods.

4. *Specialty stores* may carry only certain kinds of food, such as produce, meats, dairy products and eggs, or fish and shellfish, or emphasize top quality and more expensive forms of all foods.

Prices in the different stores vary. Supermarket prices usually are comparatively low, based on the lower cost of purchasing huge quantities of food. However, variations are found not only among the chains but even among stores in the same chain and in the same general area. The food buyer must investigate and keep track of trends and variations in such stores. These large supermarkets usually carry products from different processors, and most carry both national brands and their own private (house) brands. The latter usually are priced a cent or two lower than the same product with a national brand label.

Discount markets often offer lower prices than do other stores, but the prices of all items in the store may not be lower. Knowledge of price trends and local costs may be valuable when shopping in discount food markets.

Prices in convenience stores usually are considerably higher than are those in supermarkets and discount stores, because convenience stores generally are limited in volume purchasing and sales. Specialty store prices almost always are higher than are prices in the other stores, but again variations can be found. However, the quality of the foods offered may be higher than that found in other stores. Many specialty stores emphasize top grades and imported foods.

The food buyer on a limited budget or one who is concerned with getting the most value for the money must be aware of price variations in the area. It is essential to compare prices, quality, and forms of food, so that the best choice may be made. For example, if a certain market consistently has lower prices on canned foods that the buyer knows are satisfactory, it may be wise to shop there when the market lists calls for many items of canned foods.

Day and time Most food stores advertise specials for certain days of the week. These specials may be the result of the stores' good buying or they may be regular items priced lower to draw customers into the store. In some cases, specials may be merchandise of a brand unknown to the food buyer, in which case a question of quality may arise. However, shopping on these days may be very advantageous. In some areas, it may be wise to know the days on which the store receives its supplies of produce and fish or any other item where freshness is of particular importance.

As mentioned earlier, the food buyer must be able to decide whether or not the items offered as specials really are bargains. Here knowledge of current prices in the area, nutrition, labeling, and food preference must be applied. A lower price may be no bargain if quality or nutritional content is less than that of a regular-priced product; if all the food will not be eaten, the money will be wasted.

Always check specials in the store: not all specials are advertised. Sometimes, an unexpected shipment of perishable fruits or vegetables is received. Often, the buyer can substitute equally nutritious special items in meal plans at a saving.

If at all possible, shopping is best done when the store is not crowded and the buyer is neither hungry nor in a hurry. Avoid hasty choices and tempting-looking items. Read the labels, consider substitutions, and determine the cost per serving to make the best choice intelligently and without pressure.

Grade Top-grade, expensive foods are very rarely needed, even for most top-quality products. In fact, lower grades of equal nutritive value may result in a better finished product. For instance, for peach cobbler flavor is important, not near-perfect shape and color. A Waldorf salad made from large, Grade-A apples will not taste better than a Waldorf salad made from top-quality smaller, less expensive apples; rib roast will not make as tasty a beef stew as will a more flavorful, less expensive chuck roast.

The wise buyer selects the right grade and quality for the intended use. Selecting the quality needed in canned and packaged foods may involve some record keeping until the differences among products are known. Making a card file of brands used with comments noted on the card is one way to develop this knowledge. Another way is to buy two different brands or grades and compare the quality with others previously checked, and enter notes on a form similar to the one shown in Chart 16–1. Next time, buy a third product to compare with the preferred brand or grade. Usually, this procedure need be done only once or twice unless new products become available or brands change.

Form The form—fresh, frozen, or canned—in which a food is purchased affects its cost, and the food buyer must rely on knowledge of seasonal and local supplies, costs of the different forms, per serving costs, acceptable substitutions and alternatives, and personal preference.

For example, canned and frozen asparagus are available year-round at different prices. But, if asparagus is grown locally for market in the spring, large supplies may make fresh asparagus a better buy than are frozen or canned. Similar fluctuations in price occur for eggs, poultry, meats, fruits, and

Chart 16–1 Comparison of quality of different brands of food

Name Product	Serving size	Number of servings	Total cost	Cost per serving	Appearance	Consistency/texture	Taste/flavor	Quality 3—excellent 2—good 1—poor	Acceptable for use in	Comments
PRODUCT										
BRANDS										
PRODUCT										
BRANDS										
PRODUCT										
BRANDS										

other foods. The wise food buyer takes advantage of these pricing shifts and makes heavy use of foods when they are abundant, lower in cost, and frequently of higher quality and flavor. Conversely, when such foods are scarce or high priced, they may be used sparingly or omitted, or frozen or canned forms selected. Obviously, a knowledge of geography, climate, and locally grown crops are important here, and significant savings and superior nutritional value may be obtained by applying such knowledge.

Form also applies to such products as sliced or grated cheese, bread crumbs and croutons, and other prepared and partially prepared foods. This aspect will be considered in Chapter 18.

Quantity The general rule is: buy only the amount of food that can be used within a reasonable time and for which proper storage space is available. Highly perishable foods, such as poultry, fresh fish, meat, and some vegetables and fruits, are best purchased in quantities that will be used within four or five days. On the other hand, if freezer space is available, it may be desirable and convenient to purchase a large quantity of a particular food when prices are very low and to freeze them for use at a later time.

Other foods with longer storage life, often called *staples*, may be purchased in larger quantities if space for storage is available. Flour, sugar, potatoes, onions, pastas, legumes, and some other foods are included in this group. In all cases, however, the food buyer will be wise to keep the storage life of such foods in mind and avoid overbuying.

Food preferences of the group to be served must be considered. Thus, purchasing a 10- or 20-pound bag of flour could be sensible for a large group that enjoys homemade breads and that has extensive storage space. A 2-pound bag might be in order for a couple who prefers commercially made bread, never eats cakes or pies, and has an efficiency kitchen with very little storage space.

However, most foods cost less per unit of measure in large containers or quantities. For example, milk usually is cheaper per quart when bought by the half-gallon or gallon; ready-to-eat cereals are cheaper when purchased in a large box than in serving-sized small boxes. In the latter case, a single serving may be more convenient, but the food buyer should weigh the additional cost against actual need. If cereals are eaten frequently and can be properly stored, the extra cost of the individual wrapping represents money wasted. If the contents of a large economy package cannot be used within its shelf life, the waste may be more expensive than is purchasing the individual packages.

All these different kinds of information cannot be gathered overnight. Effort is required to collect it and to shape it into the pattern of knowledge needed for constant reference. As one develops the habit of learning and remembering the different points and aspects, the process becomes much easier and less effort is involved. Some manager-buyers find the process a challenge to their ingenuity and creativity; others find it a chore. The second group often becomes very capable simply because they view the whole process as a necessary evil, and their skill helps them to accomplish the goal of nutritionally sound meals at lower cost without unnecessary delays.

The market list

Ideally, the manager-buyer never sets out to shop until the market list has been thought out and written down in detail. Using a well-organized, complete list saves time and energy by ensuring that all ingredients are on hand for preparing the planned meals. It also prevents frustration and the need to make last-minute changes in meal preparation. Further, a complete list helps the buyer to ignore unneeded, but appealingly merchandised, products.

A market list can be made on a card or on a sheet of paper quite easily by starting at the corners and edges. Use each corner or section for a different category of food. For example, the first entries in the list shown in Chart 16-2 are butter, lettuce, coffee, pork chops, plastic wrap, and orange juice. Add additional entries directly above or under, keeping the categories separate. Then, each type of item can be selected in the different sections of the market without retracing steps.

List entries are based on needed staples and items necessary for meal plans made for the week or other time period. If the buyer feels that substitutions may be desirable or required for particular items, a question mark or other notation can be made beside those entries or possible alternatives may be noted.

Once in the market, the food buyer can proceed from section to section,

Chart 16-2 *A sample market list*

1 lb. butter	1 head lettuce	1 lb. coffee
1 qt. milk	2 grapefruits	1 can tomatoes, stewed
	1 bag spinach	1 pkg. dry milk
		1 qt. ice cream
1 lb. ground beef	liquid detergent	1 pkg. frozen peas
2 pork chops	plastic wrap	2 cans orange juice

locating and deciding on purchases with a minimum of unnecessary delay. Unexpected specials can be thought over and any changes in meal plans made on the basis of knowledge of all needs.

Most supermarkets arrange foods for psychological effect, a fact that many people do not realize. Necessities, such as breads and dairy products, frequently are placed near the back of the market. Fresh fruits and vegetables have great appeal, so they often are displayed in the first section of the store. It is more logical to begin shopping in the meat section, because substitutions made there may require selection of different produce than that on the market list. Selecting the meat first, therefore, may save the buyer from having to return to the produce section to exchange earlier selections for others more suited to the substituted meat.

The food buyer also meets marketing psychology face-to-face when waiting in line at the check-out counter. All those little colorful items stacked around the counter are planned to attract and tempt the unwary buyer who has nothing to do but wait. The wise buyer will ignore these items unless the list chances to call specifically for one of them—perhaps, razor blades or transistor batteries.

Once home, the shrewd food buyer will properly store and use all the foods purchased. Barring unexpected guests or an emergency, he or she will avoid trips to the market—and a well-stocked cupboard and a creative manager-cook may even take care of such emergencies.

Store to storage

It never is wise to delay the return home after shopping. Prompt attention to foods and their correct storage retains flavor, texture, and quality. Avoid letting frozen foods thaw or allowing meat, fish, and other highly perishable foods to become too warm. In hot weather, never leave perishable foods in a closed car. When possible, it is best to do marketing last, so that the foods are taken home without delay.

Meal management

To assemble the different dishes for a meal so that all are ready to serve at the same time requires extensive organization. With experience, the new cook learns how to manage all the details and the process becomes semiautomatic. The skill can be developed by looking at the overall job of serving a meal and

Organization and management of meals 283

then making out and using a time chart and a work chart for it. After the meal, a careful evaluation will pinpoint the areas that need refinement and improvement. As the process is repeated, expertise develops, all the details fall into place, and a meal can be assembled with comparative ease. Paper planning and evaluation then need be done only for special or festive meals.

Organizational planning

The steps used in planning the preparation of a meal can best be illustrated by using an example. Let us assume that food is in the kitchen and equipment is available to prepare the following meal for two persons:

Broiled Meat Loaf
Asparagus   Buttered Potatoes
Spinach Salad with Walnuts
Strawberry Tart
Milk or Tea

First read the recipes (pages 283–288) to determine the tasks and to estimate the time needed for each one. Then, list the tasks and the times required on a worksheet like the one shown in Chart 16-3 (page 286). For this example, the listing (Chart 16-4) (page 287) shows that preparation for this meal must begin about two hours before serving time. Suppose that you do not have the two hours to give on that day. There are three choices: partially prepare some of the foods the night, morning, or day before; have someone assist in preparing the food; or simplify the menu.

Broiled Meat Loaf

1½ lb. ground beef
⅔ C. milk
½ C. fine dry bread crumbs
3 T. chili sauce
½ C. onion, finely chopped
1½ t. salt
¼ t. pepper
½ C. barbecue sauce   *(continued)*

1. Combine ground beef, milk, bread crumbs, chili sauce, onion, salt, and pepper; mix well.
2. Pack into an oiled 5- or 6-cup ring mold. Chill thoroughly, if possible.
3. Loosen meat loaf with spatula; unmold on broiler rack or ring of aluminum foil placed on rack of broiler pan. Cut holes in foil to allow juice to drain.
4. Broil 6 inches from heat for 20 to 25 minutes. Cover loosely with aluminum foil if meat begins to overbrown.
5. Brush with barbecue sauce and broil an additional 5 minutes.

Asparagus

1 lb. asparagus
4 C. water
1 t. salt
1 T. butter

1. Wash asparagus and snap or cut off the lower part of the stalks.
2. Place water and salt in a saucepan and bring to a boil.
3. Add asparagus and cook 8 to 12 minutes, or until tender.
4. Drain thoroughly and add butter.

Buttered Potatoes

3 C. water
½ t. salt
4 small potatoes (well shaped)
1 T. butter
2 T. parsley, chopped

1. Place water and salt in small saucepan and bring to a boil.
2. Peel potatoes and add to boiling water. Cook 20 to 25 minutes or until tender.
3. Remove pan from heat and drain water from potatoes.
4. Add butter and return pan to burner to evaporate all water and to coat potatoes in butter.
5. Sprinkle with chopped parsley.

Spinach Salad with Walnuts

1 bunch (about ⅓ lb.) raw spinach, washed and dried
¼ C. red onion, sliced into thin rings
¼ C. walnuts, coarsely chopped
⅛ C. white raisins
½ small lemon, juice of
⅛ C. olive oil
salt and pepper
pomegranate seeds

1. Remove stems from spinach. Chop leaves coarsely and chill.
2. Combine spinach, onion, walnuts, and raisins.
3. Combine lemon juice, olive oil, salt, and pepper; toss with spinach mixture just before serving.
4. Garnish with pomegranate seeds.

Cookie-Dough Pastry

2 C. flour	2 t. lemon rind, grated
3 T. sugar	¾ C. margarine
½ t. salt	1 egg

1. Using an electric mixer or your fingers, mix flour, sugar, salt, lemon rind, and margarine until margarine is coarsely blended in.
2. Add egg to flour mixture, and mix to a smooth dough.
3. Place in plastic bag and chill about 1 hour.
4. On floured cloth, roll to a thickness of ⅛ inch to ¼ inch.
5. Roll dough over rolling pin and place in flan pan.
6. Bake in 176.7°C (350°F) oven until pastry is just beginning to brown, about 20 minutes.

Strawberry Tart

Crème Pâtissière

½ C. sugar
3 egg yolks

Chart 16–3 *Tasks, listed in descending order of time required*

Recipes or task	Total time (in minutes)

⅓ C. flour
1 C. milk, scalded
½ T. butter
1 T. vanilla

1 recipe Cookie-Dough Pastry, baked in shell
1 pt. basket strawberries, washed and hulled
½ C. currant jelly

1. To make Crème Pâtissière, beat together sugar and egg yolks.
2. Beat in flour.
3. Beat milk into egg mixture and return to heavy-bottom saucepan. Cook over moderate heat until mixture begins to bubble.
4. Lower heat and cook 1 to 2 minutes. Stir constantly with a rubber or wooden spatula to prevent scorching.
5. Remove from heat, and beat in butter and vanilla.
6. Cool.
7. Spoon mixture into baked cookie-dough shell.
8. Arrange strawberries, whole or cut in half, over cream filling.
9. Warm currant jelly over low heat, and brush or spoon over strawberries to glaze.

Chart 16–4 *Recipe time chart*

Food or task	Preparation, including cleanup	Cooking, including cleanup	Serving	Total time
Meat loaf	15 min.	30 min.	5 min.	50 min.
Asparagus	8 min.	12 min. plus 5 min. to bring water to boil	—	25 min.
Potatoes	5 min.	25 min.	—	30 min.
Spinach salad	7 min.	—	4 min.	16 min.
Salad dressing	5 min.			
Strawberry Tart				65 min.
Shell	30 min.	20 min.		
Filling	15 min.	15 min.		
Berries	5 min.	—		
Glaze	2 min.	2 min.		
Assemblage	13 min.	—		
Setting table	10 min.			10 min.
Making beverage	5 min.			5 min.
TOTAL	2 hours			

After some thought, Strawberry Parfait, a very quick dessert, is chosen instead of the tart. Enter the change in the listing (Chart 16-5). Now, the time required to prepare the meal is just one hour.

Strawberry Parfait

1 pt. basket strawberries, washed, hulled, and sliced
2 T. sugar
1 pt. vanilla ice cream

1. Gently toss together strawberries and sugar.
2. In a tall glass, alternate layers of ice cream with strawberries. Store in freezer until serving time.

Chart 16-5 *Revised recipe time chart*

Food or task	Preparation, including cleanup	Cooking, including cleanup	Serving	Total time
Meat loaf	15 min.	30 min.	5 min.	50 min.
Asparagus	8 min.	12 min. plus 5 min. to bring water to boil.	—	25 min.
Potatoes	5 min.	25 min.		30 min.
Spinach	7 min.	—	4 min.	16 min.
Salad dressing	5 min.	—	—	
Strawberry parfait	5 min.	—	5 min.	10 min.
Setting table	10 min.	—	—	10 min.
Making beverage	5 min.	—	—	5 min.
TOTAL	1 hour			

Next, make out a clock-time schedule. This involves setting the times at which you will do the different tasks. This evaluation and sequencing of tasks is the best way to dovetail them. The clock-time schedule for this meal is shown in Chart 16–6. The broiling time required for the meat loaf indicates that it should be prepared first and put in the broiler; the potatoes are prepared and set to cook next, since they also require a certain period for cooking. The remaining tasks are scheduled afterward, with setting the table and readying the serving dishes worked into an empty 10 minutes.

In some cases, it may be necessary to change more than one dish in a meal to arrive at a schedule that fits the available time. In other cases, it may be possible to prepare a dish earlier in the day or the day before, and refrigerate it until serving time.

Evaluation

After the meal, or perhaps the next morning, think over the meal—its preparation and the finished products. Then, fill out a form like Chart 16–7 to locate any trouble spots. A little study of the filled-in form may show that a particular recipe took longer than expected or presented some kind of problem. If so, both recipe and product may be assessed to pinpoint the snag and work out a solution by noting comments on a sheet of paper under the headings shown in Chart 16–8. Notes can be made on the same paper to serve as a reference the next time the recipe is used. If a specific solution does not appear, it may be that more time should be allotted for preparation or other recipes selected when planning menus.

These procedures may be followed as frequently as the manager-cook may wish. In a comparatively short time, however, all the steps may not be necessary because previous experience helps the cook in all aspects and dovetailing of task and timing will become automatic.

Chart 16-6 *Worksheet*

Meal manager–Cook _____ Assistant _____

Clock-time schedule

Actual clock time to begin	Recipe or task[a]	Assistant check
6:30	Mix meat loaf and shape to bake	
6:45	Bake meat loaf, prepare salad ingredients	
6:51	Prepare potatoes	
6:56	Cook potatoes	
6:59	Prepare asparagus	
7:07	Start water for asparagus to heat	
7:08	Prepare strawberries and store in refrigerator	
7:12	Cook asparagus	
7:13	Set table and set out serving containers	
7:20	Prepare beverage	
7:24	Drain asparagus and add butter; drain potatoes and toss with parsley and butter	
7:26	Toss salad	
7:30	Serve dinner	

[a] Place a check by item your assistant is to do.

Chart 16-7 *Evaluation of meal*

Kitchen organization?

Menu nutritionally balanced?

Aesthetically pleasing menu?

1. Color? _____

2. Flavor? _____

3. Texture? _____

4. Form? _____

Quality of prepared foods?

Serving method satisfactory?

Comments and thoughts for improvement:

Chart 16–8

Evaluation of

Was preparation method correct?

Was product ready on time?

Was it served at correct temperature?

Was too much or too little prepared?

Problem or trouble spots:

Possible solutions:

Chapter 17 Table appointments and meal service

A century ago, many houses had large kitchens, separate dining rooms, and pantries that provided storage space for foods, kitchen equipment, and the table appointments that were not used regularly. Large sideboards or cabinets in the dining room were used to store table linens and flatware. Many households had servants, and the work of planning, preparing, and serving meals often was the responsibility of more than one person.

Today, large kitchens, pantries, and separate dining rooms are increasingly rare, as houses and apartments become smaller and storage space, more limited. Many dining areas are adjacent to or at one side of the kitchen; other dwellings are arranged so that meals are eaten at one end of the living room. Counters designed for eating, with chair stools that slide underneath out of the way, often are used in both houses and apartments. Whatever the space arrangement may be, the tasks of the meal manager-cook usually include the details of arranging the table and serving the meals. Time, space, life style, and individual preference usually determine the table appointments and the meal service used.

The emphasis in today's world on being one's self influences the manner in which foods are presented. This individual expression may include table appointments and meal service. The guidelines are based on logic, orderliness, and convenience. These are the same guidelines on which table settings and service were originally established.

Table appointments

Tablecloths, place mats, dinnerware, glassware, and flatware are available in a great variety of materials and patterns, ranging from very simple to elaborate.

Decorative pieces—such as candlesticks and containers to hold floral centerpieces, fruits, or vegetables—are equally abundant.

Tablecloths, place mats, and napkins

These items, traditionally called *table linens*, are now made in many different fibers and combinations of fibers, patterns, and colors. Those that require little or no special care often are selected and may be used for all but the most formal of meals. For convenience or for dramatic presentation, meals also may be served on a bare table.

Tables vary in size and must be measured before a cloth is purchased. A tablecloth should overhang the table's edge by 6 to 10 inches, balancing the appearance of the table. Linen damask cloths, used today only for formal dinners, often have a deeper overhang. Breakfast and luncheon cloths usually are smaller, with less overhang, but individual preference often is the deciding factor. Napkins range in size from 12 to 18 inches square for breakfast and lunch, to the very large, 24- to 27-inch, squares some people prefer for dinner.

If food is to be served at the table, use of a silence cloth or an asbestos pad may be wise to protect the tabletop from hot dishes. A silence cloth usually hangs over the table's edge slightly; an asbestos pad does not.

Color and pattern must be considered, keeping dinnerware and glassware in mind, to avoid conflicting combinations. Patterned cloths and mats with plain dinnerware or plain cloths and mats with patterned dinnerware in pleasing color contrast provide attractive table settings. Color and design allow for creativity and expression of personality.

Dinnerware

The term *dinnerware* includes plates, bowls, cups, saucers, and serving dishes used at the table. Several other terms are used: many people speak of *china* or simply *dishes*.

Kinds Dinnerware may be made of clay in a process that involves *firing* (baking) the pieces at high heat. The firing temperature affects the strength and durability of the dinnerware. Fine china, china, stoneware, fine earthenware, earthenware, and pottery are the different qualities of dinnerware. These types are listed in descending order.

Fine china, sometimes called *porcelain*, is stronger, thinner, and more translucent than are the others. It does not crack or chip easily and is considered to be the best dinnerware. Prices vary but usually are high. *Bone china* is fine china that has had bone ash added to its clay. *China*, or *semiporcelain*, is softer than porcelain, because it is fired at a lower heat. It will chip more readily than will porcelain, but it is quite satisfactory if given reasonable care. *Stoneware* is dense, nonporous, and opaque; it will not chip as easily as will earthenware. Both *fine earthenware* and *earthenware* are thick, porous, and opaque; and they will chip. Earthenwares are fired at relatively low temperatures. *Pottery* is a heavy ware, processed at still lower temperatures than earthenware. It chips and cracks quite readily, and the *glaze* (outer coating) will *craze* (change appearance) easily. *Pyroceram*, a snowy white, hard ceramic, is durable, will not chip, and may be used from refrigerator to range to table. It may break if dropped. *Melamine* plastic dinnerware is light and chip- and break-resistant. In time, this ware will stain from coffee, tea, and other foods, and, even though some stains can be removed, it may look unattractive. Melamine will scratch from abrasives and cannot be exposed to high heat, although it can be put in a dishwasher.

Patterns and colors All types of dinnerware are made in a range of patterns and colors. Gold is used on porcelain and semiporcelain. Shapes vary widely, from traditional to highly stylized, and some dinnerware is designed so that it can be stacked in a comparatively small space. Since dinnerware may be used for many years, careful consideration of pattern and color is needed for continued enjoyment over the years.

Selection Dinnerware is most commonly sold in sets of a certain number of pieces so that the buyer may purchase the quantity needed according to the number of people in the household. Usually sets include enough dinner and salad plates, cups, and saucers for 2, 4, 6, 8, or 12 people. In some cases, a pattern is available both in sets and in "open stock," so additional or replacement pieces may be purchased with the set or at a later time. Some manufacturers offer set patterns in open stock, only at a special sale (perhaps once a year), and extra pieces may be purchased then.

Other dinnerware may be purchased a place setting at a time. A place setting usually includes a dinner plate, salad plate, a cup and saucer, and a bread-and-butter plate. Bowls, serving dishes, creamers, and sugar bowls are purchased separately. As many pieces or settings as are needed can be collected over a period of time.

Durability, cost, storage space, and personal preference—including the shape of the cup and the cup handle—all enter into the decision of which dinnerware to purchase. Since the dinnerware is the background for foods served, color and pattern coordination with other table appointments is desirable. A careful selection of one small set or a harmonizing combination of good quality dinnerware that may be added to and lived with over the years can be both adequate and satisfactory.

Flatware

Flatware is a collective term for the forks, knives, spoons, and serving implements used at a meal. These pieces also are called *table silver,* although silver is not the only metal used in them. Stainless steel, silverplate, and sterling silver are the most commonly used metals for flatware.

Stainless steel flatware is made in a variety of styles and patterns and in several grades. Pieces may be plain or patterned; the handles may be plain or of plastic, wood, or bone. The better grades of stainless steel flatware are very satisfactory, since this metal is durable, easy to care for, and attractive. However, good-quality stainless steel ware is not inexpensive, and it may need to be dried by hand directly after it is washed to prevent water-spotting.

Silverplated flatware is made by coating a metal alloy base with silver. It is produced in different grades, and the better grades have extra plating at wear points, such as the bowls of spoons, and a heavier coating of silver throughout. Good grades of silverplate will last for many years, while the life of the lesser grades varies considerably. Prices vary according to grade.

Sterling silver is nearly pure silver (92.5 percent) with copper added to harden it. The cost of sterling silver is very high, but with care it will last for several generations. Often, sterling silver is handed down from parents to children to grandchildren, and it is a cherished form of flatware.

Sterling silver, like silverplate, must be cleaned fairly often with a special cleanser to remove the *tarnish* (dark discoloration) that forms on its surface. Sterling is more likely to be scratched than is silverplate, and therefore, some people prefer to wash and dry it by hand. Others prefer the *patina* (many minute scratches) that develops over years of use.

Vermeil flatware is goldplate over sterling or stainless steel and is very expensive. It does not tarnish. *Dirlyte,* a gold-color alloy, also does not need polishing but cannot be used in dishwashers. Other novelty flatware—some with wooden, bone, or mother-of-pearl handles—require special care.

Flatware is sold (like dinnerware) in sets, in place settings, or in individual pieces. Many people purchase a minimum of pieces at first and gradually add to them as their budget allows. Comparatively plain patterns are considered a wiser choice than are elaborate ones, because they do not conflict with dinnerware patterns and colors, but they do show scratches more readily. Care, cost, and individual preference are the major determining factors in deciding which type of flatware to purchase.

Glassware

Beverage glasses, plates, bowls, and other pieces made of glass all add greatly to table attractiveness. Good glassware is just as serviceable as is chinaware and may be combined with it as desired. A dessert served in a glass bowl or plate or a few flowers in a glass container in the center of the table add a special touch that is most welcome at any time of year. In summer, a fresh fruit or vegetable salad on a glass plate looks cool and appetizing.

Glassware is made of sand, and lead or lime; it also may have minerals added to give color. Glassware is made in several qualities, ranging from very expensive hand-blown crystal to molded ware, which is moderately priced or inexpensive. Glass made with lime also is inexpensive. Clear and colored glass are available in a wide range of styles and patterns.

When selecting glass, it is best to think of the way it will look with the dinnerware and flatware. Simple patterns in good quality glass or crystal that is smooth and clear usually are considered the wisest choices, since they will harmonize with the other pieces for better effect. For practical reasons, a moderately priced, open-stock pattern for everyday use is desirable.

Fondue pots, chafing dishes, and warming trays

A fondue of cheese, meat, fish, or fruit and cake is an easy way to serve an entrée or dessert. For cheese fondues, use a pottery or ceramic pot set over an alcohol or butane burner on moderate heat. For dipping fruit or cake, use a small pottery or metal pot, over a candle, to keep the chocolate warm. Use a metal pot with sloping sides—to help prevent the fat from splattering—placed over an alcohol or butane burner for heating the oil for beef or fish fondue. Special fondue forks—9 to 10 inches long with insulated handles—and special fondue plates with separate sections for meat fondues are used.

Many meal managers may find chafing dishes convenient for serving foods, especially when entertaining. Chafing dishes may be made of aluminum, brass, copper, silver, and stainless steel. An alcohol burner or canned heat is the source of heat. These dishes are primarily used to keep foods warm. They have a water pan in which the blazer pan (containing the food) is placed and covered, if desired. Electric warming trays with temperature controls are available in different sizes. They also are convenient for holding foods at serving temperature.

Decorative pieces

Many people feel that an attractive decoration of some sort in the center of the table adds a great deal to meals. Almost any decoration of suitable size may be used: a few flowers or some green leaves in a bowl, an arrangement of smooth beach stones and shells on a small tray.

Table decorations for family meals can be made from any number of objects, provided they are clean. Grasses, gourds, a saucer of freshly washed glass marbles, or a first-grader's clay sculpture can be turned into an interesting, attractive decoration. Use table decorations that are low enough not to interfere with conversation. Color and type of centerpieces are selected to coordinate with the dinnerware and other table appointments and also with the menu. For example, daisies, rather than roses, are a better choice for a meal with hamburgers.

For the evening meal and/or special dinners, candle holders of glass, chinaware, or metal, holding tall candles, add appeal to a table. Arranged in pairs or groups, with fat or thin candles—white or colored—candles give a table a festive look and, at the same time, suggest a peaceful, enjoyable meal. The flickering light of the candles should be above or well below eye level of the diners.

Setting the table

Except for very formal dinners, the rules for setting a dining table are not ironclad, they are only guidelines. Settings necessarily vary from meal to meal, depending on the foods served and the family's or group's preferences.

The cover

A place setting, usually called the *cover*, includes the dinnerware, flatware, glassware, and napkin one diner will use to eat the meal. Because people need room to move about as they eat, it is best to allow about 25 inches per cover.

Since the plate is centered on the cover right in front of the diner, flatware is placed on the sides. Usually the forks are placed at the left of the plate, and the knife and spoon(s), on the right. Plate and flatware are one inch from the edge of the table. The pieces of flatware are positioned according to use, as shown in Figures 17–1 a, b, and c. Photograph (a) shows the forks arranged for a meal in which the salad is to be served after the main course. In photograph (b), the salad is to be the first course, so the salad fork is on the far left. In photograph (c) salad is to be served along with the main course.

Forks are placed with tines pointing up; spoons, with the bowls up; and knives, with the cutting edge toward the plate. The napkin usually is placed just to the left of the fork, folded so that the diner can easily unfold it. In other than formal service, the dessert fork or spoon may be placed above the plate, parallel to the table's edge with the handle to the right. When it is located here, the diner is not likely to become confused and use it during the main course. The dessert flatware may be placed with the serving of dessert.

The bread-and-butter plate, if used, is placed just above the fork, with the butter spreader laid at the top of the plate, in the center parallel to the table's edge, or along the plate's right side, perpendicular to the table's edge.

The salad plate, if salad is served along with entrée, is set slightly to the left of and below the bread-and-butter plate. Sometimes the salad plate also is used for bread and butter and, in that case, the dinner knife is used as a spreader and the butter spreader and plate are omitted.

The water glass is placed at the top of the knife and any other glass to its right, slightly closer to the table's edge.

Serving dishes

Dishes of food that are going to be served at the table are placed in front of the person who will serve them. The serving implement is laid to the right of the dish; if two implements are to be used, they are usually placed side by side to the right of the container. If preferred, the serving implements may be laid at the server's cover, to the right of the spoon. When meat is to be carved at the table, the meat platter is placed in front of the server's cover. The carving knife and fork are placed in front of the server's cover, as shown in Figure 17–2.

Serving dishes containing bread or rolls, butter, relishes, and similar food should be placed in a convenient area at opposite ends of the table, to be passed after the main course has been served. Usually, the table decoration is

a

b

Table appointments and meal service 301

c

Figure 17-1 (a) *A place setting indicating the salad is to be served after the main course.* (b) *The salad is the first course.* (c) *The salad is to be served with the main course.*

set in the center of the table, but it may be at one end or side, depending on the number of covers for the meal.

If more than three people are at the table, using extra sets of salt and pepper shakers is very convenient. They may be placed in line with the water goblets.

When dessert is served at the table, all dishes used at the main course are removed. The dessert and serving implements are placed in front of the server's cover, and the serving plates or bowls are placed on the cover.

Buffet table

For a buffet, at which the diners serve themselves, place napkins, flatware, dinnerware, and serving dishes on the table in a logical arrangement. As shown in Figure 17-3, place the serving dishes at convenient intervals with

Figure 17-2 *Dinner table set for a family meal, compromise service.*

Figure 17-3 *A buffet table.*

serving implements beside them. Napkins, flatware, and beverage containers may be on the buffet or set on dining tables if they are used. The table decoration may be centered or at the side of the table, depending on the location of the table.

Service

The meal service used by a family or group depends on the amount of space available, the number of people to be served, the amount of time in which to eat, and the preferences of the members. Generally, a family works out a pattern of serving that suits the members and adapts it, with or without slight change, when guests are present.

Several types of meal service are used in this country, but all may be adapted to the individual situation. All of these presume that meals are eaten at a table and obviously must be altered for meals eaten at a counter.

Plate service

Food is placed on the plates in the kitchen, and the plates are brought to the table, which has been set with the needed flatware, glassware, condiments, and so on. If coffee or tea is to be served with the main course, creamer and sugar bowl also are on the table. The hot beverage may be poured in the kitchen or at the table, as preferred. When the main course is finished, the table is cleared by one of the group, and dessert is served in the kitchen and brought in to the diners.

This service is quick and simple, and works very well if the number of diners is fairly small. If one person clears the table while another places dessert on the individual plates in the kitchen, there is a minimum of delay between courses.

Family service

For this service, the table is set with all needed flatware and glassware, and a dinner plate is set at each place. All serving implements are placed on the table. The food is brought from the kitchen in serving dishes and placed on the table or on a serving cart. The diners serve themselves as the serving

Figure 17-4 *Dessert (lemon curd tarts) and beverage to be served from a cart.*

dishes are passed from person to person around the table. The same procedure may be followed for dessert (Figure 17-4) after the table has been cleared, or it may be served at the table.

Like plate service, this procedure is informal and easy, and many families use it. When young children are at the table, their plates may be served or they may be helped by an older person, particularly if the serving dishes are large and heavy.

Compromise service

The table is set with flatware and glassware, and the dinner plates are stacked at one place. Traditionally, this place was where the father or head of the household sat. Serving dishes are set in front of this place with serving implements. The food is placed on the plates by the server, and the plates are passed from person to person until all at the table are served. Occasionally, salads or desserts are served from the kitchen.

For this service, the table must be large enough to accommodate all the serving dishes. If a roast is carved at the table, there must be adequate room for the platter and the carving knife and fork. The carver needs space to work in and sometimes his or her salad plate and/or glasses may be removed temporarily.

English service

This meal service originally was a formal style in which the head of the household served the meat. A servant carried the plate to the opposite end or side of the table, where the vegetables were served by the hostess. The servant then took the filled plate to a diner, and the process was repeated until all were served.

The traditional procedure often is modified so that two individuals serve the food, and the plates are passed from hand to hand. Dessert usually is served at the table by one individual.

Here again, a table large enough for the serving dishes is needed. If a large number of people are to be served, considerable time may be taken in passing the plates around.

Russian service

For this very formal service, servants, side or serving tables, and adequate space are needed. While it may be used in the home, usually Russian service is practiced only in hotels or restaurants, and, even there, it usually is modified.

The table is set with flatware, glassware, and a place or service plate at each place. Servants or waiters set the smaller plate holding the first course—cold or hot—on the service plate. When the first course is finished, the waiter removes both plates, and the plate containing the next course is immediately set down. The waiter may serve the food to each guest or present the food to each guest to serve themselves. No serving dishes of food are put on the table at any time, since all the courses are brought to the diner by the waiter.

After the salad course, the salad plates are removed from the table, and dessert plates and flatware are laid at each place. The dessert course is then brought in and set before the diners. Finger bowls, placed when the dessert service was laid down or after dessert is served, are used and black coffee, in demitasse cups, is served.

If this service is used in the home for a very formal dinner, trained servants, correct table appointments, and kitchen staff are essential, so no hesitations or delays develop.

Buffet service

This form of service is best used when the number of people to be served is too large for the dining table or too large for the available staff. Very often, informal entertaining uses buffet service, and, when carefully planned, it is comparatively easy.

The serving table is arranged so that the diners start at one point and proceed around the table or to the other end, assembling their food as they go. Plates are located at the starting point, and serving dishes of foods with serving implements are located around the table in logical order. Beverages may be on the same table or on a smaller table in another place to lessen crowding at the main table. Beverages also may be served to guests after they are seated.

If the diners are to hold their plates on their knees while they eat, the food must be planned so that only a fork or spoon is needed. Often trays or small tables are provided when space allows, so that eating is more comfortable. The diners may serve themselves from the buffet or a side table and be seated at the dining table. Foods for this type of buffet also must be easily served, but they may include foods that must be cut.

When the diners have finished the first course, the host or hostess or person assisting usually removes the plates to the kitchen. Individual servings of dessert are brought in and given to the diners. Coffee and tea also may be served individually, if not available with the main course, or the diners may help themselves from a dessert buffet and/or from the beverage table.

Service for outdoor meals

Many Americans are in the habit of eating meals outdoors on a patio, on a terrace, near a fireplace, or by a barbecue pit. For these meals, the food may be cooked indoors or outdoors, or some may be cooked in each location. Depending on preference, table appointments may be those that are used indoors, or plastic or paper ones. Buffet, family, or plate service may be used. If no particular service is used, the meal tends to resemble a picnic.

Outdoor meals also may be served at a table set as for use indoors, with family or plate service used. In hot weather when appetites lag, a meal served on an attractively set table on a shady porch or patio may have more appeal than has one served indoors in the same familiar setting.

Chapter 18 Meals for special situations

Manager-cooks may be faced with planning and preparing meals, week in and week out, for a group of people whose schedules and food needs vary widely. Time for food preparation may be very limited, and the question of using many convenience foods may arise. Income may dictate very careful control of food money. Packed lunches may be needed for convenience or budgetary reasons by members who work. Young children may be included in the group, and their special nutritional needs must be accommodated. Weight control may be necessary by some members. And it also is possible that the manager-cook, having mastered techniques to handle all these different situations, may find cooking a fascinating, rewarding endeavor and be anxious to make wider explorations into cookery.

Time-controlled meals

The key factors in limited-time meal preparation are a thoroughly organized kitchen and carefully thought out plans. Locating equipment according to work areas and good planning will give the manager-cook a fighting chance for success.

Cooking methods

The quickest cooking methods for meat are broiling, pan-frying, and stir-frying. All three methods require tender meat or meat that has been tenderized, for satisfactory results. Steaks and chops (for broiling), breaded veal cutlets (for pan-frying), and boned chicken breasts and fish fillets (for pan-frying or quick poaching) are all comparatively expensive. However, less expensive ground meats can be used for broiling and very thin strips of meat can be used for stir-frying for quick cooking.

Quickly prepared vegetables—fresh, frozen, or canned—usually are planned when time is short. Many salads require very little time, especially if fruits and vegetables that require a minimum of preparation are used. Desserts may be raw fruits and cheese, frappes made from frozen fruit, commercial ice cream or sherbet with fruit sauces, or other quickly prepared dishes.

Collect recipes that require only a short preparation time, and try them out as the need arises. It is helpful to note successful menus and food combinations for future planning use; variations of these basic meals and recipes often can be developed quite easily.

Prepreparation

When food is brought home from the market, many prepreparation steps can be done to save time later. Many vegetables may be washed and dried; some may be prepared for cooking. Wash and remove the stems from spinach, for example, to ready it for cooking and to provide a supply of crisp leaves for salad. Clean, wash, and store asparagus upright in ½ inch water, and it is ready to cook. Salad greens may be washed, dried, and refrigerated, ready to combine as desired.

Depending on when they will be used, citrus fruits and pineapple may be peeled, sectioned, and refrigerated in covered containers. Apples may be washed, dried, and refrigerated or placed in a bowl, to be eaten from the hand.

If a large roast has been purchased to cut into meal-sized sections, the cutting may be done and the pieces stored separately. Whole chicken can be cut up or boned, and it may be frozen—properly wrapped—for later use. Whole fish may be treated similarly.

Preparation of food ahead of time

Depending on the schedule, it may be possible to prepare ready-to-cook- or other foods the day before they are to be served. A few minutes may be found on weekends, evenings after the meal, or in the morning, when a dish can be prepared and then refrigerated, frozen, or stored.

Casseroles, soups, stews, molded salads, and desserts often can be prepared or partly prepared ahead of serving. Often, small amounts of leftover foods in the refrigerator can be used up in these products, avoiding waste. And, some dishes taste better when their flavors have time to blend—potato salad, chicken salad, spaghetti sauces, stews, and some soups are examples.

When a few extra minutes are available, prepare a recipe in a larger-than-needed amount, divide it into meal sized portions, and wrap and freeze it for a later meal. Mixing more than one meat loaf (freezing others for later baking) or preparing and cooking (then dividing and freezing for later use) spaghetti meat sauce will require very little more time than does the preparation of one meat loaf or of one batch of sauce.

Planning to have leftover or plannedover foods for another meal saves money, preparation, and cooking time. Any number of second-meal uses are possible for meats, poultry, and fish. As an example, Figures 18–1 a through d show how three entrées may be made from plannedovers from a large roast turkey. Leftover fruits may be combined with other fruits or used in sauces; leftover stew, with rice added to thicken it, makes stuffing for peppers or tomatoes; and cooked vegetables can be blended with milk or meat stock, for soup.

Plannedovers can be combined with canned products so that the resulting dish has no resemblance to its earlier form. Thus, add a small piece of roast and some gravy to canned soup or combine the roast and gravy with fresh, canned, or frozen vegetables in a casserole. The roast beef and green beans shown in Figure 18–2 a, for example, can be served at dinner one day and then appear in another meal as roast beef salad (Figure 18–2b).

In all cases, whether meals are planned for plannedovers or for new ingredients, the first consideration—despite time limitations—should be the nutritional values of all foods served. Frequent poorly planned or hastily assembled meals without proper nutritional planning are undesirable.

Equipment

Learning to use and make the most of the available equipment saves time. A chopping blade or a pastry blender that is clumsily used will exasperate the cook and slow down meal preparation; and a wire whisk used with a heavy, slow hand will not turn out a light, airy egg-white foam.

Good utensils and tools that perform properly are a great asset to the cook with limited preparation time. Each piece will perform as expected, and no aggravating problems will arise as the work moves along. Good knives, kept sharp, are particularly important, so that no time is lost fumbling about with dull blades.

The more expensive appliances—blenders, pressure saucepans, electric fry pans—may be worth their cost in preparing time-controlled meals. Ovens or slow cookers with timers also may be desirable. However, select foods, cooking times, and temperatures very carefully when using timers, to avoid the development of harmful micro-organisms in the cooked products. The microwave oven may be worthwhile in some situations for quick thawing or cooking. Each manager-cook should consider the service provided versus the cost of these appliances to determine whether or not they are desirable additions.

Convenience foods

Foods that are fully prepared—like brown-and-serve rolls, baked frozen pies, and canned soups—or partially prepared—like cake, pudding, and pastry mixes—are called *convenience foods.* These products are available in a multitude of varieties and forms in every market. In one sense, almost every food is now a convenience food—fruits and vegetables may be frozen, eggs are packed in cartons, and meats are cut, packaged, and wrapped.

Many convenience foods carry an extra cost, that of the "hidden chef"— the skill, time, and energy used to assemble the product from the raw ingredients or to combine ingredients to the particular state in which the product is purchased. In some cases, this extra cost may be very high; in others, it may be insignificant or nonexistent: the product may be processed in large quantities, harvested during peak production, or transported in bulk quantity. The very fancy pastries sold by some bakeries may carry high hidden costs; frozen orange juice concentrate often costs less than does orange juice squeezed at home.

Although it frequently is overlooked, the packaging cost also is included in the price of convenience foods. The price of a ready-to-serve frozen cake includes the cost of the light aluminum foil pan it was baked in, and muffins packed in a plastic tray shaped like a muffin pan are priced to include the tray's cost.

The nutritional values and calorie content of these foods may or may not be equal to that of similar foods prepared at home. In each case, check the label and consider the order of ingredients in the listing.

Using convenience foods saves preparation and, frequently, cooking time, and each manager-cook must consider whether or not the cost balances the time and energy involved. In addition, lack of skill for preparing a wide variety of foods may be a consideration.

a

b

Meals for special situations 313

c

d

Figure 18-1 (a) *Small roast turkey with plannedovers.* (b) *Sliced turkey.*
(c) *Turkey-filled crepes.* (d) *Turkey croquettes.*

Figure 18-2 (a) *Roast beef, baked potatoes, and green beans, planned for more than one meal.*

Dollar-controlled meals

Low-cost meals must and can be as nutritious, interesting, and appetizing as any other meals (Figure 18-3). The manager-cook who is concerned with cost must be more flexible in planning meals, to allow the use of any and all unexpected food bargains. Many manager-cooks who work with limited food budgets serve meals that are nutritionally more sound than are those prepared by persons who have unlimited funds, because they must use their food knowledge to better advantage.

Each group of foods includes expensive forms and forms that are less expensive. A gourmet meal may be prepared by using the less expensive ground beef for the more expensive beef filet (refer to Figure 13-3). The manager-cook must be able to recognize both forms (Table 18-1). The less expensive forms can be used in many recipes with a little adjustment. For example, reconstituted dry milk and margarine can substitute for cream in many sauces, puddings, and pie fillings.

Figure 18-2 (b) *Beef salad, as plannedover meal.*

Planning

In addition to planning meals carefully for a particular number of days, the manager-cook can hold down food costs by:

1. selecting the quality of foods necessary for the intended recipe
2. storing the foods correctly, so that no food spoils
3. purchasing quantities in line with the available storage space
4. using highly perishable foods before those that have a longer storage life (*no food will ever be wasted*)
5. using specials whenever possible
6. using locally grown fruits and vegetables in quantity when they are in season
7. purchasing large quantities of frequently used staples, if storage space permits (assuming a saving over small quantity per unit cost)
8. buying a whole chicken or a large roast, to cut up at home

Figure 18-3 *Beef Roulades, red cabbage, and noodles.*

9. using plannedovers (saving food costs and cooking time)
10. carefully considering convenience foods, in terms of their nutritional value and cost per serving

Convenience items whose cost is less at certain times of the year may be wise buys, but nutritional value for the money must be the determining factor. And, foods that supply only calories and all nonnutritional foods and beverages will be very carefully considered or omitted from the market list for dollar-controlled meals.

Preparing

Once food is purchased and properly stored, every effort should be made to see that none of it is wasted. Prepare only the amounts needed for each meal, unless plannedovers are involved. Promptly use all leftovers in other dishes, or properly wrap and freeze them for later use.

The ability to make different sauces allows for greater variety in low-cost meals. Different flavor combinations can be developed in sauces, to be used

Table 18-1 *Expensive and less expensive food forms*

Food group	Less expensive form	More expensive form
Milk and milk products	Dry milk Evaporated milk Margarine Bulk (American) cheeses	Home-delivered fluid milk Whipped butter Sliced, vacuum-packaged, and imported cheeses
Meat group	Large pieces of meat and poultry (to be cut at home) Beef liver and some other variety meats Poultry, whole Cod Canned, mixed clams Less-tender meat cuts—chuck roast, round steak Ground meat, especially ground meat with soybean extender (TVP) Meat and dry beans or legumes Eggs	Cut-up, ready-to-cook meat and poultry Calf's liver, sweetbreads Poultry, cup up or by sections Salmon Shellfish Tender cuts—rib roast, porterhouse steak, filets Sandwich meats Prepared, ready-to-cook or cooked meats, frozen or delicatessen Frozen scrambled eggs
Fruits and vegetables	In season, locally End of season Canned food sales Market brands of canned or frozen foods Frozen orange juice Frozen, dark green leafy vegetables Bulk carrots	Out of season, locally Name brands of canned or frozen foods Ready-to-use orange juice Frozen vegetables in sauce Carrots with tops Exotic foods
Cereals and grains	Cook-at-home cereals Bulk packages (cereals) Day-old bakery products Boxes of biscuit and pancake mix Bulk packages of rice	Ready-to-serve cereals Individual packages (cereals) Ready-to-serve bakery products Specialty breads Frozen, heat-and-serve waffles and breads Seasoned or partially cooked rice

with plannedovers or with foods served for the first time. Often a dish that is not one of a group's or family's favorites can be improved with a good sauce.

Increasing knowledge

The more the manager-cook can learn about the options available in purchasing and preparing food, the better the meals prepared will be. All food sources in the community should be investigated and reevaluated periodically. Large urban areas may have a farmers' market where produce can be purchased at low prices, and, in some sections of the country, consumers have formed food co-ops, which may offer savings in cost of foods purchased. Such savings, however, depend on the skill and expertise of the individuals who purchase food for the co-op.

Many local libraries have a wide range of cookbooks and other books about food. Extension-service home economists can advise about food matters generally or specifically. Federal and state governments provide bulletins, pamphlets, and reports about food. Daily newspapers often have special food-related features and articles. Additional information may be obtained by attending classes of community and state colleges.

Food to go

A packed meal is a challenge, because it must provide part of the daily nutritional requirements of the individual who eats it and it must be aesthetically appealing. It also must consist of food that can be prepared in the time available at an affordable cost, and the food must travel well and be easy to handle during eating.

Planning

While nutritional value is important, the paramount concern is to use foods that can be safely packed, to prevent the growth of micro-organisms. Thoroughly chill all products that contain protein foods (salads and sandwiches), stuffed eggs, and fried chicken before they are packed. In warm weather or when the food must be held in a warm place, as for a picnic, use an insulated food carrier with ice or refreezable plastic ice.

Insulated bottles, jugs, and jars are available in a wide range of shapes and sizes. Many have glass linings and must be handled carefully to avoid breaking them.

Brown-bag lunches can be a problem if no refrigeration is available on the job. It may be necessary to pack the sandwich spread in an insulated jar and wrap the bread or bun separately, to be combined just before the food is eaten. Refreezable plastic ice can be packaged with the prepared sandwich or protein food, or small insulated boxes or bags may be used to provide a variety in these lunches. Otherwise, use only those foods that can be safely held without refrigeration.

Preparing

Many cooks do not have a great deal of time in which to prepare a packed lunch. Therefore, some prefer to assemble a lunch the night before and to refrigerate it overnight. Lunches prepared at night often are more interesting and cost less than do last-minute lunches, because time and thought can be given to the food.

Other cooks prefer to prepare the different foods needed—cheese fingers, carrot and celery sticks, fresh fruit, and sandwich fillings—ahead of time and to refrigerate them. The lunch then is assembled in the morning when all the ingredients are thoroughly chilled.

Ingredients for packaged-to-go sandwiches also may be prepared in quantity and frozen for use over a period of time. However, since eggs, mayonnaise, and lettuce do not freeze satisfactorily, sandwiches prepared and frozen for later use must be made with butter, margarine, mustard, or cream cheese. Among the fillings that may be satisfactorily frozen are: sliced chicken or turkey with cranberry jelly; tuna, water chestnut, chopped olives, and grated onion; thinly sliced pork or beef roast in barbecue sauce; chicken, cream cheese, curry powder, nuts, and coconut. Meat turnovers also may be frozen. Wrap and place each sandwich in an airtight freezer bag or box.

Monotony in brown-bag lunches can be avoided by using imagination. Add a handful of raisins, a few dates, a special sauce, a salad, a dessert (in a small tightly covered container with a plastic spoon or fork), or any other safe, unexpected food as a welcome change. Pickled beets, marinated green beans, or a few pieces of raw cauliflower or zucchini add appeal and nutrition to bag lunches. When lunch is packed for others, a quick note or short cartoon may add a bit of interest for the diner.

Meals for young children

Adequate nutrition is of the utmost importance for young children, whose bodies are building bone, teeth, and muscle. All foods served to children should be carefully planned and prepared for maximum retention of nutrients.

Table 14-1 lists the nutritional requirements for children and may be used in planning daily foods for three meals and two snacks. Usually, the meals planned for the family or group easily can be adapted for children, if the general basic rules for childrens' food are applied.

Undesirable foods

All foods with high sugar content should be avoided or served in very limited quantity. These foods provide mostly calories, not the nutritional value needed. Sugars, especially those which cling to the teeth, promote cavities and may be a contributing factor to overweight; and both these problems are easier to avoid than to deal with once they develop.

Water, low-fat milk, and fruit and vegetable juices are desirable beverages for children. The caffeine in tea and coffee, the sugar and caffeine in cola drinks, and the sugar in other commercially produced soft drinks make them highly undesirable.

Foods that are highly spiced or that have high fat content, including fried foods, are best avoided or served only in limited amounts, because they may cause digestive upsets in children.

Eating habits

As was mentioned in Chapter 15, a child's eating habits are formed before he or she has any understanding of food. Therefore, the manager-cook has a dual responsibility both to see that a child's food is nutritious and to help the child to establish good eating habits. If a child has access only to nutritionally valuable foods, many problems can be avoided. Overweight, which can develop from eating too great a quantity of food, can be controlled by serving only adequate amounts of nutritional foods to meet the child's needs. Allowing the child to select the amount to be eaten may be the only guide line needed: all too often the habit of overeating begins when well-meaning adults encourage or demand that a child clean his or her plate. The habit of eating too much food, established early in life, also can lead to obesity and all the troubles associated with excess weight.

Many children dislike foods with strong flavors, like onions and steamed cabbage. They also tend to prefer foods that they can recognize and object to casseroles or other "mixed foods" that puzzle or confuse them. New foods frequently are met with suspicion. The best practice is to offer a small amount of a new food and ask the child to taste it. If the food is accepted, it can be used in the meal and thereafter; if it is refused, nothing need be said, and the meal can proceed without it. Rejected foods should be offered periodically because they may be accepted at a later time. In all cases, use a wide variety of foods, to ensure the child an adequate supply of all needed nutrients, as well as to develop an acceptance of many foods.

Small servings are best, so that a child does not feel required to eat what appears to be a very large amount. If wanted, second servings are given. Serve finger foods, which a child can hold onto easily, if handling a fork is still difficult. Using a small bowl and a spoon for chopped foods or foods that tend to spread over the plate, like creamed chicken or applesauce, also helps the child.

Many children like to be involved in meal preparation, and allowing them to help develops interest and openmindedness about foods. Also, children who have helped to prepare food are more likely to eat it, at the table. Sharp kitchen tools must be avoided when children work in the kitchen, until their manual dexterity allows them to handle tools carefully.

Atmosphere

Mealtimes should be comfortable for children, physically and emotionally. Overtired children may have no interest in food, so a brief rest before eating often is desirable. It is helpful to use chairs suitable for body size at the table, and to serve on smaller plates so that the smaller servings look appropriate. Skill in handling a knife and fork does not develop overnight, so avoid criticism. Encouragement and a congenial atmosphere are conducive to the development of eating skills and good food habits.

Meal planning

Meals planned for the family may be adapted for young children, as is shown in the following example.

For the following dinner,

> Roast Chicken with Gravy
> Buttered Asparagus
> Baked Potatoes with Chive Sour Cream
> Orange Salad   Honey Dressing
> Fruit Cream Tarts
> Milk   Coffee

adjustments are made as listed below:

1. *Chicken.* Omit the gravy. Cut the chicken into small pieces. If the food is served at the table, place the children's servings in paper baking cups on the serving platter.
2. *Potato.* Omit the sour cream. Cut the potato into small chunks, for finger food.
3. *Asparagus.* Cut the vegetable into pieces for use as a finger food or, if the children are old enough, for eating with a fork.
4. *Salad.* Omit the dressing. Cut the lettuce into small pieces.
5. *Tart.* Put the filling into small serving containers, not tart shells. Cut the fruit into bite-sized pieces and arrange the pieces on top of the filling to resemble the tarts for the adults.
6. *Milk.* Use low-fat milk.

Snacks

Ready-to-eat nutritional foods are the best snack foods for children. A snack should be interesting and easy to eat. Any of the following foods are desirable.

Fruit
apple wedges
apricots, fresh or dried
   seeds removed if necessary
bananas
fruit kabobs
grapes, seedless
melon cubes
orange and grapefruit sections
orange wedges, peels partially
   loosened

pineapple cubes
pear wedges
plums, seeds removed if
   necessary
strawberries
raisins
prunes, seeds removed

Breads and cereals
melba toast, whole wheat

whole-grain cereal nibbles
whole-wheat bread sticks with
   sesame or caraway seeds
whole-wheat crackers

Vegetables
carrot sticks and curls
cauliflower, raw or crisp-cooked
cherry tomatoes
cucumber sticks
green peas, in pod
tomato wedges
turnip sticks
zucchini sticks

Beverages, with little or no sugar
fruit slushes or frappes
milk
orange-yogurt popsicle
orange-milk sherbet

Prepared snacks
cheese fingers with whole-
   wheat crackers
cream cheese and chopped nut
   balls
cream cheese and raisin
   balls
cream cheese and clam dip,
   with crackers or raw vegetables
finger sandwiches: whole-
   wheat bread or
   crackers; peanut butter with
   banana, raisins, or grated
   carrots; cheese; egg salad
hard-cooked eggs
meat balls
meat turnovers
muffin pizza
sliced-ham rolls
yogurt with fruit slices or
   chunks

If problems arise in adjusting meals or nutritional requirements for children, use the evaluation form shown in Chart 18–1 in planning.

Weight control

Maintaining the recommended weight for height and age is important for all individuals, because being underweight or overweight can adversely affect health. Underweight individuals may have less resistance to disease, and the growth rate of the underweight child or adolescent may be slowed. Overweight is a serious complication in many diseases, and death rates from heart, circulatory, and kidney disease are higher for obese persons than they are for those of the correct weight. Obese individuals also are more likely to develop diabetes and diseases involving the kidneys and gallbladder. During pregnancy or surgery, excess weight is both a hazard and a complication.

Chart 18–1 *Nutritional evaluation for children*

Food groups	Number of daily servings needed	Number of servings					Total number of[a] servings
		Breakfast	Snack	Lunch	Snack	Dinner	
MILK AND MILK PRODUCTS[b]							
Under age 9	2–3						
Age 9–12	3 or more						
Teenagers	4 or more						
MEAT, FISH, POULTRY, EGGS[c] OR DRY LEGUMES	2 or more						
FRUITS AND VEGETABLES	4 or more						
Oranges, grapefruit, cabbage, green pepper, cantaloupe, or strawberries	1						
Dark green or deep yellow vegetables	1						
Other fruits and vegetables	2 or more						
BREADS AND CEREALS	4 or more						

[a] Additional calories to be added as necessary from extra servings. Sources of iodine (seafoods and iodized salt) and iron (liver, egg yolks, beef, dark green vegetables, whole grain cereals) must be included.

[b] One serving equals 8 oz. milk equals 1½ oz. cheddar cheese or 1½ C. cottage cheese (approximately).

[c] 1 serving equals 3 oz. meat; 2 eggs contain the protein content of 2 oz. meat (approximately).

The daily caloric requirements for the individuals the manager-cook plans for are likely to vary, depending on age, sex, and degree of activity. Often this range in requirements may be handled by smaller servings or by second helpings. Meals also may be planned so that those who need fewer calories omit certain dishes or parts of dishes, such as desserts, sauces, and gravies. Meals are based on the requirements of the majority of the group; additional needs also can be met with planned snacks.

Underweight

Below-normal weight may be caused by inadequate quantity or quality of food, poor absorption of food, or disease. Thorough examination by a physician is desirable, to determine whether or not any physical problems are involved. If the individual is underweight because of poor eating habits, a new eating pattern must be established. Usually, this problem can be handled with meal plans that will increase the daily intake of needed nutrients and calories.

The individual may be so in the habit of eating small quantities of food that increasing the intake is difficult. Sometimes this problem can be managed by slowly increasing portions at each meal. In other cases, it may be necessary for the manager-cook to plan for five or six smaller meals. High-calorie snacks can be planned between meals, provided that they do not reduce the appetite for regular meals.

In all cases, daily intake should be planned to include a good supply of high-quality protein, as well as all the other nutrients required. Vitamin and mineral supplements may be prescribed by a physician. In planning, the manager-cook can accommodate the need for increased nutritional caloric intake in many ways. Dried fruits and nuts, which need no preparation, can be planned for between-meal snacks. To increase the foods' nutritive and caloric value, skim-milk powder may be added to the underweight individual's portions of soup, pudding, and beverage. The powder also may be added to liquid milk for use with dry or cooked cereals and as a beverage. Fat intake also may be increased, but only to the extent that it does not interfere with the next meal.

For a child, it may be desirable to plan a rest period during the day and/or just before meals to reduce the calories burned and to prevent the child from being too tired to eat. A quiet activity can be planned with the child's capabilities and interests in mind. Overemphasizing the problem seldom is advisable.

Overweight

In some cases, an extra 5 or 10 pounds is gained because an individual has become less active over a period of time—perhaps from driving a car instead of walking, riding escalators instead of climbing stairs, or playing golf instead of tennis. In other cases, a person may have continued the eating habits established in childhood and adolescence, past the age at which the body's energy needs decrease. These extra pounds usually can be lost by decreasing the total caloric intake and increasing activities to burn more calories. Frequently, all that one needs is smaller servings and, less of the high-calorie foods. This may mean refusing the sour cream on the potato, the Roquefort dressing on the salad, or the pie for dessert. These adjustments present few problems for the manager-cook.

Excessive overweight, however, must be handled with a long-range plan. The gradual increase in pounds, added year by year, may have gone unnoticed or have been ignored. This slow weight gain may be due to established eating habits, decreased activity, or the gradual decrease in calories needed by the body after age 25. In these cases, new eating patterns must be developed as weight is reduced. Sometimes psychological aspects are involved, and, in a few cases, metabolic problems may be involved. In these latter cases, the basic causes for overeating or for the physical problem must be determined so that the individual may make the needed readjustments.

In all cases, an obese person should be carefully examined by a physician before a weight-control program is begun, to determine the cause of the obesity. Medical supervision should continue during the program, since adjustments may be needed. Usually, the physician or the dietitian provides guidelines and lists of foods which the manager-cook can consider in working out the needed meal plans.

Generally, the daily caloric intake is set at a certain number, and meals must be planned with permitted foods that are high in nutritive content, to meet the daily requirements. Fats of all types are restricted, as are "empty-calorie" foods, such as sugar and alcohol. Lean meats, such as lamb, veal, and chicken, and fish provide the needed protein, and the vegetables and fruits with low calorie content are used freely. Carbohydrates usually are included in limited amounts. Skim milk is included in the diet, since it provides both protein and minerals.

The daily food may be planned for three meals or for more meals of smaller size, according to the dieter's preference and schedule. In either case, the manager-cook should use as wide a variety of foods as is possible, to avoid monotony. Planning these meals over the long period of time that usually is involved in returning an obese individual to desired weight while meeting the needs of other family members is a challenge for the manager-cook. Further, once the desired weight is reached, meals must be planned to maintain the individual at that weight, in line with the newly established eating pattern.

Cooking as a hobby

After acquiring the knowledge, skills, and techniques for basic food preparation, many cooks find great satisfaction in the challenge of using the art and science of food to create masterpieces, either in an individual presentation of a food or in a complete meal. Thus, a new hobby is discovered.

Many hours can be spent reading and browsing through magazines and cookbooks in search of new and exciting ways to prepare an old standby or for new or hitherto unused foods and recipes. More hours may be spent browsing in gourmet and cookery shops, searching for unusual items for use in preparing or presenting foods. Some cooks start their own gourmet club; others enroll in art courses, to collect further knowledge of color and design, or in specialty cooking classes, for new techniques. Some cooks have a great deal of time to give to their new hobby; others find new recipes or combinations to fit their available time.

One way to develop this hobby is to explore new foods. Different foods and different preparation methods are found even in the different sections of this country. The climate, the nationality of the original settlers, and the locally grown foods influence food patterns in each area, although borderlines do not really exist. Our marketing and transportation systems are so well developed that almost all foods are available in all sections and are readily used in many areas. Table 18–2 lists some of the foods that frequently appear in different sections of the United States.

If the foods seem unusual, read about the climate, the people, the way of life to provide the background information that will make the foods and recipes more understandable. Magazines, newspapers and books can provide ways to interpret unfamiliar recipes, making them seem quite logical for the area from which they came. Some of the foods may not be available in markets but must be searched for in specialty shops.

For some cooks, the only way to use the different new recipes is to adapt them to the food pattern with which the cook is familiar and comfortable. Working out the proportions in a recipe and the preparation method can be an absorbing task, which may lead to a new addition to the cook's repertory of regularly served foods.

Table 18-2 *Regional foods in the United States*

Area	Food
Northeast	Steamed lobster Clam chowder Codfish balls Boston baked beans Indian pudding
Southeast	Crisp fried chicken Barbecued pork Smithfield and country-cured hams Deviled crab Corn bread Grits Black-eyed peas with tomatoes Peach cobbler Key lime pie
South Central	Oysters Rockefeller Shrimp creole Jambalaya Tomatoes with okra Rice and red beans Pecan pie
North Central and Midwestern	Beef steaks and roasts Country-cured hams Cheeses
Northwest	Steam-baked salmon Broiled salmon steaks Steamed crabs Huckleberry pie Apples, raw and cooked
Southwest	Sourdough breads Steamed crabs Abalone Artichokes Mexican-American cooking Patio barbecues
Hawaii	Mahimahi and other fish Pork Chicken Pineapple Papaya Coconut Soy sauce Poi
Alaska	Reindeer Salmon and other fish Bear Elk Whale

When foods from foreign countries are investigated, the cook may feel that some of the typical menus list so many foods that the meal could not be prepared without several assistants. However, some of the foods and ways to present them may seem very desirable, and the creative cook can take advantage of the ideas and build around them. Often, a most interesting meal can be built around foreign dishes. Sometimes a cooking method or use of an unfamiliar utensil—a crepe pan, fondue pot, or Chinese wok, for example—will seem to have great merit, and after using the method or utensil, the cook will find that familiar foods also benefit from the new method. As an example, Chinese menus are not practical for many American cooks: many different dishes of meat, fish, or poultry are served, depending on the number of diners. However, a particular entrée may be chosen and used as the basis for planning the remainder of a meal. The cook also may discover that the wok, which is used in many Oriental food preparations, is an excellent pan for stir-frying, for browning small pieces of meat, or even for preparing a stew. And the person who understands the cooking technique will discover that the iron fry pan is equally effective for stir-frying.

Table 18–3 gives the American adaptations of menus strongly influenced

Table 18–3 *Foreign foods*

Country	Accompaniments	Menus
China	Chopsticks Sit at table	Corn Velvet Soup Stir-fry Beef and Asparagus Chinese Rice Cucumber-Watercress Salad Chestnut Chinoiserie Tea
India	Eat with fingers or flatware Sit at table	Lamb Curry with chutneys, condiments Green Beans Rice Rayta (yogurt, tomato, cucumber, and onions) Halva (a milk fruit pudding)
Japan	Chopsticks Sit on the floor	Yakatori Spinach-Sushi (vinegared rice) Ginger Sundae Tea or Shrimp and Vegetable Tempura Rice Tea

by Chinese, Indian, and Japanese foods. These meals can be further enhanced by using table appointments and colors that represent the tables of the country involved, and the food may be served as it is in that country.

Exploring the food customs and habits of other countries is an avenue to many enjoyable hours of learning, which can be undertaken as the schedule allows. There is no pressure of deadlines to be met or exams to be taken, and the only requirements are curiosity, interest, and enthusiasm. Over the years, following the food hobby can yield hundreds of hours of pleasurable food preparation, presentation, and dining.

Appendices

Appendix A

Nutritive values of the edible part of foods

(Dashes (—) denote lack of reliable data for a constituent believed to be present in measurable amount)

Item No. (A)	Foods, approximate measures, units, and weight (edible part unless footnotes indicate otherwise) (B)		Water (C) Grams	Food energy (D) Percent	Pro-tein (E) Calories	Fat (F) Grams
	DAIRY PRODUCTS (CHEESE, CREAM, IMITATION CREAM, MILK; RELATED PRODUCTS)					
	Butter. See Fats, oils; related products, items 103-108.					
	Cheese:					
	Natural:					
1	Blue-----------------------	1 oz-------------------	28	42	100	6	8
2	Camembert (3 wedges per 4-oz container).	1 wedge----------------	38	52	115	8	9
	Cheddar:					
3	Cut pieces-----------------	1 oz-------------------	28	37	115	7	9
4		1 cu in-----------------	17.2	37	70	4	6
5	Shredded-------------------	1 cup------------------	113	37	455	28	37
	Cottage (curd not pressed down):					
	Creamed (cottage cheese, 4% fat):					
6	Large curd-----------------	1 cup------------------	225	79	235	28	10
7	Small curd-----------------	1 cup------------------	210	79	220	26	9
8	Low fat (2%)---------------	1 cup------------------	226	79	205	31	4
9	Low fat (1%)---------------	1 cup------------------	226	82	165	28	2
10	Uncreamed (cottage cheese dry curd, less than 1/2% fat).	1 cup------------------	145	80	125	25	1
11	Cream----------------------	1 oz-------------------	28	54	100	2	10
	Mozzarella, made with—					
12	Whole milk-----------------	1 oz-------------------	28	48	90	6	7
13	Part skim milk-------------	1 oz-------------------	28	49	80	8	5
	Parmesan, grated:					
14	Cup, not pressed down------	1 cup------------------	100	18	455	42	30
15	Tablespoon-----------------	1 tbsp-----------------	5	18	25	2	2
16	Ounce----------------------	1 oz-------------------	28	18	130	12	9
17	Provolone------------------	1 oz-------------------	28	41	100	7	8
	Ricotta, made with—					
18	Whole milk-----------------	1 cup------------------	246	72	1,790	28	32
19	Part skim milk-------------	1 cup------------------	246	74	340	28	19
20	Romano---------------------	1 oz-------------------	28	31	110	9	8
21	Swiss----------------------	1 oz-------------------	28	37	105	8	8
	Pasteurized process cheese:					
22	American-------------------	1 oz-------------------	28	39	105	6	9
23	Swiss----------------------	1 oz-------------------	28	42	95	7	7
24	Pasteurized process cheese food, American.	1 oz-------------------	28	43	95	6	7
25	Pasteurized process cheese spread, American.	1 oz-------------------	28	48	82	5	6
	Cream, sweet:					
26	Half-and-half (cream and milk)-	1 cup------------------	242	81	315	7	28
27		1 tbsp-----------------	15	81	20	Trace	2
28	Light, coffee, or table--------	1 cup------------------	240	74	470	6	46
29		1 tbsp-----------------	15	74	30	Trace	3

SOURCE: *Home and Garden Bulletin*, no. 72 (Washington, D.C.: U.S. Department of Agriculture, rev. April 1977).

\multicolumn{13}{	c	}{NUTRIENTS IN INDICATED QUANTITY}
\multicolumn{3}{	c	}{Fatty Acids}										
Satu-rated (total)	\multicolumn{2}{c	}{Unsaturated}	Carbo-hydrate	Calcium	Phos-phorus	Iron	Potas-sium	Vitamin A value	Thiamin	Ribo-flavin	Niacin	Ascorbic acid
	Oleic	Lino-leic										
(G)	(H)	(I)	(J)	(K)	(L)	(M)	(N)	(O)	(P)	(Q)	(R)	(S)
Grams	Grams	Grams	Grams	Milli-grams	Milli-grams	Milli-grams	Milli-grams	Inter-national units	Milli-grams	Milli-grams	Milli-grams	Milli-grams
5.3	1.9	0.2	1	150	110	0.1	73	200	0.01	0.11	0.3	0
5.8	2.2	.2	Trace	147	132	.1	71	350	.01	.19	.2	0
6.1	2.1	.2	Trace	204	145	.2	28	300	.01	.11	Trace	0
3.7	1.3	.1	Trace	124	88	.1	17	180	Trace	.06	Trace	0
24.2	8.5	.7	1	815	579	.8	111	1,200	.03	.42	.1	0
6.4	2.4	.2	6	135	297	.3	190	370	.05	.37	.3	Trace
6.0	2.2	.2	6	126	277	.3	177	340	.04	.34	.3	Trace
2.8	1.0	.1	8	155	340	.4	217	160	.05	.42	.3	Trace
1.5	.5	.1	6	138	302	.3	193	80	.05	.37	.3	Trace
.4	.1	Trace	3	46	151	.3	47	40	.04	.21	.2	0
6.2	2.4	.2	1	23	30	.3	34	400	Trace	.06	Trace	0
4.4	1.7	.2	1	163	117	.1	21	260	Trace	.08	Trace	0
3.1	1.2	.1	1	207	149	.1	27	180	.01	.10	Trace	0
19.1	7.7	.3	4	1,376	807	1.0	107	700	.05	.39	.3	0
1.0	.4	Trace	Trace	69	40	Trace	5	40	Trace	.02	Trace	0
5.4	2.2	.1	1	390	229	.3	30	200	.01	.11	.1	0
4.8	1.7	.1	1	214	141	.1	39	230	.01	.09	Trace	0
20.4	7.1	.7	7	509	389	.9	257	1,210	.03	.48	.3	0
12.1	4.7	.5	13	669	449	1.1	308	1,060	.05	.46	.2	0
—	—	—	1	302	215	—	—	160	—	.11	Trace	0
5.0	1.7	.2	1	272	171	Trace	31	240	.01	.10	Trace	0
5.6	2.1	.2	Trace	174	211	.1	46	340	.01	.10	Trace	0
4.5	1.7	.1	1	219	216	.2	61	230	Trace	.08	Trace	0
4.4	1.7	.1	2	163	130	.2	79	260	.01	.13	Trace	0
3.8	1.5	.1	2	159	202	.1	69	220	.01	.12	Trace	0
17.3	7.0	.6	10	254	230	.2	314	260	.08	.36	.2	2
1.1	.4	Trace	1	16	14	Trace	19	20	.01	.02	Trace	Trace
28.8	11.7	1.0	9	231	192	.1	292	1,730	.08	.36	.1	2
1.8	.7	.1	1	14	12	Trace	18	110	Trace	.02	Trace	Trace

NUTRITIVE VALUES OF THE EDIBLE PART OF FOODS—Continued

Item No. (A)	Foods, approximate measures, units, and weight (edible part unless footnotes indicate otherwise) (B)		Water (C)	Food energy (D)	Protein (E)	Fat (F)
		Grams	Percent	Calories	Grams	Grams
	Whipping, unwhipped (volume about double when whipped):					
30	Light----------------------- 1 cup----------------------	239	64	700	5	74
31	1 tbsp---------------------	15	64	45	Trace	5
32	Heavy----------------------- 1 cup----------------------	238	58	820	5	88
33	1 tbsp---------------------	15	58	80	Trace	6
34	Whipped topping, (pressurized)- 1 cup----------------------	60	61	155	2	13
35	1 tbsp---------------------	3	61	10	Trace	1
36	Cream, sour--------------------- 1 cup----------------------	230	71	495	7	48
37	1 tbsp---------------------	12	71	25	Trace	3
	Cream products, imitation (made with vegetable fat): Sweet: Creamers:					
38	Liquid (frozen)------------ 1 cup----------------------	245	77	335	2	24
39	1 tbsp---------------------	15	77	20	Trace	1
40	Powdered------------------ 1 cup----------------------	94	2	515	5	33
41	1 tsp----------------------	2	2	10	Trace	1
	Whipped topping:					
42	Frozen--------------------- 1 cup----------------------	75	50	240	1	19
43	1 tbsp---------------------	4	50	15	Trace	1
44	Powdered, made with whole milk. 1 cup----------------------	80	67	150	3	10
45	1 tbsp---------------------	4	67	10	Trace	Trace
46	Pressurized---------------- 1 cup----------------------	70	60	185	1	16
47	1 tbsp---------------------	4	60	10	Trace	1
48	Sour dressing (imitation sour cream) made with nonfat dry milk. 1 cup----------------------	235	75	415	8	39
49	1 tbsp---------------------	12	75	20	Trace	2
	Ice cream. See Milk desserts, frozen (items 75-80).					
	Ice milk. See Milk desserts, frozen (items 81-83).					
	Milk: Fluid:					
50	Whole (3.3% fat)------------- 1 cup----------------------	244	88	150	8	8
	Lowfat (2%):					
51	No milk solids added------- 1 cup----------------------	244	89	120	8	5
	Milk solids added:					
52	Label claim less than 10 g of protein per cup. 1 cup----------------------	245	89	125	9	5
53	Label claim 10 or more grams of protein per cup (protein fortified). 1 cup----------------------	246	88	135	10	5
	Lowfat (1%):					
54	No milk solids added------ 1 cup----------------------	244	90	100	8	3
	Milk solids added:					
55	Label claim less than 10 g of protein per cup. 1 cup----------------------	245	90	105	9	2
56	Label claim 10 or more grams of protein per cup (protein fortified). 1 cup----------------------	246	89	120	10	3
	Nonfat (skim):					
57	No milk solids added------ 1 cup----------------------	245	91	85	8	Trace

[1] Vitamin A value is largely from beta-carotene used for coloring. Riboflavin value for items 40-41 apply to products with added riboflavin.

	NUTRIENTS IN INDICATED QUANTITY											
	Fatty Acids											
Satu- rated (total)	Unsaturated Oleic	Lino- leic	Carbo- hydrate	Calcium	Phos- phorus	Iron	Potas- sium	Vitamin A value	Thiamin	Ribo- flavin	Niacin	Ascorbic acid
(G)	(H)	(I)	(J)	(K)	(L)	(M)	(N)	(O)	(P)	(Q)	(R)	(S)
Grams	Grams	Grams	Grams	Milli- grams	Milli- grams	Milli- grams	Milli- grams	Inter- national units	Milli- grams	Milli- grams	Milli- grams	Milli- grams
46.2	18.3	1.5	7	166	146	0.1	231	2,690	0.06	0.30	0.1	1
2.9	1.1	.1	Trace	10	9	Trace	15	170	Trace	.02	Trace	Trace
54.8	22.2	2.0	7	154	149	.1	179	3,500	.05	.26	.1	1
3.5	1.4	.1	Trace	10	9	Trace	11	220	Trace	.02	Trace	Trace
8.3	3.4	.3	7	61	54	Trace	88	550	.02	.04	Trace	0
.4	.2	Trace	Trace	3	3	Trace	4	30	Trace	Trace	Trace	0
30.0	12.1	1.1	10	268	195	.1	331	1,820	.08	.34	.2	2
1.6	.6	.1	1	14	10	Trace	17	90	Trace	.02	Trace	Trace
22.8	.3	Trace	28	23	157	.1	467	[1]220	0	0	0	0
1.4	Trace	0	2	1	10	Trace	29	[1]10	0	0	0	0
30.6	.9	Trace	52	21	397	.1	763	[1]190	0	[1].16	0	0
.7	Trace	0	1	Trace	8	Trace	16	[1]Trace	0	[1]Trace	0	0
16.3	1.0	.2	17	5	6	.1	14	[1]650	0	0	0	0
.9	.1	Trace	1	Trace	Trace	Trace	1	[1]30	0	0	0	0
8.5	.6	.1	13	72	69	Trace	121	[1]290	.02	.09	Trace	1
.4	Trace	Trace	1	4	3	Trace	6	[1]10	Trace	Trace	Trace	Trace
13.2	1.4	.2	11	4	13	Trace	13	[1]330	0	0	0	0
.8	.1	Trace	1	Trace	1	Trace	1	[1]20	0	0	0	0
31.2	4.4	1.1	11	266	205	.1	380	[1]20	.09	.38	.2	2
1.6	.2	.1	1	14	10	Trace	19	[1]Trace	.01	.02	Trace	Trace
5.1	2.1	.2	11	291	228	.1	370	[2]310	.09	.40	.2	2
2.9	1.2	.1	12	297	232	.1	377	500	.10	.40	.2	2
2.9	1.2	.1	12	313	245	.1	397	500	.10	.42	.2	2
3.0	1.2	.1	14	352	276	.1	447	500	.11	.48	.2	3
1.6	.7	.1	12	300	235	.1	381	500	.10	.41	.2	2
1.5	.6	.1	12	313	245	.1	397	500	.10	.42	.2	2
1.8	.7	.1	14	349	273	.1	444	500	.11	.47	.2	3
.3	.1	Trace	12	302	247	.1	406	500	.09	.37	.2	2

[2]Applies to product without added vitamin A. With added vitamin A, value is 500 International Units (I.U.).

NUTRITIVE VALUES OF THE EDIBLE PART OF FOODS—Continued

Item No. (A)	Foods, approximate measures, units, and weight (edible part unless footnotes indicate otherwise) (B)		Water (C) Percent	Food energy (D) Calories	Protein (E) Grams	Fat (F) Grams
		Grams				
	DAIRY PRODUCTS (CHEESE, CREAM, IMITATION CREAM, MILK; RELATED PRODUCTS)—Con.					
	Milk—Continued					
	Fluid—Continued					
	Nonfat (skim)—Continued					
	Milk solids added:					
58	Label claim less than 10 g of protein per cup.	1 cup — 245	90	90	9	1
59	Label claim 10 or more grams of protein per cup (protein fortified).	1 cup — 246	89	100	10	1
60	Buttermilk	1 cup — 245	90	100	8	2
	Canned:					
	Evaporated, unsweetened:					
61	Whole milk	1 cup — 252	74	340	17	19
62	Skim milk	1 cup — 255	79	200	19	1
63	Sweetened, condensed	1 cup — 306	27	980	24	27
	Dried:					
64	Buttermilk	1 cup — 120	3	465	41	7
	Nonfat instant:					
65	Envelope, net wt., 3.2 oz[5]	1 envelope — 91	4	325	32	1
66	Cup[7]	1 cup — 68	4	245	24	Trace
	Milk beverages:					
	Chocolate milk (commercial):					
67	Regular	1 cup — 250	82	210	8	8
68	Lowfat (2%)	1 cup — 250	84	180	8	5
69	Lowfat (1%)	1 cup — 250	85	160	8	3
70	Eggnog (commercial)	1 cup — 254	74	340	10	19
	Malted milk, home-prepared with 1 cup of whole milk and 2 to 3 heaping tsp of malted milk powder (about 3/4 oz):					
71	Chocolate	1 cup of milk plus 3/4 oz of powder — 265	81	235	9	9
72	Natural	1 cup of milk plus 3/4 oz of powder — 265	81	235	11	10
	Shakes, thick:[8]					
73	Chocolate, container, net wt., 10.6 oz.	1 container — 300	72	355	9	8
74	Vanilla, container, net wt., 11 oz.	1 container — 313	74	350	12	
	Milk desserts, frozen:					
	Ice cream:					
	Regular (about 11% fat):					
75	Hardened	1/2 gal — 1,064	61	2,155	38	115
76		1 cup — 133	61	270	5	1
77		3-fl oz container — 50	61	100	2	5
78	Soft serve (frozen custard)	1 cup — 173	60	375	7	2
79	Rich (about 16% fat), hardened.	1/2 gal — 1,188	59	2,805	33	190
80		1 cup — 148	59	350	4	2
	Ice milk:					
81	Hardened (about 4.3% fat)	1/2 gal — 1,048	69	1,470	41	4
82		1 cup — 131	69	185	5	

[3] Applies to product without vitamin A added.
[4] Applies to product with added vitamin A. Without added vitamin A, value is 20 International Units (I.U.).
[5] Yields 1 qt of fluid milk when reconstituted according to package directions.

336

	NUTRIENTS IN INDICATED QUANTITY											
	Fatty Acids											
Saturated (total)	Unsaturated		Carbohydrate	Calcium	Phosphorus	Iron	Potassium	Vitamin A value	Thiamin	Riboflavin	Niacin	Ascorbic acid
	Oleic	Linoleic										
(G)	(H)	(I)	(J)	(K)	(L)	(M)	(N)	(O)	(P)	(Q)	(R)	(S)
Grams	Grams	Grams	Grams	Milligrams	Milligrams	Milligrams	Milligrams	International units	Milligrams	Milligrams	Milligrams	Milligrams
0.4	0.1	Trace	12	316	255	0.1	418	500	0.10	0.43	0.2	2
.4	.1	Trace	14	352	275	.1	446	500	.11	.48	.2	3
1.3	.5	Trace	12	285	219	.1	371	[3]80	.08	.38	.1	2
11.6	5.3	0.4	25	657	510	.5	764	[3]610	.12	.80	.5	5
.3	.1	Trace	29	738	497	.7	845	[4]1,000	.11	.79	.4	3
16.8	6.7	.7	166	868	775	.6	1,136	[3]1,000	.28	1.27	.6	8
4.3	1.7	.2	59	1,421	1,119	.4	1,910	[3]260	.47	1.90	1.1	7
.4	.1	Trace	47	1,120	896	.3	1,552	[6]2,160	.38	1.59	.8	5
.3	.1	Trace	35	837	670	.2	1,160	[6]1,610	.28	1.19	.6	4
5.3	2.2	.2	26	280	251	.6	417	[3]300	.09	.41	.3	2
3.1	1.3	.1	26	284	254	.6	422	500	.10	.42	.3	2
1.5	.7	.1	26	287	257	.6	426	500	.10	.40	.2	2
11.3	5.0	.6	34	330	278	.5	420	890	.09	.48	.3	4
5.5	—	—	29	304	265	.5	500	330	.14	.43	.7	2
6.0	—	—	27	347	307	.3	529	380	.20	.54	1.3	2
5.0	2.0	.2	63	396	378	.9	672	260	.14	.67	.4	0
5.9	2.4	.2	56	457	361	.3	572	360	.09	.61	.5	0
71.3	28.8	2.6	254	1,406	1,075	1.0	2,052	4,340	.42	2.63	1.1	6
8.9	3.6	.3	32	176	134	.1	257	540	.05	.33	.1	1
3.4	1.4	.1	12	66	51	Trace	96	200	.02	.12	.1	Trace
13.5	5.9	.6	38	236	199	.4	338	790	.08	.45	.2	1
118.3	47.8	4.3	256	1,213	927	.8	1,771	7,200	.36	2.27	.9	5
14.7	6.0	.5	32	151	115	.1	221	900	.04	.28	.1	1
28.1	11.3	1.0	232	1,409	1,035	1.5	2,117	1,710	.61	2.78	.9	6
3.5	1.4	.1	29	176	129	.1	265	210	.08	.35	.1	1

[6] Applies to product with added vitamin A.
[7] Weight applies to product with label claim of 1 1/3 cups equal 3.2 oz.
[8] Applies to products made from thick shake mixes and that do not contain added ice cream. Products made from milk shake mixes are higher in fat and usually contain added ice cream.

NUTRITIVE VALUES OF THE EDIBLE PART OF FOODS—Continued

Item No. (A)	Foods, approximate measures, units, and weight (edible part unless footnotes indicate otherwise) (B)		Water (C) Percent	Food energy (D) Calories	Protein (E) Grams	Fat (F) Grams
83	Soft serve (about 2.6% fat)	1 cup	175	70	225	8	5
84	Sherbet (about 2% fat)	1/2 gal	1,542	66	2,160	17	31
85		1 cup	193	66	270	2	4
	Milk desserts, other:						
86	Custard, baked	1 cup	265	77	305	14	15
	Puddings:						
	From home recipe:						
	Starch base:						
87	Chocolate	1 cup	260	66	385	8	12
88	Vanilla (blancmange)	1 cup	255	76	285	9	10
89	Tapioca cream	1 cup	165	72	220	8	8
	From mix (chocolate) and milk:						
90	Regular (cooked)	1 cup	260	70	320	9	8
91	Instant	1 cup	260	69	325	8	7
	Yogurt:						
	With added milk solids:						
	Made with lowfat milk:						
92	Fruit-flavored[9]	1 container, net wt., 8 oz	227	75	230	10	3
93	Plain	1 container, net wt., 8 oz	227	85	145	12	4
94	Made with nonfat milk	1 container, net wt., 8 oz	227	85	125	13	Trace
	Without added milk solids:						
95	Made with whole milk	1 container, net wt., 8 oz	227	88	140	8	7

EGGS

	Eggs, large (24 oz per dozen):						
	Raw:						
96	Whole, without shell	1 egg	50	75	80	6	6
97	White	1 white	33	88	15	3	Trace
98	Yolk	1 yolk	17	49	65	3	6
	Cooked:						
99	Fried in butter	1 egg	46	72	85	5	6
100	Hard-cooked, shell removed	1 egg	50	75	80	6	6
101	Poached	1 egg	50	74	80	6	6
102	Scrambled (milk added) in butter. Also omelet.	1 egg	64	76	95	6	7

FATS, OILS; RELATED PRODUCTS

	Butter:						
	Regular (1 brick or 4 sticks per lb):						
103	Stick (1/2 cup)	1 stick	113	16	815	1	92
104	Tablespoon (about 1/8 stick).	1 tbsp	14	16	100	Trace	12
105	Pat (1 in square, 1/3 in high; 90 per lb).	1 pat	5	16	35	Trace	4
	Whipped (6 sticks or two 8-oz containers per lb).						
106	Stick (1/2 cup)	1 stick	76	16	540	1	61
107	Tablespoon (about 1/8 stick).	1 tbsp	9	16	65	Trace	8
108	Pat (1 1/4 in square, 1/3 in high; 120 per lb).	1 pat	4	16	25	Trace	3

[9] Content of fat, vitamin A, and carbohydrate varies. Consult the label when precise values are needed for special diets.

	NUTRIENTS IN INDICATED QUANTITY												
	Fatty Acids												
Saturated (total)	Unsaturated		Carbohydrate	Calcium	Phosphorus	Iron	Potassium	Vitamin A value	Thiamin	Riboflavin	Niacin	Ascorbic acid
	Oleic	Linoleic										
(G)	(H)	(I)	(J)	(K)	(L)	(M)	(N)	(O)	(P)	(Q)	(R)	(S)
Grams	*Grams*	*Grams*	*Grams*	*Milligrams*	*Milligrams*	*Milligrams*	*Milligrams*	*International units*	*Milligrams*	*Milligrams*	*Milligrams*	*Milligrams*
2.9	1.2	0.1	38	274	202	0.3	412	180	0.12	0.54	0.2	1
19.0	7.7	.7	469	827	594	2.5	1,585	1,480	.26	.71	1.0	31
2.4	1.0	.1	59	103	74	.3	198	190	.03	.09	.1	4
6.8	5.4	.7	29	297	310	1.1	387	930	.11	.50	.3	1
7.6	3.3	.3	67	250	255	1.3	445	390	.05	.36	.3	1
6.2	2.5	.2	41	298	232	Trace	352	410	.08	.41	.3	2
4.1	2.5	.5	28	173	180	.7	223	480	.07	.30	.2	2
4.3	2.6	.2	59	265	247	.8	354	340	.05	.39	.3	2
3.6	2.2	.3	63	374	237	1.3	335	340	.08	.39	.3	2
1.8	.6	.1	42	343	269	.2	439	[10]120	.08	.40	.2	1
2.3	.8	.1	16	415	326	.2	531	[10]150	.10	.49	.3	2
.3	.1	Trace	17	452	355	.2	579	[10]20	.11	.53	.3	2
4.8	1.7	.1	11	274	215	.1	351	280	.07	.32	.2	1
1.7	2.0	.6	1	28	90	1.0	65	260	.04	.15	Trace	0
0	0	0	Trace	4	4	Trace	45	0	Trace	.09	Trace	0
1.7	2.1	.6	Trace	26	86	.9	15	310	.04	.07	Trace	0
2.4	2.2	.6	1	26	80	.9	58	290	.03	.13	Trace	0
1.7	2.0	.6	1	28	90	1.0	65	260	.04	.14	Trace	0
1.7	2.0	.6	1	28	90	1.0	65	260	.04	.13	Trace	0
2.8	2.3	.6	1	47	97	.9	85	310	.04	.16	Trace	0
57.3	23.1	2.1	Trace	27	26	.2	29	[11]3,470	.01	.04	Trace	0
7.2	2.9	.3	Trace	3	3	Trace	4	[11]430	Trace	Trace	Trace	0
2.5	1.0	.1	Trace	1	1	Trace	1	[11]150	Trace	Trace	Trace	0
38.2	15.4	1.4	Trace	18	17	.1	20	[11]2,310	Trace	.03	Trace	0
4.7	1.9	.2	Trace	2	2	Trace	2	[11]290	Trace	Trace	Trace	0
1.9	.8	.1	Trace	1	1	Trace	1	[11]120	0	Trace	Trace	0

[10] Applies to product made with milk containing no added vitamin A.
[11] Based on year-round average.

NUTRITIVE VALUES OF THE EDIBLE PART OF FOODS—Continued

Item No.	Foods, approximate measures, units, and weight (edible part unless footnotes indicate otherwise)		Water	Food energy	Protein	Fat
(A)	(B)		(C)	(D)	(E)	(F)
		Grams	Percent	Calories	Grams	Grams
	FATS, OILS; RELATED PRODUCTS—Con.					
109	Fats, cooking (vegetable shortenings). 1 cup	200	0	1,770	0	200
110	1 tbsp	13	0	110	0	13
111	Lard------ 1 cup	205	0	1,850	0	205
112	1 tbsp	13	0	115	0	13
	Margarine:					
	Regular (1 brick or 4 sticks per lb):					
113	Stick (1/2 cup)------- 1 stick	113	16	815	1	92
114	Tablespoon (about 1/8 stick)- 1 tbsp	14	16	100	Trace	12
115	Pat (1 in square, 1/3 in high; 90 per lb). 1 pat	5	16	35	Trace	4
116	Soft, two 8-oz containers per lb. 1 container	227	16	1,635	1	184
117	1 tbsp	14	16	100	Trace	12
	Whipped (6 sticks per lb):					
118	Stick (1/2 cup)------- 1 stick	76	16	545	Trace	61
119	Tablespoon (about 1/8 stick)- 1 tbsp	9	16	70	Trace	8
	Oils, salad or cooking:					
120	Corn------ 1 cup	218	0	1,925	0	218
121	1 tbsp	14	0	120	0	14
122	Olive------ 1 cup	216	0	1,910	0	216
123	1 tbsp	14	0	120	0	14
124	Peanut------ 1 cup	216	0	1,910	0	216
125	1 tbsp	14	0	120	0	14
126	Safflower------ 1 cup	218	0	1,925	0	218
127	1 tbsp	14	0	120	0	14
128	Soybean oil, hydrogenated (partially hardened). 1 cup	218	0	1,925	0	218
129	1 tbsp	14	0	120	0	14
130	Soybean-cottonseed oil blend, hydrogenated. 1 cup	218	0	1,925	0	218
131	1 tbsp	14	0	120	0	14
	Salad dressings:					
	Commercial:					
	Blue cheese:					
132	Regular------ 1 tbsp	15	32	75	1	8
133	Low calorie (5 Cal per tsp) 1 tbsp	16	84	10	Trace	1
	French:					
134	Regular------ 1 tbsp	16	39	65	Trace	6
135	Low calorie (5 Cal per tsp) 1 tbsp	16	77	15	Trace	1
	Italian:					
136	Regular------ 1 tbsp	15	28	85	Trace	9
137	Low calorie (2 Cal per tsp) 1 tbsp	15	90	10	Trace	1
138	Mayonnaise------ 1 tbsp	14	15	100	Trace	11
	Mayonnaise type:					
139	Regular------ 1 tbsp	15	41	65	Trace	6
140	Low calorie (8 Cal per tsp) 1 tbsp	16	81	20	Trace	2
141	Tartar sauce, regular------ 1 tbsp	14	34	75	Trace	8
	Thousand Island:					
142	Regular------ 1 tbsp	16	32	80	Trace	8
143	Low calorie (10 Cal per tsp) 1 tbsp	15	68	25	Trace	2
	From home recipe:					
144	Cooked type[13]------ 1 tbsp	16	68	25	1	2

[12] Based on average vitamin A content of fortified margarine. Federal specifications for fortified margarine require a minimum of 15,000 International Units (I.U.) of vitamin A per pound.

	NUTRIENTS IN INDICATED QUANTITY											
	Fatty Acids											
Satu-rated (total)	Unsaturated		Carbo-hydrate	Calcium	Phos-phorus	Iron	Potas-sium	Vitamin A value	Thiamin	Ribo-flavin	Niacin	Ascorbic acid
	Oleic	Lino-leic										
(G)	(H)	(I)	(J)	(K)	(L)	(M)	(N)	(O)	(P)	(Q)	(R)	(S)
Grams	Grams	Grams	Grams	Milli-grams	Milli-grams	Milli-grams	Milli-grams	Inter-national units	Milli-grams	Milli-grams	Milli-grams	Milli-grams
48.8	88.2	48.4	0	0	0	0	0	—	0	0	0	0
3.2	5.7	3.1	0	0	0	0	0	—	0	0	0	0
81.0	83.8	20.5	0	0	0	0	0	0	0	0	0	0
5.1	5.3	1.3	0	0	0	0	0	0	0	0	0	0
16.7	42.9	24.9	Trace	27	26	.2	29	[12]3,750	.01	.04	Trace	0
2.1	5.3	3.1	Trace	3	3	Trace	4	[12]470	Trace	Trace	Trace	0
.7	1.9	1.1	Trace	1	1	Trace	1	[12]170	Trace	Trace	Trace	0
32.5	71.5	65.4	Trace	53	52	.4	59	[12]7,500	.01	.08	.1	0
2.0	4.5	4.1	Trace	3	3	Trace	4	[12]470	Trace	Trace	Trace	0
11.2	28.7	16.7	Trace	18	17	.1	20	[12]2,500	Trace	.03	Trace	0
1.4	3.6	2.1	Trace	2	2	Trace	2	[12]310	Trace	Trace	Trace	0
27.7	53.6	125.1	0	0	0	0	0	—	0	0	0	0
1.7	3.3	7.8	0	0	0	0	0	—	0	0	0	0
30.7	154.4	17.7	0	0	0	0	0	—	0	0	0	0
1.9	9.7	1.1	0	0	0	0	0	—	0	0	0	0
37.4	98.5	67.0	0	0	0	0	0	—	0	0	0	0
2.3	6.2	4.2	0	0	0	0	0	—	0	0	0	0
20.5	25.9	159.8	0	0	0	0	0	—	0	0	0	0
1.3	1.6	10.0	0	0	0	0	0	—	0	0	0	0
31.8	93.1	75.6	0	0	0	0	0	—	0	0	0	0
2.0	5.8	4.7	0	0	0	0	0	—	0	0	0	0
38.2	63.0	99.6	0	0	0	0	0	—	0	0	0	0
2.4	3.9	6.2	0	0	0	0	0		0	0	0	0
1.6	1.7	3.8	1	12	11	Trace	6	30	Trace	.02	Trace	Trace
.5	.3	Trace	1	10	8	Trace	5	30	Trace	.01	Trace	Trace
1.1	1.3	3.2	3	2	2	.1	13	—	—	—	—	—
.1	.1	.4	2	2	2	.1	13	—	—	—	—	—
1.6	1.9	4.7	1	2	1	Trace	2	Trace	Trace	Trace	Trace	—
.1	.1	.4	Trace	Trace	1	Trace	2	Trace	Trace	Trace	Trace	—
2.0	2.4	5.6	Trace	3	4	.1	5	40	Trace	.01	Trace	—
1.1	1.4	3.2	2	2	4	Trace	1	30	Trace	Trace	Trace	—
.4	.4	1.0	2	3	4	Trace	1	40	Trace	Trace	Trace	—
1.5	1.8	4.1	1	3	4	.1	11	30	Trace	Trace	Trace	Trace
1.4	1.7	4.0	2	2	3	.1	18	50	Trace	Trace	Trace	Trace
.4	.4	1.0	2	2	3	.1	17	50	Trace	Trace	Trace	Trace
.5	.6	.3	2	14	15	.1	19	80	.01	.03	Trace	Trace

[13] Fatty acid values apply to product made with regular-type margarine.

NUTRITIVE VALUES OF THE EDIBLE PART OF FOODS–Continued

Item No. (A)	Foods, approximate measures, units, and weight (edible part unless footnotes indicate otherwise) (B)		Water (C) Percent	Food energy (D) Calories	Protein (E) Grams	Fat (F) Grams
		Grams				
	FISH, SHELLFISH, MEAT, POULTRY; RELATED PRODUCTS					
	Fish and shellfish:					
145	Bluefish, baked with butter or margarine.	3 oz	85	68	135	22	4
	Clams:					
146	Raw, meat only	3 oz	85	82	65	11	1
147	Canned, solids and liquid	3 oz	85	86	45	7	1
148	Crabmeat (white or king), canned, not pressed down.	1 cup	135	77	135	24	3
149	Fish sticks, breaded, cooked, frozen (stick, 4 by 1 by 1/2 in).	1 fish stick or 1 oz	28	66	50	5	3
150	Haddock, breaded, fried[14]	3 oz	85	66	140	17	5
151	Ocean perch, breaded, fried[14]	1 fillet	85	59	195	16	11
152	Oysters, raw, meat only (13-19 medium Selects).	1 cup	240	85	160	20	4
153	Salmon, pink, canned, solids and liquid.	3 oz	85	71	120	17	5
154	Sardines, Atlantic, canned in oil, drained solids.	3 oz	85	62	175	20	9
155	Scallops, frozen, breaded, fried, reheated.	6 scallops	90	60	175	16	8
156	Shad, baked with butter or margarine, bacon.	3 oz	85	64	170	20	10
	Shrimp:					
157	Canned meat	3 oz	85	70	100	21	1
158	French fried[16]	3 oz	85	57	190	17	9
159	Tuna, canned in oil, drained solids.	3 oz	85	61	170	24	7
160	Tuna salad[17]	1 cup	205	70	350	30	22
	Meat and meat products:					
161	Bacon, (20 slices per lb, raw), broiled or fried, crisp.	2 slices	15	8	85	4	8
	Beef,[18] cooked:					
	Cuts braised, simmered or pot roasted:					
162	Lean and fat (piece, 2 1/2 by 2 1/2 by 3/4 in).	3 oz	85	53	245	23	16
163	Lean only from item 162	2.5 oz	72	62	140	22	5
	Ground beef, broiled:					
164	Lean with 10% fat	3 oz or patty 3 by 5/8 in	85	60	185	23	10
165	Lean with 21% fat	2.9 oz or patty 3 by 5/8 in	82	54	235	20	17
	Roast, oven cooked, no liquid added:					
	Relatively fat, such as rib:					
166	Lean and fat (2 pieces, 4 1/8 by 2 1/4 by 1/4 in).	3 oz	85	40	375	17	33
167	Lean only from item 166	1.8 oz	51	57	125	14	7
	Relatively lean, such as heel of round:					
168	Lean and fat (2 pieces, 4 1/8 by 2 1/4 by 1/4 in).	3 oz	85	62	165	25	7

[14] Dipped in egg, milk or water, and breadcrumbs; fried in vegetable shortening.
[15] If bones are discarded, value for calcium will be greatly reduced.
[16] Dipped in egg, breadcrumbs, and flour or batter.

	NUTRIENTS IN INDICATED QUANTITY											
	Fatty Acids											
Saturated (total)	Unsaturated		Carbohydrate	Calcium	Phosphorus	Iron	Potassium	Vitamin A value	Thiamin	Riboflavin	Niacin	Ascorbic acid
	Oleic	Linoleic										
(G)	(H)	(I)	(J)	(K)	(L)	(M)	(N)	(O)	(P)	(Q)	(R)	(S)
Grams	Grams	Grams	Grams	Milligrams	Milligrams	Milligrams	Milligrams	International units	Milligrams	Milligrams	Milligrams	Milligrams
—	—	—	0	25	244	0.6	—	40	0.09	0.08	1.6	—
—	—	—	2	59	138	5.2	154	90	.08	.15	1.1	8
0.2	Trace	Trace	2	47	116	3.5	119	—	.01	.09	.9	—
.6	0.4	0.1	1	61	246	1.1	149	—	.11	.11	2.6	—
—	—	—	2	3	47	.1	—	0	.01	.02	.5	—
1.4	2.2	1.2	5	34	210	1.0	296	—	.03	.06	2.7	2
2.7	4.4	2.3	6	28	192	1.1	242	—	.10	.10	1.6	—
1.3	.2	.1	8	226	343	13.2	290	740	.34	.43	6.0	—
.9	.8	.1	0	[15]167	243	.7	307	60	.03	.16	6.8	—
3.0	2.5	.5	0	372	424	2.5	502	190	.02	.17	4.6	—
—	—	—	9	—	—	—	—	—	—	—	—	—
—	—	—	0	20	266	.5	320	30	.11	.22	7.3	—
.1	.1	Trace	1	98	224	2.6	104	50	.01	.03	1.5	—
2.3	3.7	2.0	9	61	162	1.7	195	—	.03	.07	2.3	—
1.7	1.7	.7	0	7	199	1.6	—	70	.04	.10	10.1	—
4.3	6.3	6.7	7	41	291	2.7	—	590	.08	.23	10.3	2
2.5	3.7	.7	Trace	2	34	.5	35	0	.08	.05	.8	—
6.8	6.5	.4	0	10	114	2.9	184	30	.04	.18	3.6	—
2.1	1.8	.2	0	10	108	2.7	176	10	.04	.17	3.3	—
4.0	3.9	.3	0	10	196	3.0	261	20	.08	.20	5.1	—
7.0	6.7	.4	0	9	159	2.6	221	30	.07	.17	4.4	—
14.0	13.6	.8	0	8	158	2.2	189	70	.05	.13	3.1	—
3.0	2.5	.3	0	6	131	1.8	161	10	.04	.11	2.6	—
2.8	2.7	.2	0	11	208	3.2	279	10	.06	.19	4.5	—

[17] Prepared with tuna, celery, salad dressing (mayonnaise type), pickle, onion, and egg.
[18] Outer layer of fat on the cut was removed to within approximately 1/2 in of the lean. Deposits of fat within the cut were not removed.

NUTRITIVE VALUES OF THE EDIBLE PART OF FOODS—Continued

Item No. (A)	Foods, approximate measures, units, and weight (edible part unless footnotes indicate otherwise) (B)		Grams	Water Per-cent (C)	Food energy Cal-ories (D)	Pro-tein Grams (E)	Fat Grams (F)
	FISH, SHELLFISH, MEAT, POULTRY; RELATED PRODUCTS—Con.						
	Meat and meat products—Continued						
	Beef,[18] cooked—Continued						
	Roast, oven cooked, no liquid added—Continued						
	Relatively lean such as heel of round—Continued						
169	Lean only from item 168	2.8 oz	78	65	125	24	3
	Steak:						
	Relatively fat—sirloin, broiled:						
170	Lean and fat (piece, 2 1/2 by 2 1/2 by 3/4 in)	3 oz	85	44	330	20	27
171	Lean only from item 170	2.0 oz	56	59	115	18	4
	Relatively lean—round, braised:						
172	Lean and fat (piece, 4 1/8 by 2 1/4 by 1/2 in)	3 oz	85	55	220	24	13
173	Lean only from item 172	2.4 oz	68	61	130	21	4
	Beef, canned:						
174	Corned beef	3 oz	85	59	185	22	10
175	Corned beef hash	1 cup	220	67	400	19	25
176	Beef, dried, chipped	2 1/2-oz jar	71	48	145	24	4
177	Beef and vegetable stew	1 cup	245	82	220	16	11
178	Beef potpie (home recipe), baked[19] (piece, 1/3 of 9-in diam. pie)	1 piece	210	55	515	21	30
179	Chili con carne with beans, canned.	1 cup	255	72	340	19	16
180	Chop suey with beef and pork (home recipe).	1 cup	250	75	300	26	17
181	Heart, beef, lean, braised	3 oz	85	61	160	27	5
	Lamb, cooked:						
	Chop, rib (cut 3 per lb with bone), broiled:						
182	Lean and fat	3.1 oz	89	43	360	18	32
183	Lean only from item 182	2 oz	57	60	120	16	6
	Leg, roasted:						
184	Lean and fat (2 pieces, 4 1/8 by 2 1/4 by 1/4 in).	3 oz	85	54	235	22	16
185	Lean only from item 184	2.5 oz	71	62	130	20	5
	Shoulder, roasted:						
186	Lean and fat (3 pieces, 2 1/2 by 2 1/2 by 1/4 in).	3 oz	85	50	285	18	23
187	Lean only from item 186	2.3 oz	64	61	130	17	6
188	Liver, beef, fried[20] (slice, 6 1/2 by 2 3/8 by 3/8 in).	3 oz	85	56	195	22	9
	Pork, cured, cooked:						
189	Ham, light cure, lean and fat, roasted (2 pieces, 4 1/8 by 2 1/4 by 1/4 in).[22]	3 oz	85	54	245	18	19
	Luncheon meat:						
190	Boiled ham, slice (8 per 8-oz pkg.).	1 oz	28	59	65	5	5
	Canned, spiced or unspiced:						
191	Slice, approx. 3 by 2 by 1/2 in.	1 slice	60	55	175	9	15

[18] Outer layer of fat on the cut was removed to within approximately 1/2 of the lean. Deposits of fat within the cut were not removed.
[19] Crust made with vegetable shortening and enriched flour.
[20] Regular-type margarine used.

	NUTRIENTS IN INDICATED QUANTITY											
	Fatty Acids											
Saturated (total)	Unsaturated		Carbohydrate	Calcium	Phosphorus	Iron	Potassium	Vitamin A value	Thiamin	Riboflavin	Niacin	Ascorbic acid
	Oleic	Linoleic										
(G)	(H)	(I)	(J)	(K)	(L)	(M)	(N)	(O)	(P)	(Q)	(R)	(S)
Grams	Grams	Grams	Grams	Milligrams	Milligrams	Milligrams	Milligrams	International units	Milligrams	Milligrams	Milligrams	Milligrams
1.2	1.0	0.1	0	10	199	3.0	268	Trace	0.06	0.18	4.3	—
11.3	11.1	.6	0	9	162	2.5	220	50	.05	.15	4.0	—
1.8	1.6	.2	0	7	146	2.2	202	10	.05	.14	3.6	—
5.5	5.2	.4	0	10	213	3.0	272	20	.07	.19	4.8	—
1.7	1.5	.2	0	9	182	2.5	238	10	.05	.16	4.1	—
4.9	4.5	.2	0	17	90	3.7	—	—	.01	.20	2.9	—
11.9	10.9	.5	24	29	147	4.4	440	—	.02	.20	4.6	—
2.1	2.0	.1	0	14	287	3.6	142	—	.05	.23	2.7	0
4.9	4.5	.2	15	29	184	2.9	613	2,400	.15	.17	4.7	17
7.9	12.8	6.7	39	29	149	3.8	334	1,720	.30	.30	5.5	6
7.5	6.8	.3	31	82	321	4.3	594	150	.08	.18	3.3	—
8.5	6.2	.7	13	60	248	4.8	425	600	.28	.38	5.0	33
1.5	1.1	.6	1	5	154	5.0	197	20	.21	1.04	6.5	1
14.8	12.1	1.2	0	8	139	1.0	200	—	.11	.19	4.1	—
2.5	2.1	.2	0	6	121	1.1	174	—	.09	.15	3.4	—
7.3	6.0	.6	0	9	177	1.4	241	—	.13	.23	4.7	—
2.1	1.8	.2	0	9	169	1.4	227	—	.12	.21	4.4	—
10.8	8.8	.9	0	9	146	1.0	206	—	.11	.20	4.0	—
3.6	2.3	.2	0	8	140	1.0	193	—	.10	.18	3.7	—
2.5	3.5	.9	5	9	405	7.5	323	[21]45,390	.22	3.56	14.0	23
6.8	7.9	1.7	0	8	146	2.2	199	0	.40	.15	3.1	—
1.7	2.0	.4	0	3	47	.8	—	0	.12	.04	.7	—
5.4	6.7	1.0	1	5	65	1.3	133	0	.19	.13	1.8	—

[21] Value varies widely.
[22] About one-fourth of the outer layer of fat on the cut was removed. Deposits of fat within the cut were not removed.

NUTRITIVE VALUES OF THE EDIBLE PART OF FOODS—Continued

Item No. (A)	Foods, approximate measures, units, and weight (edible part unless footnotes indicate otherwise) (B)		Water (C) Grams	Food energy (D) Per-cent	Pro-tein (E) Cal-ories	Fat (F) Grams
	Pork, fresh,[18] cooked: Chop, loin (cut 3 per lb with bone), broiled:					
192	Lean and fat	2.7 oz	78	42	305	19	25
193	Lean only from item 192	2 oz	56	53	150	17	9
	Roast, oven cooked, no liquid added:					
194	Lean and fat (piece, 2 1/2 by 2 1/2 by 3/4 in).	3 oz	85	46	310	21	24
195	Lean only from item 194	2.4 oz	68	55	175	20	10
	Shoulder cut, simmered:					
196	Lean and fat (3 pieces, 2 1/2 by 2 1/2 by 1/4 in).	3 oz	85	46	320	20	26
197	Lean only from item 196	2.2 oz	63	60	135	18	6
	Sausages (see also Luncheon meat (items 190-191)):					
198	Bologna, slice (8 per 8-oz pkg.).	1 slice	28	56	85	3	8
199	Braunschweiger, slice (6 per 6-oz pkg.).	1 slice	28	53	90	4	8
200	Brown and serve (10-11 per 8-oz pkg.), browned.	1 link	17	40	70	3	6
201	Deviled ham, canned	1 tbsp	13	51	45	2	4
202	Frankfurter (8 per 1-lb pkg.), cooked (reheated).	1 frankfurter	56	57	170	7	15
203	Meat, potted (beef, chicken, turkey), canned.	1 tbsp	13	61	30	2	2
204	Pork link (16 per 1-lb pkg.), cooked.	1 link	13	35	60	2	6
	Salami:					
205	Dry type, slice (12 per 4-oz pkg.).	1 slice	10	30	45	2	4
206	Cooked type, slice (8 per 8-oz pkg.).	1 slice	28	51	90	5	7
207	Vienna sausage (7 per 4-oz can).	1 sausage	16	63	40	2	3
	Veal, medium fat, cooked, bone removed:					
208	Cutlet (4 1/8 by 2 1/4 by 1/2 in), braised or broiled.	3 oz	85	60	185	23	9
209	Rib (2 pieces, 4 1/8 by 2 1/4 by 1/4 in), roasted.	3 oz	85	55	230	23	14
	Poultry and poultry products: Chicken, cooked:					
210	Breast, fried,[23] bones removed, 1/2 breast (3.3 oz with bones).	2.8 oz	79	58	160	26	5
211	Drumstick, fried,[23] bones removed (2 oz with bones).	1.3 oz	38	55	90	12	4
212	Half broiler, broiled, bones removed (10.4 oz with bones).	6.2 oz	176	71	240	42	7
213	Chicken, canned, boneless	3 oz	85	65	170	18	10
214	Chicken a la king, cooked (home recipe).	1 cup	245	68	470	27	34
215	Chicken and noodles, cooked (home recipe).	1 cup	240	71	365	22	18

[18]Outer layer of fat on the cut was removed to within approximately 1/2 in of the lean. Deposits of fat within the cut were not removed.

	NUTRIENTS IN INDICATED QUANTITY											
	Fatty Acids											
Satu-rated (total)	Unsaturated		Carbo-hydrate	Calcium	Phos-phorus	Iron	Potas-sium	Vitamin A value	Thiamin	Ribo-flavin	Niacin	Ascorbic acid
	Oleic	Lino-leic										
(G)	(H)	(I)	(J)	(K)	(L)	(M)	(N)	(O)	(P)	(Q)	(R)	(S)
Grams	Grams	Grams	Grams	Milli-grams	Milli-grams	Milli-grams	Milli-grams	Inter-national units	Milli-grams	Milli-grams	Milli-grams	Milli-grams
8.9	10.4	2.2	0	9	209	2.7	216	0	0.75	0.22	4.5	—
3.1	3.6	.8	0	7	181	2.2	192	0	.63	.18	3.8	—
8.7	10.2	2.2	0	9	218	2.7	233	0	.78	.22	4.8	—
3.5	4.1	.8	0	9	211	2.6	224	0	.73	.21	4.4	—
9.3	10.9	2.3	0	9	118	2.6	158	0	.46	.21	4.1	—
2.2	2.6	.6	0	8	111	2.3	146	0	.42	.19	3.7	—
3.0	3.4	.5	Trace	2	36	.5	65	—	.05	.06	.7	—
2.6	3.4	.8	1	3	69	1.7	—	1,850	.05	.41	2.3	—
2.3	2.8	.7	Trace	—	—	—	—	—	—	—	—	—
1.5	1.8	.4	0	1	12	.3	—	0	.02	.01	.2	—
5.6	6.5	1.2	1	3	57	.8	—	—	.08	.11	1.4	—
—	—	—	0	—	—	—	—	—	Trace	.03	.2	—
2.1	2.4	.5	Trace	1	21	.3	35	0	.10	.04	.5	—
1.6	1.6	.1	Trace	1	28	.4	—	—	.04	.03	.5	—
3.1	3.0	.2	Trace	3	57	.7	—	—	.07	.07	1.2	—
1.2	1.4	.2	Trace	1	24	.3	—	—	.01	.02	.4	—
4.0	3.4	.4	0	9	196	2.7	258	—	.06	.21	4.6	—
6.1	5.1	.6	0	10	211	2.9	259	—	.11	.26	6.6	—
1.4	1.8	1.1	1	9	218	1.3	—	70	.04	.17	11.6	—
1.1	1.3	.9	Trace	6	89	.9	—	50	.03	.15	2.7	—
2.2	2.5	1.3	0	16	355	3.0	483	160	.09	.34	15.5	—
3.2	3.8	2.0	0	18	210	1.3	117	200	.03	.11	3.7	3
12.7	14.3	3.3	12	127	358	2.5	404	1,130	.10	.42	5.4	12
5.9	7.1	3.5	26	26	247	2.2	149	430	.05	.17	4.3	Trace

[2,3] Vegetable shortening used.

Item No. (A)	Foods, approximate measures, units, and weight (edible part unless footnotes indicate otherwise) (B)			Water (C)	Food energy (D)	Protein (E)	Fat (F)
			Grams	*Percent*	*Calories*	*Grams*	*Grams*
	FISH, SHELLFISH, MEAT, POULTRY; RELATED PRODUCTS–Con.						
	Poultry and poultry products–Continued						
	Chicken chow mein:						
216	Canned	1 cup	250	89	95	7	Trace
217	From home recipe	1 cup	250	78	255	31	10
218	Chicken potpie (home recipe), baked,[19] piece (1/3 or 9-in diam. pie).	1 piece	232	57	545	23	31
	Turkey, roasted, flesh without skin:						
219	Dark meat, piece, 2 1/2 by 1 5/8 by 1/4 in.	4 pieces	85	61	175	26	7
220	Light meat, piece, 4 by 2 by 1/4 in.	2 pieces	85	62	150	28	3
	Light and dark meat:						
221	Chopped or diced	1 cup	140	61	265	44	9
222	Pieces (1 slice white meat, 4 by 2 by 1/4 in with 2 slices dark meat, 2 1/2 by 1 5/8 by 1/4 in).	3 pieces	85	61	160	27	5
	FRUITS AND FRUIT PRODUCTS						
	Apples, raw, unpeeled, without cores:						
223	2 3/4-in diam. (about 3 per lb with cores).	1 apple	138	84	80	Trace	1
224	3 1/4 in diam. (about 2 per lb with cores).	1 apple	212	84	125	Trace	1
225	Applejuice, bottled or canned[24]	1 cup	248	88	120	Trace	Trace
	Applesauce, canned:						
226	Sweetened	1 cup	255	76	230	1	Trace
227	Unsweetened	1 cup	244	89	100	Trace	Trace
	Apricots:						
228	Raw, without pits (about 12 per lb with pits).	3 apricots	107	85	55	1	Trace
229	Canned in heavy sirup (halves and sirup).	1 cup	258	77	220	2	Trace
	Dried:						
230	Uncooked (28 large or 37 medium halves per cup).	1 cup	130	25	340	7	1
231	Cooked, unsweetened, fruit and liquid.	1 cup	250	76	215	4	1
232	Apricot nectar, canned	1 cup	251	85	145	1	Trace
	Avocados, raw, whole, without skins and seeds:						
233	California, mid- and late-winter (with skin and seed, 3 1/8-in diam.; wt., 10 oz).	1 avocado	216	74	370	5	37
234	Florida, late summer and fall (with skin and seed, 3 5/8-in diam.; wt., 1 lb).	1 avocado	304	78	390	4	33
235	Banana without peel (about 2.6 per lb with peel).	1 banana	119	76	100	1	Trace
236	Banana flakes	1 tbsp	6	3	20	Trace	Trace

[19]Crust made with vegetable shortening and enriched flour.
[24]Also applies to pasteurized apple cider.

	NUTRIENTS IN INDICATED QUANTITY											
	Fatty Acids											
Satu-rated (total)	Unsaturated Oleic	Lino-leic	Carbo-hydrate	Calcium	Phos-phorus	Iron	Potas-sium	Vitamin A value	Thiamin	Ribo-flavin	Niacin	Ascorbic acid
(G)	(H)	(I)	(J)	(K)	(L)	(M)	(N)	(O)	(P)	(Q)	(R)	(S)
Grams	Grams	Grams	Grams	Milli-grams	Milli-grams	Milli-grams	Milli-grams	Inter-national units	Milli-grams	Milli-grams	Milli-grams	Milli-grams
—	—	—	18	45	85	1.3	418	150	0.05	0.10	1.0	13
2.4	3.4	3.1	10	58	293	2.5	473	280	.08	.23	4.3	10
11.3	10.9	5.6	42	70	232	3.0	343	3,090	.34	.31	5.5	5
2.1	1.5	1.5	0	—	—	2.0	338	—	.03	.20	3.6	—
.9	.6	.7	0	—	—	1.0	349	—	.04	.12	9.4	—
2.5	1.7	1.8	0	11	351	2.5	514	—	.07	.25	10.8	—
1.5	1.0	1.1	0	7	213	1.5	312	—	.04	.15	6.5	—
—	—	—	20	10	14	.4	152	120	.04	.03	.1	6
—	—	—	31	15	21	.6	233	190	.06	.04	.2	8
—	—	—	30	15	22	1.5	250	—	.02	.05	.2	[25]2
—	—	—	61	10	13	1.3	166	100	.05	.03	.1	[25]3
—	—	—	26	10	12	1.2	190	100	.05	.02	.1	[25]2
—	—	—	14	18	25	.5	301	2,890	.03	.04	.6	11
—	—	—	57	28	39	.8	604	4,490	.05	.05	1.0	10
—	—	—	86	87	140	7.2	1,273	14,170	.01	.21	4.3	16
—	—	—	54	55	88	4.5	795	7,500	.01	.13	2.5	8
—	—	—	37	23	30	.5	379	2,380	.03	.03	.5	[26]36
5.5	22.0	3.7	13	22	91	1.3	1,303	630	.24	.43	3.5	30
6.7	15.7	5.3	27	30	128	1.8	1,836	880	.33	.61	4.9	43
—	—	—	26	10	31	.8	440	230	.06	.07	.8	12
—	—	—	5	2	6	.2	92	50	.01	.01	.2	Trace

[25] Applies to product without added ascorbic acid. For value of product with added ascorbic acid, refer to label.
[26] Based on product with label claim of 45% of U.S. RDA in 6 fl oz.

NUTRITIVE VALUES OF THE EDIBLE PART OF FOODS—Continued

Item No. (A)	Foods, approximate measures, units, and weight (edible part unless footnotes indicate otherwise) (B)		Water (C)	Food energy (D)	Protein (E)	Fat (F)
		Grams	Percent	Calories	Grams	Grams
237	Blackberries, raw--------------	1 cup----------------- 144	85	85	2	1
238	Blueberries, raw--------------	1 cup----------------- 145	83	90	1	1
	Cantaloup. See Muskmelons (item 271).					
	Cherries:					
239	Sour (tart), red, pitted, canned, water pack.	1 cup----------------- 244	88	105	2	Trace
240	Sweet, raw, without pits and stems.	10 cherries----------- 68	80	45	1	Trace
241	Cranberry juice cocktail, bottled, sweetened.	1 cup----------------- 253	83	165	Trace	Trace
242	Cranberry sauce, sweetened, canned, strained.	1 cup----------------- 277	62	405	Trace	1
	Dates:					
243	Whole, without pits----------	10 dates------------- 80	23	220	2	Trace
244	Chopped---------------------	1 cup----------------- 178	23	490	4	1
245	Fruit cocktail, canned, in heavy sirup.	1 cup----------------- 255	80	195	1	Trace
	Grapefruit:					
	Raw, medium, 3 3/4-in diam. (about 1 lb 1 oz):					
246	Pink or red-----------------	1/2 grapefruit with peel[28] 241	89	50	1	Trace
247	White-----------------------	1/2 grapefruit with peel[28] 241	89	45	1	Trace
248	Canned, sections with sirup--	1 cup----------------- 254	81	180	2	Trace
	Grapefruit juice:					
249	Raw, pink, red, or white-----	1 cup----------------- 246	90	95	1	Trace
	Canned, white:					
250	Unsweetened-----------------	1 cup----------------- 247	89	100	1	Trace
251	Sweetened-------------------	1 cup----------------- 250	86	135	1	Trace
	Frozen, concentrate, unsweetened:					
252	Undiluted, 6-fl oz can------	1 can----------------- 207	62	300	4	1
253	Diluted with 3 parts water by volume.	1 cup----------------- 247	89	100	1	Trace
254	Dehydrated crystals, prepared with water (1 lb yields about 1 gal).	1 cup----------------- 247	90	100	1	Trace
	Grapes, European type (adherent skin), raw:					
255	Thompson Seedless------------	10 grapes------------- 50	81	35	Trace	Trace
256	Tokay and Emperor, seeded types-	10 grapes[30]--------- 60	81	40	Trace	Trace
	Grapejuice:					
257	Canned or bottled-----------	1 cup----------------- 253	83	165	1	Trace
	Frozen concentrate, sweetened:					
258	Undiluted, 6-fl oz can------	1 can----------------- 216	53	395	1	Trace
259	Diluted with 3 parts water by volume.	1 cup----------------- 250	86	135	1	Trace
260	Grape drink, canned----------	1 cup----------------- 250	86	135	Trace	Trace
261	Lemon, raw, size 165, without peel and seeds (about 4 per lb with peels and seeds).	1 lemon--------------- 74	90	20	1	Trace
	Lemon juice:					
262	Raw------------------------	1 cup----------------- 244	91	60	1	Trace
263	Canned, or bottled, unsweetened-	1 cup----------------- 244	92	55	1	Trace
264	Frozen, single strength, unsweetened, 6-fl oz can.	1 can----------------- 183	92	40	1	Trace
	Lemonade concentrate, frozen:					
265	Undiluted, 6-fl oz can------	1 can----------------- 219	49	425	Trace	Trace
266	Diluted with 4 1/3 parts water by volume.	1 cup----------------- 248	89	105	Trace	Trace

[25] Applies to product without added ascorbic acid. For value of product with added ascorbic acid, refer to label.
[27] Based on product with label claim of 100% of U.S. RDA in 6 fl oz.
[28] Weight includes peel and membranes between sections. Without these parts, the weight of the edible portion is 123 g for item 246 and 118 g for item 247.
[29] For white-fleshed varieties, value is about 20 International Units (I.U.) per cup; for red-fleshed varieties, 1,080 I.U.
[30] Weight includes seeds. Without seeds, weight of the edible portion is 57 g.

	NUTRIENTS IN INDICATED QUANTITY										
	Fatty Acids										
Satu-rated (total)	Unsaturated		Carbo-hydrate	Calcium	Phos-phorus	Iron	Potas-sium	Vitamin A value	Thiamin	Ribo-flavin	Niacin	Ascorbic acid
	Oleic	Lino-leic										
(G)	(H)	(I)	(J)	(K)	(L)	(M)	(N)	(O)	(P)	(Q)	(R)	(S)
Grams	Grams	Grams	Grams	Milli-grams	Milli-grams	Milli-grams	Milli-grams	Inter-national units	Milli-grams	Milli-grams	Milli-grams	Milli-grams
—	—	—	19	46	27	1.3	245	290	0.04	0.06	0.6	30
—	—	—	22	22	19	1.5	117	150	.04	.09	.7	20
			26	37	32	.7	317	1,660	.07	.05	.5	12
			12	15	13	.3	129	70	.03	.04	.3	7
—	—	—	42	13	8	.8	25	Trace	.03	.03	.1	[27]81
			104	17	11	.6	83	60	.03	.03	.1	6
—	—	—	58	47	50	2.4	518	40	.07	.08	1.8	0
—	—	—	130	105	112	5.3	1,153	90	.16	.18	3.9	0
—	—	—	50	23	31	1.0	411	360	.05	.03	1.0	5
—	—	—	13	20	20	.5	166	540	.05	.02	.2	44
—	—	—	12	19	19	.5	159	10	.05	.02	.2	44
—	—	—	45	33	36	.8	343	30	.08	.05	.5	76
—	—	—	23	22	37	.5	399	([29])	.10	.05	.5	93
			24	20	35	1.0	400	20	.07	.05	.5	84
			32	20	35	1.0	405	30	.08	.05	.5	78
—	—	—	72	70	124	.8	1,250	60	.29	.12	1.4	286
			24	25	42	.2	420	20	.10	.04	.5	96
—	—	—	24	22	40	.2	412	20	.10	.05	.5	91
—	—	—	9	6	10	.2	87	50	.03	.02	.2	2
—	—	—	10	7	11	.2	99	60	.03	.02	.2	2
			42	28	30	.8	293	—	.10	.05	.5	[25]Trace
—	—	—	100	22	32	.9	255	40	.13	.22	1.5	[31]32
—	—	—	33	8	10	.3	85	10	.05	.08	.5	[31]10
—	—	—	35	8	10	.3	88	—	[32].03	[32].03	.3	([32])
—	—	—	6	19	12	.4	102	10	.03	.01	.1	39
—	—	—	20	17	24	.5	344	50	.07	.02	.2	112
—	—	—	19	17	24	.5	344	50	.07	.02	.2	102
—	—	—	13	13	16	.5	258	40	.05	.02	.2	81
—	—	—	112	9	13	.4	153	40	.05	.06	.7	66
—	—	—	28	2	3	.1	40	10	.01	.02	.2	17

[31] Applies to product without added ascorbic acid. With added ascorbic acid, based on claim that 6 fl oz of reconstituted juice contain 45% or 50% of the U.S. RDA, value in milligrams is 108 or 120 for a 6-fl oz can (item 258), 36 or 40 for 1 cup of diluted juice (item 259).

[32] For products with added thiamin and riboflavin but without added ascorbic acid, values in milligrams would be 0.60 for thiamin, 0.80 for riboflavin, and trace for ascorbic acid. For products with only ascorbic acid added, value varies with the brand. Consult the label.

NUTRITIVE VALUES OF THE EDIBLE PART OF FOODS—Continued

Item No. (A)	Foods, approximate measures, units, and weight (edible part unless footnotes indicate otherwise) (B)		Water (C)	Food energy (D)	Protein (E)	Fat (F)
		Grams	Percent	Calories	Grams	Grams
	FRUITS AND FRUIT PRODUCTS—Con.					
	Limeade concentrate, frozen:					
267	Undiluted, 6-fl oz can---------- 1 can--------------------	218	50	410	Trace	Trace
268	Diluted with 4 1/3 parts water by volume. 1 cup--------------------	247	89	100	Trace	Trace
	Limejuice:					
269	Raw------------------------- 1 cup--------------------	246	90	65	1	Trace
270	Canned, unsweetened--------- 1 cup--------------------	246	90	65	1	Trace
	Muskmelons, raw, with rind, without seed cavity:					
271	Cantaloup, orange-fleshed (with rind and seed cavity, 5-in diam., 2 1/3 lb). 1/2 melon with rind[33]-----	477	91	80	2	Trace
272	Honeydew (with rind and seed cavity, 6 1/2-in diam., 5 1/4 lb). 1/10 melon with rind[33]----	226	91	50	1	Trace
	Oranges, all commercial varieties, raw:					
273	Whole, 2 5/8-in diam., without peel and seeds (about 2 1/2 per lb with peel and seeds). 1 orange------------------	131	86	65	1	Trace
274	Sections without membranes------ 1 cup--------------------	180	86	90	2	Trace
	Orange juice:					
275	Raw, all varieties-------------- 1 cup--------------------	248	88	110	2	Trace
276	Canned, unsweetened------------ 1 cup--------------------	249	87	120	2	Trace
	Frozen concentrate:					
277	Undiluted, 6-fl oz can-------- 1 can--------------------	213	55	360	5	Trace
278	Diluted with 3 parts water by volume. 1 cup--------------------	249	87	120	2	Trace
279	Dehydrated crystals, prepared with water (1 lb yields about 1 gal). 1 cup--------------------	248	88	115	1	Trace
	Orange and grapefruit juice: Frozen concentrate:					
280	Undiluted, 6-fl oz can-------- 1 can--------------------	210	59	330	4	1
281	Diluted with 3 parts water by volume. 1 cup--------------------	248	88	110	1	Trace
282	Papayas, raw, 1/2-in cubes-------- 1 cup--------------------	140	89	55	1	Trace
	Peaches: Raw:					
283	Whole, 2 1/2-in diam., peeled, pitted (about 4 per lb with peels and pits). 1 peach-------------------	100	89	40	1	Trace
284	Sliced------------------------ 1 cup--------------------	170	89	65	1	Trace
	Canned, yellow-fleshed, solids and liquid (halves or slices):					
285	Sirup pack-------------------- 1 cup--------------------	256	79	200	1	Trace
286	Water pack-------------------- 1 cup--------------------	244	91	75	1	Trace
	Dried:					
287	Uncooked--------------------- 1 cup--------------------	160	25	420	5	1
288	Cooked, unsweetened, halves and juice. 1 cup--------------------	250	77	205	3	1

[33] Weight includes rind. Without rind, the weight of the edible portion is 272 g for item 271 and 149 g for item 272.

	NUTRIENTS IN INDICATED QUANTITY												
	Fatty Acids												
Satu-rated (total)	Unsaturated		Carbo-hydrate	Calcium	Phos-phorus	Iron	Potas-sium	Vitamin A value	Thiamin	Ribo-flavin	Niacin	Ascorbic acid
	Oleic	Lino-leic										
(G)	(H)	(I)	(J)	(K)	(L)	(M)	(N)	(O)	(P)	(Q)	(R)	(S)
Grams	Grams	Grams	Grams	Milli-grams	Milli-grams	Milli-grams	Milli-grams	Inter-national units	Milli-grams	Milli-grams	Milli-grams	Milli-grams
—	—	—	108	11	13	0.2	129	Trace	0.02	0.02	0.2	26
—	—	—	27	3	3	Trace	32	Trace	Trace	Trace	Trace	6
—	—	—	22	22	27	.5	256	20	.05	.02	.2	79
—	—	—	22	22	27	.5	256	20	.05	.02	.2	52
—	—	—	20	38	44	1.1	682	9,240	.11	.08	1.6	90
—	—	—	11	21	24	.6	374	60	.06	.04	.9	34
—	—	—	16	54	26	.5	263	260	.13	.05	.5	66
—	—	—	22	74	36	.7	360	360	.18	.07	.7	90
—	—	—	26	27	42	.5	496	500	.22	.07	1.0	124
—	—	—	28	25	45	1.0	496	500	.17	.05	.7	100
—	—	—	87	75	126	.9	1,500	1,620	.68	.11	2.8	360
—	—	—	29	25	42	.2	503	540	.23	.03	.9	120
—	—	—	27	25	40	.5	518	500	.20	.07	1.0	109
—	—	—	78	61	99	.8	1,308	800	.48	.06	2.3	302
—	—	—	26	20	32	.2	439	270	.15	.02	.7	102
—	—	—	14	28	22	.4	328	2,450	.06	.06	.4	78
—	—	—	10	9	19	.5	202	[34]1,330	.02	.05	1.0	7
—	—	—	16	15	32	.9	343	[34]2,260	.03	.09	1.7	12
—	—	—	51	10	31	.8	333	1,100	.03	.05	1.5	8
—	—	—	20	10	32	.7	334	1,100	.02	.07	1.5	7
—	—	—	109	77	187	9.6	1,520	6,240	.02	.30	8.5	29
—	—	—	54	38	93	4.8	743	3,050	.01	.15	3.8	5

[34] Represents yellow-fleshed varieties. For white-fleshed varieties, value is 50 International Units (I.J.) for 1 peach, 90 I.U. for 1 cup of slices.

NUTRITIVE VALUES OF THE EDIBLE PART OF FOODS—Continued

Item No. (A)	Foods, approximate measures, units, and weight (edible part unless footnotes indicate otherwise) (B)		Water (C) Percent	Food energy (D) Calories	Protein (E) Grams	Fat (F) Grams
		Grams				
	Frozen, sliced, sweetened:					
289	10-oz container	1 container	284	77	250	1	Trace
290	Cup	1 cup	250	77	220	1	Trace
	Pears:					
	Raw, with skin, cored:					
291	Bartlett, 2 1/2-in diam. (about 2 1/2 per lb with cores and stems).	1 pear	164	83	100	1	1
292	Bosc, 2 1/2-in diam. (about 3 per lb with cores and stems).	1 pear	141	83	85	1	1
293	D'Anjou, 3-in diam. (about 2 per lb with cores and stems).	1 pear	200	83	120	1	1
294	Canned, solids and liquid, sirup pack, heavy (halves or slices).	1 cup	255	80	195	1	1
	Pineapple:					
295	Raw, diced	1 cup	155	85	80	1	Trace
	Canned, heavy sirup pack, solids and liquid:					
296	Crushed, chunks, tidbits	1 cup	255	80	190	1	Trace
	Slices and liquid:					
297	Large	1 slice; 2 1/4 tbsp liquid.	105	80	80	Trace	Trace
298	Medium	1 slice; 1 1/4 tbsp liquid.	58	80	45	Trace	Trace
299	Pineapple juice, unsweetened, canned.	1 cup	250	86	140	1	Trace
	Plums:					
	Raw, without pits:					
300	Japanese and hybrid (2 1/8-in diam., about 6 1/2 per lb with pits).	1 plum	66	87	30	Trace	Trace
301	Prune-type (1 1/2-in diam., about 15 per lb with pits).	1 plum	28	79	20	Trace	Trace
	Canned, heavy sirup pack (Italian prunes), with pits and liquid:					
302	Cup	1 cup[36]	272	77	215	1	Trace
303	Portion	3 plums; 2 3/4 tbsp liquid.[36]	140	77	110	1	Trace
	Prunes, dried, "softenized," with pits:					
304	Uncooked	4 extra large or 5 large prunes.[36]	49	28	110	1	Trace
305	Cooked, unsweetened, all sizes, fruit and liquid.	1 cup[36]	250	66	255	2	1
306	Prune juice, canned or bottled	1 cup	256	80	195	1	Trace
	Raisins, seedless:					
307	Cup, not pressed down	1 cup	145	18	420	4	Trace
308	Packet, 1/2 oz (1 1/2 tbsp)	1 packet	14	18	40	Trace	Trace
	Raspberries, red:					
309	Raw, capped, whole	1 cup	123	84	70	1	1
310	Frozen, sweetened, 10-oz container	1 container	284	74	280	2	1
	Rhubarb, cooked, added sugar:					
311	From raw	1 cup	270	63	380	1	Trace
312	From frozen, sweetened	1 cup	270	63	385	1	1

[27]Based on product with label claim of 100% of U.S. RDA in 6 fl oz.
[35]Value represents products with added ascorbic acid. For products without added ascorbic acid, value in milligrams is 116 for a 10-oz container, 103 for 1 cup.

354

	NUTRIENTS IN INDICATED QUANTITY												
	Fatty Acids												
Satu-rated (total)	Unsaturated		Carbo-hydrate	Calcium	Phos-phorus	Iron	Potas-sium	Vitamin A value	Thiamin	Ribo-flavin	Niacin	Ascorbic acid
	Oleic	Lino-leic										
(G)	(H)	(I)	(J)	(K)	(L)	(M)	(N)	(O)	(P)	(Q)	(R)	(S)
Grams	Grams	Grams	Grams	Milli-grams	Milli-grams	Milli-grams	Milli-grams	Inter-national units	Milli-grams	Milli-grams	Milli-grams	Milli-grams
—	—	—	64	11	37	1.4	352	1,850	0.03	0.11	2.0	[35]116
—	—	—	57	10	33	1.3	310	1,630	.03	.10	1.8	[35]103
—	—	—	25	13	18	.5	213	30	.03	.07	.2	7
—	—	—	22	11	16	.4	83	30	.03	.06	.1	6
—	—	—	31	16	22	.6	260	40	.04	.08	.2	8
—	—	—	50	13	18	.5	214	10	.03	.05	.3	3
—	—	—	21	26	12	.8	226	110	.14	.05	.3	26
—	—	—	49	28	13	.8	245	130	.20	.05	.5	18
—	—	—	20	12	5	.3	101	50	.08	.02	.2	7
—	—	—	11	6	3	.2	56	30	.05	.01	.1	4
—	—	—	34	38	23	.8	373	130	.13	.05	.5	[27]80
—	—	—	8	8	12	.3	112	160	.02	.02	.3	4
—	—	—	6	3	5	.1	48	80	.01	.01	.1	1
—	—	—	56	23	26	2.3	367	3,130	.05	.05	1.0	5
—	—	—	29	12	13	1.2	189	1,610	.03	.03	.5	3
—	—	—	29	22	34	1.7	298	690	.04	.07	.7	1
—	—	—	67	51	79	3.8	695	1,590	.07	.15	1.5	2
—	—	—	49	36	51	1.8	602	—	.03	.03	1.0	5
—	—	—	112	90	146	5.1	1,106	30	.16	.12	.7	1
—	—	—	11	9	14	.5	107	Trace	.02	.01	.1	Trace
—	—	—	17	27	27	1.1	207	160	.04	.11	1.1	31
—	—	—	70	37	48	1.7	284	200	.06	.17	1.7	60
—	—	—	97	211	41	1.6	548	220	.05	.14	.8	16
—	—	—	98	211	32	1.9	475	190	.05	.11	.5	16

[36]Weight includes pits. After removal of the pits, the weight of the edible portion is 258 g for item 302, 133 g for item 303, 43 g for item 304, and 213 g for item 305.

NUTRITIVE VALUES OF THE EDIBLE PART OF FOODS—Continued

Item No. (A)	Foods, approximate measures, units, and weight (edible part unless footnotes indicate otherwise) (B)		Water (C)	Food energy (D)	Protein (E)	Fat (F)
		Grams	Percent	Calories	Grams	Grams
	FRUITS AND FRUIT PRODUCTS—Con.					
	Strawberries:					
313	Raw, whole berries, capped	1 cup	149	90	55	1	1
	Frozen, sweetened:					
314	Sliced, 10-oz container	1 container	284	71	310	1	1
315	Whole, 1-lb container (about 1 3/4 cups).	1 container	454	76	415	2	1
316	Tangerine, raw, 2 3/8-in diam., size 176, without peel (about 4 per lb with peels and seeds).	1 tangerine	86	87	40	1	Trace
317	Tangerine juice, canned, sweetened.	1 cup	249	87	125	1	Trace
318	Watermelon, raw, 4 by 8 in wedge with rind and seeds (1/16 of 32 2/3-lb melon, 10 by 16 in).	1 wedge with rind and seeds[37]	926	93	110	2	1
	GRAIN PRODUCTS					
	Bagel, 3-in diam.:					
319	Egg	1 bagel	55	32	165	6	2
320	Water	1 bagel	55	29	165	6	1
321	Barley, pearled, light, uncooked	1 cup	200	11	700	16	2
	Biscuits, baking powder, 2-in diam. (enriched flour, vegetable shortening):					
322	From home recipe	1 biscuit	28	27	105	2	5
323	From mix	1 biscuit	28	29	90	2	3
	Breadcrumbs (enriched):[38]					
324	Dry, grated	1 cup	100	7	390	13	5
	Soft. See White bread (items 349-350).					
	Breads:					
325	Boston brown bread, canned, slice, 3 1/4 by 1/2 in.[38]	1 slice	45	45	95	2	1
	Cracked-wheat bread (3/4 enriched wheat flour, 1/4 cracked wheat):[38]					
326	Loaf, 1 lb	1 loaf	454	35	1,195	39	10
327	Slice (18 per loaf)	1 slice	25	35	65	2	1
	French or vienna bread, enriched:[38]					
328	Loaf, 1 lb	1 loaf	454	31	1,315	41	14
	Slice:					
329	French (5 by 2 1/2 by 1 in)	1 slice	35	31	100	3	1
330	Vienna (4 3/4 by 4 by 1/2 in).	1 slice	25	31	75	2	1
	Italian bread, enriched:					
331	Loaf, 1 lb	1 loaf	454	32	1,250	41	4
332	Slice, 4 1/2 by 3 1/4 by 3/4 in.	1 slice	30	32	85	3	Trace
	Raisin bread, enriched:[38]					
333	Loaf, 1 lb	1 loaf	454	35	1,190	30	13
334	Slice (18 per loaf)	1 slice	25	35	65	2	1

[37] Weight includes rind and seeds. Without rind and seeds, weight of the edible portion is 426 g.
[38] Made with vegetable shortening.

	Fatty Acids		Carbo-hydrate	Calcium	Phos-phorus	Iron	Potas-sium	Vitamin A value	Thiamin	Ribo-flavin	Niacin	Ascorbic acid
Satu-rated (total)	Unsaturated											
	Oleic	Lino-leic										
(G)	(H)	(I)	(J)	(K)	(L)	(M)	(N)	(O)	(P)	(Q)	(R)	(S)
Grams	Grams	Grams	Grams	Milli-grams	Milli-grams	Milli-grams	Milli-grams	Inter-national units	Milli-grams	Milli-grams	Milli-grams	Milli-grams
—	—	—	13	31	31	1.5	244	90	0.04	0.10	0.9	88
—	—	—	79	40	48	2.0	318	90	.06	.17	1.4	151
—	—	—	107	59	73	2.7	472	140	.09	.27	2.3	249
—	—	—	10	34	15	.3	108	360	.05	.02	.1	27
—	—	—	30	44	35	.5	440	1,040	.15	.05	.2	54
—	—	—	27	30	43	2.1	426	2,510	.13	.13	.9	30
0.5	0.9	0.8	28	9	43	1.2	41	30	.14	.10	1.2	0
.2	.4	.6	30	8	41	1.2	42	0	.15	.11	1.4	0
.3	.2	.8	158	32	378	4.0	320	0	.24	.10	6.2	0
1.2	2.0	1.2	13	34	49	.4	33	Trace	.08	.08	.7	Trace
.6	1.1	.7	15	19	65	.6	32	Trace	.09	.08	.8	Trace
1.0	1.6	1.4	73	122	141	3.6	152	Trace	.35	.35	4.8	Trace
.1	.2	.2	21	41	72	.9	131	[39]0	.06	.04	.7	0
2.2	3.0	3.9	236	399	581	9.5	608	Trace	1.52	1.13	14.4	Trace
.1	.2	.2	13	22	32	.5	34	Trace	.08	.06	.8	Trace
3.2	4.7	4.6	251	195	386	10.0	408	Trace	1.80	1.10	15.0	Trace
.2	.4	.4	19	15	30	.8	32	Trace	.14	.08	1.2	Trace
.2	.3	.3	14	11	21	.6	23	Trace	.10	.06	.8	Trace
.6	.3	1.5	256	77	349	10.0	336	0	1.80	1.10	15.0	0
Trace	Trace	.1	17	5	23	.7	22	0	.12	.07	1.0	0
3.0	4.7	3.9	243	322	395	10.0	1,057	Trace	1.70	1.07	10.7	Trace
.2	.3	.2	13	18	22	.6	58	Trace	.09	.06	.6	Trace

[39] Applies to product made with white cornmeal. With yellow cornmeal, value is 30 International Units (I.U.).

NUTRITIVE VALUES OF THE EDIBLE PART OF FOODS—Continued

Item No. (A)	Foods, approximate measures, units, and weight (edible part unless footnotes indicate otherwise) (B)		Water (C)	Food energy (D)	Protein (E)	Fat (F)
			Grams	Per-cent	Cal-ories	Grams	Grams
	Rye Bread:						
	American, light (2/3 enriched wheat flour, 1/3 rye flour):						
335	Loaf, 1 lb	1 loaf	454	36	1,100	41	5
336	Slice (4 3/4 by 3 3/4 by 7/16 in).	1 slice	25	36	60	2	Trace
	Pumpernickel (2/3 rye flour, 1/3 enriched wheat flour):						
337	Loaf, 1 lb	1 loaf	454	34	1,115	41	5
338	Slice (5 by 4 by 3/8 in)	1 slice	32	34	80	3	Trace
	White bread, enriched:[38]						
	Soft-crumb type:						
339	Loaf, 1 lb	1 loaf	454	36	1,225	39	15
340	Slice (18 per loaf)	1 slice	25	36	70	2	1
341	Slice, toasted	1 slice	22	25	70	2	1
342	Slice (22 per loaf)	1 slice	20	36	55	2	1
343	Slice, toasted	1 slice	17	25	55	2	1
344	Loaf, 1 1/2 lb	1 loaf	680	36	1,835	59	22
345	Slice (24 per loaf)	1 slice	28	36	75	2	1
346	Slice, toasted	1 slice	24	25	75	2	1
347	Slice (28 per loaf)	1 slice	24	36	65	2	1
348	Slice, toasted	1 slice	21	25	65	2	1
349	Cubes	1 cup	30	36	80	3	1
350	Crumbs	1 cup	45	36	120	4	1
	Firm-crumb type:						
351	Loaf, 1 lb	1 loaf	454	35	1,245	41	17
352	Slice (20 per loaf)	1 slice	23	35	65	2	1
353	Slice, toasted	1 slice	20	24	65	2	1
354	Loaf, 2 lb	1 loaf	907	35	2,495	82	34
355	Slice (34 per loaf)	1 slice	27	35	75	2	1
356	Slice, toasted	1 slice	23	24	75	2	1
	Whole-wheat bread:						
	Soft-crumb type:[38]						
357	Loaf, 1 lb	1 loaf	454	36	1,095	41	12
358	Slice (16 per loaf)	1 slice	28	36	65	3	1
359	Slice, toasted	1 slice	24	24	65	3	1
	Firm-crumb type:[38]						
360	Loaf, 1 lb	1 loaf	454	36	1,100	48	14
361	Slice (18 per loaf)	1 slice	25	36	60	3	1
362	Slice, toasted	1 slice	21	24	60	3	1
	Breakfast cereals:						
	Hot type, cooked:						
	Corn (hominy) grits, degermed:						
363	Enriched	1 cup	245	87	125	3	Trace
364	Unenriched	1 cup	245	87	125	3	Trace
365	Farina, quick-cooking, enriched.	1 cup	245	89	105	3	Trace
366	Oatmeal or rolled oats	1 cup	240	87	130	5	2
367	Wheat, rolled	1 cup	240	80	180	5	1
368	Wheat, whole-meal	1 cup	245	88	110	4	1
	Ready-to-eat:						
369	Bran flakes (40% bran), added sugar, salt, iron, vitamins.	1 cup	35	3	105	4	1
370	Bran flakes with raisins, added sugar, salt, iron, vitamins.	1 cup	50	7	145	4	1

[38] Made with vegetable shortening.
[40] Applies to white varieties. For yellow varieties, value is 150 International Units (I.U.).

NUTRIENTS IN INDICATED QUANTITY

	Fatty Acids											
Satu-rated (total)	Unsaturated Oleic	Lino-leic	Carbo-hydrate	Calcium	Phos-phorus	Iron	Potas-sium	Vitamin A value	Thiamin	Ribo-flavin	Niacin	Ascorbic acid
(G)	(H)	(I)	(J)	(K)	(L)	(M)	(N)	(O)	(P)	(Q)	(R)	(S)
Grams	Grams	Grams	Grams	Milli-grams	Milli-grams	Milli-grams	Milli-grams	Inter-national units	Milli-grams	Milli-grams	Milli-grams	Milli-grams
0.7	0.5	2.2	236	340	667	9.1	658	0	1.35	0.98	12.9	0
Trace	Trace	.1	13	19	37	.5	36	0	.07	.05	.7	0
.7	.5	2.4	241	381	1,039	11.8	2,059	0	1.30	.93	8.5	0
.1	Trace	.2	17	27	73	.8	145	0	.09	.07	.6	0
3.4	5.3	4.6	229	381	440	11.3	476	Trace	1.80	1.10	15.0	Trace
.2	.3	.3	13	21	24	.6	26	Trace	.10	.06	.8	Trace
.2	.3	.3	13	21	24	.6	26	Trace	.08	.06	.8	Trace
.2	.2	.2	10	17	19	.5	21	Trace	.08	.05	.7	Trace
.2	.2	.2	10	17	19	.5	21	Trace	.06	.05	.7	Trace
5.2	7.9	6.9	343	571	660	17.0	714	Trace	2.70	1.65	22.5	Trace
.2	.3	.3	14	24	27	.7	29	Trace	.11	.07	.9	Trace
.2	.3	.3	14	24	27	.7	29	Trace	.09	.07	.9	Trace
.2	.3	.2	12	20	23	.6	25	Trace	.10	.06	.8	Trace
.2	.3	.2	12	20	23	.6	25	Trace	.08	.06	.8	Trace
.2	.3	.3	15	25	29	.8	32	Trace	.12	.07	1.0	Trace
.3	.5	.5	23	38	44	1.1	47	Trace	.18	.11	1.5	Trace
3.9	5.9	5.2	228	435	463	11.3	549	Trace	1.80	1.10	15.0	Trace
.2	.3	.3	12	22	23	.6	28	Trace	.09	.06	.8	Trace
.2	.3	.3	12	22	23	.6	28	Trace	.07	.06	.8	Trace
7.7	11.8	10.4	455	871	925	22.7	1,097	Trace	3.60	2.20	30.0	Trace
.2	.3	.3	14	26	28	.7	33	Trace	.11	.06	.9	Trace
.2	.3	.3	14	26	28	.7	33	Trace	.09	.06	.9	Trace
2.2	2.9	4.2	224	381	1,152	13.6	1,161	Trace	1.37	.45	12.7	Trace
.1	.2	.2	14	24	71	.8	72	Trace	.09	.03	.8	Trace
.1	.2	.2	14	24	71	.8	72	Trace	.07	.03	.8	Trace
2.5	3.3	4.9	216	449	1,034	13.6	1,238	Trace	1.17	.54	12.7	Trace
.1	.2	.3	12	25	57	.8	68	Trace	.06	.03	.7	Trace
.1	.2	.3	12	25	57	.8	68	Trace	.05	.03	.7	Trace
Trace	Trace	.1	27	2	25	.7	27	[40]Trace	.10	.07	1.0	0
Trace	Trace	.1	27	2	25	.2	27	[40]Trace	.05	.02	.5	0
Trace	Trace	.1	22	147 [41]113		([42])	25	0	.12	.07	1.0	0
.4	.8	.9	23	22	137	1.4	146	0	.19	.05	.2	0
—	—	—	41	19	182	1.7	202	0	.17	.07	2.2	0
—	—	—	23	17	127	1.2	118	0	.15	.05	1.5	0
—	—	—	28	19	125	12.4	137	1,650	.41	.49	4.1	12
—	—	—	40	28	146	17.7	154	2,350	.58	.71	5.8	18

[41] Applies to products that do not contain di-sodium phosphate. If di-sodium phosphate is an ingredient, value is 162 mg.
[42] Value may range from less than 1 mg to about 8 mg depending on the brand. Consult the label.

NUTRITIVE VALUES OF THE EDIBLE PART OF FOODS—Continued

Item No. (A)	Foods, approximate measures, units, and weight (edible part unless footnotes indicate otherwise) (B)		Water (C) Grams	Food energy (D) Per-cent	Pro-tein (E) Cal-ories	Fat (F) Grams
	GRAIN PRODUCTS—Con.					
	Breakfast cereals—Continued					
	Ready-to-eat—Continued					
	Corn flakes:					
371	Plain, added sugar, salt, iron, vitamins.	1 cup	25	4	95	2 Trace
372	Sugar-coated, added salt, iron, vitamins.	1 cup	40	2	155	2 Trace
373	Corn, puffed, plain, added sugar, salt, iron, vitamins.	1 cup	20	4	80	2 1
374	Corn, shredded, added sugar, salt, iron, thiamin, niacin.	1 cup	25	3	95	2 Trace
375	Oats, puffed, added sugar, salt, minerals, vitamins.	1 cup	25	3	100	3 1
	Rice, puffed:					
376	Plain, added iron, thiamin, niacin.	1 cup	15	4	60	1 Trace
377	Presweetened, added salt, iron, vitamins.	1 cup	28	3	115	1 0
378	Wheat flakes, added sugar, salt, iron, vitamins.	1 cup	30	4	105	3 Trace
	Wheat, puffed:					
379	Plain, added iron, thiamin, niacin.	1 cup	15	3	55	2 Trace
380	Presweetened, added salt, iron, vitamins.	1 cup	38	3	140	3 Trace
381	Wheat, shredded, plain	1 oblong biscuit or 1/2 cup spoon-size biscuits.	25	7	90	2 1
382	Wheat germ, without salt and sugar, toasted.	1 tbsp	6	4	25	2 1
383	Buckwheat flour, light, sifted	1 cup	98	12	340	6 1
384	Bulgur, canned, seasoned	1 cup	135	56	245	8 4
	Cake icings. See Sugars and Sweets (items 532-536).					
	Cakes made from cake mixes with enriched flour:[46]					
	Angelfood:					
385	Whole cake (9 3/4-in diam. tube cake).	1 cake	635	34	1,645	36 1
386	Piece, 1/12 of cake	1 piece	53	34	135	3 Trace
	Coffeecake:					
387	Whole cake (7 3/4 by 5 5/8 by 1 1/4 in).	1 cake	430	30	1,385	27 41
388	Piece, 1/6 of cake	1 piece	72	30	230	5 7
	Cupcakes, made with egg, milk, 2 1/2-in diam.:					
389	Without icing	1 cupcake	25	26	90	1 3
390	With chocolate icing	1 cupcake	36	22	130	2 5
	Devil's food with chocolate icing:					
391	Whole, 2 layer cake (8- or 9-in diam.).	1 cake	1,107	24	3,755	49 136
392	Piece, 1/16 of cake	1 piece	69	24	235	3 8
393	Cupcake, 2 1/2-in diam	1 cupcake	35	24	120	2 4

[43] Value varies with the brand. Consult the label.
[44] Value varies with the brand. Consult the label.
[45] Applies to product with added ascorbic acid. Without added ascorbic acid, value is trace.

	NUTRIENTS IN INDICATED QUANTITY											
	Fatty Acids											
Satu-rated (total)	Unsaturated Oleic	Unsaturated Lino-leic	Carbo-hydrate	Calcium	Phos-phorus	Iron	Potas-sium	Vitamin A value	Thiamin	Ribo-flavin	Niacin	Ascorbic acid
(G)	(H)	(I)	(J)	(K)	(L)	(M)	(N)	(O)	(P)	(Q)	(R)	(S)
Grams	Grams	Grams	Grams	Milli-grams	Milli-grams	Milli-grams	Milli-grams	Inter-national units	Milli-grams	Milli-grams	Milli-grams	Milli-grams
—	—	—	21	(⁴³)	9	0.6	30	1,180	0.29	0.35	2.9	9
—	—	—	37	1	10	1.0	27	1,880	.46	.56	4.6	14
—	—	—	16	4	18	2.3	—	940	.23	.28	2.3	7
—	—	—	22	1	10	.6	—	0	.11	.05	.5	0
—	—	—	19	44	102	2.9	—	1,180	.29	.35	2.9	9
—	—	—	13	3	14	.3	15	0	.07	.01	.7	0
—	—	—	26	3	14 ⁴⁴1.1		43	1,250	.38	.43	5.0	⁴⁵15
—	—	—	24	12	83	(⁴³)	81	1,410	.35	.42	3.5	11
—	—	—	12	4	48	.6	51	0	.08	.03	1.2	0
—	—	—	33	7	52 ⁴⁴1.6		63	1,680	.50	.57	6.7	⁴⁵20
—	—	—	20	11	97	.9	87	0	.06	.03	1.1	0
—	—	—	3	3	70	.5	57	10	.11	.05	.3	1
0.2	0.4	0.4	78	11	86	1.0	314	0	.08	.04	.4	0
—	—	—	44	27	263	1.9	151	0	.08	.05	4.1	0
—	—	—	377	603	756	2.5	381	0	.37	.95	3.6	0
—	—	—	32	50	63	.2	32	0	.03	.08	.3	0
11.7	16.3	8.8	225	262	748	6.9	469	690	.82	.91	7.7	1
2.0	2.7	1.5	38	44	125	1.2	78	120	.14	.15	1.3	Trace
.8	1.2	.7	14	40	59	.3	21	40	.05	.05	.4	Trace
2.0	1.6	.6	21	47	71	.4	42	60	.05	.06	.4	Trace
50.0	44.9	17.0	645	653	1,162	16.6	1,439	1,660	1.06	1.65	10.1	1
3.1	2.8	1.1	40	41	72	1.0	90	100	.07	.10	.6	Trace
1.6	1.4	.5	20	21	37	.5	46	50	.03	.05	.3	Trace

⁴⁶Excepting angelfood cake, cakes were made from mixes containing vegetable shortening; icings, with butter.

NUTRITIVE VALUES OF THE EDIBLE PART OF FOODS—Continued

Item No.	Foods, approximate measures, units, and weight (edible part unless footnotes indicate otherwise)		Water	Food energy	Protein	Fat
(A)	(B)		(C)	(D)	(E)	(F)
		Grams	Percent	Calories	Grams	Grams
	Gingerbread:					
394	Whole cake (8-in square)------- 1 cake------------------	570	37	1,575	18	39
395	Piece, 1/9 of cake------------ 1 piece-----------------	63	37	175	2	4
	White, 2 layer with chocolate icing:					
396	Whole cake (8- or 9-in diam.)-- 1 cake------------------	1,140	21	4,000	44	122
397	Piece, 1/16 of cake----------- 1 piece-----------------	71	21	250	3	8
	Yellow, 2 layer with chocolate icing:					
398	Whole cake (8- or 9-in diam.)-- 1 cake------------------	1,108	26	3,735	45	125
399	Piece, 1/16 of cake----------- 1 piece-----------------	69	26	235	3	8
	Cakes made from home recipes using enriched flour:[47]					
	Boston cream pie with custard filling:					
400	Whole cake (8-in diam.)-------- 1 cake------------------	825	35	2,490	41	78
401	Piece, 1/12 of cake----------- 1 piece-----------------	69	35	210	3	6
	Fruitcake, dark:					
402	Loaf, 1-lb (7 1/2 by 2 by 1 1/2 in). 1 loaf------------------	454	18	1,720	22	69
403	Slice, 1/30 of loaf----------- 1 slice----------------	15	18	55	1	2
	Plain, sheet cake:					
	Without icing:					
404	Whole cake (9-in square)----- 1 cake------------------	777	25	2,830	35	108
405	Piece, 1/9 of cake----------- 1 piece-----------------	86	25	315	4	12
	With uncooked white icing:					
406	Whole cake (9-in square)----- 1 cake------------------	1,096	21	4,020	37	129
407	Piece, 1/9 of cake----------- 1 piece-----------------	121	21	445	4	14
	Pound:[49]					
408	Loaf, 8 1/2 by 3 1/2 by 3 1/4 in. 1 loaf------------------	565	16	2,725	31	170
409	Slice, 1/17 of loaf----------- 1 slice----------------	33	16	160	2	10
	Spongecake:					
410	Whole cake (9 3/4-in diam. tube cake). 1 cake------------------	790	32	2,345	60	45
411	Piece, 1/12 of cake----------- 1 piece-----------------	66	32	195	5	4
	Cookies made with enriched flour:[50] [51]					
	Brownies with nuts:					
	Home-prepared, 1 3/4 by 1 3/4 by 7/8 in:					
412	From home recipe------------- 1 brownie---------------	20	10	95	1	6
413	From commercial recipe------- 1 brownie---------------	20	11	85	1	4
414	Frozen, with chocolate icing,[52] 1 1/2 by 1 3/4 by 7/8 in. 1 brownie---------------	25	13	105	1	5
	Chocolate chip:					
415	Commercial, 2 1/4-in diam., 3/8 in thick. 4 cookies----------------	42	3	200	2	9
416	From home recipe, 2 1/3-in diam. 4 cookies----------------	40	3	205	2	12
417	Fig bars, square (1 5/8 by 1 5/8 by 3/8 in) or rectangular (1 1/2 by 1 3/4 by 1/2 in). 4 cookies----------------	56	14	200	2	3
418	Gingersnaps, 2-in diam., 1/4 in thick. 4 cookies----------------	28	3	90	2	2
419	Macaroons, 2 3/4-in diam., 1/4 in thick. 2 cookies----------------	38	4	180	2	9
420	Oatmeal with raisins, 2 5/8-in diam., 1/4 in thick. 4 cookies----------------	52	3	235	3	8

[47] Excepting spongecake, vegetable shortening used for cake portion; butter, for icing.
If butter or margarine used for cake portion, vitamin A values would be higher.
[48] Applies to product made with a sodium aluminum-sulfate type baking powder. With a low-sodium type baking powder containing potassium, value would be about twice the amount shown.

362

	NUTRIENTS IN INDICATED QUANTITY											
	Fatty Acids											
Satu-rated (total)	Unsaturated		Carbo-hydrate	Calcium	Phos-phorus	Iron	Potas-sium	Vitamin A value	Thiamin	Ribo-flavin	Niacin	Ascorbic acid
	Oleic	Lino-leic										
(G)	(H)	(I)	(J)	(K)	(L)	(M)	(N)	(O)	(P)	(Q)	(R)	(S)
Grams	Grams	Grams	Grams	Milli-grams	Milli-grams	Milli-grams	Milli-grams	Inter-national units	Milli-grams	Milli-grams	Milli-grams	Milli-grams
9.7	16.6	10.0	291	513	570	8.6	1,562	Trace	0.84	1.00	7.4	Trace
1.1	1.8	1.1	32	57	63	.9	173	Trace	.09	.11	.8	Trace
48.2	46.4	20.0	716	1,129	2,041	11.4	1,322	680	1.50	1.77	12.5	2
3.0	2.9	1.2	45	70	127	.7	82	40	.09	.11	.8	Trace
47.8	47.8	20.3	638	1,008	2,017	12.2	1,208	1,550	1.24	1.67	10.6	2
3.0	3.0	1.3	40	63	126	.8	75	100	.08	.10	.7	Trace
23.0	30.1	15.2	412	553	833	8.2	[48]734	1,730	1.04	1.27	9.6	2
1.9	2.5	1.3	34	46	70	.7	[48]61	140	.09	.11	.8	Trace
14.4	33.5	14.8	271	327	513	11.8	2,250	540	.72	.73	4.9	2
.5	1.1	.5	9	11	17	.4	74	20	.02	.02	.2	Trace
29.5	44.4	23.9	434	497	793	8.5	[48]614	1,320	1.21	1.40	10.2	2
3.3	4.9	2.6	48	55	88	.9	[48]68	150	.13	.15	1.1	Trace
42.2	49.5	24.4	694	548	822	8.2	[48]669	2,190	1.22	1.47	10.2	2
4.7	5.5	2.7	77	61	91	.8	[48]74	240	.14	.16	1.1	Trace
42.9	73.1	39.6	273	107	418	7.9	345	1,410	.90	.99	7.3	0
2.5	4.3	2.3	16	6	24	.5	20	80	.05	.06	.4	0
13.1	15.8	5.7	427	237	885	13.4	687	3,560	1.10	1.64	7.4	Trace
1.1	1.3	.5	36	20	74	1.1	57	300	.09	.14	.6	Trace
1.5	3.0	1.2	10	8	30	.4	38	40	.04	.03	.2	Trace
.9	1.4	1.3	13	9	27	.4	34	20	.03	.02	.2	Trace
2.0	2.2	.7	15	10	31	.4	44	50	.03	.03	.2	Trace
2.8	2.9	2.2	29	16	48	1.0	56	50	.10	.17	.9	Trace
3.5	4.5	2.9	24	14	40	.8	47	40	.06	.06	.5	Trace
.8	1.2	.7	42	44	34	1.0	111	60	.04	.14	.9	Trace
.7	1.0	.6	22	20	13	.7	129	20	.08	.06	.7	0
—	—	—	25	10	32	.3	176	0	.02	.06	.2	0
2.0	3.3	2.0	38	11	53	1.4	192	30	.15	.10	1.0	Trace

[49] Equal weights of flour, sugar, eggs, and vegetable shortening.
[50] Products are commercial unless otherwise specified.
[51] Made with enriched flour and vegetable shortening except for macaroons which do not contain flour or shortening.
[52] Icing made with butter.

NUTRITIVE VALUES OF THE EDIBLE PART OF FOODS—Continued

Item No.	Foods, approximate measures, units, and weight (edible part unless footnotes indicate otherwise)		Water	Food energy	Protein	Fat
(A)	(B)		(C)	(D)	(E)	(F)
		Grams	Percent	Calories	Grams	Grams
	GRAIN PRODUCTS—Con.					
	Cookies made with enriched flour[50] [51]—Continued					
421	Plain, prepared from commercial chilled dough, 2 1/2-in diam., 1/4 in thick.	4 cookies------------------	48	5	240	2	12
422	Sandwich type (chocolate or vanilla), 1 3/4-in diam., 3/8 in thick.	4 cookies------------------	40	2	200	2	9
423	Vanilla wafers, 1 3/4-in diam., 1/4 in thick.	10 cookies-----------------	40	3	185	2	6
	Cornmeal:						
424	Whole-ground, unbolted, dry form.	1 cup---------------------	122	12	435	11	5
425	Bolted (nearly whole-grain), dry form.	1 cup---------------------	122	12	440	11	4
	Degermed, enriched:						
426	Dry form------------------	1 cup---------------------	138	12	500	11	2
427	Cooked--------------------	1 cup---------------------	240	88	120	3	Trace
	Degermed, unenriched:						
428	Dry form------------------	1 cup---------------------	138	12	500	11	2
429	Cooked--------------------	1 cup---------------------	240	88	120	3	Trace
	Crackers:[38]						
430	Graham, plain, 2 1/2-in square--	2 crackers----------------	14	6	55	1	1
431	Rye wafers, whole-grain, 1 7/8 by 3 1/2 in.	2 wafers------------------	13	6	45	2	Trace
432	Saltines, made with enriched flour.	4 crackers or 1 packet----	11	4	50	1	1
	Danish pastry (enriched flour), plain without fruit or nuts:[54]						
433	Packaged ring, 12 oz------------	1 ring--------------------	340	22	1,435	25	80
434	Round piece, about 4 1/4-in diam. by 1 in.	1 pastry------------------	65	22	275	5	15
435	Ounce--------------------------	1 oz----------------------	28	22	120	2	7
	Doughnuts, made with enriched flour:[38]						
436	Cake type, plain, 2 1/2-in diam., 1 in high.	1 doughnut----------------	25	24	100	1	5
437	Yeast-leavened, glazed, 3 3/4-in diam., 1 1/4 in high.	1 doughnut----------------	50	26	205	3	11
	Macaroni, enriched, cooked (cut lengths, elbows, shells):						
438	Firm stage (hot)---------------	1 cup---------------------	130	64	190	7	1
	Tender stage:						
439	Cold macaroni-----------------	1 cup---------------------	105	73	115	4	Trace
440	Hot macaroni------------------	1 cup---------------------	140	73	155	5	1
	Macaroni (enriched) and cheese:						
441	Canned[55]----------------------	1 cup---------------------	240	80	230	9	10
442	From home recipe (served hot)[56]-	1 cup---------------------	200	58	430	17	22
	Muffins made with enriched flour:[38]						
	From home recipe:						
443	Blueberry, 2 3/8-in diam., 1 1/2 in high.	1 muffin------------------	40	39	110	3	4
444	Bran--------------------------	1 muffin------------------	40	35	105	3	4
445	Corn (enriched degermed cornmeal and flour), 2 3/8-in diam., 1 1/2 in high.	1 muffin------------------	40	33	125	3	4

[38] Made with vegetable shortening.
[50] Products are commercial unless otherwise specified.
[51] Made with enriched flour and vegetable shortening except for macaroons which do not contain flour or shortening.
[53] Applies to yellow varieties; white varieties contain only a trace.

364

	NUTRIENTS IN INDICATED QUANTITY										
	Fatty Acids										
Satu-rated (total)	Unsaturated Oleic	Lino-leic	Carbo-hydrate	Calcium	Phos-phorus	Iron	Potas-sium	Vitamin A value	Thiamin	Ribo-flavin	Niacin	Ascorbic acid
(G)	(H)	(I)	(J)	(K)	(L)	(M)	(N)	(O)	(P)	(Q)	(R)	(S)
Grams	Grams	Grams	Grams	Milli-grams	Milli-grams	Milli-grams	Milli-grams	Inter-national units	Milli-grams	Milli-grams	Milli-grams	Milli-grams
3.0	5.2	2.9	31	17	35	0.6	23	30	0.10	0.08	0.9	0
2.2	3.9	2.2	28	10	96	.7	15	0	.06	.10	.7	0
—	—	—	30	16	25	.6	29	50	.10	.09	.8	0
.5	1.0	2.5	90	24	312	2.9	346	[53]620	.46	.13	2.4	0
.5	.9	2.1	91	21	272	2.2	303	[53]590	.37	.10	2.3	0
.2	.4	.9	108	8	137	4.0	166	[53]610	.61	.36	4.8	0
Trace	.1	.2	26	2	34	1.0	38	[53]140	.14	.10	1.2	0
.2	.4	.9	108	8	137	1.5	166	[53]610	.19	.07	1.4	0
Trace	.1	.2	26	2	34	.5	38	[53]140	.05	.02	.2	0
.3	.5	.3	10	6	21	.5	55	0	.02	.08	.5	0
—	—	—	10	7	50	.5	78	0	.04	.03	.2	0
.3	.5	.4	8	2	10	.5	13	0	.05	.05	.4	0
24.3	31.7	16.5	155	170	371	6.1	381	1,050	.97	1.01	8.6	Trace
4.7	6.1	3.2	30	33	71	1.2	73	200	.18	.19	1.7	Trace
2.0	2.7	1.4	13	14	31	.5	32	90	.08	.08	.7	Trace
1.2	2.0	1.1	13	10	48	.4	23	20	.05	.05	.4	Trace
3.3	5.8	3.3	22	16	33	.6	34	25	.10	.10	.8	0
—	—	—	39	14	85	1.4	103	0	.23	.13	1.8	0
—	—	—	24	8	53	.9	64	0	.15	.08	1.2	0
—	—	—	32	11	70	1.3	85	0	.20	.11	1.5	0
4.2	3.1	1.4	26	199	182	1.0	139	260	.12	.24	1.0	Trace
8.9	8.8	2.9	40	362	322	1.8	240	860	.20	.40	1.8	Trace
1.1	1.4	.7	17	34	53	.6	46	90	.09	.10	.7	Trace
1.2	1.4	.8	17	57	162	1.5	172	90	.07	.10	1.7	Trace
1.2	1.6	.9	19	42	68	.7	54	[57]120	.10	.10	.7	Trace

[54]Contains vegetable shortening and butter.
[55]Made with corn oil.
[56]Made with regular margarine.
[57]Applies to product made with yellow cornmeal.

NUTRITIVE VALUES OF THE EDIBLE PART OF FOODS—Continued

Item No. (A)	Foods, approximate measures, units, and weight (edible part unless footnotes indicate otherwise) (B)		Water (C) Percent	Food energy (D) Calories	Protein (E) Grams	Fat (F) Grams
			Grams				
446	Plain, 3-in diam., 1 1/2 in high.	1 muffin	40	38	120	3	4
	From mix, egg, milk:						
447	Corn, 2 3/8-in diam., 1 1/2 in high.[58]	1 muffin	40	30	130	3	4
448	Noodles (egg noodles), enriched, cooked.	1 cup	160	71	200	7	2
449	Noodles, chow mein, canned	1 cup	45	1	220	6	11
	Pancakes, (4-in diam.):[38]						
450	Buckwheat, made from mix (with buckwheat and enriched flours), egg and milk added.	1 cake	27	58	55	2	2
	Plain:						
51	Made from home recipe using enriched flour.	1 cake	27	50	60	2	2
452	Made from mix with enriched flour, egg and milk added.	1 cake	27	51	60	2	2
	Pies, piecrust made with enriched flour, vegetable shortening (9-in diam.):						
	Apple:						
453	Whole	1 pie	945	48	2,420	21	105
454	Sector, 1/7 of pie	1 sector	135	48	345	3	15
	Banana cream:						
455	Whole	1 pie	910	54	2,010	41	85
456	Sector, 1/7 of pie	1 sector	130	54	285	6	12
	Blueberry:						
457	Whole	1 pie	945	51	2,285	23	102
458	Sector, 1/7 of pie	1 sector	135	51	325	3	15
	Cherry:						
459	Whole	1 pie	945	47	2,465	25	107
460	Sector, 1/7 of pie	1 sector	135	47	350	4	15
	Custard:						
461	Whole	1 pie	910	58	1,985	56	101
462	Sector, 1/7 of pie	1 sector	130	58	285	8	14
	Lemon meringue:						
463	Whole	1 pie	840	47	2,140	31	86
464	Sector, 1/7 of pie	1 sector	120	47	305	4	12
	Mince:						
465	Whole	1 pie	945	43	2,560	24	109
466	Sector, 1/7 of pie	1 sector	135	43	365	3	16
	Peach:						
467	Whole	1 pie	945	48	2,410	24	101
468	Sector, 1/7 of pie	1 sector	135	48	345	3	14
	Pecan:						
469	Whole	1 pie	825	20	3,450	42	189
470	Sector, 1/7 of pie	1 sector	118	20	495	6	27
	Pumpkin:						
471	Whole	1 pie	910	59	1,920	36	102
472	Sector, 1/7 of pie	1 sector	130	59	275	5	15
473	Piecrust (home recipe) made with enriched flour and vegetable shortening, baked.	1 pie shell, 9-in diam.	180	15	900	11	60
474	Piecrust mix with enriched flour and vegetable shortening, 10-oz pkg. prepared and baked.	Piecrust for 2-crust pie, 9-in diam.	320	19	1,485	20	93

[38] Made with vegetable shortening.

	NUTRIENTS IN INDICATED QUANTITY											
	Fatty Acids											
Satu-rated (total)	Unsaturated		Carbo-hydrate	Calcium	Phos-phorus	Iron	Potas-sium	Vitamin A value	Thiamin	Ribo-flavin	Niacin	Ascorbic acid
	Oleic	Lino-leic										
(G)	(H)	(I)	(J)	(K)	(L)	(M)	(N)	(O)	(P)	(Q)	(R)	(S)
Grams	Grams	Grams	Grams	Milli-grams	Milli-grams	Milli-grams	Milli-grams	Inter-national units	Milli-grams	Milli-grams	Milli-grams	Milli-grams
1.0	1.7	1.0	17	42	60	0.6	50	40	0.09	0.12	0.9	Trace
1.2	1.7	.9	20	96	152	.6	44	[57]100	.08	.09	.7	Trace
—	—	—	37	16	94	1.4	70	110	.22	.13	1.9	0
—	—	—	26	—	—	—	—	—	—	—	—	—
.8	.9	.4	6	59	91	.4	66	60	.04	.05	.2	Trace
.5	.8	.5	9	27	38	.4	33	30	.06	.07	.5	Trace
.7	.7	.3	9	58	70	.3	42	70	.04	.06	.2	Trace
27.0	44.5	25.2	360	76	208	6.6	756	280	1.06	.79	9.3	9
3.9	6.4	3.6	51	11	30	.9	108	40	.15	.11	1.3	2
26.7	33.2	16.2	279	601	746	7.3	1,847	2,280	.77	1.51	7.0	9
3.8	4.7	2.3	40	86	107	1.0	264	330	.11	.22	1.0	1
24.8	43.7	25.1	330	104	217	9.5	614	280	1.03	.80	10.0	28
3.5	6.2	3.6	47	15	31	1.4	88	40	.15	.11	1.4	4
28.2	45.0	25.3	363	132	236	6.6	992	4,160	1.09	.84	9.8	Trace
4.0	6.4	3.6	52	19	34	.9	142	590	.16	.12	1.4	Trace
33.9	38.5	17.5	213	874	1,028	8.2	1,247	2,090	.79	1.92	5.6	0
4.8	5.5	2.5	30	125	147	1.2	178	300	.11	.27	.8	0
26.1	33.8	16.4	317	118	412	6.7	420	1,430	.61	.84	5.2	25
3.7	4.8	2.3	45	17	59	1.0	60	200	.09	.12	.7	4
28.0	45.9	25.2	389	265	359	13.3	1,682	20	.96	.86	9.8	9
4.0	6.6	3.6	56	38	51	1.9	240	Trace	.14	.12	1.4	1
24.8	43.7	25.1	361	95	274	8.5	1,408	6,900	1.04	.97	14.0	28
3.5	6.2	3.6	52	14	39	1.2	201	990	.15	.14	2.0	4
27.8	101.0	44.2	423	388	850	25.6	1,015	1,320	1.80	.95	6.9	Trace
4.0	14.4	6.3	61	55	122	3.7	145	190	.26	.14	1.0	Trace
37.4	37.5	16.6	223	464	628	7.3	1,456	22,480	.78	1.27	7.0	Trace
5.4	5.4	2.4	32	66	90	1.0	208	3,210	.11	.18	1.0	Trace
14.8	26.1	14.9	79	25	90	3.1	89	0	.47	.40	5.0	0
22.7	39.7	23.4	141	131	272	6.1	179	0	1.07	.79	9.9	0

[57] Applies to product made with yellow cornmeal.
[58] Made with enriched degermed cornmeal and enriched flour.

367

NUTRITIVE VALUES OF THE EDIBLE PART OF FOODS—Continued

Item No. (A)	Foods, approximate measures, units, and weight (edible part unless footnotes indicate otherwise) (B)		Water (C)	Food energy (D)	Protein (E)	Fat (F)
			Grams	Percent	Calories	Grams	Grams
	GRAIN PRODUCTS—Con.						
475	Pizza (cheese) baked, 4 3/4-in sector; 1/8 of 12-in diam. pie.[19]	1 sector	60	45	145	6	4
	Popcorn, popped:						
476	Plain, large kernel	1 cup	6	4	25	1	Trace
477	With oil (coconut) and salt added, large kernel.	1 cup	9	3	40	1	2
478	Sugar coated	1 cup	35	4	135	2	1
	Pretzels, made with enriched flour:						
479	Dutch, twisted, 2 3/4 by 2 5/8 in.	1 pretzel	16	5	60	2	1
480	Thin, twisted, 3 1/4 by 2 1/4 by 1/4 in.	10 pretzels	60	5	235	6	3
481	Stick, 2 1/4 in long	10 pretzels	3	5	10	Trace	Trace
	Rice, white, enriched:						
482	Instant, ready-to-serve, hot	1 cup	165	73	180	4	Trace
	Long grain:						
483	Raw	1 cup	185	12	670	12	1
484	Cooked, served hot	1 cup	205	73	225	4	Trace
	Parboiled:						
485	Raw	1 cup	185	10	685	14	1
486	Cooked, served hot	1 cup	175	73	185	4	Trace
	Rolls, enriched:[38]						
	Commercial:						
487	Brown-and-serve (12 per 12-oz pkg.), browned.	1 roll	26	27	85	2	2
488	Cloverleaf or pan, 2 1/2-in diam., 2 in high.	1 roll	28	31	85	2	2
489	Frankfurter and hamburger (8 per 11 1/2-oz pkg.).	1 roll	40	31	120	3	2
490	Hard, 3 3/4-in diam., 2 in high.	1 roll	50	25	155	5	2
491	Hoagie or submarine, 11 1/2 by 3 by 2 1/2 in.	1 roll	135	31	390	12	4
	From home recipe:						
492	Cloverleaf, 2 1/2-in diam., 2 in high.	1 roll	35	26	120	3	3
	Spaghetti, enriched, cooked:						
493	Firm stage, "al dente," served hot.	1 cup	130	64	190	7	1
494	Tender stage, served hot	1 cup	140	73	155	5	1
	Spaghetti (enriched) in tomato sauce with cheese:						
495	From home recipe	1 cup	250	77	260	9	9
496	Canned	1 cup	250	80	190	6	2
	Spaghetti (enriched) with meat balls and tomato sauce:						
497	From home recipe	1 cup	248	70	330	19	12
498	Canned	1 cup	250	78	260	12	10
499	Toaster pastries	1 pastry	50	12	200	3	6
	Waffles, made with enriched flour, 7-in diam.:[38]						
500	From home recipe	1 waffle	75	41	210	7	7
501	From mix, egg and milk added	1 waffle	75	42	205	7	8

[19]Crust made with vegetable shortening and enriched flour.
[38]Made with vegetable shortening.

	NUTRIENTS IN INDICATED QUANTITY											
	Fatty Acids											
Satu-rated (total)	Unsaturated		Carbo-hydrate	Calcium	Phos-phorus	Iron	Potas-sium	Vitamin A value	Thiamin	Ribo-flavin	Niacin	Ascorbic acid
	Oleic	Lino-leic										
(G)	(H)	(I)	(J)	(K)	(L)	(M)	(N)	(O)	(P)	(Q)	(R)	(S)
Grams	Grams	Grams	Grams	Milli-grams	Milli-grams	Milli-grams	Milli-grams	Inter-national units	Milli-grams	Milli-grams	Milli-grams	Milli-grams
1.7	1.5	0.6	22	86	89	1.1	67	230	0.16	0.18	1.6	4
Trace	.1	.2	5	1	17	.2	—	—	—	.01	.1	0
1.5	.2	.2	5	1	19	.2	—	—	—	.01	.2	0
.5	.2	.4	30	2	47	.5	—	—	—	.02	.4	0
—	—	—	12	4	21	.2	21	0	.05	.04	.7	0
—	—	—	46	13	79	.9	78	0	.20	.15	2.5	0
—	—	—	2	1	4	Trace	4	0	.01	.01	.1	0
Trace	Trace	Trace	40	5	31	1.3	—	0	.21	([59])	1.7	0
.2	.2	.2	149	44	174	5.4	170	0	.81	.06	6.5	0
.1	.1	.1	50	21	57	1.8	57	0	.23	.02	2.1	0
.2	.1	.2	150	111	370	5.4	278	0	.81	.07	6.5	0
.1	.1	.1	41	33	100	1.4	75	0	.19	.02	2.1	0
.4	.7	.5	14	20	23	.5	25	Trace	.10	.06	.9	Trace
.4	.6	.4	15	21	24	.5	27	Trace	.11	.07	.9	Trace
.5	.8	.6	21	30	34	.8	38	Trace	.16	.10	1.3	Trace
.4	.6	.5	30	24	46	1.2	49	Trace	.20	.12	1.7	Trace
.9	1.4	1.4	75	58	115	3.0	122	Trace	.54	.32	4.5	Trace
.8	1.1	.7	20	16	36	.7	41	30	.12	.12	1.2	Trace
—	—	—	39	14	85	1.4	103	0	.23	.13	1.8	0
—	—	—	32	11	70	1.3	85	0	.20	.11	1.5	0
2.0	5.4	.7	37	80	135	2.3	408	1,080	.25	.18	2.3	13
.5	.3	.4	39	40	88	2.8	303	930	.35	.28	4.5	10
3.3	6.3	.9	39	124	236	3.7	665	1,590	.25	.30	4.0	22
2.2	3.3	3.9	29	53	113	3.3	245	1,000	.15	.18	2.3	5
—	—	—	36	[60]54	[60]67	1.9	[60]74	500	.16	.17	2.1	([60])
2.3	2.8	1.4	28	85	130	1.3	109	250	.17	.23	1.4	Trace
2.8	2.9	1.2	27	179	257	1.0	146	170	.14	.22	.9	Trace

[59] Product may or may not be enriched with riboflavin. Consult the label.
[60] Value varies with the brand. Consult the label.

NUTRITIVE VALUES OF THE EDIBLE PART OF FOODS–Continued

Item No.	Foods, approximate measures, units, and weight (edible part unless footnotes indicate otherwise)			Water	Food energy	Protein	Fat
(A)	(B)			(C)	(D)	(E)	(F)
			Grams	Percent	Calories	Grams	Grams
	Wheat flours: All-purpose or family flour, enriched:						
502	Sifted, spooned---------------	1 cup-------------------	115	12	420	12	1
503	Unsifted, spooned-------------	1 cup-------------------	125	12	455	13	1
504	Cake or pastry flour, enriched, sifted, spooned.	1 cup-------------------	96	12	350	7	1
505	Self-rising, enriched, unsifted, spooned.	1 cup-------------------	125	12	440	12	1
506	Whole-wheat, from hard wheats, stirred.	1 cup-------------------	120	12	400	16	2
	LEGUMES (DRY), NUTS, SEEDS; RELATED PRODUCTS						
	Almonds, shelled:						
507	Chopped (about 130 almonds)-----	1 cup-------------------	130	5	775	24	70
508	Slivered, not pressed down (about 115 almonds).	1 cup-------------------	115	5	690	21	62
	Beans, dry: Common varieties as Great Northern, navy, and others: Cooked, drained:						
509	Great Northern---------------	1 cup-------------------	180	69	210	14	1
510	Pea (navy)------------------	1 cup-------------------	190	69	225	15	1
	Canned, solids and liquid: White with—						
511	Frankfurters (sliced)-----	1 cup-------------------	255	71	365	19	18
512	Pork and tomato sauce-----	1 cup-------------------	255	71	310	16	7
513	Pork and sweet sauce------	1 cup-------------------	255	66	385	16	12
514	Red kidney----------------	1 cup-------------------	255	76	230	15	1
515	Lima, cooked, drained----------	1 cup-------------------	190	64	260	16	1
516	Blackeye peas, dry, cooked (with residual cooking liquid).	1 cup-------------------	250	80	190	13	1
517	Brazil nuts, shelled (6-8 large kernels).	1 oz--------------------	28	5	185	4	19
518	Cashew nuts, roasted in oil-------	1 cup-------------------	140	5	785	24	64
	Coconut meat, fresh:						
519	Piece, about 2 by 2 by 1/2 in---	1 piece------------------	45	51	155	2	16
520	Shredded or grated, not pressed down.	1 cup-------------------	80	51	275	3	28
521	Filberts (hazelnuts), chopped (about 80 kernels).	1 cup-------------------	115	6	730	14	72
522	Lentils, whole, cooked----------	1 cup-------------------	200	72	210	16	Trace
523	Peanuts, roasted in oil, salted (whole, halves, chopped).	1 cup-------------------	144	2	840	37	72
524	Peanut butter------------------	1 tbsp------------------	16	2	95	4	8
525	Peas, split, dry, cooked----------	1 cup-------------------	200	70	230	16	1
526	Pecans, chopped or pieces (about 120 large halves).	1 cup-------------------	118	3	810	11	84
527	Pumpkin and squash kernels, dry, hulled.	1 cup-------------------	140	4	775	41	65
528	Sunflower seeds, dry, hulled------	1 cup-------------------	145	5	810	35	69
	Walnuts: Black:						
529	Chopped or broken kernels-----	1 cup-------------------	125	3	785	26	74
530	Ground (finely)---------------	1 cup-------------------	80	3	500	16	47
531	Persian or English, chopped (about 60 halves).	1 cup-------------------	120	4	780	18	77

NUTRIENTS IN INDICATED QUANTITY												
Fatty Acids												
Satu-rated (total)	Unsaturated		Carbo-hydrate	Calcium	Phos-phorus	Iron	Potas-sium	Vitamin A value	Thiamin	Ribo-flavin	Niacin	Ascorbic acid
	Oleic	Lino-leic										
(G)	(H)	(I)	(J)	(K)	(L)	(M)	(N)	(O)	(P)	(Q)	(R)	(S)
Grams	Grams	Grams	Grams	Milli-grams	Milli-grams	Milli-grams	Milli-grams	Inter-national units	Milli-grams	Milli-grams	Milli-grams	Milli-grams
0.2	0.1	0.5	88	18	100	3.3	109	0	0.74	0.46	6.1	0
.2	.1	.5	95	20	109	3.6	119	0	.80	.50	6.6	0
.1	.1	.3	76	16	70	2.8	91	0	.61	.38	5.1	0
.2	.1	.5	93	331	583	3.6	—	0	.80	.50	6.6	0
.4	.2	1.0	85	49	446	4.0	444	0	.66	.14	5.2	0
5.6	47.7	12.8	25	304	655	6.1	1,005	0	.31	1.20	4.6	Trace
5.0	42.2	11.3	22	269	580	5.4	889	0	.28	1.06	4.0	Trace
—	—	—	38	90	266	4.9	749	0	.25	.13	1.3	0
—	—	—	40	95	281	5.1	790	0	.27	.13	1.3	0
—	—	—	32	94	303	4.8	668	330	.19	.15	3.3	Trace
2.4	2.8	.6	48	138	235	4.6	536	330	.20	.08	1.5	5
4.3	5.0	1.1	54	161	291	5.9	—	—	.15	.10	1.3	—
—	—	—	42	74	278	4.6	673	10	.13	.10	1.5	—
—	—	—	49	55	293	5.9	1,163	—	.25	.11	1.3	—
—	—	—	35	43	238	3.3	573	30	.40	.10	1.0	—
4.8	6.2	7.1	3	53	196	1.0	203	Trace	.27	.03	.5	—
12.9	36.8	10.2	41	53	522	5.3	650	140	.60	.35	2.5	—
14.0	.9	.3	4	6	43	.8	115	0	.02	.01	.2	1
24.8	1.6	.5	8	10	76	1.4	205	0	.04	.02	.4	2
5.1	55.2	7.3	19	240	388	3.9	810	—	.53	—	1.0	Trace
—	—	—	39	50	238	4.2	498	40	.14	.12	1.2	0
13.7	33.0	20.7	27	107	577	3.0	971	—	.46	.19	24.8	0
1.5	3.7	2.3	3	9	61	.3	100	—	.02	.02	2.4	0
—	—	—	42	22	178	3.4	592	80	.30	.18	1.8	—
7.2	50.5	20.0	17	86	341	2.8	712	150	1.01	.15	1.1	2
11.8	23.5	27.5	21	71	1,602	15.7	1,386	100	.34	.27	3.4	—
8.2	13.7	43.2	29	174	1,214	10.3	1,334	70	2.84	.33	7.8	—
6.3	13.3	45.7	19	Trace	713	7.5	575	380	.28	.14	.9	—
4.0	8.5	29.2	12	Trace	456	4.8	368	240	.18	.09	.6	—
8.4	11.8	42.2	19	119	456	3.7	540	40	.40	.16	1.1	2

NUTRITIVE VALUES OF THE EDIBLE PART OF FOODS–Continued

Item No.	Foods, approximate measures, units, and weight (edible part unless footnotes indicate otherwise)		Water	Food energy	Protein	Fat
(A)	(B)		(C)	(D)	(E)	(F)
			Grams	Percent	Calories	Grams	Grams
	SUGARS AND SWEETS						
	Cake icings:						
	Boiled, white:						
532	Plain------------------------	1 cup---------------------	94	18	295	1	0
533	With coconut------------------	1 cup---------------------	166	15	605	3	13
	Uncooked:						
534	Chocolate made with milk and butter.	1 cup---------------------	275	14	1,035	9	38
535	Creamy fudge from mix and water.	1 cup---------------------	245	15	830	7	16
536	White------------------------	1 cup---------------------	319	11	1,200	2	21
	Candy:						
537	Caramels, plain or chocolate----	1 oz----------------------	28	8	115	1	3
	Chocolate:						
538	Milk, plain-------------------	1 oz----------------------	28	1	145	2	9
539	Semisweet, small pieces (60 per oz).	1 cup or 6-oz pkg---------	170	1	860	7	61
540	Chocolate-coated peanuts--------	1 oz----------------------	28	1	160	5	12
541	Fondant, uncoated (mints, candy corn, other).	1 oz----------------------	28	8	105	Trace	1
542	Fudge, chocolate, plain---------	1 oz----------------------	28	8	115	1	3
543	Gum drops----------------------	1 oz----------------------	28	12	100	Trace	Trace
544	Hard-------------------------	1 oz----------------------	28	1	110	0	Trace
545	Marshmallows------------------	1 oz----------------------	28	17	90	1	Trace
	Chocolate-flavored beverage powders (about 4 heaping tsp per oz):						
546	With nonfat dry milk-----------	1 oz----------------------	28	2	100	5	1
547	Without milk------------------	1 oz----------------------	28	1	100	1	1
548	Honey, strained or extracted------	1 tbsp--------------------	21	17	65	Trace	0
549	Jams and preserves---------------	1 tbsp--------------------	20	29	55	Trace	Trace
550		1 packet------------------	14	29	40	Trace	Trace
551	Jellies------------------------	1 tbsp--------------------	18	29	50	Trace	Trace
552		1 packet------------------	14	29	40	Trace	Trace
	Sirups:						
	Chocolate-flavored sirup or topping:						
553	Thin type---------------------	1 fl oz or 2 tbsp----------	38	32	90	1	1
554	Fudge type--------------------	1 fl oz or 2 tbsp----------	38	25	125	2	5
	Molasses, cane:						
555	Light (first extraction)-------	1 tbsp--------------------	20	24	50	—	—
556	Blackstrap (third extraction)-	1 tbsp--------------------	20	24	45	—	—
557	Sorghum-----------------------	1 tbsp--------------------	21	23	55	—	—
558	Table blends, chiefly corn, light and dark.	1 tbsp--------------------	21	24	60	0	0
	Sugars:						
559	Brown, pressed down------------	1 cup---------------------	220	2	820	0	0
	White:						
560	Granulated--------------------	1 cup---------------------	200	1	770	0	0
561		1 tbsp--------------------	12	1	45	0	0
562		1 packet------------------	6	1	23	0	0
563	Powdered, sifted, spooned into cup.	1 cup---------------------	100	1	385	0	0

	NUTRIENTS IN INDICATED QUANTITY											
	Fatty Acids											
Satu-rated (total)	Unsaturated Oleic	Lino-leic	Carbo-hydrate	Calcium	Phos-phorus	Iron	Potas-sium	Vitamin A value	Thiamin	Ribo-flavin	Niacin	Ascorbic acid
(G)	(H)	(I)	(J)	(K)	(L)	(M)	(N)	(O)	(P)	(Q)	(R)	(S)
Grams	Grams	Grams	Grams	Milli-grams	Milli-grams	Milli-grams	Milli-grams	Inter-national units	Milli-grams	Milli-grams	Milli-grams	Milli-grams
0	0	0	75	2	2	Trace	17	0	Trace	0.03	Trace	0
11.0	.9	Trace	124	10	50	0.8	277	0	0.02	.07	0.3	0
23.4	11.7	1.0	185	165	305	3.3	536	580	.06	.28	.6	1
5.1	6.7	3.1	183	96	218	2.7	238	Trace	.05	.20	.7	Trace
12.7	5.1	.5	260	48	38	Trace	57	860	Trace	.06	Trace	Trace
1.6	1.1	.1	22	42	35	.4	54	Trace	.01	.05	.1	Trace
5.5	3.0	.3	16	65	65	.3	109	80	.02	.10	.1	Trace
36.2	19.8	1.7	97	51	255	4.4	553	30	.02	.14	.9	0
4.0	4.7	2.1	11	33	84	.4	143	Trace	.10	.05	2.1	Trace
.1	.3	.1	25	4	2	.3	1	0	Trace	Trace	Trace	0
1.3	1.4	.6	21	22	24	.3	42	Trace	.01	.03	.1	Trace
—	—	—	25	2	Trace	.1	1	0	0	Trace	Trace	0
—	—	—	28	6	2	.5	1	0	0	0	0	0
—	—	—	23	5	2	.5	2	0	0	Trace	Trace	0
.5	.3	Trace	20	167	155	.5	227	10	.04	.21	.2	1
.4	.2	Trace	25	9	48	.6	142	—	.01	.03	.1	0
0	0	0	17	1	1	.1	11	0	Trace	.01	.1	Trace
—	—	—	14	4	2	.2	18	Trace	Trace	.01	Trace	Trace
—	—	—	10	3	1	.1	12	Trace	Trace	Trace	Trace	Trace
—	—	—	13	4	1	.3	14	Trace	Trace	.01	Trace	1
—	—	—	10	3	1	.2	11	Trace	Trace	Trace	Trace	1
.5	.3	Trace	24	6	35	.6	106	Trace	.01	.03	.2	0
3.1	1.6	.1	20	48	60	.5	107	60	.02	.08	.2	Trace
—	—	—	13	33	9	.9	183	—	.01	.01	Trace	—
—	—	—	11	137	17	3.2	585	—	.02	.04	.4	—
—	—	—	14	35	5	2.6	—	—	—	.02	Trace	—
0	0	0	15	9	3	.8	1	0	0	0	0	0
0	0	0	212	187	42	7.5	757	0	.02	.07	.4	0
0	0	0	199	0	0	.2	6	0	0	0	0	0
0	0	0	12	0	0	Trace	Trace	0	0	0	0	0
0	0	0	6	0	0	Trace	Trace	0	0	0	0	0
0	0	0	100	0	0	.1	3	0	0	0	0	0

NUTRITIVE VALUES OF THE EDIBLE PART OF FOODS—Continued

Item No. (A)	Foods, approximate measures, units, and weight (edible part unless footnotes indicate otherwise) (B)		Water (C)	Food energy (D)	Protein (E)	Fat (F)
		Grams	Percent	Calories	Grams	Grams

VEGETABLE AND VEGETABLE PRODUCTS

	Asparagus, green:						
	Cooked, drained:						
	Cuts and tips, 1 1/2- to 2-in lengths:						
564	From raw--------------------	1 cup--------------------	145	94	30	3	Trace
565	From frozen-----------------	1 cup--------------------	180	93	40	6	Trace
	Spears, 1/2-in diam. at base:						
566	From raw--------------------	4 spears-----------------	60	94	10	1	Trace
567	From frozen-----------------	4 spears-----------------	60	92	15	2	Trace
568	Canned, spears, 1/2-in diam. at base.	4 spears-----------------	80	93	15	2	Trace
	Beans:						
	Lima, immature seeds, frozen, cooked, drained:						
569	Thick-seeded types (Fordhooks)	1 cup--------------------	170	74	170	10	Trace
570	Thin-seeded types (baby limas)	1 cup--------------------	180	69	210	13	Trace
	Snap:						
	Green:						
	Cooked, drained:						
571	From raw (cuts and French style).	1 cup--------------------	125	92	30	2	Trace
	From frozen:						
572	Cuts--------------------	1 cup--------------------	135	92	35	2	Trace
573	French style------------	1 cup--------------------	130	92	35	2	Trace
574	Canned, drained solids (cuts).	1 cup--------------------	135	92	30	2	Trace
	Yellow or wax:						
	Cooked, drained:						
575	From raw (cuts and French style).	1 cup--------------------	125	93	30	2	Trace
576	From frozen (cuts)--------	1 cup--------------------	135	92	35	2	Trace
577	Canned, drained solids (cuts).	1 cup--------------------	135	92	30	2	Trace
	Beans, mature. See Beans, dry (items 509-515) and Blackeye peas, dry (item 516).						
	Bean sprouts (mung):						
578	Raw--------------------------	1 cup--------------------	105	89	35	4	Trace
579	Cooked, drained-------------	1 cup--------------------	125	91	35	4	Trace
	Beets:						
	Cooked, drained, peeled:						
580	Whole beets, 2-in diam.------	2 beets------------------	100	91	30	1	Trace
581	Diced or sliced------------	1 cup--------------------	170	91	55	2	Trace
	Canned, drained solids:						
582	Whole beets, small---------	1 cup--------------------	160	89	60	2	Trace
583	Diced or sliced------------	1 cup--------------------	170	89	65	2	Trace
584	Beet greens, leaves and stems, cooked, drained.	1 cup--------------------	145	94	25	2	Trace
	Blackeye peas, immature seeds, cooked and drained:						
585	From raw--------------------	1 cup--------------------	165	72	180	13	1
586	From frozen-----------------	1 cup--------------------	170	66	220	15	1
	Broccoli, cooked, drained:						
	From raw:						
587	Stalk, medium size----------	1 stalk------------------	180	91	45	6	1
588	Stalks cut into 1/2-in pieces	1 cup--------------------	155	91	40	5	Trace
	From frozen:						
589	Stalk, 4 1/2 to 5 in long-----	1 stalk------------------	30	91	10	1	Trace
590	Chopped--------------------	1 cup--------------------	185	92	50	5	1
	Brussels sprouts, cooked, drained:						
591	From raw, 7-8 sprouts (1 1/4- to 1 1/2-in diam.).	1 cup--------------------	155	88	55	7	1
592	From frozen-----------------	1 cup--------------------	155	89	50	5	Trace

374

	NUTRIENTS IN INDICATED QUANTITY											
	Fatty Acids											
Satu-	Unsaturated		Carbo-	Calcium	Phos-	Iron	Potas-	Vitamin	Thiamin	Ribo-	Niacin	Ascorbic
rated	Oleic	Lino-	hydrate		phorus		sium	A value		flavin		acid
(total)		leic										
(G)	(H)	(I)	(J)	(K)	(L)	(M)	(N)	(O)	(P)	(Q)	(R)	(S)
Grams	Grams	Grams	Grams	Milli-grams	Milli-grams	Milli-grams	Milli-grams	Inter-national units	Milli-grams	Milli-grams	Milli-grams	Milli-grams
—	—	—	5	30	73	0.9	265	1,310	0.23	0.26	2.0	38
—	—	—	6	40	115	2.2	396	1,530	.25	.23	1.8	41
—	—	—	2	13	30	.4	110	540	.10	.11	.8	16
—	—	—	2	13	40	.7	143	470	.10	.08	.7	16
—	—	—	3	15	42	1.5	133	640	.05	.08	.6	12
—	—	—	32	34	153	2.9	724	390	.12	.09	1.7	29
—	—	—	40	63	227	4.7	709	400	.16	.09	2.2	22
—	—	—	7	63	46	.8	189	680	.09	.11	.6	15
—	—	—	8	54	43	.9	205	780	.09	.12	.5	7
—	—	—	8	49	39	1.2	177	690	.08	.10	.4	9
—	—	—	7	61	34	2.0	128	630	.04	.07	.4	5
—	—	—	6	63	46	.8	189	290	.09	.11	.6	16
—	—	—	8	47	42	.9	221	140	.09	.11	.5	8
—	—	—	7	61	34	2.0	128	140	.04	.07	.4	7
—	—	—	7	20	67	1.4	234	20	.14	.14	.8	20
—	—	—	7	21	60	1.1	195	30	.11	.13	.9	8
—	—	—	7	14	23	.5	208	20	.03	.04	.3	6
—	—	—	12	24	39	.9	354	30	.05	.07	.5	10
—	—	—	14	30	29	1.1	267	30	.02	.05	.2	5
—	—	—	15	32	31	1.2	284	30	.02	.05	.2	5
—	—	—	5	144	36	2.8	481	7,400	.10	.22	.4	22
—	—	—	30	40	241	3.5	625	580	.50	.18	2.3	28
—	—	—	40	43	286	4.8	573	290	.68	.19	2.4	15
—	—	—	8	158	112	1.4	481	4,500	.16	.36	1.4	162
—	—	—	7	136	96	1.2	414	3,880	.14	.31	1.2	140
—	—	—	1	12	17	.2	66	570	.02	.03	.2	22
—	—	—	9	100	104	1.3	392	4,810	.11	.22	.9	105
—	—	—	10	50	112	1.7	423	810	.12	.22	1.2	135
—	—	—	10	33	95	1.2	457	880	.12	.16	.9	126

NUTRITIVE VALUES OF THE EDIBLE PART OF FOODS–Continued

Item No.	Foods, approximate measures, units, and weight (edible part unless footnotes indicate otherwise)		Water	Food energy	Pro-tein	Fat
(A)	(B)		(C)	(D)	(E)	(F)
			Grams	Percent	Calories	Grams	Grams
	VEGETABLE AND VEGETABLE PRODUCTS–Con.						
	Cabbage:						
	Common varieties:						
	Raw:						
593	Coarsely shredded or sliced-	1 cup------------------	70	92	15	1	Trace
594	Finely shredded or chopped--	1 cup------------------	90	92	20	1	Trace
595	Cooked, drained---------------	1 cup------------------	145	94	30	2	Trace
596	Red, raw, coarsely shredded or sliced.	1 cup------------------	70	90	20	1	Trace
597	Savoy, raw, coarsely shredded or sliced.	1 cup------------------	70	92	15	2	Trace
598	Cabbage, celery (also called pe-tsai or wongbok), raw, 1-in pieces.	1 cup------------------	75	95	10	1	Trace
599	Cabbage, white mustard (also called bokchoy or pakchoy), cooked, drained.	1 cup------------------	170	95	25	2	Trace
	Carrots:						
	Raw, without crowns and tips, scraped:						
600	Whole, 7 1/2 by 1 1/8 in, or strips, 2 1/2 to 3 in long.	1 carrot or 18 strips----	72	88	30	1	Trace
601	Grated-------------------------	1 cup------------------	110	88	45	1	Trace
602	Cooked (crosswise cuts), drained	1 cup------------------	155	91	50	1	Trace
	Canned:						
603	Sliced, drained solids--------	1 cup------------------	155	91	45	1	Trace
604	Strained or junior (baby food)	1 oz (1 3/4 to 2 tbsp)---	28	92	10	Trace	Trace
	Cauliflower:						
605	Raw, chopped-------------------	1 cup------------------	115	91	31	3	Trace
	Cooked, drained:						
606	From raw (flower buds)--------	1 cup------------------	125	93	30	3	Trace
607	From frozen (flowerets)--------	1 cup------------------	180	94	30	3	Trace
	Celery, Pascal type, raw:						
608	Stalk, large outer, 8 by 1 1/2 in, at root end.	1 stalk----------------	40	94	5	Trace	Trace
609	Pieces, diced------------------	1 cup------------------	120	94	20	1	Trace
	Collards, cooked, drained:						
610	From raw (leaves without stems)-	1 cup------------------	190	90	65	7	1
611	From frozen (chopped)----------	1 cup------------------	170	90	50	5	1
	Corn, sweet:						
	Cooked, drained:						
612	From raw, ear 5 by 1 3/4 in---	1 ear[61]----------------	140	74	70	2	1
	From frozen:						
613	Ear, 5 in long----------------	1 ear[61]----------------	229	73	120	4	1
614	Kernels-----------------------	1 cup------------------	165	77	130	5	1
	Canned:						
615	Cream style-------------------	1 cup------------------	256	76	210	5	2
	Whole kernel:						
616	Vacuum pack------------------	1 cup------------------	210	76	175	5	1
617	Wet pack, drained solids----	1 cup------------------	165	76	140	4	1
	Cowpeas. See Blackeye peas. (Items 585-586).						
	Cucumber slices, 1/8 in thick (large, 2 1/8-in diam.; small, 1 3/4-in diam.):						
618	With peel----------------------	6 large or 8 small slices	28	95	5	Trace	Trace

[61]Weight includes cob. Without cob, weight is 77 g for item 612, 126 g for item 613.

	NUTRIENTS IN INDICATED QUANTITY										
	Fatty Acids											
Satu-	Unsaturated		Carbo-	Calcium	Phos-	Iron	Potas-	Vitamin	Thiamin	Ribo-	Niacin	Ascorbic
rated	Oleic	Lino-	hydrate		phorus		sium	A value		flavin		acid
(total)		leic										
(G)	(H)	(I)	(J)	(K)	(L)	(M)	(N)	(O)	(P)	(Q)	(R)	(S)
Grams	Grams	Grams	Grams	Milli-	Milli-	Milli-	Milli-	Inter-	Milli-	Milli-	Milli-	Milli-
				grams	grams	grams	grams	national	grams	grams	grams	grams
								units				
—	—	—	4	34	20	0.3	163	90	0.04	0.04	0.02	33
—	—	—	5	44	26	.4	210	120	.05	.05	.3	42
—	—	—	6	64	29	.4	236	190	.06	.06	.4	48
—	—	—	5	29	25	.6	188	30	.06	.04	.3	43
			3	47	38	.6	188	140	.04	.06	.2	39
—	—	—	2	32	30	.5	190	110	.04	.03	.5	19
—	—	—	4	252	56	1.0	364	5,270	.07	.14	1.2	26
			7	27	26	.5	246	7,930	.04	.04	.4	6
—	—	—	11	41	40	.8	375	12,100	.07	.06	.7	9
—	—	—	11	51	48	.9	344	16,280	.08	.08	.8	9
			10	47	34	1.1	186	23,250	.03	.05	.6	3
			2	7	6	.1	51	3,690	.01	.01	.1	1
—	—	—	6	29	64	1.3	339	70	.13	.12	.8	90
—	—	—	5	26	53	.9	258	80	.11	.10	.8	69
			6	31	68	.9	373	50	.07	.09	.7	74
			2	16	11	.1	136	110	.01	.01	.1	4
			5	47	34	.4	409	320	.04	.04	.4	11
—	—	—	10	357	99	1.5	498	14,820	.21	.38	2.3	144
—	—	—	10	299	87	1.7	401	11,560	.10	.24	1.0	56
			16	2	69	.5	151	[62]310	.09	.08	1.1	7
—	—	—	27	4	121	1.0	291	[62]440	.18	.10	2.1	9
—	—	—	31	5	120	1.3	304	[62]580	.15	.10	2.5	8
			51	8	143	1.5	248	[62]840	.08	.13	2.6	13
—	—	—	43	6	153	1.1	204	[62]740	.06	.13	2.3	11
			33	8	81	.8	160	[62]580	.05	.08	1.5	7
—	—	—	1	7	8	.3	45	70	.01	.01	.1	3

[62] Based on yellow varieties. For white varieties, value is trace.

377

NUTRITIVE VALUES OF THE EDIBLE PART OF FOODS—Continued

Item No. (A)	Foods, approximate measures, units, and weight (edible part unless footnotes indicate otherwise) (B)		Water (C) Per-cent	Food energy (D) Cal-ories	Pro-tein (E) Grams	Fat (F) Grams
		Grams				
619	Without peel------------------	6 1/2 large or 9 small pieces.	28	96	5	Trace	Trace
620	Dandelion greens, cooked, drained-	1 cup------------------	105	90	35	2	1
621	Endive, curly (including escarole), raw, small pieces.	1 cup------------------	50	93	10	1	Trace
	Kale, cooked, drained:						
622	From raw (leaves without stems and midribs).	1 cup------------------	110	88	45	5	1
623	From frozen (leaf style)--------	1 cup------------------	130	91	40	4	1
	Lettuce, raw:						
	Butterhead, as Boston types:						
624	Head, 5-in diam--------------	1 head[63]-------------	220	95	25	2	Trace
625	Leaves-----------------------	1 outer or 2 inner or 3 heart leaves.	15	95	Trace	Trace	Trace
	Crisphead, as Iceberg:						
626	Head, 6-in diam--------------	1 head[64]-------------	567	96	70	5	1
627	Wedge, 1/4 of head-----------	1 wedge---------------	135	96	20	1	Trace
628	Pieces, chopped or shredded---	1 cup-----------------	55	96	5	Trace	Trace
629	Looseleaf (bunching varieties including romaine or cos), chopped or shredded pieces.	1 cup-----------------	55	94	10	1	Trace
630	Mushrooms, raw, sliced or chopped-	1 cup-----------------	70	90	20	2	Trace
631	Mustard greens, without stems and midribs, cooked, drained.	1 cup-----------------	140	93	30	3	1
632	Okra pods, 3 by 5/8 in, cooked----	10 pods---------------	106	91	30	2	Trace
	Onions:						
	Mature:						
	Raw:						
633	Chopped------------------	1 cup-----------------	170	89	65	3	Trace
634	Sliced-------------------	1 cup-----------------	115	89	45	2	Trace
635	Cooked (whole or sliced), drained.	1 cup-----------------	210	92	60	3	Trace
636	Young green, bulb (3/8 in diam.) and white portion of top.	6 onions--------------	30	88	15	Trace	Trace
637	Parsley, raw, chopped------------	1 tbsp----------------	4	85	Trace	Trace	Trace
638	Parsnips, cooked (diced or 2-in lengths).	1 cup-----------------	155	82	100	2	1
	Peas, green:						
	Canned:						
639	Whole, drained solids---------	1 cup-----------------	170	77	150	8	1
640	Strained (baby food)----------	1 oz (1 3/4 to 2 tbsp)--	28	86	15	1	Trace
641	Frozen, cooked, drained-------	1 cup-----------------	160	82	110	8	Trace
642	Peppers, hot, red, without seeds, dried (ground chili powder, added seasonings).	1 tsp-----------------	2	9	5	Trace	Trace
	Peppers, sweet (about 5 per lb, whole), stem and seeds removed:						
643	Raw--------------------------	1 pod-----------------	74	93	15	1	Trace
644	Cooked, boiled, drained--------	1 pod-----------------	73	95	15	1	Trace
	Potatoes, cooked:						
645	Baked, peeled after baking (about 2 per lb, raw).	1 potato--------------	156	75	145	4	Trace
	Boiled (about 3 per lb, raw):						
646	Peeled after boiling----------	1 potato--------------	137	80	105	3	Trace
647	Peeled before boiling---------	1 potato--------------	135	83	90	3	Trace
	French-fried, strip, 2 to 3 1/2 in long:						
648	Prepared from raw-------------	10 strips-------------	50	45	135	2	7
649	Frozen, oven heated-----------	10 strips-------------	50	53	110	2	4
650	Hashed brown, prepared from frozen.	1 cup-----------------	155	56	345	3	18
	Mashed, prepared from—						
	Raw:						
651	Milk added------------------	1 cup-----------------	210	83	135	4	2

[63] Weight includes refuse of outer leaves and core. Without these parts, weight is 163 g.
[64] Weight includes core. Without core, weight is 539 g.

	NUTRIENTS IN INDICATED QUANTITY											
	Fatty Acids											
Satu- rated (total)	Unsaturated		Carbo- hydrate	Calcium	Phos- phorus	Iron	Potas- sium	Vitamin A value	Thiamin	Ribo- flavin	Niacin	Ascorbic acid
	Oleic	Lino- leic										
(G)	(H)	(I)	(J)	(K)	(L)	(M)	(N)	(O)	(P)	(Q)	(R)	(S)
Grams	Grams	Grams	Grams	Milli- grams	Milli- grams	Milli- grams	Milli- grams	Inter- national units	Milli- grams	Milli- grams	Milli- grams	Milli- grams
—	—	—	1	5	5	0.1	45	Trace	0.01	0.01	0.1	3
—	—	—	7	147	44	1.9	244	12,290	.14	.17	—	19
—	—	—	2	41	27	.9	147	1,650	.04	.07	.3	5
—	—	—	7	206	64	1.8	243	9,130	.11	.20	1.8	102
—	—	—	7	157	62	1.3	251	10,660	.08	.20	.9	49
—	—	—	4	57	42	3.3	430	1,580	.10	.10	.5	13
—	—	— Trace	5	4	.3	40	150	.01	.01 Trace	1
—	—	—	16	108	118	2.7	943	1,780	.32	.32	1.6	32
—	—	—	4	27	30	.7	236	450	.08	.08	.4	8
—	—	—	2	11	12	.3	96	180	.03	.03	.2	3
—	—	—	2	37	14	.8	145	1,050	.03	.04	.2	10
—	—	—	3	4	81	.6	290	Trace	.07	.32	2.9	2
—	—	—	6	193	45	2.5	308	8,120	.11	.20	.8	67
—	—	—	6	98	43	.5	184	520	.14	.19	1.0	21
—	—	—	15	46	61	.9	267	[65]Trace	.05	.07	.3	17
—	—	—	10	31	41	.6	181	[65]Trace	.03	.05	.2	12
—	—	—	14	50	61	.8	231	[65]Trace	.06	.06	.4	15
—	—	—	3	12	12	.2	69	Trace	.02	.01	.1	8
—	—	— Trace	7	2	.2	25	300	Trace	.01 Trace	6
—	—	—	23	70	96	.9	587	50	.11	.12	.2	16
—	—	—	29	44	129	3.2	163	1,170	.15	.10	1.4	14
—	—	—	3	3	18	.3	28	140	.02	.03	.3	3
—	—	—	19	30	138	3.0	216	960	.43	.14	2.7	21
—	—	—	1	5	4	.3	20	1,300	Trace	.02	.2	Trace
—	—	—	4	7	16	.5	157	310	.06	.06	.4	94
—	—	—	3	7	12	.4	109	310	.05	.05	.4	70
—	—	—	33	14	101	1.1	782	Trace	.15	.07	2.7	31
—	—	—	23	10	72	.8	556	Trace	.12	.05	2.0	22
—	—	—	20	8	57	.7	385	Trace	.12	.05	1.6	22
1.7	1.2	3.3	18	8	56	.7	427	Trace	.07	.04	1.6	11
1.1	.8	2.1	17	5	43	.9	326	Trace	.07	.01	1.3	11
4.6	3.2	9.0	45	28	78	1.9	439	Trace	.11	.03	1.6	12
.7	.4	Trace	27	50	103	.8	548	40	.17	.11	2.1	21

[65]Value based on white-fleshed varieties. For yellow-fleshed varieties, value in International Units (I.U.) is 70 for item 633, 50 for item 634, and 80 for item 635.

NUTRITIVE VALUES OF THE EDIBLE PART OF FOODS—Continued

Item No. (A)	Foods, approximate measures, units, and weight (edible part unless footnotes indicate otherwise) (B)		Water (C)	Food energy (D)	Protein (E)	Fat (F)
			Grams	Percent	Calories	Grams	Grams
	VEGETABLE AND VEGETABLE PRODUCTS—Con.						
	Potatoes, cooked—Continued						
	Mashed, prepared from—Continued						
	Raw—Continued						
652	Milk and butter added------	1 cup------------------	210	80	195	4	9
653	Dehydrated flakes (without milk), water, milk, butter, and salt added.	1 cup------------------	210	79	195	4	7
654	Potato chips, 1 3/4 by 2 1/2 in oval cross section.	10 chips---------------	20	2	115	1	8
655	Potato salad, made with cooked salad dressing.	1 cup------------------	250	76	250	7	7
656	Pumpkin, canned------------	1 cup------------------	245	90	80	2	1
657	Radishes, raw (prepackaged) stem ends, rootlets cut off.	4 radishes-------------	18	95	5	Trace	Trace
658	Sauerkraut, canned, solids and liquid.	1 cup------------------	235	93	40	2	Trace
	Southern peas. See Blackeye peas (items 585-586).						
	Spinach:						
659	Raw, chopped--------------	1 cup------------------	55	91	15	2	Trace
	Cooked, drained:						
660	From raw------------------	1 cup------------------	180	92	40	5	1
	From frozen:						
661	Chopped----------------	1 cup------------------	205	92	45	6	1
662	Leaf-------------------	1 cup------------------	190	92	45	6	1
663	Canned, drained solids----	1 cup------------------	205	91	50	6	1
	Squash, cooked:						
664	Summer (all varieties), diced, drained.	1 cup------------------	210	96	30	2	Trace
665	Winter (all varieties), baked, mashed.	1 cup------------------	205	81	130	4	1
	Sweetpotatoes:						
	Cooked (raw, 5 by 2 in; about 2 1/2 per lb):						
666	Baked in skin, peeled---------	1 potato---------------	114	64	160	2	1
667	Boiled in skin, peeled--------	1 potato---------------	151	71	170	3	1
668	Candied, 2 1/2 by 2-in piece----	1 piece----------------	105	60	175	1	3
	Canned:						
669	Solid pack (mashed)-----------	1 cup------------------	255	72	275	5	1
670	Vacuum pack, piece 2 3/4 by 1 in.	1 piece----------------	40	72	45	1	Trace
	Tomatoes:						
671	Raw, 2 3/5-in diam. (3 per 12 oz pkg.).	1 tomato[66]-----------	135	94	25	1	Trace
672	Canned, solids and liquid------	1 cup------------------	241	94	50	2	Trace
673	Tomato catsup------------------	1 cup------------------	273	69	290	5	1
674		1 tbsp-----------------	15	69	15	Trace	Trace
	Tomato juice, canned:						
675	Cup--------------------------	1 cup------------------	243	94	45	2	Trace
676	Glass (6 fl oz)--------------	1 glass----------------	182	94	35	2	Trace
677	Turnips, cooked, diced---------	1 cup------------------	155	94	35	1	Trace
	Turnip greens, cooked, drained:						
678	From raw (leaves and stems)-----	1 cup------------------	145	94	30	3	Trace
679	From frozen (chopped)-----------	1 cup------------------	165	93	40	4	Trace
680	Vegetables, mixed, frozen, cooked-	1 cup------------------	182	83	115	6	1

[66] Weight includes cores and stem ends. Without these parts, weight is 123 g.
[67] Based on year-round average. For tomatoes marketed from November through May, value is about 12 mg; from June through October, 32 mg.

	NUTRIENTS IN INDICATED QUANTITY											
	Fatty Acids											
Satu-rated (total)	Unsaturated Oleic	Lino-leic	Carbo-hydrate	Calcium	Phos-phorus	Iron	Potas-sium	Vitamin A value	Thiamin	Ribo-flavin	Niacin	Ascorbic acid
(G)	(H)	(I)	(J)	(K)	(L)	(M)	(N)	(O)	(P)	(Q)	(R)	(S)
Grams	Grams	Grams	Grams	Milli-grams	Milli-grams	Milli-grams	Milli-grams	Inter-national units	Milli-grams	Milli-grams	Milli-grams	Milli-grams
5.6	2.3	0.2	26	50	101	0.8	525	360	0.17	0.11	2.1	19
3.6	2.1	.2	30	65	99	.6	601	270	.08	.08	1.9	11
2.1	1.4	4.0	10	8	28	.4	226	Trace	.04	.01	1.0	3
2.0	2.7	1.3	41	80	160	1.5	798	350	.20	.18	2.8	28
—	—	—	19	61	64	1.0	588	15,680	.07	.12	1.5	12
—	—	—	1	5	6	.2	58	Trace	.01	.01	.1	5
—	—	—	9	85	42	1.2	329	120	.07	.09	.5	33
—	—	—	2	51	28	1.7	259	4,460	.06	.11	.3	28
—	—	—	6	167	68	4.0	583	14,580	.13	.25	.9	50
—	—	—	8	232	90	4.3	683	16,200	.14	.31	.8	39
—	—	—	7	200	84	4.8	688	15,390	.15	.27	1.0	53
—	—	—	7	242	53	5.3	513	16,400	.04	.25	.6	29
—	—	—	7	53	53	.8	296	820	.11	.17	1.7	21
—	—	—	32	57	98	1.6	945	8,610	.10	.27	1.4	27
—	—	—	37	46	66	1.0	342	9,230	.10	.08	.8	25
—	—	—	40	48	71	1.1	367	11,940	.14	.09	.9	26
2.0	.8	.1	36	39	45	.9	200	6,620	.06	.04	.4	11
—	—	—	63	64	105	2.0	510	19,890	.13	.10	1.5	36
—	—	—	10	10	16	.3	80	3,120	.02	.02	.2	6
—	—	—	6	16	33	.6	300	1,110	.07	.05	.9	[6,7]28
—	—	—	10	[6,8]14	46	1.2	523	2,170	.12	.07	1.7	41
—	—	—	69	60	137	2.2	991	3,820	.25	.19	4.4	41
—	—	—	4	3	8	.1	54	210	.01	.01	.2	2
—	—	—	10	17	44	2.2	552	1,940	.12	.07	1.9	39
—	—	—	8	13	33	1.6	413	1,460	.09	.05	1.5	29
—	—	—	8	54	37	.6	291	Trace	.06	.08	.5	34
—	—	—	5	252	49	1.5	—	8,270	.15	.33	.7	68
—	—	—	6	195	64	2.6	246	11,390	.08	.15	.7	31
—	—	—	24	46	115	2.4	348	9,010	.22	.13	2.0	15

[6,8] Applies to product without calcium salts added. Value for products with calcium salts added may be as much as 63 mg for whole tomatoes, 241 mg for cut forms.

NUTRITIVE VALUES OF THE EDIBLE PART OF FOODS—Continued

Item No. (A)	Foods, approximate measures, units, and weight (edible part unless footnotes indicate otherwise) (B)			Water (C)	Food energy (D)	Protein (E)	Fat (F)
			Grams	Percent	Calories	Grams	Grams

MISCELLANEOUS ITEMS

Baking powders for home use:
  Sodium aluminum sulfate:

681	With monocalcium phosphate monohydrate.	1 tsp	3.0	2	5	Trace	Trace
682	With monocalcium phosphate monohydrate, calcium sulfate.	1 tsp	2.9	1	5	Trace	Trace
683	Straight phosphate	1 tsp	3.8	2	5	Trace	Trace
684	Low sodium	1 tsp	4.3	2	5	Trace	Trace
685	Barbecue sauce	1 cup	250	81	230	4	17

Beverages, alcoholic:

| 686 | Beer | 12 fl oz | 360 | 92 | 150 | 1 | 0 |

  Gin, rum, vodka, whisky:

687	80-proof	1 1/2-fl oz jigger	42	67	95	—	—
688	86-proof	1 1/2-fl oz jigger	42	64	105	—	—
689	90-proof	1 1/2-fl oz jigger	42	62	110	—	—

  Wines:

| 690 | Dessert | 3 1/2-fl oz glass | 103 | 77 | 140 | Trace | 0 |
| 691 | Table | 3 1/2-fl oz glass | 102 | 86 | 85 | Trace | 0 |

Beverages, carbonated, sweetened, nonalcoholic:

692	Carbonated water	12 fl oz	366	92	115	0	0
693	Cola type	12 fl oz	369	90	145	0	0
694	Fruit-flavored sodas and Tom Collins mixer.	12 fl oz	372	88	170	0	0
695	Ginger ale	12 fl oz	366	92	115	0	0
696	Root beer	12 fl oz	370	90	150	0	0

Chili powder. See Peppers, hot, red (item 642).
Chocolate:

| 697 | Bitter or baking | 1 oz | 28 | 2 | 145 | 3 | 15 |

  Semisweet, see Candy, chocolate (item 539).

698	Gelatin, dry	1, 7-g envelope	7	13	25	6	Trace
699	Gelatin dessert prepared with gelatin dessert powder and water.	1 cup	240	84	140	4	0
700	Mustard, prepared, yellow	1 tsp or individual serving pouch or cup.	5	80	5	Trace	Trace

Olives, pickled, canned:

| 701 | Green | 4 medium or 3 extra large or 2 giant.[69] | 16 | 78 | 15 | Trace | 2 |
| 702 | Ripe, Mission | 3 small or 2 large[69] | 10 | 73 | 15 | Trace | 2 |

Pickles, cucumber:

703	Dill, medium, whole, 3 3/4 in long, 1 1/4-in diam.	1 pickle	65	93	5	Trace	Trace
704	Fresh-pack, slices 1 1/2-in diam., 1/4 in thick.	2 slices	15	79	10	Trace	Trace
705	Sweet, gherkin, small, whole, about 2 1/2 in long, 3/4-in diam.	1 pickle	15	61	20	Trace	Trace
706	Relish, finely chopped, sweet	1 tbsp	15	63	20	Trace	Trace

Popcorn. See items 476-478.

| 707 | Popsicle, 3-fl oz size | 1 popsicle | 95 | 80 | 70 | 0 | 0 |

[69]Weight includes pits. Without pits, weight is 13 g for item 701, 9 g for item 702.

	NUTRIENTS IN INDICATED QUANTITY											
	Fatty Acids											
Satu-rated (total)	Unsaturated		Carbo-hydrate	Calcium	Phos-phorus	Iron	Potas-sium	Vitamin A value	Thiamin	Ribo-flavin	Niacin	Ascorbic acid
	Oleic	Lino-leic										
(G)	(H)	(I)	(J)	(K)	(L)	(M)	(N)	(O)	(P)	(Q)	(R)	(S)
Grams	Grams	Grams	Grams	Milli-grams	Milli-grams	Milli-grams	Milli-grams	Inter-national units	Milli-grams	Milli-grams	Milli-grams	Milli-grams
0	0	0	1	58	87	—	5	0	0	0	0	0
0	0	0	1	183	45	—	—	0	0	0	0	0
0	0	0	1	239	359	—	6	0	0	0	0	0
0	0	0	2	207	314	—	471	0	0	0	0	0
2.2	4.3	10.0	20	53	50	2.0	435	900	.03	.03	.8	13
0	0	0	14	18	108	Trace	90	—	.01	.11	2.2	—
0	0	0	Trace	—	—	—	1	—	—	—	—	—
0	0	0	Trace	—	—	—	1	—	—	—	—	—
0	0	0	Trace	—	—	—	1	—	—	—	—	—
0	0	0	8	8	—	—	77	—	.01	.02	.2	—
0	0	0	4	9	10	.4	94	—	Trace	.01	.1	—
0	0	0	29	—	—	—	—	0	0	0	0	0
0	0	0	37	—	—	—	—	0	0	0	0	0
0	0	0	45	—	—	—	—	0	0	0	0	0
0	0	0	29	—	—	—	0	0	0	0	0	0
0	0	0	39	—	—	—	0	0	0	0	0	0
8.9	4.9	.4	8	22	109	1.9	235	20	.01	.07	.4	0
0	0	0	0	—	—	—	—	—	—	—	—	—
0	0	0	34	—	—	—	—	—	—	—	—	—
—	—	—	Trace	4	4	.1	7	—	—	—	—	—
.2	1.2	.1	Trace	8	2	.2	7	40	—	—	—	—
.2	1.2	.1	Trace	9	1	.1	2	10	Trace	Trace	—	—
—	—	—	1	17	14	.7	130	70	Trace	.01	Trace	4
—	—	—	3	5	4	.3	—	20	Trace	Trace	Trace	1
—	—	—	5	2	2	.2	—	10	Trace	Trace	Trace	1
—	—	—	5	3	2	.1	—	—	—	—	—	—
0	0	0	18	0	—	Trace	—	0	0	0	0	0

NUTRITIVE VALUES OF THE EDIBLE PART OF FOODS—Continued

Item No. (A)	Foods, approximate measures, units, and weight (edible part unless footnotes indicate otherwise) (B)		Water (C)	Food energy (D)	Protein (E)	Fat (F)
		Grams	Percent	Calories	Grams	Grams
	MISCELLANEOUS ITEMS—Con.					
	Soups:					
	Canned, condensed:					
	Prepared with equal volume of milk:					
708	Cream of chicken------------- 1 cup--------------------	245	85	180	7	10
709	Cream of mushroom----------- 1 cup--------------------	245	83	215	7	14
710	Tomato---------------------- 1 cup--------------------	250	84	175	7	7
	Prepared with equal volume of water:					
711	Bean with pork-------------- 1 cup--------------------	250	84	170	8	6
712	Beef broth, bouillon, consomme. 1 cup--------------------	240	96	30	5	0
713	Beef noodle----------------- 1 cup--------------------	240	93	65	4	3
714	Clam chowder, Manhattan type (with tomatoes, without milk). 1 cup--------------------	245	92	80	2	3
715	Cream of chicken------------ 1 cup--------------------	240	92	95	3	6
716	Cream of mushroom----------- 1 cup--------------------	240	90	135	2	10
717	Minestrone------------------ 1 cup--------------------	245	90	105	5	3
718	Split pea------------------- 1 cup--------------------	245	85	145	9	3
719	Tomato---------------------- 1 cup--------------------	245	91	90	2	3
720	Vegetable beef-------------- 1 cup--------------------	245	92	80	5	2
721	Vegetarian------------------ 1 cup--------------------	245	92	80	2	2
	Dehydrated:					
722	Bouillon cube, 1/2 in------- 1 cube-------------------	4	4	5	1	Trace
	Mixes:					
	Unprepared:					
723	Onion---------------------- 1 1/2-oz pkg ------------	43	3	150	6	5
	Prepared with water:					
724	Chicken noodle------------ 1 cup--------------------	240	95	55	2	1
725	Onion---------------------- 1 cup--------------------	240	96	35	1	1
726	Tomato vegetable with noodles. 1 cup--------------------	240	93	65	1	1
727	Vinegar, cider--------------------- 1 tbsp-------------------	15	94	Trace	Trace	0
728	White sauce, medium, with enriched flour. 1 cup--------------------	250	73	405	10	31
	Yeast:					
729	Baker's, dry, active------------- 1 pkg--------------------	7	5	20	3	Trace
730	Brewer's, dry-------------------- 1 tbsp-------------------	8	5	25	3	Trace

[70] Value may vary from 6 to 60 mg.

384

	NUTRIENTS IN INDICATED QUANTITY											
	Fatty Acids											
Satu-rated (total)	Unsaturated		Carbo-hydrate	Calcium	Phos-phorus	Iron	Potas-sium	Vitamin A value	Thiamin	Ribo-flavin	Niacin	Ascorbic acid
	Oleic	Lino-leic										
(G)	(H)	(I)	(J)	(K)	(L)	(M)	(N)	(O)	(P)	(Q)	(R)	(S)
Grams	Grams	Grams	Grams	Milli-grams	Milli-grams	Milli-grams	Milli-grams	Inter-national units	Milli-grams	Milli-grams	Milli-grams	Milli-grams
4.2	3.6	1.3	15	172	152	0.5	260	610	0.05	0.27	0.7	2
5.4	2.9	4.6	16	191	169	.5	279	250	.05	.34	.7	1
3.4	1.7	1.0	23	168	155	.8	418	1,200	.10	.25	1.3	15
1.2	1.8	2.4	22	63	128	2.3	395	650	.13	.08	1.0	3
0	0	0	3	Trace	31	.5	130	Trace	Trace	.02	1.2	—
.6	.7	.8	7	7	48	1.0	77	50	.05	.07	1.0	Trace
.5	.4	1.3	12	34	47	1.0	184	880	.02	.02	1.0	—
1.6	2.3	1.1	8	24	34	.5	79	410	.02	.05	.5	Trace
2.6	1.7	4.5	10	41	50	.5	98	70	.02	.12	.7	Trace
.7	.9	1.3	14	37	59	1.0	314	2,350	.07	.05	1.0	—
1.1	1.2	.4	21	29	149	1.5	270	440	.25	.15	1.5	1
.5	.5	1.0	16	15	34	.7	230	1,000	.05	.05	1.2	12
—	—	—	10	12	49	.7	162	2,700	.05	.05	1.0	—
—	—	—	13	20	39	1.0	172	2,940	.05	.05	1.0	—
—	—	—	Trace	—	—	—	4	—	—	— —	—	—
1.1	2.3	1.0	23	42	49	.6	238	30	.05	.03	.3	6
—	—	—	8	7	19	.2	19	50	.07	.05	.5	Trace
—	—	—	6	10	12	.2	58	Trace	Trace	Trace	Trace	2
—	—	—	12	7	19	.2	29	480	.05	.02	.5	5
0	0	0	1	1	1	.1	15	—	—	—	—	—
19.3	7.8	.8	22	288	233	.5	348	1,150	.12	.43	.7	2
—	—	—	3	3	90	1.1	140	Trace	.16	.38	2.6	Trace
—	—	—	3	[70]17	140	1.4	152	Trace	1.25	.34	3.0	Trace

385

Appendix B

Temperature conversion for Fahrenheit and Celsius

To convert degrees Fahrenheit to degrees Celsius, use the formula:

$$(°F - 32°) \times 5/9$$

To convert degrees Celsius to degrees Fahrenheit, use the formula:

$$(9/5 \times °C) + 32°$$

Convert Fahrenheit to Celsius by reading up from °F to the diagonal line, and then left to read °C.

Reverse to convert Celsius to Fahrenheit.

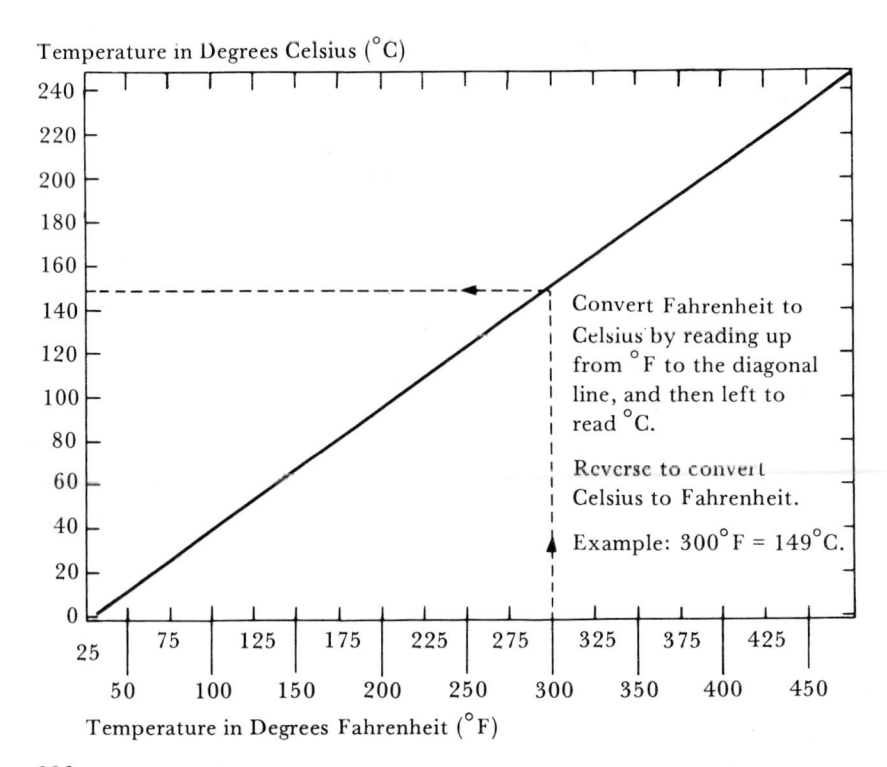

Example: 300°F = 149°C.

Appendix C

Essential and desirable kitchen equipment[a]

Essential	Desirable
Preparation	
1 can opener	1 grater
1 bottle opener	1 cheese slicer
1 can key punch	1 pair kitchen scissors
1 good-quality sharpening stone	1 corkscrew
1 cutting board, wood or plastic	1 meat mallet
1 chef's knife, 10″ or 12″, high-carbon steel or high-carbon stainless steel	1 bread knife, serrated blade
	1 garlic press
1 paring knife, 6″, high-carbon steel or high-carbon stainless steel	1 large wire whisk, fine wires
	1 small wire whisk
2 rubber spatulas	1 colander
2 wooden spoons or flat-bottomed stirrers	1 large strainer, fine mesh
	1 small strainer, fine mesh
1 set measuring spoons	1 juicer
1 rotary beater	1 2-cup measuring cup
1 set graduated measuring cups	1 pastry brush
1 8-ounce liquid measuring cup	1 rolling pin
1 set 3 graduated-size mixing bowls	1 flour sifter
1 vegetable brush	1 pastry blender
Cooking	
1 small pancake turner	1 deep-fat frying thermometer
1 pair tongs	1 meat thermometer
1 cooking fork	1 slotted spatula
1 slotted spoon	1 long-handled cooking fork
4 potholders	1 2-qt. saucepan with heavy bottom
1 1-qt. saucepan with cover	2 8″ round cake pans
1 2-qt. saucepan with cover	2 wire cooling racks
1 4–6 qt. pot with cover	1 8″ pie pan
1 8″ saucepan or skillet with cover	1 muffin pan, nonstick
1 7″ nonstick fry pan	1 11″ × 15″ jelly-roll pan
1 8–10″ cast iron fry pan	
1 8″ × 8″ × 2″ baking pan	
1 5″ × 7″ loaf pan	
1 6″ casserole or soufflé dish	
1 7″ × 11″ baking pan	
2 custard cups	

[a]Equipment needed will depend upon the individual situation.

(continued)

Essential	Desirable
Storing food Glass jars and covers Plastic bags Plastic refrigerator containers and lids Aluminum foil Plastic wrap 1 2-qt. bottle or plastic container for fruit juice	
Cleaning 1 dish brush 2 sponges 2 dishcloths 8–10 dishtowels Scouring pads Soap powder Detergent Sanitizer (chlorine laundry bleach or hypochlorite)	
	Miscellaneous 1 toaster 1 portable electric beater 1 electric blender 1 lettuce spinner 1 pastry bag and tubes 1 pastry cutter wheel 1 egg slicer

Appendix D

Equivalents and substitutions

Food	Amount	Equivalent	Substitution
Fruits			
Apples	4 medium-size	4 C. sliced	
Lemons			
Whole	1	2–3 T. juice	
		2 t. rind	
Juice	1 t.		½ t. vinegar
Limes	1	1½–2 T. juice	
Oranges	1 medium-size	6–8 T. juice	
		2–3 t. rind	
Strawberries	10 oz. pkg. frozen	1 C. sliced fresh plus ⅓ C. sugar	
Vegetables			
Cabbage	1 small head	4 C. shredded	
Carrots	1 lb.	2½ C. sliced	
Chives	1 T. chopped fresh		1 t. freeze-dried
Garlic	1 clove fresh		1 t. garlic salt
			⅛ t. garlic powder
Onions	2 t. minced		1 t. onion powder
Potatoes	4 medium-size	4 C. sliced raw	
	1 lb. raw (3 medium-size)	2 C. mashed	
Tomatoes			
Whole	1 C. canned		1⅓ C. chopped fresh tomatoes simmered 10 min.
Juice	1 C.		½ C. tomato sauce plus ½ C. water
Eggs			
Whole	1 large	3 T. slightly beaten	2 yolks plus 1 T. water (in cookies)
			2 yolks (in custards, cream fillings, and similar mixtures)

Food	Amount	Equivalent	Substitution
Whites	6–7 large	1 C.	
Yolks	11–12 large	1 C.	
Milk and milk products			
Butter	1 stick (¼ lb.)	½ C.	7 T. vegetable shortening
	4 sticks (1 lb.)	2 C.	4 sticks margarine
Cheese			
Grated	4 oz. Cheddar cheese	1 C.	Cheese of your choice (Swiss, Monterey Jack)
Cottage	½ lb.	1 C.	
Cream	1 C. 18–20%		⅞ C. milk 3 T. butter or margarine
	1 C. 36–40%		¾ C. milk ⅓ C. butter or margarine
Heavy	½ pt.	2 C. whipped	
Sour	1 C.		1 T. lemon juice plus evaporated milk to equal 1 C.
Margarine	1 stick (¼ lb.)	½ C.	1 stick butter 7 T. vegetable shortening
Milk, Homogenized	1 C.	⅞ C. skim plus 2 T. fat	⅓ C. powdered plus water to equal 1 C. ½ C. evaporated plus ½ C. water 1 C. fruit juice or potato water (in baking)
Buttermilk	1 C.		1 T. vinegar plus sweet milk to equal 1 C.
Evaporated	14½ oz. can	1⅔ C.	
	6 oz. can	¾ C.	
Sweetened, condensed	15½ oz. can	1⅓ C.	
Liquid			Vegetable or fruit juices, water, red or white wine, milk, bouillon, leftover liquid from fruits or vegetables

Equivalents and substitutions

Food	Amount	Equivalent	Substitution
Breads			
Bread crumbs			
Dry	1 slice	⅓ C.	
Soft	1 slice	¾ C.	
Cracker			
Saltine	7, coarsely crumbled	1 C.	
	9, finely crumbled	1 C.	
Graham	9, coarsely crumbled	1 C.	
	11, finely crumbled	1 C.	
Small vanilla wafers	20, coarsely crumbled	1 C.	
	30, finely crumbled	1 C.	
Zwieback	4, coarsely crumbled	1 C.	
	9, finely crumbled	1 C.	
Flour, thickeners, and leavening agents			
Flour, all purpose	1 lb.	4 C. sifted	
	1 C. sifted		1 C. plus 2 T. cake flour
			⅞ C. cornmeal
			1 C. graham flour
			1 C. rye flour
			1½ C. bran
			1½ C. bread crumbs
			1 C. rolled oats
Flour, cake	1 lb.	4¾–5 C. sifted	
	1 C. sifted		⅞ C. sifted all-purpose flour (⅞ C. equals 1 C. less 2 T.)
Flour, whole wheat	1 lb.	3½ C. unsifted	
Flour as a thickener	1 T.		1½ t. cornstarch
			2 t. quick-cooking tapioca
			1 whole egg
			2 egg whites or 2 egg yolks
			2 T. granular cereal
			1½ t. arrowroot

Food	Amount	Equivalent	Substitution
Cornstarch	1 T.		2 T. flour
Gelatin as a thickener	1 (1/4 oz.) envelope	1 T.	
Leavening agents			
Baking powder	1 t.		1/2 t. cream of tartar plus 1/4 t. baking soda
Yeast, fresh, compressed	1 cake	2/3 oz.	2 1/2 t. dry yeast
Yeast, dry, granular	1 pkg.	1/4 oz.	2/3 oz. fresh
Sugar			
White	1 lb.	2 C.	
	1 C.		1 1/3 C. brown sugar, lightly packed
			1 1/2 C. powdered sugar
			1 C. honey, minus 1/4 to 1/3 C. liquid
			1 C. molasses plus 1/4–1/2 t. soda (omit baking powder)
			1 1/4 C. corn syrup minus 1/4 C. liquid
Brown, packed	1 lb.	2 1/3 C.	
Powdered	1 lb.	3 1/2 C.	
Honey	2/3 C.		1 C. sugar plus 1/3 C. water
Corn syrup	1 1/2 C.		1 C. sugar plus 1/2 C. water
Chocolate	1 oz.		3 T. cocoa plus 1 T. shortening
Grains, pastas, and legumes			
Cornmeal	1 lb.	3 C.	
	1 C. uncooked	4 C. cooked	

Equivalents and substitutions

Food	Amount	Equivalent	Substitution
Rice	1 lb.	2 C.	
	1 C. uncooked	3–3½ C. cooked	
Macaroni	1 lb.	4 C.	
	1 C. uncooked	2–2¼ C. cooked	
Noodles	1 C. uncooked	1¾ C. cooked	
Spaghetti	½ lb. uncooked	2 C. uncooked	
	1 C. uncooked	2 C. cooked	
Beans			
Kidney	2⅔ C. uncooked	6¼ C. cooked	
Lima	3 C. uncooked	7 C. cooked	
Peas, split	2 C. uncooked	5 C. cooked	
White	2 C. uncooked	6 C. cooked	
Fish			
Shrimp	1½ lb. raw shrimp	1 lb. raw, shelled and deveined	12 oz. canned shrimp
Oysters	2 dozen small or medium, in shell	1 pint shucked	
Poultry			
Chicken	3½ lb., drawn	2 C. cooked, diced	
Chicken broth	1 C.		1 chicken bouillon cube or 1 envelope chicken extract dissolved in 1 C. boiling water
			1 C. canned chicken broth
Meat			
Beef			
Uncooked	1 lb. ground	2 C.	
Cooked	1 lb. minced	3 C.	
Beef broth	1 C.		1 beef bouillon cube or 1 envelope instant beef broth or 1 t. beef extract dissolved in 1 C. water
Pork, ground	½ lb.		½ lb. sausage meat
Ham, cooked and diced	1½ C.		12 oz. can pork luncheon meat, diced

Food	Amount	Equivalent	Substitution
Spices, herbs, and seasonings			
Fresh	1 T.	1 t. dried	
Allspice	1 t.		½ t. cinnamon plus ⅛ t. ground cloves
Cinnamon sugar	¼ C.		¼ C. sugar plus 1 t. cinnamon
Garlic	1 small clove		⅛ t. garlic powder
Italian seasoning	1 t.		¼ t. *each* oregano, basil, thyme, rosemary, plus dash cayenne pepper
Oregano	1 t.		1 t. marjoram
Pumpkin pie spice	1 t.		½ t. cinnamon, ¼ t. ginger, ⅛ t. *each* ground nutmeg, ground cloves
Other seasonings and condiments			
Ketchup	½ C.		½ C. Chili sauce
			½ C. tomato sauce plus 2 T. sugar, 1 T. vinegar, ⅛ t. ground cloves
Tabasco sauce	Few drops		Dash cayenne pepper
Tartar sauce	½ C.		6 T. mayonnaise plus 2 T. chopped pickle relish
Worcestershire sauce	1 t.		1 t. bottled steak sauce

Glossary

al dente—(firm to the bite) the desirable state of doneness for pasta

all-purpose flour—a wheat flour suitable for all types of home cookery; also called *general-purpose flour*

amino acid—an organic compound that contains an amino group (nitrogen and hydrogen); an organic compound that is a structural part of proteins

amoebic dysentery—a disease caused by a parasite in food

bake, baked, baking—to cook with dry heat in an oven; for meat, roasting

barbecue, barbecued, barbecuing—to cook slowly over dry heat; also, to baste with a sauce while cooking slowly over dry heat

barley—a small grain used in soups and as a cooked dish, usually a hot cereal

basal metabolism—the minimum amount of energy needed by the body for the vital body processes to function

Basic Four—the four food groups developed by the USDA for use in planning nutritionally adequate meals

Basic Seven—the seven food groups developed by the USDA before the Basic Four were formulated

baste, basted, basting—to moisten the surface of food with liquid during dry-heat cooking, as in basting a chicken

batter—a thin mixture of flour, liquid, fat, and other ingredients used for pancakes, crepes, waffles, or cakes; a seasoned mixture used to coat foods before frying

bean sprouts—the small, new shoots of growth that develop when beans (usually soybeans) are kept moist

binding agent—a substance that causes ingredients to hold together

biological score—an indication of the quality of a food's protein

blanch, blanched, blanching—to immerse vegetables in scalding water to stop enzyme action; a process used to aid in the removal of skins from some fruits and nuts

blend, blended, blending—to mix ingredients together thoroughly

boil, boiled, boiling—to heat water until it moves actively in the pan; to cook a food in water or other liquid that is boiling

botulism—a serious, frequently fatal illness that is caused by the toxin produced in food by *Clostridium botulinum*

braise, braised, braising—to cook in a small quantity of liquid in a covered pan

bran—the outer, protective layers of a kernel of grain

broil, broiled, broiling—to cook food in direct contact with the heat or flame

brown rice—unpolished rice, from which only the outside layer has been removed

brucellosis—a disease that is transmitted to people by the milk of an infected cow; also called *undulant fever*

bulgur—a food made by parboiling and cracking kernels of wheat; bulgur is used widely in the Middle East and is available in this country

buttermilk—the thin liquid left when the fat of milk is churned into butter; a milk product made commercially by adding lactic-acid bacteria to low-fat or skim milk

candle, candled, candling—to pass whole eggs in front of a bright light, for inspection and grading before marketing

capon—a castrated male chicken; a plump, meaty bird that usually is roasted

carcass—the body of a meat animal after it has been prepared for the wholesale market

carbon dioxide—the gas formed in food that acts as a leavener, making a baked product expand or rise *catalyst*—a substance that starts or affects the speed of a reaction, but which is not a part of that reaction

cereal—a plant that produces grains; a breakfast food

chickpea—see **legume**

chinaware—a collective term for the dishes used for serving food at a meal

chlorophyll—the green coloring matter found in plants

chop, chopped, chopping—to cut into small pieces with a knife or chopping blade

Clostridium botulinum—a toxin-producing bacterium that causes botulism

Clostridium perfringens—a micro-organism that causes food poisoning

coagulation—the thickening process that develops when proteins are cooked; a thickened mass, as in the clotting of blood

coddle, coddled, coddling—to heat or cook for one to five minutes in almost-simmering water

coenzyme—a substance, frequently a vitamin, that activates an enzyme

cold cuts—see **luncheon meats**

collagen—a protein constituent of connective tissues; a substance that holds cells together

connective tissue—a substance that holds meat together; connective tissue may be heavy and tough

contaminated—containing dirt, mold, bacteria, or other foreign matter; unfit for human consumption

convenience food—a food product that is partially or fully prepared before it is marketed

converted rice—rice that has been treated with hot water and steam to aid in retaining part of the vitamins and minerals normally removed by milling

core—the fibrous center of fruit, which holds the seeds; the woody, center stalk around which leaves curl and head, as in lettuce and cabbage

cornmeal—a grainy, coarse product made from corn that is used for quick breads and some desserts

cover—the flatware, glassware, dinnerware, and napkin needed by one person for a meal *cracked wheat*—unmilled wheat kernels broken into small pieces

cream, creamed, creaming—to blend fat and sugar together until the mixture is light and fluffy; the process is used in cake making

curd—a semisolid substance, formed by bacteria in milk, from which cheese is made; a fruit filling used in tart shells

curdle, curdled, curdling—to separate; a process that can occur when milk or milk-egg mixtures are subjected to too high cooking temperatures or are cooked for too long a period of time

cure, cured, curing—to preserve meat by a chemical process; to age cheese

cut into, cutting in—to reduce fat to small pieces in flour; the process is used to make pastry and some quick breads

deaminization—the removal of the nitrogen-containing molecule from an amino acid

deep-frying—see **fry**

dental caries—tooth decay

digestion—the conversion of foods into a form that can be absorbed from the intestinal tract into the body

dinnerware—the plates, cups, saucers, and other items onto which food is put for a meal

dough—a thick mixture of flour, liquid, and other ingredients from which breads are made; dough may or may not contain yeast

draw, drawn, drawing—to remove all entrails from poultry

durum wheat—a hard wheat that has high gluten content; the wheat is used to make pastas

earthenware—a type of dinnerware that includes semiporcelain and pottery

emulsion—the suspension of oil in liquid, as oil and vinegar; the mixture must be held together by a third substance, an *emulsifier*, as in mayonnaise, or held together temporarily by vigorous mixing, as in vinaigrette dressing

endosperm—the part of a seed or grain that contains the protein and starch

enriched flour—flour to which some nutrients have been added after milling

Endamoeba histolytica—a parasite that causes amoebic dysentery *entrée*—the main dinner dish or course

enzyme—a substance formed in living cells, which acts as a catalyst to cause specific reactions

epithelial tissue—the protective membrane that lines the mouth, esophagus, respiratory tract, and other parts of the body

ethylene gas—a gas released by fruit as it ripens

evaporated milk—whole milk with about 60 percent of its water content removed

extend, extended, extending—to add one ingredient (*extender*) to another, to increase the quantity of the second

extender—see **extend**

farina—a type of cereal, usually enriched, made by grinding the endosperm of the wheat kernel

fatty acids—organic acids that combine with glycerol to form fats

fermentation—a bacterial action in food, which causes a change of some kind in the food

filet—the tenderloin; a boneless piece of meat that has been removed from rib and sirloin sections of a beef or pork carcass

fillet—a lengthwise, boneless, or nearly boneless, slice from the side of a fish

flan—a pielike product with only a bottom crust, made in a special pan

flatware—the knives, forks, spoons, and serving implements used to eat or serve food

flute, fluted, fluting—to shape the edge of pastry into a pattern with the fingers

foam—the light, airy mixture produced by beating the whites of eggs with a whisk or rotary beater, used as the basis for meringues, soufflés, and omelets; also may be produced from yolks or whole eggs, as for sponge cakes

fold, folded, folding—to incorporate ingredients into a light mixture by cutting a spoon or rubber spatula straight down through the mixture to the bottom, across the bowl bottom, and back up the side, turning the wrist and spatula accordingly

foodborne infection—an illness transmitted to human beings by micro-organisms in food *fortified*—a food to which nutrients have been added, as is vitamin D to milk

fricassee, fricasseed, fricasseeing—to cook, as in braising; the term is used with chicken

fry, fried, frying—to cook in a small amount of hot fat in a frying pan (pan-frying); to cook in a large amount of hot fat in a deep pan (deep-frying)

garbanzo—see **legume**

garnish, garnished, garnishing—to decorate a food product to enhance its appearance

gel—a soft solid

germ—the innermost section of a kernel of grain, as wheat germ

giblets—the heart, liver, and gizzard of poultry

glycerol—the portion of molecule of fat with which the fatty acids are combined

GRAS list—a list of additives that have been recognized as safe

green shrimp—raw, uncooked shrimp

glaze, glazed, glazing—to apply a thin translucent coating (*glaze*) to a cooked product to decorate it

gluten—a protein substance in flour that strengthens dough

grass-fed cattle—cattle, usually beef, that have been fed on grass before slaughter, not fattened in feed lots

grits—a cereal food processed from corn

groats—grain kernels, usually oats, from which the hulls have been removed

hard meringue—a stiffly beaten egg-white foam, containing large proportions of sugar, that is shaped and baked

hard wheat—a type of wheat that has more protein than does soft wheat; hard wheat is considered to be the most desirable type for flour for bread making

heifer—a young female beef animal that has not had a calf

hidden chef—the time, skill, and energy used in combining, and perhaps cooking, a convenience food

hominy—corn kernels from which hull and germ have been removed mechanically or by soaking in lye; often used as a vegetable

homogenized milk—milk that has been processed so that the fat remains distributed and will not rise to the top of the container.

hormone—a secretion, from glands or cells of the body, that causes special responses

hydrogenation—the process by which hydrogen is added to an oil to form a semisolid or solid fat

instantized flour—a finely milled flour that does not need to be sifted; this flour is best used in sauces and gravies (other recipes may need adjustment); also called *instant blending* flour

intestinal mucosa—the cells of villi on walls of the intestines, which absorb nutrients

jell—to set or to become a solid mass

julienne—cut into long, thin strips

knead, kneaded, kneading—to apply pressure with the heels of the hand to dough, as in making bread

lard—the fat of hogs, used for pastry; the best lard comes from around the abdominal cavity

larding—thin, narrow strips of fat laid over or through lean meat to keep it from drying out during roasting

lattice top—the top layer on a pie in which pastry strips are interwoven to form a lattice

leavener—a substance or process that causes a product to expand during cooking; air, steam, or carbon dioxide gas; also called *leavening* and *leavening agent*

legume—a type of vegetable whose seeds are dried and used for food; peas, beans, lentils, and chickpeas (garbanzos)

lentil—see **legume**

lighten—the process of stirring to loosen that is used for cornmeal and whole-wheat flour instead of sifting

liquid alkali—a kitchen cleanser used to dissolve and remove soil and grease

luncheon meats—cooked, ground-meat mixtures formed into a loaf and usually sliced as for sandwiches; pickle and pimiento loaf, liver loaf, and so on

macrocytic anemia—a blood condition in which the blood contains larger-than-normal-sized red blood cells along with low levels of hemoglobin, leukocytes, and platelets; also called *megaloblastic anemia*

macronutrients—those mineral elements needed by the human body in comparatively large amounts; more than 50 parts per 1,000,000 of body weight

marbled, marbling—streaked; as fat is streaked through the lean muscle of meat

marinate, marinated, marinating—to soak in liquid to add flavor

metabolism—a series of chemical changes that occur within the body as the nutrients are absorbed through the intestinal walls and used for the body's processes and building or replacing the body's tissues

metabolize, metabolized, metabolizing—to use a nutrient in the body for the body's processes or building or replacing the body's tissues

micronutrients—those mineral elements needed by the human body in comparatively small or trace amounts; less than 50 parts per 1,000,000 of body weight

micro-organism—a very small organism, visible only under a microscope

milling—the mechanical process used to make grain into different food forms

muscle—the lean part in meats

microwave—an electromagnetic wave of energy produced by an electric charge and converted into heat when absorbed by food

nondairy product—a creamlike liquid that contains no real milk or cream; used widely in coffee as a whitener

nutritional anemia—a condition of the blood in which the blood has low hemoglobin level and smaller-than-normal-sized red blood cells; this anemia is related to deficiency of iron and/or protein especially during periods of growth

osmosis—the passage of liquids through a semipermeable membrane

osmotic pressure—the pressure that develops when substances, such as protein, mineral salts, or sugars, are more concentrated on one side of a membrane or cells walls than they are on the other; the pressure that causes fluids or water to pass through a semipermeable membrane which separates solutions of unequal concentrations

oxidation—a chemical change that occurs when a substance is combined with oxygen, as when carbohydrates combine with oxygen to release energy

oxidized—burned; a carbohydrate is oxidized to produce energy, water, and carbon dioxide

pan-broil—to cook food by direct contact with a very hot, heavy pan; the fat is poured off as it accumulates

pan-fry—see **fry**

parboiled rice—see **converted rice**

pasta—macaroni or other shaped product made from durum wheat, such as spaghetti, shells, bows, and so on

pasteurized milk—milk that has been heated to 63°C (145°F) and held at that temperature for 30 minutes, or heated to 71°C (161°F) and held for 15 seconds; the process is used to destroy micro-organisms that may be present in milk

pastry cloth—a floured cloth on which pastry is rolled out

pastry sock—the cover for a rolling pin used to roll out pastry

pastry shell—a shaped pastry, baked or unbaked, into which pie filling is poured

peel, peeled, peeling—to remove the outer layer of a fruit or vegetable

pernicious anemia—a condition of the blood in which there is a low red blood count and larger-than-normal-sized red blood cells; the disorder is related to a deficiency of vitamin B_{12}

photosynthesis—the process by which carbohydrates are formed in plants by the reaction of sunlight on the plants' chlorophyll

place setting—the flatware or chinaware needed for one cover

poach, poached, poaching—to cook gently in hot, simmering water or other liquid

porcelain—a very strong and durable type of dinnerware that is slow to chip or crack and that is expensive

pottery—a type of earthenware that is heavy, easily cracked and chipped, and comparatively inexpensive

precursor—a substance from which the body synthesizes another substance

provitamin—a substance that can be changed into a vitamin in the body

purging—the process used to clean out the stomachs of raw clams

quick bread—any of several breads or muffins using quick-acting leavening agents, such as baking powder or baking soda and an acid

rancidity—a chemical change in fats, due to oxidation, that results in undesirable flavor and taste in foods

reconstitute, reconstituted, reconstituting—to mix a dry substance with water, as in reconstituted dry milk

reduce, reduced, reducing—to boil a liquid, evaporating some of it and leaving a smaller quantity to concentrate the flavor

rehydrate, rehydrated, rehydrating—to return moisture to a dried (*hydrated*) food

ribbon—to beat together sugar and egg yolks until they fall from the beater or whip in the form of a ribbon

roast, roasted, roasting—to cook in an uncovered pan in dry heat in an oven, usually meat or poultry

Rock Cornish hen—a small bird developed by cross breeding; a kind of poultry

Salmonella—a micro-organism in food that causes illness

sanitizer—a liquid used to destroy certain micro-organisms

satiety value—the ability of a food to keep an individual from feeling hungry; satiety value is related to the length of time a food stays in the stomach

sausage—ground meat and seasonings packed into casings or sold in bulk, such as frankfurters, liverwurst, knockwurst, and so on

sauté, sautéed, sautéing—to brown or cook in a small amount of fat

scorch, scorched, scorching—to burn slightly onto the sides or bottom of a pan

score, scored, scoring—to make shallow cuts on the surface of a food with a knife

scum—the film that collects on the top of milk when it is heated or on the liquid in which other foods are cooked

SDA—see **specific dynamic action**

self-rising flour—flour to which salt and leavening ingredients have been added

semipermeable—allowing the passage of liquids; usually, a membrane or tissue

semiporcelain—a type of earthenware that is of good serviceability, less chip- and crack-resistant than porcelain, and moderately priced *shelf life*—the length of time a stored nonrefrigerated food will keep

shelf spoilage—the deterioration or spoiling of food during nonrefrigerated storage

shorten, shortened, shortening—to use fat to make a flour mixture tender; the fat used (*shortening*); a product that contains fat (*shortened*)

shuck, shucked, shucking—to remove from the shell, as in oysters; to remove from outer wrapping, as in corn

silence cloth—a heavy pad or pad-type cloth used under a tablecloth to protect the table's top

silverplate—a type of flatware made by coating a metal alloy form with silver

simmer, simmered, simmering—to cook in hot water just under the active boiling stage

skewer—a long, thin, metal pin or rod used to hold food together during cooking

skim, skimmed, skimming—to remove cream, fat, or scum from the surface of a liquid

skimmed milk—milk from which the cream (or fat) has been removed

smoke point—the temperature at which hot fat begins to smoke

soft wheat—a type of wheat that has less protein than does hard wheat; soft wheat makes a powdery, soft flour

special—a supermarket item sold at a particular price to attract customers; the price may or may not be lower than usual

specific dynamic action—(SDA) the amount of energy used by the body from the foods for the intake of those foods into the body

spore—the inactive or nongrowing form of some micro-organisms

split peas—see **legume**

spring wheat—wheat that is planted in the spring and harvested in the fall

squab—a young pigeon used for food; a type of poultry

Staphylococcus aureus—a micro-organism that forms a poisonous toxin in foods

staying quality—see **satiety value**

steam, steamed, steaming—to cook on a rack over boiling water

steer—a castrated male beef animal

stew, stewed, stewing—to simmer in liquid in a covered pan

still-frozen—frozen without stirring

stir-frozen—frozen with stirring

synthesis—the production of a substance in the body from other substances

table linens—tablecloths, place mats, and napkins used on a dining table at mealtime

tart—a small filled pastry usually with no top crust

tenderizer—a substance used to make a meat tender, such as a marinade, commercial product, and so on

textured vegetable protein—(TVP) soy protein processed into a small shape or powder, which is used to increase the volume of foods or as a food itself

thickener—a substance that is added to foods to make a product less runny or more viscous

toxin—a poisonous substance produced in foods by some micro-organisms

Trichinella spiralis—a parasitic worm found in the muscles of some hogs

trichinosis—the disease caused by ingesting trichinae

truss, trussed, trussing—to tie poultry legs and tail

turnover—a pastry made by folding the pastry dough back over the filling and sealing the edges

TVP—see **textured vegetable protein**

uncured—not held for a time to age or ripen; the term usually is used with cheese

undulant fever—see **brucellosis**

unshortened—made without any fat, as in unshortened cake

USDA—United States Department of Agriculture

variety meats—brains, heart, kidney, liver, sweetbreads, tongue, and tripe of meat animals

vinaigrette—a type of salad dressing

virus A—a virus that causes infectious hepatitis

wheat germ—see **germ**

whey—the watery liquid left when milk solids are made into cheese

whip, whipped, whipping—to beat briskly with a rotary beater or whisk

whole-wheat flour—a flour made from the whole kernel of wheat; also called graham flour

wild rice—the seed of a wild grass; not a true rice

winter wheat—wheat planted in the fall and harvested in early summer

wok—a cooking pan with slanted sides used for stir-frying foods

young hen—a female turkey less than seven months old

young tom—male turkey less than seven months old

Bibliography

Adams, C. F., *Nutritive Value of American Foods in Common Units.* Agriculture Handbook, no. 456. Washington, D.C.: U.S. Government Printing Office, 1975.

Bennion, M., and Hughes, O. *Introductory Foods.* 6th ed. New York: Macmillan, 1974.

Burton, B. T. *Human Nutrition.* 3rd ed. New York: McGraw-Hill, 1976.

Ehrenkranz, F., and Inman, L. *Equipment in the Home.* 3rd ed. New York: Harper & Row, 1973.

Gifft, H., et al. *Nutrition, Behavior, and Change.* Englewood Cliffs, N.J.: Prentice-Hall, 1972.

Guthrie, H. *Introductory Nutrition,* 3rd. ed. Saint Louis: Mosby Co., 1975.

Kinder, F. *Meal Management.* 4th ed. New York: Macmillan, 1973.

Lowenberg, M. E., et al. *Food and Man.* 2nd ed. New York: Wiley, 1974.

Lundberg, G. *Principles of Food Science.* Vols. 1 and 2. New York: Macmillan, 1968.

McWilliams, M. *Nutrition for the Growing Years.* 2nd ed. New York: Wiley, 1975.

Peckham, G. C. *Foundations of Food Preparation.* 3rd ed. New York: Macmillan, 1974.

Peet, L. J., et al. *Household Equipment.* 7th ed. New York: Wiley, 1975.

Stare, F. J., and McWilliams, M. *Living Nutrition.* New York: Wiley, 1973.

Lorenz, K., and Dilsaver, W. *Mile High Cakes for the Seventies.* Bulletin 556-S. Fort Collins, Colo.: Colorado State University Experimental Station, 1972.

Vail, G. E., et al. *Foods.* 7th ed. Boston: Houghton Mifflin, 1978.

Van Zante, H. J. *The Microwave Oven.* Boston: Houghton Mifflin, 1973.

Wilson, E. D., et al. *Principles of Nutrition.* 3rd ed. New York: Wiley, 1975.

Wilson, P. *Household Equipment: Selection and Management.* Boston: Houghton Mifflin, 1975.

Index

Absorption
 defined, 242
 and transportation, 243
Additives, 247–249
Al dente, defined, 150
Amino acids, essential, 221–222
Amoebic dysentery, 5
Anemia
 macrocytic, 239
 nutritional, 229
 pernicious, 240
Antioxidant, defined, 234
Artichoke, technique for cutting raw, *illus.* 46–47
Ascorbic acid (vitamin C), 231, 240–241
Asparagus, 285–286
 and butter lettuce salad, *illus.* 58
Avocado, cutting, *illus.* 66–67

Bacteria, 1, 3
 Brucella, 4
 causing illness or death, 5–6
 causing infection, 4
 Clostridium botulinum, 3, 6
 Clostridium perfringens, 6
 lactic-acid, 3
 Salmonella, 4
 Staphylococcus aureus, 5
Baking
 of bread, 109–111
 of eggs and egg dishes (custards and soufflés), 81
 of fish and shellfish, 164
 of fruits, 28–29
 of vegetables, 50
Baking powder, 105, 106
Barbecuing
 of meat, 205
 of poultry, 179
Barley, 155
Basal metabolism, 229, 243
Basic Four food groups, 254, 255
 nutrients found in, 256–257

Basic Seven food groups, 254
Basting, defined, 179
Batter(s)
 definition of, 106–107
 thick, 107
 thin, 107
Beans, 156
Beef, 187
 roast, and plannedovers, *illus.* 314–316
 see also Meat
Beri-beri, 236
Biotin, 231, 235, 239
Blanching, 45
Blood stream, 243
Boiling
 of eggs, 83
 of fish and shellfish, 164–165
 of fruits, 29
 of vegetables, 49–50
Botulism, 6
Braising, of meat, 208
Bran, 149
Bread(s), 102
 baking, 109–111
 ingredients in, 102–106
 leaveners in, 105–106
 mixing methods for making, 106–109
 nutritional value of, 102, 356–359
 preparation of, 106
 selection of, *illus.* 103
 storage of, 111
 yeast, *illus.* 109–110
Broccoli, cooked, *illus.,* 49
Broiling
 of fish and shellfish, 163
 of fruits, 29
 of meat, 202, *illus.* 204–205, 206
 pan-, of meat, 202–205
 of poultry, 179
Brown-bag lunches, 319
Brucella bacteria, 4

Index

Brucellosis, 4
Buffet
  service, 306
  setting table for, 301–303, *illus.* 302
Bulgur, 150
Butter, 88, 90
  clarified, 98
  nutritive values of, 338–339
  preparation of, 98
  storage of, 96
Buttermilk, 89, 106
  storage of, 93

Cake(s), 131, *illus.* 147
  baking of, 141–143
    oven temperature for, 141
    pan location for, 142
    testing for doneness of, 142–143
  carrot, 131
  desirable characteristics of, 143
  fillings, 143–145, 146–147
  frostings, 143, 145–147
  genoise, 131
  ingredients for, 131–133
    eggs, 133
    fat, 132
    flour, 132
    leaveners, 133
    liquid, 132
    sugar, 132–133
  made from prepared cake and pudding mixes, 136, *illus.* 136
  making, altitude and, 133–134
  mixing methods, 134–137
    angel food cake, 135
    cake mixes, 136–137
    chiffon cakes, 135
    shortened cakes, 134–135
    sponge cake, 135–136
    unshortened cakes, 135–136
  nutritional value of, 131, 360–363
  shortened and unshortened, 131–132
  sponge, *illus.* 145

Cake fillings, 143–145
  spreading, 146–147
Cake frostings, 143, 145
  cooked, 146
  nutritive values of, 372–373
  spreading, 146–147
  uncooked, 145–146
Cake pans, *illus.* 140–141
  preparation of, 140–141
  selection of, 137
Calcium, 225
Calorie, defined, 219
Candling, defined, 75
Capons, 171. *See also* Poultry
Carbohydrates
  food sources of, 218
  problems related to, 219
  recommended dietary allowances of, 219
  uses of, in the body, 219
Carbon dioxide, 105, 106
Carcass, beef, 187
  wholesale and retail cuts of, *illus.* 191
Caries, dental, carbohydrates and, 219
Carotene, 231, 232
Carotenoids, 231
Carrot curls, *illus.* 71
Celery
  fans, *illus.* 70
  technique for chopping, *illus.* 45
Cellulose, 33
Celsius, temperature conversion for Fahrenheit and, 386
Cereals and cereal products, 148, 149
  barley, 155
  corn, 154
  nutritional value of, 148–149, 358–361
  oats, 154–155
  rice, 152–154
  selection and storage of, 156–157
  wheat, 150

Chafing dishes, 297–298
Cheese, 88
    forms of, 91
    gourmandise, *illus.* 93
    mold on, 2
    nutritive values of, 332–333
    pepper, *illus.* 92–93
    preparation of, 99
    storage of, 96
Chicken
    bite-sized pieces of, for salad, *illus.* 69
    cashew, *illus.* 183
    and cashew salad, *illus.* 60
    see also Poultry
China, 294–295
    bone, 295
    fine, 294–295
Chlorine, 227
Chlorophyll, 218
Cholesterol, 221
Chromium, 230–231
Chuck roasts, *illus.* 193
Citric acid, action of molds on beet molasses to produce, 2
Clams, 158, 160, 161
    preparation of, 162–163
    purging of, 163
Clostridium botulinum, 3, 6
Clostridium perfringens, 6
Coagulation, defined, 79
Cobalamin, *see* Vitamin B$_{12}$
Cobalt, 230–231
Coenzymes, defined, 235 and 235n
Collagen, 241
Convenience foods, 195, 311
Cookies, nutritive values of, 362–365
Cooking as a hobby, 327–330
Copper, 230–231
Corn cereals, 154
Cornmeal, 104, 106, 154
Cover, defined, 298–299
Crab, 158, 159–160, 161
Craze, of pottery glaze, defined, 295

Cream, 88
    kinds of, 90
    nutritive values of, 332–335
    sour, 90, 98
    storage of, 96
    whipping, 90, 97, 130
Crepes, *illus.* 108
Cretinism, 229
Crust, crumb, 121–123
Crustaceans, 158
Curd, 79
Curdling, defined, 79, 97
Curing, defined, 188

Dairy products
    kinds of, 88–91
    nutritional value of, 88, 332–338
    preparation of, 96–99
    selection of, 91–92
    storage of, 93–96
Deaminization, defined, 222
Department of the Interior, 159
Desserts, frozen milk, 88, 99–101
Dietary allowances, recommended, 215–218, 246
Diets, 252. *See also* Weight control
Digestion, defined, 242
Dinnerware
    defined, 294
    kinds of, 294–295
    patterns and colors of, 295
    selection of, 295–296
Dirlyte, 296
Dishes, *see* Dinnerware
Dish washing
    automatic, 11
    hand, 9–11
    precautions, 11–12
Dough(s)
    cobbler, 129
    definition of, 107
    soft, 107
    yeast, 107–109
Duck, *see* Poultry

Earthenware, 294, 295
  fine, 294, 295
Eggs, 74
  cooking methods, 81–87
    baking of, 81
    coddled, 83
    custards and puddings, preparing stirred, 86–87
    fried, 83–84
    hard-cooked, 83
    omelets, 84, *illus.* 84–85
    poached, 83
    scrambled, 84
    soft-cooked, 83
    soufflé, *illus.* 82
  nutritional value of, 74, 76, 338
  preparation of, 79–81
    coagulation of, 79
    egg-white foams, 80–81
    emulsions, 81
    meringue, *illus.* 80
  selection of, 74–77
    considerations in, 75–76
    and consumer dollar, 76–77
    grading of, 75
    size of, 75
  serving suggestions for, 87
  storage of, 77–79
    cooked, 79
    fresh, 77
    fresh versus not-so-fresh, *illus.* 76
    frozen, 79
  stuffed and garnished, *illus.* 86
Emulsions, 81
Enamelware, 267
Endamoeba histolytica, 5
Endosperm, 149
Enzymes, defined, 224 and 224n
Equivalents and substitutions, 389–394
Eviscerate, defined, 170
Extenders, 188, 189

Fahrenheit and Celsius, temperature conversion for, 386
Farina, 150
Fats
  food sources of, 220
  nutritive values of, 338–341
  problems related to, 221
  recommended dietary allowances of, 220
  uses of, in the body, 220
FDA, *see* Food and Drug Administration
Fettucine, *illus.* 152
Fillings, *see* Cake fillings; Pastry fillings
Firing, of dinnerware, defined, 294
Fish, 158
  cooking methods for, 163–166
    baking, 164
    broiling, 163
    chowders and soups, preparing, 165–166
    fillet, *illus.* 165–166
    frying, 164
    poaching, 165
    steaming and boiling, 164
  inspection and grading system for, 159
  nutritional value of, 158–159, 342–343
  poisonous, 7
  preparation of, 162–163
  retail forms of, 159
  selection of, 160–162
    amount to buy, 161–162
  serving of, *illus.* 167–168
  serving suggestions for, 166
  storage of, 162
Fish flour, 158–159
Flans, 113
  apple, *illus.* 114, 127
  pastry for, *illus.* 122
Flatware
  kinds of, 296

Flatware *(Continued)*
 selection of, 296–297
Flour
 fish, 158–159
 mixtures, mixing methods for, 106–109
 preparation of, 106
 rye, 104
 soy, 104, 156
 wheat, 102–104, 157
Fluorine, 229–230
Fondue pots, 297
Food buying, 275–282
 basic knowledge needed for, 275–276
 choice of store for, 276–277
 day and time for, 277–278
 of fresh versus processed forms, 278, 280
 market list for, 281–282
 prompt storage after, 282
 quantity considerations in, 280–281
 selection of grade and quality in, 278
Food and Drug Administration (FDA), 244, 247, 272
Food to go, 318–319
 planning of, 318–319
 preparation of, 319
Food selection, factors affecting, 250–253
 availability, 250
 diets, 252
 economics, 252–253
 family traditions and customs, 250–251
 habit, 251
 individual life styles and daily schedules, 253
 likes, dislikes, and preferences, 251–252
 meal manager-cook, 253
 psychological aspects, 253
 season, 252

Foreign foods, 329–330
Fowl (or stewing hen), 171. *See also* Poultry
Fricasseeing, 183–184
Frosting, *see* Cake frostings
Fruits, 17
 cooking methods for, 28–29
  baking, 28–29
  broiling, 29
  poaching, 29
  stewing or boiling, 29
 nutritional value of, 17–18, 348–357
  effects of cooking and freezing on nutrients, 18
  effects of preparation on nutrients, 18
 preparation of, 26–28
  dehydrated (dried), 27–28
  fresh, 26
  frozen, 27
  in gelatin mixtures, 28
 selection of, 18–20
  considerations in, 18–20
  and consumer dollar, 20
  fresh versus canned or frozen, 20
 serving suggestions for, 32
 storage of, 20–26
  canned and frozen, 21
  cooked, 26
  fresh, 20–21
Frying
 deep-fat, of vegetables, 51–53
 of eggs, 83–84
 of fish and shellfish, 164
 oven-, of poultry, 183
 pan-, of meat, 206
 of poultry, 182
 stir-, of vegetables, 51

Germ, 149
Giblets, 172
Glassware, 297

Index

Glaze, defined, 295
Glazes, 145
Goiter, endemic, 229
Goose, see Poultry
Grading system, USDA's
   for eggs, 75
   for fruits and vegetables, 18–19, 35
   for meat, 189, 190
   for poultry, 170
Grain(s), 148
   products, nutritive values of, 356–371
   see also Cereals and cereal products
Granola, *illus.* 149
GRAS list, 247
Gravy, making, 210–211
Grits, 154

Hams, mold on country-cured, 2
Hemorrhages, 241
Hepatitis, viral infectious, 4
Herbs, 63–68
Hominy, 154
Hormones, defined, 224 and n
Hydrogenation, defined, 105 and n

Icings, 145. *See also* Cake frostings
Illness, control of food-related, 7–12
   care of foods, 8
   cleanliness of food handlers, 7–8
   sanitation in dish washing, 9–12
   sanitation for kitchen and equipment, 8–9
Infections, food and, 3–5
   bacteria, 4
   parasites, 5
   viruses, 4
International Units (I.U.), 232
Intestinal mucosa, 243
Iodine, 229
Iron, 228–229

Jams and jellies, mold on, 2

Kitchen arrangement, 273–275
   cleaning area, 274
   cooking area, 274
   planning area, 274
   preparation area, 273
   reorganization of work areas, 274–275
Kitchen equipment, 266–273
   beating and blending tools, 270–271
   essential and desirable, 387–388
   knives, 270
   materials used in, 267, 268–269
   measurers, 270
   microwave ovens, 271–273
   miscellaneous tools, 271
   pans, 267
   turning and stirring tools, 270

Labeling, food, 276
   additive labeling, 247–249
   ingredient listing, 244–245
   nutritional labeling, 245–247
Lactose, 219
Lamb and mutton, 187–188. *See also* Meat
Leaveners, 105–106
Legumes, 148
   beans, 156
   dried, 155–156
   lentils, 155
   nutritional value of, 148–149, 370–371
   peas, 155
   selection and storage of, 156–157
Lentils, 155
Lettuce, 57
   drying, 62–63
   removing core of iceberg, *illus.* 61
   washing, 61–62, *illus.* 62
Linoleic acid, 220, 221
Lobster, 158, 160, 161–162
Lymphatic system, 243

Macronutrients, 223–224
Magnesium, 226
Manganese, 230–231
Marbling, in meats, defined, 186
Margarine, 90–91
　nutritive values of, 340–341
　storage of, 96
Marinating, 63, *illus.* 201
　tenderizing by, 198
Market list, 281–282
Meal management, 282–289
　clock-time schedule for, 289, 290
　evaluation of, 289, 291–292
　organizational planning for, 283–289
Meal patterns, 253–258
　caloric requirements for, 256–258
　nutritional guides for, 254–255
　nutritional requirements for, 256
　tailoring of, 258
Meals, dollar-controlled, 314–318
　increasing knowledge of food for, 318
　planning of, 315–316
　preparation of, 316–318
Meals, time-controlled, 308–311
　cooking methods for, 308–309
　equipment for, 310–311
　preparation of food ahead of time, 309–310
　prepreparation of, 309
Meals for young children, 320–323
　atmosphere for, 321
　establishing good eating habits in, 320–321
　planning of, 321–322
　and snack foods, 322–323
　undesirable foods for, 320
Meat, 186
　cooking methods for, dry-heat, 199–206, 209
　　barbecuing, 205
　　broiling, 202, *illus.* 204–205, 206
　　pan-broiling, 202–205

　　pan-frying, 206
　　roasting, 199–202, 203
　cooking methods for, moist-heat, 199, 206–208, *illus.* 207, 209
　　braising, 208
　　microwave cooking, 208
　　stewing, 208
　cuts of, 190–192
　inspection and grading of, 189, 190
　kinds of, 187–189
　　beef, 187
　　cured, 188
　　lamb and mutton, 187–188
　　luncheon, 188–189
　　pork, 187
　　sausage, 188
　　variety, 188
　　veal, 187
　nutritional value of, 186–187, 342–347
　preparation of, 197–199
　　frozen meats, 198–199
　　tenderizing, 198
　selection of, 192–195
　　amount to buy, 192–193
　　chuck roasts, *illus.* 193
　　convenience meats and meat dishes, 195
　　nutritional value and cost, 193–194
　　other considerations in, 195
　　quality, 192
　　soybean products, 194
　serving suggestions for, 209–211
　storage of, freezer, 197
　　cooked meat, 197
　　fresh meat, 197
　storage of, refrigerator, 196–197
　　cooked meat, 196–197
　　fresh meat, 196
Meat loaf, broiled
　with Brussels sprouts, *illus.* 210
　recipe for, 283–285

Melamine, 295
Menu planning
  factors affecting, 258–263
  problem areas in, 263–265
Metabolism, 243
  basal, 243
Metabolized, defined, 219
Micronutrients, 223–224
Micro-organisms found in food, 1–3
  bacteria, 3
  growing and spore forms of, 2
  molds, 2
  yeasts, 2–3
Microwave cooking
  advantages and disadvantages of, 272–273
  of meats, 208
  safety of, 272
  uses of, 271–272
  of vegetables, 53
Milk, 88–89
  curdling of, 97
  desserts, frozen, 88, 99–101
    nutritive value of, 336–339
  kinds of, 89–90
  nutritional value of, 88, 334–337
  preparation of, 96–97
  scorching or burning of, 97
  scum formation on, 97
  selection of, 91–92
  storage of, 93–96
Minerals, 223–231
  calcium, 225
  chlorine, 227
  fluorine, 229–230
  iodine, 229
  iron, 228–229
  magnesium, 226
  phosphorus, 225
  potassium, 226–227
  sodium, 227
  sulfur, 227–228
  zinc, 230
Molds, 1, 2

Mollusks, 158
Molybdenum, 230–231
Muffins, *illus.* 112
Mushrooms
  fluted, *illus.* 54
  poisonous, 6–7
  rinsed and drained, *illus.* 43
  washing of, *illus.* 43

National Academy of Science-National Research Council, 246
  Food and Nutrition Board (FNB) of, 215, 219
Niacin (nicotinic acid), 231, 235, 237–238
Nickel, 230–231
Nicotinic acid, *see* Niacin

Oats, oatmeal, 154–155
Oils, nutritive values of, 338–339
Onion
  brushes, *illus.* 52, 60
  technique for producing chopped, *illus.* 44
Osmosis, 63
  defined, 26, 224
Osteoporosis, 230
Oxidized, defined, 219
Oysters, 158, 160, 161

Pantothenic acid, 231, 235, 238
Parasites
  Endamoeba histolytica, 5
  Trichinella spiralis, 5
Paratyphoid, 4
Pasta, 149, 150
Pastry, cookie-dough, 121, *illus.* 127, 287
  forming, 121
  mixing, 121
  repairing torn dough, *illus.* 123
  trimming and baking, 121

Pastry, standard, 115–121
  baking filled shell, 120–121
  baking unfilled shell, 118–120
  fluting, *illus.* 120
  folding into pan, *illus.* 118
  forming, 117
  making, 115, *illus.* 116–117
  mixing, 115
  nutritive values of, 366–367
  trimming, 117–118, *illus.* 119
Pastry fillings, 124–125
  cooked-pudding, 128–129
    cream, 128–129
    lemon, 129
  custard, 128
  fruit, 125–126
    fresh fruit and unbaked pastry, 126
    frozen or canned fruit and unbaked pastry, 126
    fruit for baked shells, 126
  meat and poultry, 129
Pastry mixes and shells, commercially prepared, 124
Patina, defined, 296
Peas, 155
Pellagra, 238
Phosphorus, 225
Photosynthesis, 218
Pie(s), 113
  nutritive values of, 366–367
  pans, 113–115
  see also Pastry, cookie-dough; Pastry, standard; Pastry fillings; Pastry mixes and shells
Piecrust, *see* Pastry, standard
Pigeons, *see* Poultry
Pineapple
  cutting and serving of, *illus.* 30–31
  fresh or frozen, not used in gelatin mixtures, 28
Plants
  food for, 1
  food-poisoning from, 6–7

Poaching
  of eggs, 83
  of fish and shellfish, 165
  of fruits, 29
  of poultry, 185
Poisoning, food, 5–7
  from animals, 7
  bacteria causing, 5–6
  from plants, 6–7
Porcelain, 295
Pork, 187. *See also* Meat
Potassium, 226–227
Potatoes, buttered, 286
Pottery, 294, 295
Poultry, 169
  cooking methods for, dry-heat, 178–183
    barbecuing, 179
    broiling, 179
    frying, 182
    oven-frying, 183
    roasting, 178–179, 182
  cooking methods for, moist-heat, 183–185
    fricasseeing, 183–184
    poaching, 185
    stewing or steaming, 184
  cutting up, *illus.* 174–178
  inspection and grading of, 170
  nutritional value of, 169–170, 346–349
  preparation of, 173–178
    frozen, 173
    kitchen sanitation, 178
    raw, 178
  retail forms of, 170–171
  selection of, 171–172
    amount to buy, 171–172
    by grade, 171
  serving suggestions for, 185
  storage of, 172–173
    cooked, 172–173
    raw, 172
  trussing of, 178–179, *illus.* 180–181

Precursor, 233
  defined, 221
Proteins, 221–222
  food sources of, 222
  problems related to, 223
  recommended dietary allowances of, 222
  uses of, in the body, 223
Provitamin A, 231
Pyridoxine (vitamin B$_6$), 231, 235, 238
Pyroceran, 295

Radishes, cutting and crisping, *illus.* 52
Recommended Dietary Allowances, 215–218
Regional foods (United States), 327–328
Riboflavin (vitamin B$_2$), 231, 235, 236–237
Rice
  kinds of, 152–154
  molded, *illus.* 153
  nutritive values of, 368–369
Rickets, 233
Roasting
  of meat, 199–202, 203
  of poultry, 178–179, 182
Rock Cornish hens, 169, 170–171. *See also* Poultry
Rye flour, 104

Salad dressings, 70–72
  calorie content of, 73
  cooked, 73
  mayonnaise, 72
  nutritive values of, 340–341
  selection of, 73
  vinaigrette (French), 72
Salade Nicoise, 63, *illus.* 34
Salad greens, 57
  nutritional value of, 57–58, 59
  selection of, 58–60
    considerations in, 59
    and consumer dollar, 60
  storage of, 61
    drying, 62–63
    washing, 61–62
Salads, 57
  and consumer dollar, 60
  fresh versus canned or frozen ingredients, 60
  nutritional value of, 57–58
  preparation of, 63–68
    making molded and frozen, 68
    mixing, 63–68
  presentation of, 68–70
    garnishes for, 69–70
    size of pieces for, 69
Salmonella bacteria, 4, 178
Salt, *see* Sodium
Satiety value, defined, 261
Sausage, 188. *See also* Meat
Scallops, 158, 160
  broiling of, 163
Scurvy, 240, 241
Selenium, 230–231
Semipermeable membrane, 26
Service, of meals, 303–307
  buffet, 306
  compromise, 305
  of dessert and beverage, 304, *illus.* 304
  English, 305
  family, 303–304
  for outdoor meals, 307
  plate, 303
  Russian, 305–306
  suggestions for, 265
Shelf life, defined, 149
Shellfish, 158
  cooking methods for, 163–166
    baking, 164
    broiling, 163
    chowders and soups, preparing, 165–166

Shellfish *(Continued)*
   frying, 164
   poaching, 165
   steaming and boiling, 165
  inspection and grading system for, 159
  nutritional value of, 158–159, 342–343
  poisonous, 7
  preparation of, 162–163
  retail forms of, 159–160
   clams, 160
   crab, 159–160
   lobster, 160
   oysters, 160
   scallops, 160
   shrimp, 160
  selection of, 160–162
   amount to buy, 161–162
  serving suggestions for, 166
  storage of, 162
Shells, hard-meringue, 123–124, *illus.* 125
  forming and baking, 124
  mixing, 123–124
Shrimp, 158, 160, 161
  deveining of, 163
  green, 161
  preparation of, 163
Silicon, 230–231
Silverplated flatware, 296
Silverware, *see* Flatware
Skewer, defined, 178–179
Smoke point, defined, 51
Sodium, 227
Soybean products, 156, 194
Soybeans, dried, 156
Soy flour, 104, 156
Spinach Salad with Walnuts, 286
Spore, defined, 2
Squab, 169. *See also* Poultry
Stainless steel flatware, 296
Staphylococcus aureus, 5
Staples, 280

Steaming
  of fish and shellfish, 164–165
  of poultry, 184
  of vegetables, 50
Sterling silver flatware, 296
Stewing
  of fruits, 29
  of meat, 208
  of poultry, 184
Stoneware, 294, 295
Strawberry Parfait, 288
Strawberry Tart, 287–288
Substitutions, equivalents and, 389–394
Sugars and sweets, nutritive values of, 372–373
Sulfur, 227–228
Sweetbreads, 188
Synthesis, defined, 221

Table appointments, 293–298
  decorative pieces, 298
  dinnerware, 294–296
  flatware, 296–297
  fondue pots, chafing dishes, and warming trays, 297–298
  glassware, 297
  tablecloths, place mats, and napkins, 294
Table setting(s), 298–303, *illus.* 300–302
  for a buffet, 301–303, *illus.* 302
  casual and formal, *illus.* 264
  cover, 298–299
  serving dishes, 299–301
Tabooleh, 150, *illus.* 151
Tarnish, defined, 296
Tarts, 113
Tenderizing, various means of, 198, *illus.* 200–201
Thiamin (vitamin B$_1$), 231, 235–236
Thyroxine, 229
Tin, 230–231
Tocopherol, 233

Index

Tomato flowers, *illus.* 56
Toppings, 129–130
  meringue, 129–130
  whipped cream, 130
Tournedos and beef sauté, *illus.* 194
Trichina, 189
Trichinella spiralis, 5
Trichinosis, 189
Tripe, 188
Trussing, *illus.* 180–181
  defined, 178–179
Tryptophan, 237
Tuberculosis, 3
Turkey, roast, 6, *illus.* 184
  with plannedovers, *illus.* 312–313
  see also Poultry
Turnips, making chrysanthemum, *illus.* 54–55
Turnovers, 113, 130
TVP (textured vegetable protein), 156
Typhoid fever, 3, 4

Undulant fever, 4
United States Department of Agriculture (USDA), 254
  grading system of
    for eggs, 75
    for fruits and vegetables, 18–19
    for meats, 189, 190
    for poultry, 170

Vanadium, 230–231
Variety meats, 188
Veal, 187. *See also* Meat
Vegetables, 33
  cooking methods for, 48–53
    baking, 50
    boiling, 49–50
    deep-fat frying, 51–53
    microwave cooking, 53
    pressure-cooking, 50
    steaming or waterless cooking, 50
    stir-frying, 51
    using canned, 53
  effect of cooking on, 47–48
    green, 47
    strong-flavored, 48
    white, red, and yellow, 48
  nutritional value of, 33–35, 374–381
    effects of cooking and freezing on nutrients, 35
    effects of preparation on nutrients, 34–35
  preparation of, 42–45
    fresh, 42
    frozen, 42–45
  selection of, 35–37
    considerations in, 35–36
    and consumer dollar, 36
    fresh versus canned or frozen, 36–37
  serving suggestions for, 53
  storage of, 37–42
    canned and frozen, 37–42
    cooked, 42
    fresh, 37
Vermeil flatware, 296
Vinaigrette, 72
Viruses, 4
Vitamin(s)
  A, 231–232
  ascorbic acid (vitamin C), 231, 240–241
  B_1, *see* Thiamin
  B_2, *see* Riboflavin
  B_6, *see* Pyridoxine
  B_{12} (cobalamin), 231, 235, 240
  biotin, 231, 235, 239
  C, *see* Ascorbic acid
  Cobalamin, *see* Vitamin B_{12}
  D, 231, 232–233
  E, 231, 233–234
  fat-soluble, 231
  folic acid (folacin), 231, 235, 239
  K, 231, 234–235

Vitamin(s) *(Continued)*
  niacin (nicotinic acid), 231, 235, 237–238
  pantothenic acid, 231, 235, 238
  pyridoxine (vitamin B$_6$), 231, 235, 238
  riboflavin (vitamin B$_2$), 231, 235, 236–237
  thiamin (vitamin B$_1$), 231, 235–236
  water soluble, 231

Warming trays, 297–298
Water, as nutrient
  problems related to, 242
  sources and requirements of, 241–242
  uses of, 242
Weight control, 323–327
  overweight, 326–327
  underweight, 325

Wheat, 150
  bulgur, 150
  cracked, 104
  farina, 150
  pasta, 150
Wheat flour, 102–104, 150, 157
  nutritive values of, 370–371
Wheat germ, 104, 150, 157

Yeast(s), 1, 2–3, 106
  bread, *illus.* 109–110
    baking of, 111
  doughs, 107–109
Yogurt, 90
  nutritive values of, 338–339
  preparation of, 98
  storage of, 93

Zinc, 230